Learning
Microsoft® Excel 97

Cathy Vento
Iris Blanc

To Our Families

Alan, Pamela, and Jaime–*I.B.*

Jim, Chris, Dirk, Tyler, Jimmy, Mindi, and Anthony–*C.V.*

Project Manager
Marni Ayers Brady
New York, NY

Technical Editor
Katherine Bernthal
Westmont, IL

Design and Layout
Elsa Johannesson
New York, NY

English Editor
Christine Ford
New York, NY

Adrion Smith
New York, NY

Marni Ayers Brady
New York, NY

Paul Wray
New York, NY

CONTENTS

CONTENTS i
INTRODUCTION AND CD-ROM INSTALLATION v
LOG OF EXERCISES ix
DIRECTORY OF FILES xii

LESSON 1
GETTING STARTED   1

    Exercise 1 2
        Start Microsoft Excel
        The Microsoft Excel 97 Window
        The Workbook Window
        The Mouse and Keyboard
        Menus, Toolbars, and Commands
        Exit Excel
        The Excel 97 Keyboard Template
    Exercise 2 10
        Select Menu Items
        Options in a Dialog Box
        Set View Preferences
        The View Menu
    Exercise 3 16
        Change Window Displays
        Help Features
        The Office Assistant
        Contents and Index
        Exit Help

LESSON 2
EXPLORE WORKSHEET   23

    Exercise 4 24
        Explore the Worksheet Using the Mouse and
        Keyboard
    Exercise 5 28
        Explore the Worksheet Using the Mouse and
        Keyboard

LESSON 3
WORKSHEET BASICS   31

    Exercise 6 32
        Enter Labels
        Make Simple Corrections
        Save a Workbook
        Close a Workbook
    Exercise 7 36
        Numeric Labels and Values
        Label Alignment
        Check for Viruses
    Exercise 8 38
        Align Labels
        Indent Text in Cells
    Exercise 9 40
        Summary
    Exercise 10 41
        Summary

LESSON 4
FILES, FORMULAS AND FORMATTING   43

    Exercise 11 44
        Use Formulas
        Mathematical Operators
        Natural Language Formulas
    Exercise 12 46
        Open Files
        Save and Save As
        Create Backup Files
        Send Files
    Exercise 13 50
        Format Data
        Use Ranges
    Exercise 14 54
        Copy Data
        Print a Worksheet
    Exercise 15 58
        Copy Formulas (Absolute and Relative Reference)
        Format Data (Bold, Italic and Underscore)
    Exercise 16 62
        Format Fractions and Mixed Numbers
        Spelling
        Look Up Reference
    Exercise 17 66
        Summary
    Exercise 18 67
        Summary

LESSON 5
**FUNCTIONS, FORMATS, FEATURES, AND PRINT
OPTIONS**   69

    Exercise 19 70
        Use Functions
        Formula Bar and Formula Palette
        Paste Function
    Exercise 20 74
        AutoCalculate
        Edit
        Copy Part of a Cell's Contents
    Exercise 21 78
        Change Column Width
        Create a Series
        Comma Format
        AutoComplete
    Exercise 22 82
        Print Options
        Print Preview
        Cell Comments
        AutoSum
    Exercise 23 86
        Page Setup (Orientation, Scale, Margins,
        Header, Footer, Etc.)
        Range Entry Using the Collapse Button

Exercise 24 90
   Page Breaks
   Headers and Footers
   Bold Text
Exercise 25 96
   Print Titles
Exercise 26 100
   Summary
Exercise 27 101
   Summary

LESSON 6
WORK WITH WORKBOOKS,
WORKSHEETS, AND TEMPLATES   **103**

Exercise 28 104
   Insert and Delete Columns and Rows
   Move (Cut/Paste)
   Drag and Drop
   Undo a Command
Exercise 29 108
   Copy and Paste Special
   Transpose Data
   Scroll Tips
   AutoCorrect
Exercise 30 112
   Freeze Titles
   Split Panes
   Copy and Paste Special (Extract Data)
   Create New Workbook
   Arrange Workbooks Window
   Save Workspace
Exercise 31 118
   Workbook Sheets
   Group Sheets
   Print Workbook
Exercise 32 122
   Named Ranges
Exercise 33 126
   Data Validation
   Copy and Paste Special
   Format Negative Numbers
Exercise 34 130
   Copy and Paste Special (Add Option)
Exercise 35 132
   Drag and Drop Between Workbooks
   Replace
Exercise 36 136
   Use Templates (Spreadsheet Solutions)
Exercise 37 140
   Original Templates
   Link Workbooks
Exercise 38 144
   3-D Formulas
   Workbook Sheets
   New (or Duplicate) Workbook Window
Exercise 39 148
   Summary

Exercise 40 150
   Summary

LESSON 7
ADVANCED FEATURES AND FUNCTIONS   **153**

Exercise 41 154
   Solve What-If Problems
   Data Tables
   Goal Seek
Exercise 42 158
   Solve What-If Problems (Data Tables)
   PMT Function
Exercise 43 162
   Insert an IF Function
   Paste Function Feature
Exercise 44 166
   IF Function
   Print Compressed Worksheet
   Conditional Sum Wizard
Exercise 45 170
   Audit Formulas
Exercise 46 174
   Enter Dates as Numerical Data
   Format Numerical Dates
Exercise 47 178
   Scenarios
   AutoFormat
   Color Buttons
Exercise 48 182
   Insert Lookup Functions
Exercise 49 186
   Vertical Lookup Function (VLOOKUP)
Exercise 50 188
   Horizontal Lookup Function (HLOOKUP)
   Lock Cells in a Worksheet
   Protect a Worksheet
Exercise 51 192
   Hide Data
   Non-Consecutive References in a Function
   Custom Views
Exercise 52 196
   Summary
Exercise 53 198
   Summary

LESSON 8
CHART AND MAP DATA   **201**

Exercise 54 202
   Chart Basics
   Select Chart Data
   Chart Elements
   Create Column, Line, and Pie Charts
   Chart Types
   Select, Size, and Edit Embedded Chart
   Enable Chart Editing

Exercise 55.. 210
   Chart Types and Subtypes
   Custom Chart Types
   Select Chart Items
   Change Legend Position
   Chart Toolbar
   Edit Chart in its Own Window
Exercise 56.. 214
   Edit Linked Chart Text
   Edit Titles and Axis Labels
   Series Labels for Pie Charts
   Move Embedded Charts
   Change Chart Colors and Patterns
Exercise 57.. 218
   Print Charts
   Print Preview Charts
   Print Embedded Charts
   Black and White Printers
   Add Data to a Chart
Exercise 58.. 222
   Change Location of Charts
   Change Orientation of Data Series
   Change Orientation of Chart Text
   Chart Options
Exercise 59.. 226
   Create Stock Charts
   Format Data Markers
   Set Scale of Value Axis
   Charts with Two Value Axes
Exercise 60.. 230
   Create an Exploded Pie Chart
   Size Plot Area or Legend in a Chart
   Create an Area Chart
Exercise 61.. 234
   Enter Line Breaks in a Cell Entry
   Add Gridlines and Data Labels
   Create a 3-D Chart
Exercise 62.. 238
   Use Map Feature
   Edit Maps
   Map Toolbar
Exercise 63.. 242
   Summary
Exercise 64.. 244
   Summary

LESSON 9
ENHANCING THE WORKSHEET   **245**

Exercise 65.. 246
   Change Font and Font Size
   Change Font Attributes (Bold, Italics and Underline)
   Rotate Text
Exercise 66.. 250
   Change Cell Colors and Patterns
   Hide Worksheet Gridlines
   Format Painter
   Set Styles
   Format Sheet Backgrounds

Exercise 67..256
   Change Cell Borders
   Insert AutoShapes
Exercise 68..260
   Page Setup Options
   Center Titles Over Selected Range
   Edit Cell Formats
   Use WordArt Feature
Exercise 69..266
   Enlarge the Printout
   Insert and Size Pictures
   Download Clip Art from the Internet
Exercise 70..270
   Use Drawing Toolbar
   Insert Objects
   Format Graphic Objects
   Adjust Row Height
Exercise 71..276
   Add and Format a Text Box
   Add Callouts
Exercise 72..280
   Summary
Exercise 73..281

LESSON 10
ANALYZING DATA   **283**

Exercise 74..284
   Create a List/Database
   Add Records and Fields to a List
   Wrap Text
   Use a Data Form
Exercise 75..288
   Name Lists
   Data Validation
Exercise 76..292
   Sort Records in a List
   Undo a Sort
Exercise 77..298
   Default Sort Order
   Create Valid Data List
Exercise 78..302
   Update Database (Find, Delete, and
   Modify Records Using a Data Form)
   Add a Field to a List
Exercise 79..306
   AutoFilter
Exercise 80..308
   Maintain Original Record Order
   Advanced Filter
Exercise 81..314
   Extract Records Using Advanced Filter
   Edit Result List
Exercise 82..316
   Filter a List with Multiple Criteria
Exercise 83..320
   Use Database (List) Functions

Exercise 84 324
   Subtotals Within a List
   Nested Subtotals
   Remove Subtotals
   Copy Subtotals
   Outline Feature
Exercise 85 330
   Use Microsoft Query Wizard
Exercise 86 334
   Use a PivotTable to Summarize List Data
Exercise 87 340
   Consolidate Data
   Create a Consolidation Table
Exercise 88 344
   Summary
Exercise 89 346
   Summary

LESSON 11
MACRO BASICS AND HYPERLINKS   349

Exercise 90 350
   Create, Name, Record, and Run Simple Macros
   Stop Recording Toolbar
   Delete Macros
Exercise 91 354
   Open File Containing Macros
   Visual Basic
   Edit a Macro
   Assign Macro to a Graphic Control
Exercise 92 358
   Hyperlinks
   Create Hyperlinks in Excel
   Hyperlink to the Internet
Exercise 93 362
   Summary

LESSON 12
SUMMARY EXERCISES   363

Exercise 94 364
   Internet Basics
   Use Internet Features
Exercise 95 370
   Finance/Portfolio Analysis (Formulas, Charting,
   Enhancements)
   Use Internet Financial Services
Exercise 96 372
   Accounting: Balance Sheet (Copy Template
   sheet, 3-D references, Consolidate Data)
   Internet Research Using Current Periodicals
Exercise 97 376
   Economics/Decision Making (Formulas,
   Copying, Editing, Multiple Worksheets,
   AutoFormat, Charting, Enhancements)
Exercise 98 378
   Sales Marketing (Lists, Subtotals, Database
   Functions, Filters, Pivot Tables)
Exercise 99 380
   Accounting/Depreciation (Formulas,
   IF Statements)
Exercise 100 384
   Accounting/Financial Reports (3-D Reference,
   Worksheets,Enhancements)

APPENDIX   389

Appendix A 390
Appendix B 394
Appendix C 396
Appendix D 399
Appendix E 400

INDEX   401

About Microsoft® Excel 97

■ Microsoft ® Excel 97 is a spreadsheet program, used for analyses and graphing of numerical data.

■ The information created in Excel 97 can be shared with other Microsoft applications. For instance, a spreadsheet created in Excel can easily be incorporated into a memo or letter created in Microsoft Word, and a chart can easily be imported into a presentation created in Microsoft PowerPoint. Data created in any other Microsoft Office 97 application (which includes Excel, Access, Word, PowerPoint, Outlook and other utility applications) can also be incorporated into Excel.

About this Book

■ Learning Excel 97 is designed to be used with the Microsoft Excel 97 application for Windows 95 on an IBM PC or compatible computer.

■ Each lesson in this book explains concepts, provides numerous exercises to apply those concepts, and illustrates the necessary keystrokes or mouse actions required to complete the exercises. Lesson summary exercises are provided at the end of each lesson to challenge and reinforce the concepts learned.

■ After completing the exercises in this book, you will be able to use the essential features of Excel 97 with ease.

How to Use this Book

■ Each exercise contains four parts:

NOTES	explain the concept and application being introduced.
EXERCISE DIRECTIONS	explain how to complete the exercise.
EXERCISES	allow you to apply the new concept.
KEYSTROKES	outline the keystroke shortcuts and mouse actions required for completing an exercise.

✓ NOTE: *Keystrokes and mouse actions are only provided when a new concept is being introduced. Therefore, if you forget the keystroke or mouse action required to perform a task, you can use either the Microsoft online Help feature or the index of this book to find the procedure.*

The Teacher's Manual

■ While this book can be used as a self-paced learning book, a comprehensive Teacher's Manual (purchased separately) is also available. The Teacher's Manual contains the following:

- Lesson objectives

- Exercise objectives

- Related vocabulary

- Points to emphasize

- Exercise settings

- A Log of Exercises, which lists filenames in exercise number order

- A Directory of Documents, which lists filenames alphabetically along with the corresponding exercise numbers.

- Solution illustrations

Companion DDC CD-ROM

■ The DDC CD-ROM that accompanies this book contains the following:

PROGRAMS:

- Excel Internet Simulation

- Multimedia Internet Browser tutorial

- Demo of DDC's Office 97 CBT (computer based training)

FILES:

- Data files

- Clip art file (from the Internet)

Excel Internet Simulation

- This simulation program allows you to complete the exercises in this book that integrate Excel 97 and the Internet without accessing the Internet. This means that you can complete the exercises without an Internet connection, therefore avoiding modems, connection time and fees, wandering to unrelated sites, and long waits for Web sites to load. It's like being live on the Internet without the inconveniences that can sometimes result.

- For example, in Exercise 95, you will be asked to conduct a search for stock prices at a search site and then incorporate the results into an Excel 97 document. Where indicated in the exercise, follow the detailed directions to launch the simulation and follow the prompts at the bottom of your screen to find the information that you need. You will then copy the results of your search and paste them directly into Excel. Even if you have never been on the Internet before, you will be able to do the exercises. As a result, you will learn how to integrate the power of Excel 97 with the power of the Internet.
(See Program Installation Instructions on the right.)

Multimedia Internet Browser Tutorial

- For the new user of the Internet, the CD-ROM includes basic computer based training on how to navigate the Internet using a browser. A browser is a program that helps manage the process of locating information on the Word Wide Web. The tutorial introduces the concepts and then shows you how to apply them.
(See Program Installation Instructions on the right.)

Demo of DDC's Office 97 CBT

- In this excerpt of DDC's Office 97 CBT (Computer Based Training), you will receive a sample of step-by-step directions, illustrations, simulations of desired keystrokes or mouse actions, and application problems. This program is designed to teach you the basic functions of Microsoft Office 97, which include: Excel 97, Word 97, PowerPoint 97 and Access 97.

Program Installation Instructions

- A separate installation is required for each program. At the designated prompt, indicate which program you wish to install: Excel Internet Simulation, Office 97 CBT or Internet Browser Tutorial. When installation of one program is complete, you may begin again from step one to install another.

System Requirements

Software	Windows 95 or Windows NT 3.51 (or higher)
Hardware	80486DX or higher, 16 MB RAM, 256 Color Monitor, and CD-ROM Drive-
Disk Space	30 MB available hard disk space for a Typical installation.

To install a program, place the DDC CD-ROM in your CD-ROM drive and follow the listed steps below:

1. **To install from Windows 95:**
   Click Start on the desktop and click Run.
   OR
   To install from Windows NT:
   Go to Program Manager in Main, click File.

2. In the Run window, begin a program installation by typing one of the following:

   - *CD-ROM drive letter:*\EX97INT\SETUP to install the **Excel Internet Simulation**.

   - *CD-ROM drive letter:*\OFFICE97\SETUP to install the **Office 97 CBT**.

   - *CD-ROM drive letter:* \NETSIM\SETUP to install the **Browser tutorial**.

3. Click NEXT at the Setup Wizard screen.

4. At the following screen, click NEXT to create a DDCPUB directory for storing program files. Then click YES to confirm the directory choice.

5. At the following screen, allow the default folder to be named DDC Publishing, and click NEXT. At the next screen, choose one of the following options based on your individual system needs:

   ✓ NOTE: *A **Typical** installation is standard for most individual installation.*

- **TYPICAL** installs a minimum number of files to the hard drive with the majority of files remaining on the CD-ROM.

  ✓ *NOTE: With this installation, the CD must remain in the CD-ROM drive when running the program.*

- **COMPACT** installs the fewest required files to the hard drive. This is the best option for portable computers and computers with little available hard disk space.

  ✓ *NOTE: With this installation, the CD must remain in the CD-ROM drive when running the program.*

- **CUSTOM** installs only those files that you choose to the hard drive. This is generally only recommended for advanced users of Innovus Multimedia software.

- **SERVER** installs the programs on a network server and enables you to then do workstation installations to any computer connected to your network. **(A separate Network Site License purchase is required for this option.)**

7. Click NEXT to begin copying the necessary files to your system.

8. Click OK at the Set Up status Window and then click YES to restart Windows.

- To launch a program, click the Start button on the Windows 95 desktop, select Programs, DDC Publishing, and then select one of the following:

  - **Ex97INT** (to start the Internet Simulation)

  - **DEMO97** (to start the Office97 CBT)

  - **NETCBT** (to start the Browser tutorial)

Network Site Licence

- If you wish to install the programs and data files that accompany this book on a network server, a Network Site License may be purchased separately from DDC Publishing. This would enable any computer workstation that is connected to the main server to access the programs and data files.

Data Files

- Since this book is designed to teach you how to use the features of Microsoft Excel 97, and not how to type, you can use data files to avoid typing long documents that are used in many of the exercises. Data files are provided on the accompanying CD-ROM in the Ex97data folder. Directions are provided in each exercise for both data file and non-data file users. For example, exercise directions will include a keyboard icon 🖮 to direct *non-data file* users to open documents that they would have created in a previous exercise, and a diskette icon 🖫 to direct *data file* users to open the document available on the CD-ROM. A typical direction might read: Open 🖮**DUES**, or open 🖫**09DUES**.

To copy data files onto a hard drive using Window 95 Explorer:

1. Open Windows 95 Explorer (Right-click on **Start** button and click **Explore**).

2. Be sure that the CD is in your CD-ROM drive. Select the CD-ROM drive letter in the **All Folders** pane of Windows 95 Explorer.

3. Click to Select the **Ex97data** folder in the **Contents of (CD-ROM Drive letter)** pane of Windows 95 Explorer.

- Drag the folder to the letter representing your hard drive (usually **C:**) in the **All Folders** pane of Windows 95 Explorer.

  NOTE: Saving files to most local area networks automatically truncates all filenames to a maximum of eight characters. Therefore, if you copy data and solution files to a local area network, some filenames on the network may differ from the filenames used in the book. You can, however, rely on the first two characters of data filenames and first three characters of solution filenames to identify the files correctly.

- A directory of data and solutions filenames are provided in the Log of Exercises section of this book.

Clip Art File

- A clip art file, **ENTE0017.WMF**, has been provided on the DDC-CD-ROM in the Clip Art folder. This file can be accessed by Excel Internet Simulation users in place of the file that is downloaded from the live Internet in exercise 69. Installation instructions are provided in the exercise directions of exercise 69.

Solution Files

- The Solution disk (purchased separately) may be used for you to compare your work with the final version or solution on disk. Each solution filename begins with the letter "S" and is followed by the exercise number and a descriptive filename. For example, **S09DUES** would contain the final solution to the exercise directions in exercise nine.

Lesson	Exercise	Filename	Data file	Solution File	Page
1	1				
	2				
	3				
2	4				
	5				
3	6	REGISTER		S06REGISTER	34
	7	PAYROLL		S07PAYROLL	37
	8	INVOICE		S08INVOICE	38
	9	DUES		S09DUES	40
	10	INVEN		S10INVEN	41
4	11	SAVINGS		S11SAVINGS	45
	12	INVOICE INV2	12INVOICE	S12INVOICE S12INV2	48
	13	SAVINGS	13SAVINGS	S13SAVINGS	52
	14	PAYROLL	14PAYROLL	S14PAYROLL	56
	15	REGISTER	15REGISTER	S15REGISTER	59
	16	BAKERY		S16BAKERY	64
	17	USEMPS		S17USEMPS	66
	18	AGENT		S18AGENT	67
5	19	SAVINGS	19SAVINGS	S19SAVINGS	72
	20	INVEN	20INVEN	S20INVEN	75
	21	FURN	21FURN	S21FURN	80
	22	PAYROLL	22PAYROLL	S22PAYROLL	84
	23	FURN	23FURN	S23FURN	89
	24	EXPENSE	24EXPENSE	S24EXPENSE	92
	25	INS	25INS	S25INS	97
	26	MUSIC	26MUSIC	S26MUSIC	100
	27	GRADES		S27GRADES	101
6	28	PAYROLL	28PAYROLL	S28PAYROLL	106
	29	INS	29INS	S29INS	110
	30	INS ISANA INSANAL	30INS	S30INS S30ISANA S30INSANAL	114
	31	PAYROLL PAYFORM	31PAYROLL	S31PAYFORM	119
	32	FURN	32FURN	S32FURN	123
	33	INVEST INVSUM	33INVEST	S33INVEST S33INVSUM	128
	34	FURN FURNSUM	34FURN	S34FURN S34FURNSUM	130
	35	INS INSQTRS	35INS	S35INS S35INSQTRS	134
	36	ADINV ZINNO		S36ADINV S36ZINNO	137

Lesson	Exercise	Filename	Data file	Solution File	Page
	37	SALCOM CHUCK PAT ROGER MOSUM	37SALCOM 37MOSUM	S37SALCOM S37CHUCK S37PAT S37ROGER S37MOSUM	142
	38	PAYFORM	38PAYFORM	S38PAYFORM	146
	39	BAKERY BREAD	39BAKERY	S39BAKERY	148 149
	40	GRADES FINSUM	40GRADES	S40GRADES S40FINSUM	150
	41	REDUCE	41REDUCE	S41REDUCE	156
	42	LOAN	42LOAN	S42LOAN	159
	43	FINSUM	43FINSUM	S43FINSUM	163
7	44	AUTO	44AUTO	S44AUTO	168
	45	RAISE	45RAISE	S45RAISE	172
	46	INVEST	46INVEST	S46INVEST	175
	47	AR	47AR	S47AR	180
	48	LOAN DREAM	48LOAN	S48DREAM	184
	49	INVEN VALUE	49INVEN	S49VALUE	186 187
	50	MAIL	50MAIL	S50MAIL	189
	51	FURN	51FURN	S51FURN	193
	52	AR	52AR	S52AR	196
	53	GRAIN BPRICE	53GRAIN	S53GRAIN S53BPRICE	198
8	54	SPORTS	54SPORTS	S54SPORTS	206
	55	SPORTS	55SPORTS	S55SPORTS	212
	56	INSQTRS	56INSQTRS	S56INSQTRS	216
	57	SPORTS	57SPORTS.	S57SPORTS	220
	58	GROW	58GROW	S58GROW	224
	59	STOCK	59STOCK	S59STOCK	228
	60	PROD	60PROD	S60PROD	231
	61	INVEST	61INVEST	S61INVEST	235
	62	USEMPS	62USEMPS	S62USEMPS	239
	63	MUSIC	63MUSIC	S63MUSIC	242
	64	FURN	64FURN	S64FURN	244
9	65	INVSUM	65INVSUM	S65INVSUM	248
	66	RAISE	66RAISE	S66RAISE	252
	67	AUTO	67AUTO	S67AUTO	258
	68	RAISE	68RAISE	S68RAISE	262
	69	MUSIC	69MUSIC	S69MUSIC	267
	70	SAVINGS	70SAVINGS	S70SAVINGS	272
	71	INSQTRS	71INSQTRS	S71INSQTRS	276
	72	FURN	72FURN	S72FURN	280

Lesson	Exercise	Filename	Data file	Solution File	Page
	73	NET	73NET	S73NET	281
10	74	EMPS	74EMPS	S74EMPS	286
	75	EMPS	75EMPS	S75EMPS	290
	76	EMPS	76EMPS	S76EMPS	294
	77	HOME	77HOME	S77HOME	299
	78	EMPS	78EMPS	S78EMPS	303
	79	EMPS	79EMPS	S79EMPS	307
	80	HOME	80HOME	S80HOME	309
	81	STORE	81STORE	S81STORE	314
	82	HOME	82HOME	S82HOME	318
	83	STORE	83STORE	S83STORE	321
	84	EMPS	84EMPS	S84EMPS	326
	85	BUDGET	85COLLEGE. MDB	S85BUDGET	329
	86	EMPS	86EMPS	S86EMPS	336
	87	EXPENSES	87EXPENSES	S87EXPENSES	341
	88	CKBK	88CKBK	S88CKBK	344
	89	ROYALE	89ROYALE	S89ROYALE	346
11	90	LIST	90LIST	S90LIST	352
	91	LIST	91LIST	S91LIST	355
	92	TOGS SPORTS	92TOGS 92SPORTS	S92TOGS S92SPORTS	360
	93	MYMACS REDUCE INVEST	93REDUCE 93INVEST	S93MYMACS S93REDUCE 93INVEST	362
12	94	TRADE	94TRADE	S94TRADE	367
	95	FOLIO	95FOLIO	S95FOLIO	370
	96	WEB		S96WEB	373
	97	CAB	97CAB	S97CAB	376
	98	JOG	98JOG	S98JOG	378
	99	DEPR	99DEPR	S99DEPR	381
	100	DECOR	100DECOR	S100DECOR	384

DIRECTORY OF FILES

Filename	Exercise
ADINV	36
AGENT	18
AR	47, 52
AUTO	44, 67
BAKERY	16, 39
BPRICE	53
BREAD	39
BUDGET	85
CAB	97
CHUCK	37
CKBK	88
DECOR	100
DEPR	99
DREAM	48
DUES	9
EMPS	74, 75, 76,78, 79, 84, 86
EXPENSE	24, 87
FINSUM	40, 43
FOLIO	95
FURN	21, 23, 32, 34, 51, 64, 72
FURNSUM	34

Filename	Exercise
GRADES	27, 40
GRAIN	53
GROW	58
HOME	77, 80, 82
INS	25, 29, 30, 35
INSANAL	30
INSQTRS	35, 56, 71
INV2	12
INVEN	10, 20, 49
INVEST	33, 46, 61, 93
INVOICE	8, 12
INVSUM	33, 65
ISANA	30
JOG	98
LIST	90, 91
LOAN	42, 48
MAIL	50
MOSUM	37
MUSIC	26, 63, 69
MYMACS	93
NET	73
PAT	37

Filename	Exercise
PAYFORM	31, 38
PAYROLL	7, 14, 22, 28, 31
PROD	60
RAISE	45, 66, 68
REDUCE	41, 93
REGISTER	6, 15
ROGER	37
ROYALE	89
SALCOM	37
SAVINGS	11, 13, 19, 70
SPORTS	54, 55, 57, 92
STOCK	59, 81, 83
TOGS	92
TRADE	94
USEMPS	17, 62
VALUE	49
WEB	373
ZINNO	36

Excel

LESSON 1

GETTING STARTED

Exercises 1-3

- Start Microsoft Excel
- The Microsoft Excel 97 Window
- The Workbook Window
- The Mouse and Keyboard
- Menus, Toolbars, and Commands
- Exit Excel
- The Excel 97 Keyboard Template
- Select Menu Items
- Options in a Dialog Box
- Set View Preferences
- The View Menu
- Change Window Displays
- Help Features
- Office Assistant
- Contents and Index
- Exit Help

Exercise 1	■ **Start Microsoft Excel** ■ **The Microsoft® Excel 97 Window** ■ **The Workbook Window** ■ **The Mouse and Keyboard** ■ **Menus, Toolbars, and Commands** ■ **Exit Excel** ■ **The Excel 97 Keyboard Template**

NOTES

Start Microsoft® Excel

■ Microsoft® Excel 97 is a spreadsheet tool that is used for analyzing, charting, and managing data. It is a powerful software application that is used extensively for personal, business, and financial solutions. Excel 97 may be started in Windows® 95 as follows:

- On the Windows 95 Taskbar: Click **Start**, highlight **Programs**, and highlight and select **Microsoft Excel**.

■ If you own Excel as part of the Microsoft® Office 97 suite, the program may be started using the method noted above or as follows:

- On the Windows 95 Taskbar: Click **Start**, highlight and select **New Office Document**, select **Blank Workbook**.

- On the Microsoft Shortcut Bar: Select **Open Office Document** and select **Blank Workbook**. (You may customize the Shortcut Bar to include an Excel icon, which will open Excel and a blank workbook simultaneously.)

The Microsoft Excel 97 Window

■ The Microsoft® Excel 97 window that displays when the program is first started appears below:

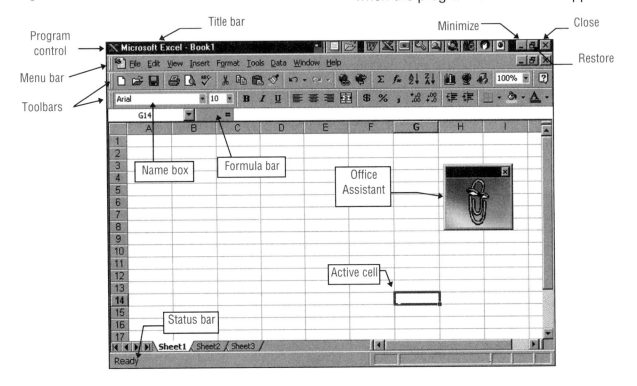

2

Note the following Excel window parts:

- The **application window title bar**, located at the top of the application window, displays the program name (Microsoft Excel), and the filename of an open workbook window when maximized. You can drag the title bar to move the Excel window, or double-click to maximize or minimize the window.

- The **program control menu icon**, located to the left of the application window title bar, can be clicked to access a drop-down menu with commands to control the Excel window.

- The application window minimize, restore and close buttons, are located on the right side of the application window title bar. Clicking the **minimize button** ▬ shrinks the Excel window to a button on the Windows 95 Taskbar. Clicking the **restore button** 🗗 reduces the Excel screen to a window on your desktop. When Excel is a window on the desktop, the **maximize button** 🗖 appears so it can be brought back to a full screen. The **close button** ☒ exits or closes the program.

- The **menu bar**, located below the Excel title bar, displays menu names from which drop-down menus may be accessed.

- The **toolbars**, located below the menu bar, contain buttons that can be used to select commands quickly without opening a menu or dialog box. Pointing to and resting the pointer on a toolbar button displays the tool name, while an explanation of the button's function is displayed on the status bar. This is called the ToolTips function.

- The **name box**, located below the toolbars and to the left of the window, displays the active cell reference, i.e. the location of your cursor.

- The **formula bar**, located next to the name box, provides a space for typing or editing cell data.

- The **mouse pointer** moves as you move the mouse. Its shape changes to signal different functions. Use the mouse pointer to select cells, menu items, toolbar buttons, or worksheets.

- The **status bar**, located at the bottom of the Excel window, displays information about the current mode, selected command, or option. At the right of the status bar is the AutoCalculate box. The results of automatically calculating selected cells using a variety of formulas are displayed here.

- The **Office Assistant** is a new online help feature. The Assistant provides context-sensitive help and offers advice, allowing you to search the index or ask questions. It tracks your actions and can suggest the next steps to take. It will be discussed further in Exercise 3.

The Workbook Window

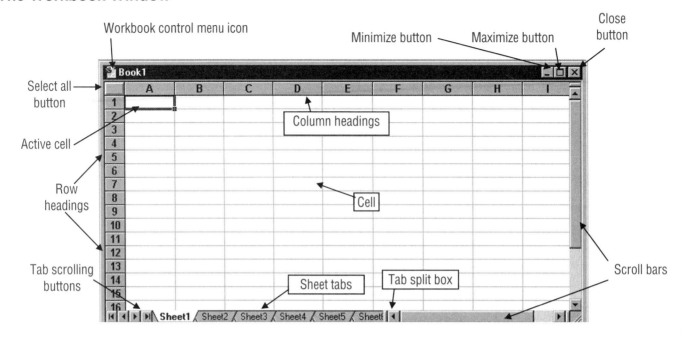

Note the following workbook window parts:

- A **workbook** (Book1) displaying the active **worksheet** (Sheet1) is the document window that opens when you start Excel 97. By default, workbooks contain three worksheets (Sheet1-Sheet3). You can have up to 255 sheets in a workbook to enter your data and formulas or to create charts and macros. Several workbooks may be open at one time.

- The **workbook window title bar** located at the top of a workbook window, displays the workbook filename. You can drag the title bar to move the window or double-click it to maximize the window size. A maximized workbook window does not have a title bar. Its filename appears on the application window title bar.

- The **workbook control menu** icon is at the left of the document window title bar. If the workbook window is maximized, its control menu icon is located on the left side of the Excel window menu bar. Clicking the document window control menu box opens a drop-down menu with commands that control the workbook window.

- The workbook window minimize, maximize, and close buttons are located on the right side of the document window title bar. Clicking the

- **minimize button** [_] shrinks the workbook window to an icon. Clicking the **maximize button** [□] enlarges the workbook to its largest size. Once the window has been maximized, the maximize button changes to the **restore button** [⮌] and these buttons are located on the right side of the Excel window menu bar. Clicking the restore button returns the workbook window to the previous size. The **close button** [X] will close the workbook window.

- **Row** and **column headings** are the areas at the left and top of the worksheet. Rows are numbered and columns are lettered. A worksheet can have up to 65,536 rows and 256 columns.

- The intersection of rows and columns forms a grid of cells. A **cell** is a single location on a worksheet in which data is stored. A cell reference refers to a column letter and row number, which are highlighted. For example, A1 is the cell reference of the cell where row 1 intersects column A. The *active cell* contains a dark outline, cell A1 in the illustration above. The cell must be active to enter data or formulas into the cell.

- When you enter data or double-click a cell, Excel displays the **insertion point**, a flashing line that indicates the cell is ready to receive data or be edited.

- When you click the **select all** button, located at the intersection of the row and column headings in the upper-left hand corner of the worksheet, all the cells in the worksheet become selected.

- The **tab scrolling** buttons located at the bottom left of the workbook window, provide a way for you to scroll to hidden sheet tabs.

- The **sheet tabs** are located next to the tab scrolling buttons, at the bottom of the workbook window. Clicking a sheet tab displays that sheet in the workbook window. The active sheet tab is shown in bold, Sheet1 in the illustration on the previous page.

- The **tab split box** is located between the sheet tabs and the horizontal scroll bar at the bottom of the workbook window. This box can be dragged to the right to display more sheet tabs or to the left to show more of the horizontal scroll bar. The mouse pointer will change to a ← | | → to denote that the split box may be dragged to the left or right.

- The **scroll bars** located at the right and bottom borders of the workbook window, are used to display areas of the workbook that are not in view. You can click a scroll arrow to move one row or column at a time, click a scroll bar to move one screen at a time, or drag a scroll box to move quickly to a desired sheet area.

The Mouse and Keyboard

- You can use the mouse or the keyboard to choose commands and perform tasks.

Using the Mouse

- When the mouse is moved on the tabletop, a corresponding movement of the mouse pointer occurs on the screen. The mouse pointer changes shape depending upon the object it is pointing to and actions it can perform. The mouse pointer will not move if the mouse is lifted up and placed back on the tabletop.

- Microsoft has introduced a new pointing device called the IntelliMouse. This device makes it easier to scroll and zoom your view of a worksheet or expand and collapse data in special formats. The mouse terminology and the corresponding actions described below will be used throughout the book:

- **Point to** — Move the mouse (on the tabletop) so the pointer touches a specific item.

- **Click** — Point to the item and quickly press and release the left mouse button.

- **Right–click** — Point to the item and quickly press and release the right mouse button.

- **Double–click** — Point to the item and press the left mouse button twice in rapid succession.

- **Drag** — Point to the item and press and hold down the left mouse button while moving the mouse. When the item is in the desired position, release the mouse button to place the item.

- **Right–drag** — Point to the item and press and hold down the right mouse button while moving the mouse. When the item is in the desired position, release the mouse button to place the item.

Using the Keyboard

- In addition to the alphanumeric keys found on most typewriters, computers contain additional keys:

- **Function keys** (F1 through F10 or F12, depending on your keyboard) perform special functions and are located across the top of an enhanced keyboard (which has 12 function keys) or on the side (which has ten function keys).

- **Modifier keys** (Shift, Alt, Ctrl) are used in conjunction with other keys to select certain commands or perform actions. To use a modifier key with another key, you must hold down the modifier key while tapping the other key.

- **Numeric keys** found on keyboards with a number pad, allow you to enter numbers quickly. When Num Lock is ON, the number keys on the pad are operational, as is the decimal point. When Num Lock is OFF, the cursor control keys (Home, PgUp, End, PgDn) are active. The numbers on the top row of the keyboard are always active.

- **Escape key** (Esc) is used to cancel some actions, commands, menus, or an entry.

- **Directional arrow keys** are used to move the active cell when in the Ready mode or the insertion point when in the Edit mode.

- **Enter keys** (there are two on most keyboards) are used to complete an entry of data into a cell.

Menus, Toolbars, and Commands

- In Excel, commands are used to change or enter data and are applied to selected cells or objects. The menu bar, shortcut menus, and toolbar buttons may be used to select commands.

- The menu bar may be used with the keyboard or the mouse.

To select a menu:

- Use the mouse to point to a menu on the menu bar and click once, or

- Press Alt + underlined letter in the menu name.

- Note the drop-down menu that appears when the File menu is selected. Several commands have icons that may be selected from the toolbar or can be added to a customized toolbar.

To select a command from the drop-down menu:

- Use the mouse to point to the command on the drop-down menu and click once, or

- Press the underlined letter in the command name, or

- Use the up or down arrow key to highlight the command, then press Enter.

  Shortcut menus are only available by using the mouse.

To access shortcut menu commands:

- Use the mouse to point to the object you want the command to act on and right-click once.

  ✓ NOTE: Not all objects display a menu when right-clicked.

- Note the pop-up menu that appears when a cell in a worksheet is right-clicked:

To select a command from the pop-up (shortcut) menu:

- Use the mouse to point to the command on the pop-up menu and click once, or

- Use the up or down arrow key to highlight the command, then press Enter.

- The toolbars provide icons that represent commands that are activated by using the mouse. Excel 97 has thirteen toolbars that may be displayed as needed. The Standard and Formatting toolbars are present by default. Toolbars may be customized by adding and deleting buttons so that your most frequently used commands are on the toolbar.

To select a command from a toolbar

- Use the mouse to point to a button and click once.

Exit Excel

- The quickest way to exit Excel with the mouse is to use the Close button in the top right corner of the screen on the Excel title bar.

The Excel 97 Keyboard Template

- To assist you in remembering special key combinations, you may use the keyboard template of frequently used commands illustrated below. The key combinations will be presented in the keystroke procedures as the corresponding topics are discussed in this text.

Command	Keys	Command	Keys	Command	Keys
Calculate active worksheet	Shift + F9	Extend selection	F8	Repeat	F4
Calculate open workbooks	F9	Find	Ctrl + F	Replace	Ctrl + H
Change reference type	F4	Format cells/object	Ctrl + 1	Save	Shift + F12
Copy selection	Ctrl + C	Go to	F5	Save As	F12
Create chart	F11	Help	F1	Select column	Ctrl + Space
Cut selection	Ctrl + X	Move to next page	F6	Select entire worksheet	Ctrl + A
Display AutoComplete	Alt + ↓	Open	Ctrl + F12	Select row	Shift + Space
Edit cell	F2	Paste	Ctrl + V	Spell check	F7
Enter current date	Ctrl + ;	Paste named reference	F3	Undo	Ctrl + Z
Enter current time	Ctrl + Shift + ;	Print	Ctrl + Shift + F12		

EXERCISE DIRECTIONS

1. Roll the mouse up, down, left, and right on the tabletop (or the mousepad).

2. Click File. Note the drop-down menu selections.

3. Click away from the File menu once to close it.

4. Click Edit. Note the drop-down menu selections.

5. Slide the mouse to the View menu. Note the drop-down menu selections.
   - Once a menu is selected you can view other sub-menus by sliding the mouse across the menu bar.

6. Close the View menu by clicking off the menu.

7. Select the Insert menu. Note the drop-down menu selections.

8. Close the Insert menu.

9. Select each remaining menu.
   ✓ *Note the drop-down menu selections of each menu.*

10. Point to any worksheet cell and right-click to open a shortcut menu. Note the pop-up menu selections.

11. Click once away from the shortcut menu to close it.

12. Point to and rest the pointer on a toolbar button to display its name. Do this procedure for all buttons on the toolbars.
    ✓ *A ToolTip displays the name of the button.*

13. Use keystrokes to select a column by pressing Ctrl+Space Bar. The column where the cursor is located will be selected. Click on any other cell to deselect the column.

14. Use keystrokes to select a row by pressing Shift+Space Bar. The row where the cursor is located will be selected. Click on any other cell to deselect the row.

15. Use keystrokes to select the entire worksheet by pressing Ctrl+A. The entire worksheet will be selected. Click on any cell to deselect the worksheet.

16. Use the mouse to select the entire worksheet by selecting the Select All button at the intersection of the row and column headings. Click on any cell to deselect the worksheet.

17. Exit Excel by clicking the close button.
    ✓ *Mouse action procedures are indicated on the left; keyboard procedures are indicated on the right. You may use either the mouse or the keystrokes, or a combination of both.*

KEYSTROKES

START EXCEL

1. Click **Start** on Taskbar........... `Ctrl` + `Esc`
2. Select **P**rograms .... `P`
3. Select **Microsoft Excel** .... `↓`

SELECT A MENU BAR ITEM

1. Click desired menu name ...... `Alt` +*letter*
2. Click desired menu item................. *letter*

SELECT A SHORTCUT MENU ITEM

1. Right–click desired object.
2. Click desired menu item.

CLOSE A MENU

Click anywhere off the menu.
OR
Press Escape .... `Esc`

VIEW TOOLBAR BUTTON DESCRIPTIONS

Point to and rest pointer on desired toolbar button.

✓ *The tool name is displayed next to the button and its purpose is shown on the Status Bar.*

EXIT WITHOUT SAVING

Press **Alt** + **F4**.............................. `Alt` + `F4`
OR
1. Click **File** menu .... `Alt` + `F`
2. Click **Exit** .... `X`
OR
Click **Close** button .... `X`

✓ *When a message box appears prompting you to save changes to the open workbook, click the **No** button. Saving a workbook will be covered in Lesson 3.*

Exercise
2

■ **Select Menu Items** ■ **Options in a Dialog Box**
■ **Set View Preferences** ■ **The View Menu**

NOTES

Select Menu Items

■ In Exercise 1, you selected menus from the menu bar. Once a menu is selected, it opens a **drop-down menu** that lists items from which you can choose. The menus Excel displays will vary. For example, if no workbook is open, Excel displays only the **File** and **Help** menus. The items on a drop-down menu will depend on the object that is selected.

Note the drop-down menus that appear when the **View** and **Tools** menus are selected:

■ Note on the Tools menu that some options appear dimmed, while others appear black. **Dimmed options** are not available for selection at this time while **black options** are.

■ A **check mark** next to a drop-down menu item means the option is currently selected.

■ A menu item followed by an **arrow** (<) opens a **submenu** with additional choices.

■ A menu item followed by an **ellipsis** (...) indicates that a **dialog box** (which requires you to provide additional information to complete a task) will be forthcoming.

Options in a Dialog Box

- A **dialog box** contains different ways to ask you for information:

  - The **title bar** identifies the title of the dialog box.

  - The **text box** is a location where you type information.

  - **Command buttons** carry out actions described on the button. When command names have an ellipsis following them, they will access another dialog box.

  - A **drop-down list** is marked with a down arrow. Clicking the drop-down list arrow accesses a short list of options. Make a choice from the options provided.

  - An **increment box** provides a space for typing a value. An up or down arrow (usually to the right of the box) gives you a way to select a value with the mouse.

  - A **named tab** is used to display options related to the tab's name in the same dialog box.

- **Option buttons** are small circular buttons marking options that appear as a set. You may choose only one option from the set. A selected option button contains a dark circle.

- **Check boxes** are small square boxes where options may be selected or deselected. A check mark "✓" within a box indicates that the option is selected. If several check boxes are offered, you may select more than one.

- A **list box** displays a list of items from which selections can be made. A list box may have a scroll bar that can be used to show hidden items in the list.

- A **scroll bar** is a horizontal or vertical bar providing scroll arrows and a scroll box that can be used to show hidden items in a list.

Note the labeled parts in the dialog box below:

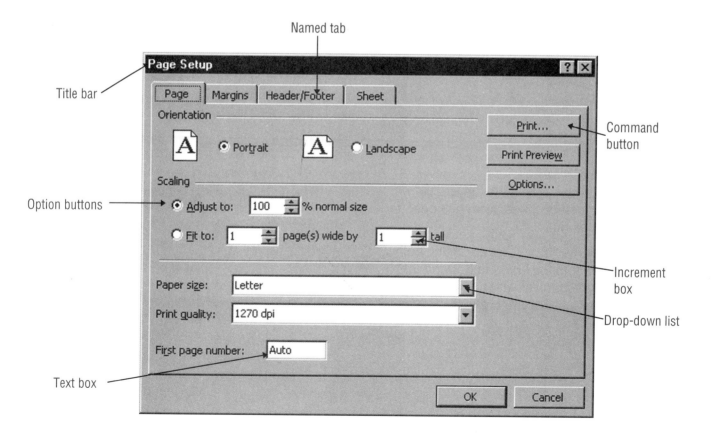

Set View Preferences

- The default view settings for windows are indicated in the View tab in the Options dialog box indicated below. To customize view preferences, select **Options** from the **Tools** menu and then select the View tab in the Options dialog box.

  To change the settings, you may deselect or select any combination of features in the View tab. The items are selected or deselected by clicking the check boxes or option buttons. When selected, check boxes contain a "✓" and option buttons contain a dark dot. In the illustration below, note the View tab in the Options dialog box and the default view settings.

Options Dialog Box

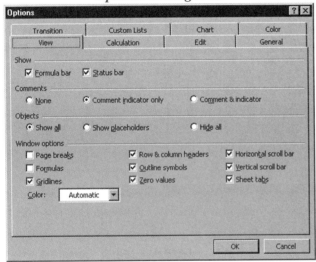

- The <u>T</u>oolbars command on the <u>V</u>iew menu displays a submenu that contains a list of available toolbars that are checked if they are currently displayed. You may select a toolbar to display it and deselect it to hide it.

  ✓ *NOTE:* *To work through the exercises in this text, the Standard and Formatting toolbars must be displayed on your screen. If these items are not displayed, follow the keystrokes at the end of this exercise.*

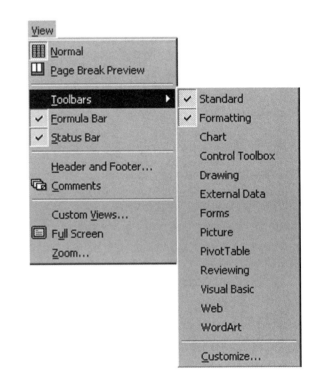

The View Menu

- A quick way to view or hide the formula or status bar is to select or deselect each option from the **View** menu.

- Note the check marks on the <u>V</u>iew menu below, which indicates that the Formula Bar and the <u>S</u>tatus Bar have been selected:

Full Screen View

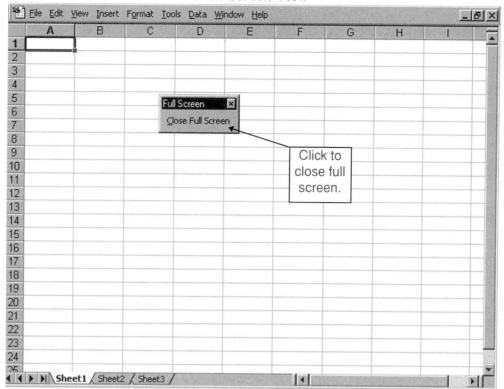

Click to close full screen.

■ The <u>V</u>iew menu contains a new option called **F<u>u</u>ll Screen** that expands the worksheet to fill the screen. As you will note in the illustration above, the toolbars are hidden and only the menu bar is displayed for commands. A <u>C</u>lose Full Screen box may appear, which can be used to return to the default view. You may also use the <u>V</u>iew menu and deselect F<u>u</u>ll Screen to close this view.

■ The <u>V</u>iew menu also contains a **Zoom** option that allows you to set the magnification of cells in a worksheet. When <u>Z</u>oom is selected, the following dialog box appears:

By clicking an option button, you can display the cells at **<u>2</u>5%**, **<u>5</u>0%**, **<u>7</u>5%**, **<u>1</u>00%**, or **20<u>0</u>%** of the normal display. The **<u>C</u>ustom** option sets the zoom percentage anywhere from 10%-400%. The **<u>F</u>it Selection** option sizes a selected range to the current window size.

✓ NOTE: *If you are using the IntelliMouse, you can hold down the Ctrl button, roll the wheel on the IntelliMouse and adjust the view by 10% increments from 10%-500%.*

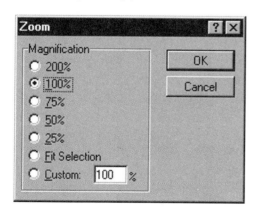

EXERCISE DIRECTIONS

1. Select Tools from the menu bar.

2. Select Options.

3. Select the View tab in the Options dialog box.

4. Deselect the Formula Bar check box.

5. Select OK.
   - ✓ *Note the change.*

6. Repeat steps 1–2.

7. Select the Formula Bar check box.

8. Select OK.
   - ✓ *Note the change.*

9. Repeat steps 1–2.

10. Make the following changes:
    a. Deselect the status bar.
    b. Deselect the vertical scroll bar and horizontal scroll bar.
    c. Click the Gridlines, Color drop-down arrow, then click the red color box in the palette.

11. Select OK.
    - ✓ *Note the changes.*

12. Restore View options to the default settings by reversing all actions listed above. The color setting is to Automatic.

13. Select View from the menu bar.

14. Select Zoom.

15. Select the 50% magnification option.

16. Select OK.
    - ✓ *Note the changes.*

17. Repeat steps 13–16 several times choosing a different magnification each time.

18. Select Zoom from the View menu.

19. Select Custom and type 300 in the text box.

20. Select OK.
    - ✓ *Note the changes.*

21. Select Zoom from the View menu.

22. Select 100% magnification to return to the default zoom setting.

23. Select OK.

24. Select Toolbars from the View menu.

25. Select the Drawing toolbar. (The toolbar will be checked. Note the buttons on the new toolbar.)

26. Repeat step 24 and deselect the Drawing toolbar.

27. Select Page Setup from the File menu.

28. Click the Margins tab.
    - ✓ *Note the margin options displayed in the dialog box.*

29. Press the Escape key to close the dialog box.

30. Select Page Setup from the File menu.

31. Practice selecting options in a dialog box:

32. Select the Page tab.
    - ✓ *Note the dialog box selections.*
    a. Click the Landscape option button to select it.
    b. Click the Paper Size drop-down arrow.
       - ✓ *Note the choices, but do not select one.*
    c. Click the Margins tab.
    d. Click the up arrow in the Top increment box until a 2 appears.
    e. Double-click in the Left increment box and type 2.5.
    f. Press Tab and type 2.5 in the Right increment box.
       - ✓ *Note effects of changes in the sample Preview.*
    g. Exit Page Setup. (Click Cancel or press Escape. The changes will not be made since you did not click OK.)

33. Select Exit from the File menu to exit Excel.

KEYSTROKES

SET VIEW PREFERENCES

1. Click **Tools** menu .... `Alt`+`T`
2. Click **Options**... .... `O`
3. Click **View** tab .... `Ctrl`+`Tab`

To set general view options:

Select or deselect desired **Show** options:

- **Formula Bar** .... `Alt`+`F`
- **Status Bar** .... `Alt`+`S`

Select or deselect desired Comments options:

- **None** .... `Alt`+`N`
- **Comment indicator only**... `Alt`+`I`
- **Comment & indicator** ...... `Alt`+`M`

Select or deselect desired Objects options:

- **Show all** .... `Alt`+`A`
- **Show place holders** .... `Alt`+`P`
- **Hide all** .... `Alt`+`D`

To set view of window options:

Select or deselect desired **Window Options**:

- **Page Breaks** .... `Alt`+`K`
- **Formulas** .... `Alt`+`R`
- **Gridlines** .... `Alt`+`G`
- **Color** .... `Alt`+`C`
- Select a color .... `⬍`
- **Row & column headers** .... `Alt`+`E`
- **Outline** symbols .... `Alt`+`O`
- **Zero** values .... `Alt`+`Z`
- **Horizontal** scroll bar .... `Alt`+`T`
- **Vertical** scroll bar .... `Alt`+`V`
- **Sheet tabs** .... `Alt`+`B`

4. Click **OK** .... `Enter`

EXIT EXCEL USING THE MENU

1. Click **File** menu .... `Alt`+`F`
2. Click **Exit** .... `X`

ZOOM

1. Click **View** menu .... `Alt`+`V`
2. Click **Zoom** .... `Z`
3. Select desired **Magnification** option:

- **200%** .... `0`
- **100%** .... `1`
- **75%** .... `7`
- **50%** .... `5`
- **25%** .... `2`

OR

a. Select **Custom** .... `C`
b. Type zoom percentage (10–400)

4. Click **OK** .... `Enter`

VIEW TOOLBARS

1. Click **View** menu .... `Alt`+`V`
2. Click **Toolbars** .... `T`
3. Click desired toolbar .... `⬍`

Exercise 3

- Change Window Displays ■ Help Features
- The Office Assistant ■ Contents and Index ■ Exit Help

NOTES

Change Window Displays

- The Minimize ▭ , Maximize ▢ and Close ☒ buttons that appear on the top line to the right of the application name (Microsoft Excel) may be used to shrink, enlarge, and close the program window on the desktop.

- Once the application window has been maximized, the maximize button is replaced with a restore button ▣ . Use the restore button to return the Excel window to its previous size.

- The minimize and maximize buttons on the title bar of the workbook window may be used to shrink, enlarge and close the workbook window within the Excel window.

- Once the workbook window has been maximized, the title bar disappears and the maximize button is replaced with a restore button to the right of the menu bar. Use the restore button to return the workbook window to its previous size.

Help Features

- There are many help features available from a variety of sources for Excel 97. Help may be accessed by clicking Help on the menu bar, or by pressing F1 (which will open the Office Assistant).

- Note the Help menu options below:

Microsoft Excel Help opens the Office Assistant which is explained below. The Assistant may also be launched using the help button ? on the toolbar.

Contents and Index displays the Contents, Index, and Find tabs in the Help Topics dialog box. The icon is not on the default toolbar but may be added by customizing the toolbar.

What's This? provides help on a particular screen item or you can access this feature by pressing Shift+F1. The mouse pointer will change to this icon ▶? to point to any screen icon or location. A help screen appears explaining the item in question.

Microsoft on the Web provides a series of links to Web sites on the Internet. When you click one of the sites, as illustrated below, you are automatically connected to your Internet service provider and your default Web browser. After you sign on, the site you selected is located and displayed. By default, Internet Explorer is the browser application used to locate the Web document.

← Web sites

16

Lotus 1-2-3 Help provides information about Excel 97 equivalents to Lotus 1-2-3 commands.

About Microsoft Excel provides system status information.

The Office Assistant

- By default, the Office Assistant appears on screen when you open Excel. However, you can launch Microsoft Excel Help and the Office Assistant by pressing the help button on the toolbar, pressing F1 or by selecting the option from the Help menu. The Office Assistant, as illustrated below, lets you search the Help index or ask questions. It also provides context-sensitive help questions and offers advice. If you leave the Assistant active, it will move out of the way of dialog boxes and track your recent actions.

- When you click on the assistant, type your question, and click Search, the requested procedures will display:

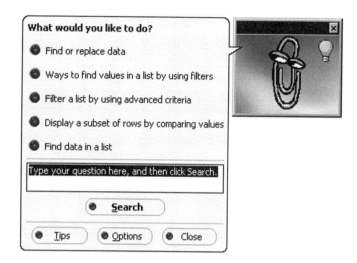

- In the illustration above, note the light bulb in the Office Assistant graphic. The light bulb indicates that a Tip is available for the current activity. When the light bulb is clicked, the tip displays, as illustrated below.

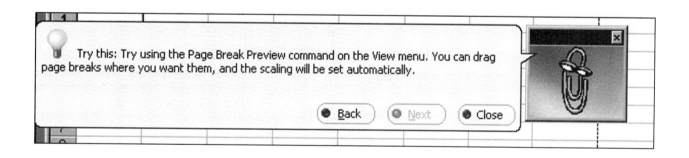

- You can control the way the Office Assistant appears on the screen as well as the kind of information it presents. Select the Options button on the Office Assistant bubble to set capabilities and tip displays on the Office Assistant dialog box, Options tab.

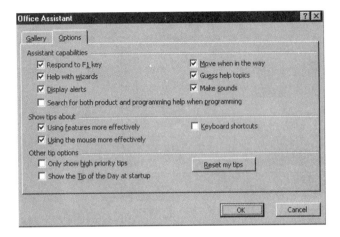

- Use the Gallery tab to customize the Office Assistant by selecting from eight other characters, two of which are illustrated below.

- You can turn off the Office Assistant by clicking the Close button on the Office Assistant title bar.

Contents and Index

- When you select <u>C</u>ontents and Index from the <u>H</u>elp menu, the Help Topics dialog box displays with three tabs. Note the illustrations on the bottom of the page.

Contents

- The contents tab displays a page listing help contents for Excel. Double-clicking on a topic presents a list of subtopics and/or display screens. Note the Excel contents page and an example of a help display screen illustrated below.

Index

- The Index tab allows you to enter the first few letters of your topic, which brings you to the index entry. Double-click the entry or select the entry and click <u>D</u>isplay. The help screen related to your topic is then displayed.

Find

- The Find tab accesses the Help database feature. It allows you to search the Help database for the occurrence of any word or phrase in a Help topic. The Index and Find features are similar; however, Find offers more options for finding a topic.

Exit Help

- To exit Help: Double-click the Help window control menu box.

  ✓ NOTE: *It may be necessary to click Cancel or Close, or press Escape to close a dialog box before exiting Help.*

 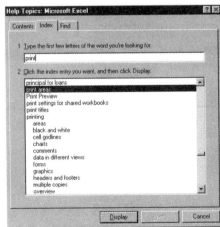 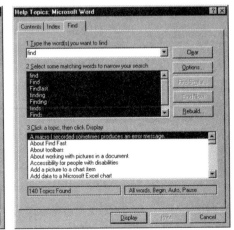

EXERCISE DIRECTIONS

1. Select Help from the menu bar. Note the selections. Deselect Help.

2. Click the Help button on the toolbar. Note the Office Assistant and question box.

3. Click Close.

4. Press F1 to access Help.

5. Type the following question: How do I minimize the window?

6. Click Search.

7. Double-click on Minimize a Workbook Window.

8. Read and then close the Help screen.

9. Click the minimize button on the title bar (which contains the software name).
   ✓ *Note the Microsoft Excel icon on the Taskbar.*

10. Click the Microsoft Excel icon to return to the program.

11. Click the restore button on the menu bar.
    ✓ *Note the Excel workbook window returns to its previous size.*

12. If the window is not maximized, click the Maximize button on the workbook window title bar.

13. Click the Minimize button on the workbook window title bar.
    ✓ *Note the workbook icon in the Excel window.*

14. Click the icon to return the workbook to a window.

15. Select Contents and Index from the Help menu.

16. Select the Contents tab if it is not active.

17. Do the following:
    a. Double-click Working with Workbooks and Worksheets from the list.
    b. Double-click the About Workbooks and Worksheets help topic.
    c. Read the topic and click on the vocabulary word worksheets to see the definition.
    d. Read the definition for active sheet.
    e. Click on the Options menu and note the Print topic option.
    f. Click on Help Topics to return to the Help Contents menu.

18. Click on the Index tab.

19. Type help in the text box.

20. Click on Help from the Web and read the topic.
    ✓ *If you have an Internet connection, use the instructions to connect to Microsoft Help on the Web.*

21. Click the Close box.

22. On the Office Assistant bubble, click Options.

23. Note the contents of the Options and Gallery tabs.

24. Close the screen.

25. Exit Excel.

KEYSTROKES

START OFFICE ASSISTANT

✓ *By default, the Office Assistant will appear when you start Excel. If the Assistant is not on the screen, use these steps to activate the Assistant.*

1. Click **Help** menu .... `Alt`+`H`

2. Click **Microsoft Excel Help** .... `H`

   OR

   Press **F1** .... `F1`

   OR

   Click **Help** button .... 🔲

   ✓ *If the Contents, Index and Find window opens instead of the Office Assistant, the F1 key option has been disabled in the Office Assistant Options dialog box. See below to change options.*

USE OFFICE ASSISTANT

1. Click Office Assistant .... `F1`

2. Type question in Assistant text box.

3. Click **Search** .... `Alt`+`S`

4. Select from list of procedures to view more information.

5. Press **Esc** .... `Esc`
   to close Help window.

CHANGE OFFICE ASSISTANT OPTIONS

1. Click Office Assistant .... `F1`

2. Click **Options** .... `Alt`+`O`

3. Click **Options** tab .... `Alt`+`O`

4. Select desired options.

5. Click **OK** .... `Enter`

   To change Office Assistant character:

   1. Click Office Assistant .... `F1`

   2. Click **Options** .... `Alt`+`O`

   3. Click **Gallery** tab .... `Alt`+`G`

   4. Select desired display.

   5. Click **OK** .... `Enter`

EXIT HELP OR HELP SCREENS

✓ *It may be necessary to click Cancel or Close, or press Esc to close a dialog box before exiting Help.*

   Click **Cancel** button .... `Cancel`

   OR

   Press **Escape** key .... `Esc`

   OR

   Click **close** button .... `X`

   OR

   Double-click

   Help Screen Control icon .... ❓

MAXIMIZE A WINDOW

Click **Maximize** button .... 🔲

✓ *After a window is maximized, the maximize button is replaced with the restore button.*

OR

1. Click **Workbook Control** icon .... 📄

2. Click **Maximize** .... `X`

USE CONTENTS AND INDEX

1. Click **Help** .... `Alt`+`H`

2. Click **Contents and Index** .... `C`

3. Click desired tab.

   Contents

   a. Double-click a topic.

   b. Double-click a submenu item or a display item.

   Index

   a. Type first letters of topic word in Step 1 text box.

   b. Select matching words in Step 2, if presented.

   c. Double-click topic in Step 2 box.

      OR

      Select topic.

   d. Click **Display** .... `Alt`+`D`

Find

✓ *The first time you use the Find Tab, Excel will prompt you to setup the Find database.*

a. Type or enter search word or phrase in Step 1 text box.

b. Select matching words in Step 2, if presented.

c. Double-click topic in Step 3 box.

   OR

   Select topic.

d. Click **Display** .... `Alt`+`D`

ACCESS SCREEN TIPS

To View Tip for Region of Screen, Menu, or Toolbar Button:

1. Point to element on screen.

2. Press Shift+F1 .... `Shift`+`F1`

3. Click What's This button .... 🔍

   OR

   Click mouse to view information about desired element.

4. Press **Escape** to close Help. .... `Esc`

To View Tips in Dialog Boxes:

Click question mark icon in dialog box.

OR

Point to option and press Shift+F1.

EXIT HELP OR HELP SCREENS

Click **Cancel** .... `Esc`

OR

Click **Close button** .... `X`

OR

Double-click **Help Screen Control** icon...

RESTORE A MAXIMIZED WINDOW

Click **Restore** button .... 🗗

✓ *After a window is restored, the restore button is replaced with the maximize button.*

OR

1. Click **Workbook Control** icon.

2. Click **R**estore .... Ⓡ

MINIMIZE A WINDOW

Click desired window **Minimize**

button .... ▁

✓ *To minimize the window, use Steps 1 and 2 below.*

OR

1. Click **Workbook Control** icon.

2. Click **Mi**_n_**imize** .... Ⓝ

NEXT LESSON

Excel

LESSON 2

EXPLORE WORKSHEET

Exercises 4-5

■ Explore the Worksheet Using the Mouse
and Keyboard

<table>
<tr><td>**Exercise**
4</td><td>■ **Explore the Worksheet Using the Mouse and Keyboard**</td></tr>
</table>

NOTES

Explore the Worksheet Using the Mouse and Keyboard

- The **active cell** is the cell that is ready to receive data or a command.

- When you change the active cell, the **name box** located on the left side of the formula bar shows the new **cell reference**.

- The cell reference identifies the location of the active cell in the worksheet by the column and row headings. Excel highlights the row number and column letter of the selected cell in a worksheet. This makes it easier to identify your worksheet selection at a glance.

- You can change the active cell in a worksheet using the mouse or keyboard. It is important to learn the keystrokes, as listed in the procedures section on page 27 that allow you to quickly move around the screen.

- The workbook window displays a limited portion of the worksheet. It is possible to view other portions of the worksheet by scrolling to the desired location.

- You can scroll to different areas in a worksheet using the mouse or keyboard. Scrolling does not change the active cell.

- There are 256 columns and 65,536 rows in a worksheet.

- Note the illustrations on the following page of the outer edges of a worksheet.

Top Left of Worksheet

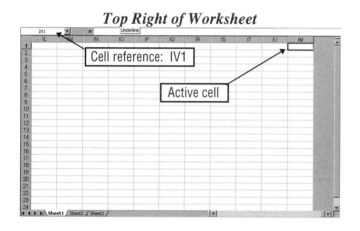

Cell reference: A1

Active cell

Bottom Left of Worksheet

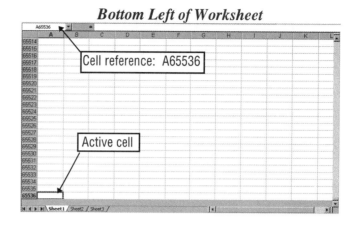

Cell reference: A65536

Active cell

Top Right of Worksheet

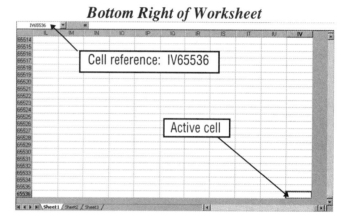

Cell reference: IV1

Active cell

Bottom Right of Worksheet

Cell reference: IV65536

Active cell

- You can scroll through the worksheet by clicking on the scroll arrows or by moving the scroll box. When you use the vertical or horizontal scroll bars, Excel displays a **ScrollTip** which indicates the row or column location.

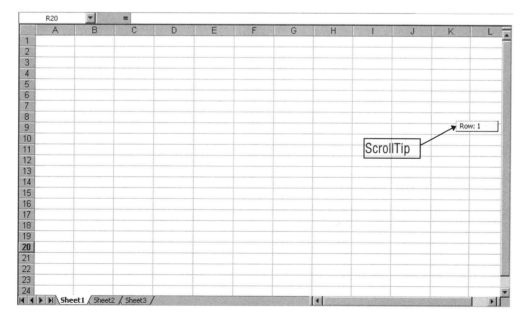

Row: 1

ScrollTip

EXERCISE DIRECTIONS

1. Click cell E5 to make it active.
   - ✓ *Note the cell reference in the name box.*

2. Press the left arrow key until cell C5 is selected.
   - ✓ *Note the cell reference in the name box.*

3. Select cell C9.
   - ✓ *Note the cell reference in the name box.*

4. Use the arrow keys to select the following cells:
   - A6
   - B14
   - G2
   - H20
   - R19
   - AA45
   - J33
   - A1

5. Click the down scroll arrow on the vertical scroll bar.
   - ✓ *Note the worksheet moves down by one row.*

6. Click the right scroll arrow on the horizontal scroll bar.
   - ✓ *Note the worksheet moves right by one column.*

7. Click the scroll bar below the scroll box on the vertical scroll bar.
   - ✓ *Note the row ScrollTip and that the worksheet moves down by one screen.*

8. Click the scroll bar to the right of the scroll box on the horizontal scroll bar.
   - ✓ *The column ScrollTip and the worksheet moves to the right by one screen.*

9. Drag the horizontal scroll box all the way to the right on the scroll bar.
   - ✓ *Note how the view of the worksheet has changed.*

10. Drag the vertical scroll box all the way down on the scroll bar.
    - ✓ *Note how the view of the worksheet has changed.*

11. Use the scroll bars or keystrokes to move in the following ways or to the parts of the worksheet listed below:
    - Down one screen
    - Up one screen
    - Right one screen
    - Left one screen
    - Lower left of worksheet
    - Top right of worksheet
    - Bottom right of worksheet

12. Exit Excel.

KEYSTROKES

CHANGE ACTIVE CELL USING THE KEYBOARD

- **One cell right**............................. →
- **One cell left**............................... ←
- **One cell down**........................... ↓
- **One cell up** .... ↑
- **One screen up** .... `Page Up`
- **One screen down**.................. `Page Down`
- **One screen right**.......... `Alt`+`Page Down`
- **One screen left** .... `Alt`+`Page Up`
- **First cell in current row**........ `Home`
- **Last cell in current row** ..... `Ctrl`+→
- **First cell in worksheet**. `Ctrl`+`Home`
- **Las occupied cell in worksheet**...................... `Ctrl`+`End`

CHANGE ACTIVE CELL USING THE MOUSE

Click desired cell.

✓ *If desired cell is not in view, use the scroll bars to move area of worksheet containing cell into view. Then click the cell.*

SCROLL USING THE MOUSE

✓ *The vertical scroll bar is located on the right side of the workbook window. The horizontal scroll bar (illustrated below) is located on the bottom of the workbook window. Excel shows the destination row or column (ScrollTips) when you drag a scroll box.*

scroll arrow — scroll box

SCROLL BAR

To scroll one column left or right:

Click left or right scroll arrow.

To scroll one row up or down:

Click up or down scroll arrow.

To scroll one screen up or down:

Click vertical scroll bar above or below the scroll box.

To scroll one screen right or left:

Click horizontal scroll bar to right or left of the scroll box.

To scroll to the beginning columns:

Drag horizontal scroll box to the extreme left of the scroll bar.

To scroll to the beginning rows:

Drag vertical scroll box to the top of the scroll bar.

To scroll quickly to an area in worksheet:

Drag scroll box to desired position on the scroll bar.

✓ *The limits of the scrolling area will depend on the location of data in the worksheet.*

To scroll quickly to the last row where data was entered:

Press Ctrl and drag vertical scroll box to the bottom of the scroll bar.

SCROLL USING THE KEYBOARD

- **One screen up** .... `Page Up`
- **One screen down**.................. `Page Down`
- **One screen right**.......... `Alt`+`Page Down`
- **One screen left** .... `Alt`+`Page Up`

Exercise

5

■ Explore the Worksheet Using the Mouse and Keyboard

NOTES

Explore the Worksheet Using the Mouse and Keyboard

■ You can also change the active cell in a worksheet by selecting the **Go To** command on the Edit menu or by pressing F5.

■ The Go To dialog box appears when Go To is selected or F5 is pressed. The Go To dialog box as illustrated, displays a list of the locations you have selected. You may reselect one of these locations by clicking on the cell address. The cell addresses are listed with the last selection on top of the list. Cell addresses are displayed with dollar signs before the row and column locations to indicate that the address is an absolute reference, or a reference to that specific location on that sheet.

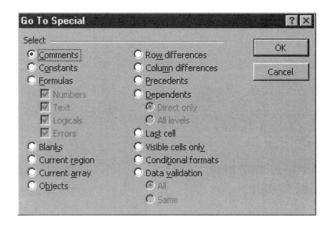

■ The Go to dialog box has a **Special** button that displays a Go To Special dialog box when clicked. The dialog box allows you to go to and select specific types of data, regions, differences, formats, etc. These selections will be discussed as they are developed in the text.

■ You can also change the active cell in a worksheet by typing or selecting a reference in the name box.

■ Note the location of the name box with an active reference displayed:

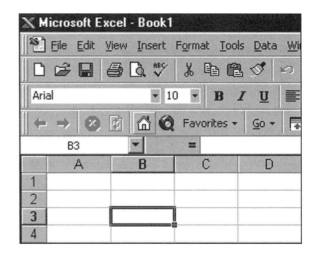

EXERCISE DIRECTIONS

1. Select Edit on the menu bar.

2. Select Go To.

3. Type A10 in the Reference text box.

4. Click OK.
   - ✓ *Note the active cell is A10.*

5. Using the Go To command, change the active cell to the following:
   - AB105
   - A8150
   - K965
   - BG200
   - C28
   - A1 (Home)
   - ✓ *Note the Go To list box displays the last four references you chose to go to.*

6. Use the Go To dialog box to reselect C28 by selecting it from the list.

7. Use the Go To dialog box and select Special.

   Review the items in the dialog box.

   Click Cancel.

8. Click in the name box on the left side of the formula bar.
   - ✓ *Note A1 becomes highlighted.*

9. Type C6 and press Enter.
   - ✓ *Note C6 is now the active cell.*

10. Using the name box, change the active cell to the following:
    - P365
    - GH67
    - IV56
    - Q80
    - Lower left of worksheet (A65536)
    - Top right of worksheet (IV1)
    - Bottom right of worksheet (IV65536)
    - Top left of worksheet (A1)

11. Press F5 and go to the following cells:
    - BC15
    - GZ495
    - DA15000

12. Close Excel.

KEYSTROKES

CHANGE ACTIVE CELL USING GO TO

1. Press **F5** F5

   OR

   a. Click **Edit** menu .... Alt + E

   b. Click **Go To** .... G

2. Type cell reference in **Reference** text box.
   - ✓ *The Go To list box displays the last four references you chose to go to.*

3. Click **OK** .... Enter

CHANGE ACTIVE CELL USING THE NAME BOX

1. Click in name box [▼] on left side of formula bar.

2. Type cell reference.

3. Press **OK** .... Enter

NEXT LESSON

Excel

LESSON 3

WORKSHEET BASICS

Exercises 6-10

- Enter Labels
- Make Simple Corrections
- Save a Workbook
- Close a Workbook
- Numeric Labels and Values
- Label Alignment
- Check for Viruses
- Align Labels
- Indent Text in Cells

Exercise 6

- ■ **Enter Labels** ■ **Make Simple Corrections**
- ■ **Save a Workbook** ■ **Close a Workbook**

NOTES

Enter Labels

- ■ The **status** of a cell is determined by the first character entered.

- ■ When an alphabetical character or a symbol (` ~ ! # % ^ & * ( ) _ \ | [ ] { } ; : ' " < > , ?) is entered as the first character in a cell, the cell contains a **label**.

- ■ By default, each cell is approximately nine characters wide; however, it is possible to view an entered label that is longer than the cell width if the cell to the right is blank. Excel 97 supports up to 32,000 characters in a cell entry.

- ■ A label is entered in the cell after you do one of the following:

  - • Press the Enter key

    OR

    Press an arrow key

    OR

    Click another cell

    OR

    Click the Enter box [✓] on the formula bar.

- ■ The contents in a label will automatically align to the left of the cell, making it a left-justified entry.

Make Simple Corrections

- ■ Before data is entered, the Backspace key may be used to correct an error. To delete the entire entry, press the Escape key or click the Cancel box [×] on the formula bar. Note the illustration of the formula bar below. After text is entered, a correction may be typed directly over the existing text. This is referred to as the **strikeover** method of correction.

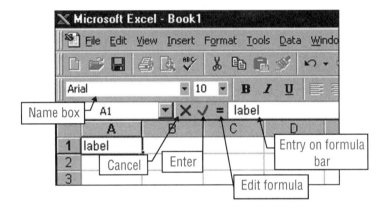

Save a Workbook

- ■ Each workbook is saved on a data disk or hard drive for future recall, and must be given a name for identification. A saved workbook is called a **file.**

- ■ Previously, a **filename** could not exceed eight characters. However, with Windows® 95, you may use descriptive filenames up to 255 characters long. Since the name has to be remembered and typed for recall, it is still advisable to limit the length of the names. When you save a file, Excel automatically adds a period and a **filename extension** (usually .XLS) to the end of the filename. Because Excel identifies file types by their extension, you should not type the filename extension.

  ✓ NOTE: *Filenames may be typed in either uppercase or lowercase characters.*

Close a Workbook

■ A workbook must be saved before closing it or all current or updated entries will be lost. If you attempt to close a workbook or exit Excel before saving, you will be asked if you want to save the changes.

✓ NOTE: *If you make a mistake and want to begin again, you may choose to close the workbook without saving it.*

■ A file may be saved by selecting Save As or Save or by clicking the **Save** button on the Standard toolbar. The Save dialog box that appears allows you to name the path, folder, and file.

Click to open a list of
drive or path options.

Select a folder within the chosen directory.

Select a drive or path.

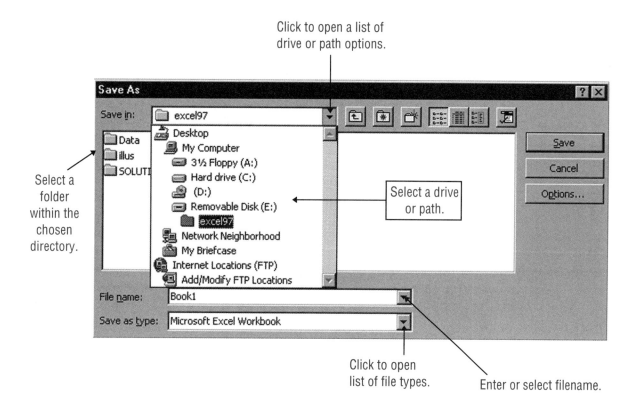

Click to open
list of file types.

Enter or select filename.

In this exercise, you will begin to create a worksheet for The Veggie Farm by entering labels. Numeric data will be entered in a later exercise.

EXERCISE DIRECTIONS

1. Go to cell B2.

2. Type your name and look at the formula bar.
   - ✓ Note the Cancel and Enter boxes to the left of the formula bar.
   - ✓ If the formula bar is not visible, see SET VIEW PREFERENCES, page 15, and follow steps to select the Formula Bar option.

3. Cancel the entry by pressing the Escape key, or by clicking the Cancel box ☒.

4. Create the worksheet below.

5. Enter the labels in the exact cell locations shown in the illustration.

6. Correct errors using the Backspace or strikeover method.

7. Save the workbook; name it **REGISTER**.

8. Close the workbook.

	A	B	C	D	E	F	G	H
1		VEGGIE FARM						
2		DAILY SALES REPORT						
3	DATE:							
4								
5	CODE	DEPARTMENT		SALES	TAX	TOTAL	% OF SALES	
6								
7	A	FRUIT						
8	B	VEGETABLES						
9	C	DAIRY						
10	D	PLANTS						
11	E	BUSHES						
12	F	FLOWERS						
13	G	SUPPLIES						

KEYSTROKES

ENTER A LABEL

✓ *Labels are left-aligned by default and cannot be calculated.*

1. Click cell .... `↑↓←→`
   to receive label.

2. Type label text.

3. Press **Enter** .... `Enter`

   OR

   Click **Enter** box .... `✓`
   on the formula bar.

   OR

   Press any **arrow** key .... `↑↓←→`
   to enter label and move to next cell.

SAVE A NEW WORKBOOK

1. Click **File** menu .... `Alt`+`F`

2. Click **Save As** .... `A`

3. To change a path:

   a. Click **Save in** .... `Alt`+`I`

   b. Click desired drive letter .... `↓`

4. To select a folder:

   Click on desired
   folder in list .... `Tab`, `↓`

5. Double–click in **File name:** .... `Alt`+`N`

6. Type filename.

7. Click **Save** .... `Alt`+`S`

CLOSE A WORKBOOK

1. Click **Close** button .... `X`

   OR

   a. Click **File** menu .... `Alt`+`F`

   b. Click **Close** .... `C`

2. If Save Changes in Workbook message appears:

   Click **Yes** .... `Y`

   to save changes to the workbook.

   ✓ *If you have not previously saved the workbook, the **Save As** dialog box appears. (See **SAVE A NEW WORKBOOK**, left.)*

   OR

   Click **No** .... `N`

   to close without saving the changes.

EXIT EXCEL

1. Click **Close** button .... `X`

   OR

   Press **Alt + F4** .... `Alt`+`F4`

   OR

   a. Click **File** menu .... `Alt`+`F`

   b. Click **Exit** .... `X`

2. If Save Changes in Workbook message appears:

   Click **Yes** .... `Y`

   to save changes to the workbook.

   ✓ *If you have not previously saved the workbook, the **Save As** dialog box appears. (See **SAVE A NEW WORKBOOK**, left.)*

   OR

   Click **No** .... `N`

   to close without saving the changes.

Exercise 7

- ■ **Numeric Labels and Values**
- ■ **Label Alignment** ■ **Check for Viruses**

NOTES

Numeric Labels and Values

- ■ When a number or a symbol (+ - . = $) is entered as the first character in a cell, the cell contains a **value**. A value is entered after you do one of the following:

  - • Press the Enter key

    OR

  - • Press an arrow key

    OR

  - • Click another cell

    OR

  - • Click the Enter box on the formula bar.

- ■ If a value is longer than the cell, Excel displays the number in scientific notation or number signs (######) appear in the cell. In this case, the column width must be reset. Setting column width will be covered in Exercise 21, page 70.

- ■ A **numeric label** is a number that will not be used in calculation. Examples of numeric labels are social security, telephone, or identification numbers. To indicate that such numbers are to be treated as labels and not values, begin the entry with an apostrophe ('), which serves as a **label prefix**. For example, if card number 12567 is entered as '12567, it will appear left-aligned as a label without the apostrophe (or label prefix). If the numeric label contains text or symbols, such as the hyphens in a social security number, Excel 97 will automatically format the data as a label.

- ■ The label prefix is not displayed on the worksheet, but is shown on the formula bar.

Label Alignment

- ■ A value automatically aligns to the right of the cell, making it a right-aligned entry. Numbers, dates, and times are considered values and are right-aligned by default.

- ■ Since labels are left-aligned and values are right-aligned in a cell, column titles (which are labels) will not appear centered over numeric data. Therefore, you may wish to set the alignment of the text or values to improve the worksheet's appearance.

- ■ Note the illustration showing the default alignments for labels, values, and numeric labels:

TEXT	◄———	left-aligned label
123	◄———	right-aligned label
123	◄———	left-aligned numeric label

Check for Viruses

- ■ Excel 97 provides a method to check workbooks for macros that might contain viruses that could damage your computer. Macros are sets of commands that are generally written to automate a worksheet, but they could contain commands to perform unwanted actions. When you enable **macro virus protection**, Excel will display a warning message each time you open a workbook that contains macros, whether harmful or harmless. You must then either open the workbook with the macros enabled or disabled based on the source of the workbook. To enable macro virus protection, select Tools, Options, the General tab, and then Macro virus protection.

In this exercise, you will create a payroll for employees of the First State Bank. GROSS PAY refers to total salary earned before taxes; NET PAY refers to salary received after taxes are deducted; Soc. Sec. Tax and Medicare Tax are designations for these mandatory deductions; and F.W.T. refers to Federal Withholding Tax.

EXERCISE DIRECTIONS

1. Create the worksheet below.

2. Enter the labels and values in the exact cell locations shown in the illustration.
   a. Enter the Card Number data as numeric labels, not values.
   b. Enter the Hourly Rate data with the decimal point.

3. Correct any errors.

4. Enable check for viruses:

5. Click Tools, Options, select the General tab, select Macro virus protection, click OK.
   ✓ *Hereafter, any files that contain macros will not open unless you disable the macros or approve the file.*

6. Save the workbook; name it **PAYROLL**.

7. Close the workbook.

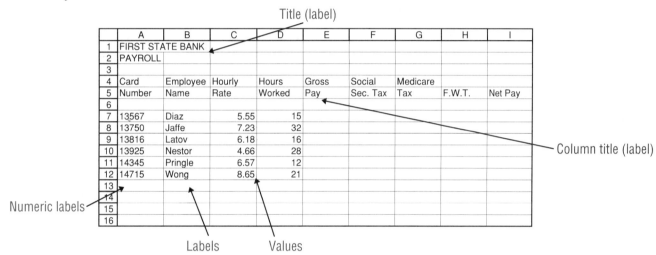

Title (label)

Column title (label)

Numeric labels

Labels   Values

	A	B	C	D	E	F	G	H	I
1	FIRST STATE BANK								
2	PAYROLL								
3									
4	Card	Employee	Hourly	Hours	Gross	Social	Medicare		
5	Number	Name	Rate	Worked	Pay	Sec. Tax	Tax	F.W.T.	Net Pay
6									
7	13567	Diaz	5.55	15					
8	13750	Jaffe	7.23	32					
9	13816	Latov	6.18	16					
10	13925	Nestor	4.66	28					
11	14345	Pringle	6.57	12					
12	14715	Wong	8.65	21					
13									
14									
15									
16									

KEYSTROKES

ENTER A NUMERIC LABEL

✓ *Numbers, entered as numeric labels, are left-aligned and cannot be calculated.*

1. Click cell..................................... ⬌
   to receive numeric label.

2. Press ' (label prefix)........................ '

3. Type number.

4. Press **Enter** .... Enter

ENTER A VALUE

✓ *Numbers, entered as values, are right-aligned and can be calculated.*

1. Click cell..................................... ⬌
   to receive value.

2. Type number.
   ✓ *Begin entry with a number from zero to nine, or a decimal point. Precede a negative number with a minus sign (-) or enclose it within parentheses ().*

3. Press **Enter**.............................. Enter
   ✓ *If Excel displays number signs (######) or the number in scientific notation, the column is not wide enough to display the value. Excel stores the value in the cell, but cannot display it. To see the entry, double-click the right border of the column heading. If the value has more than eight decimal places, Excel automatically rounds it to eight places.*

ENABLE OR DISABLE CHECK FOR VIRUSES

✓ *This setting will display a warning whenever a file is opened that contains a macro. You must then either approve the file, disable the macro, or cancel the open command.*

4. Click **Tools**.......................... Alt + T

5. Click **Options** .... O

6. Click the **General** tab.

7. Select or deselect **Macro virus protection**.................................... T

8. Click **OK** .... Enter

Exercise 8

■ Align Labels ■ Indent Text in Cells

Formatting Toolbar

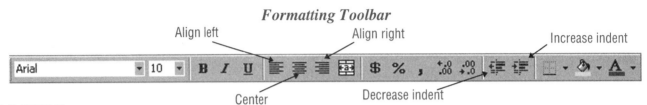

Align left   Align right   Increase indent

Center   Decrease indent

NOTES

Align Labels

■ Note the label and value entries in the worksheet on the right. The label text is left-aligned while the values are right-aligned in the cell. Column title labels above numeric data may be centered or right-aligned to improve the appearance of the worksheet.

■ You can align a label by using the **alignment buttons** on the Formatting toolbar.

■ Labels may also be aligned by selecting the cell(s) containing the label(s) to align and choosing an alignment through the menu system.

TEXT	←	left-aligned label
TEXT	←	centered label
TEXT	←	right-aligned label
123	←	right-aligned value
123	←	left-aligned value

■ When entering labels that consist of values and text, such as an address, Excel 97 will format the entry as a left-aligned label and you won't need to use a label prefix.

Indent Text in Cells

■ Indentation is a new horizontal alignment option in Excel 97. It lets you align text away from the left edge of the cell. You can indent cell text quickly by using the Increase Indent button on the Formatting toolbar, as illustrated above. You can also set the indentation of text within cells by using the Format, Cells, Alignment commands.

■ Note the illustration of the alignment and indent buttons on the Formatting toolbar above. Depending on the size of your monitor, the Increase or Decrease buttons may or may not appear.

In this exercise you will create an invoice. An invoice is a bill provided to a buyer by a seller. UNIT PRICE refers to the price of one unit quoted by the way the item is packaged for sale. For example, the unit price for pencils may be quoted by the dozen.

EXERCISE DIRECTIONS

1. Create the worksheet on the right.

2. Enter the labels and values in the exact cell locations shown in the illustration, using the following features:
   a. Indent the address text (in rows 3 and 4) for Office Barn Supplies Co.

   b. Right-align the labels UNIT PRICE and TOTAL PRICE, to match the alignment of the data for those columns.
   c. Center the numbers in the QUANTITY column.
   d. Enter the stock numbers as numeric labels, using the label prefix.
   e. Correct any errors.

3. Save the workbook; name it **INVOICE**.

4. Close the workbook.

	A	B	C	D	E	F	G	H	I
1				INVOICE					
2			OFFICE BARN SUPPLIES CO.						
3			345 Paperpoint Boulevard						
4			Beverly Hills, CA 90210						
5									
6	SOLD TO:	Barbara Taylor							
7		45 First Street							
8		Beverly Hills, CA 90210							
9									
10	TERMS:	30 days							
11									
12						STOCK	UNIT	TOTAL	
13	QUANTITY	UNIT	DESCRIPTION			NUMBER	PRICE	PRICE	
14									
15	5	Dozen	Pencils #2			234324	2.47		
16	4	Boxes	Folders - Legal Size			543234	7.86		
17	2	Boxes	Disks - 3.5"			354354	8.21		
18									
19									
20									

Callouts: Indented text, Right-aligned labels, Centered values, Numeric labels

KEYSTROKES

SELECT (HIGHLIGHT) A RANGE OF CELLS USING THE MOUSE

1. Point to interior of first cell to select.
   - ✓ *Pointer becomes a ✛ .*
2. Drag through adjacent cells until desired cells are highlighted.

SELECT (HIGHLIGHT) A RANGE OF CELLS USING THE KEYBOARD

1. Press **arrow keys** .... [⤢]
   until first cell to select is outlined.
2. Press **Shift + arrow keys** .... [Shift] + [⤢]
   until adjacent cells to select are highlighted.

ALIGN LABELS USING THE TOOLBAR

1. Select cell(s) containing label(s).
   —FROM FORMATTING TOOLBAR—
2. Click **Align Left** button .... [≣]
   OR
   Click **Center button** .... [≣]
   OR
   Click **Align Right** button .... [≣]

ALIGN LABELS USING THE MENU

Aligns data in labels horizontally or vertically in cells.

1. Select cell(s) containing label(s) to align.
2. Complete the following:
   a. Click **Format** menu .... [Alt] + [O]
   b. Click **Cells** .... [E]

OR

   a. Right-click a selected cell.
   b. Click **Format Cells** .... [F]
3. Click **Alignment** tab .... [Ctrl] + [Tab]
4. Click **Horizontal** .... [Alt] + [H]
5. Select horizontal alignment ... [↓] [Enter]
6. Click **Vertical** .... [Alt] + [V]
7. Select vertical alignment .... [↓] [Enter]
8. Click **Indent** .... [Tab], [↑] [↓]
9. Select text controls, if desired:
   - **Wrap Text** .... [Alt] + [W]
   - **Shrink to Fit** .... [Alt] + [K]
   - **Merge cells** .... [Alt] + [M]
10. Click **OK** .... [Enter]

Exercise
9

■ **Summary**

You want to keep track of the Senior Dues paid by students at Wagner High School. Data provided includes student names, school identification numbers, dates of birth (entered as numeric labels), and fees paid to date.

EXERCISE DIRECTIONS

1. Include a two-line report title and indent the second line of the heading.

2. Use the data and steps below to create the worksheet.

STUDENT NAME	ID NO.	BIRTH DATE	SENIOR DUES
Allison, John	2314	03/14/80	75
Darkin, Bill	4376	12/02/81	75
Gallina, Lawrence	7543	02/28/80	55
Johnson, Sean	3265	05/12/81	55
Marks, Samuel	5376	08/30/81	35
Potter, George	2943	04/19/80	25
Ryan, Mike	4328	11/07/81	50
Timmons, Robert	3178	10/27/81	50

   a. Allow two columns for STUDENT NAME data.

   b. Enter ID. NO. data as numeric labels.

   c. Center all entries in the ID. NO. column including the column title.

   d. Right–align the column title for the BIRTH DATE and SENIOR DUES columns.

3. Save the workbook; name it **DUES**.

4. Close the workbook.

Exercise

10

■ **Summary**

Mr. Manifold, the owner of the Cruiser Repair Shop, has asked you to prepare an inventory listing the items he stocks in his repair shop with the item numbers, unit cost, and selling price of each item.

EXERCISE DIRECTIONS

1. Include an appropriate two-line worksheet title and indent the second line of the title.

2. Use the data below to create the worksheet.

3. Leave a blank column (column C) between ITEM and UNIT COST.

4. Center the ITEM NUMBER and ITEM headings.

5. Enter ITEM NUMBER data as numeric labels.

6. Right-align column labels for UNIT COST and SELLING PRICE.

ITEM NUMBER	ITEM	UNIT COST	SELLING PRICE
142	carburetor	120	168
321	spark plugs	2	3
093	tires	55	77
393	brakes	60	84
659	alarm	125	195
572	mats	45	63
175	battery	45	70
421	radio	185	265
932	fan belt	15	28

7. Save the workbook; name it **INVEN**.

8. Close the workbook.

NEXT LESSON

Excel

LESSON 4

FILES, FORMULAS AND FORMATTING

Exercises 11-18

- Use Formulas
- Mathematical Operators
- Natural Language Formulas
- Open Files
- Save and Save As
- Create Backup Files
- Send Files
- Format Data
- Use Ranges
- Copy Data
- Print a Worksheet
- Copy Formulas (Absolute and Relative Reference)
- Format Data (Bold, Italic and Underline)
- Format Fractions and Mixed Numbers
- Spelling
- Look Up Reference

Exercise 11

- ■ **Use Formulas**
- ■ **Mathematical Operators**
- ■ **Natural Language Formulas**

NOTES

Use Formula

- ■ A **formula** is an instruction to calculate a number.

- ■ A formula is entered in the cell where the answer should appear. As you type the formula, it appears in the cell and in the **formula bar**. After a formula is entered, the answer is displayed in the cell and the formula is displayed in the formula bar.

- ■ **Cell references**, or cell addresses, and **mathematical operators**, or math symbols, are used to develop formulas. The cell reference can be typed or inserted into a formula. An equal sign (=) must precede a formula. For example, the formula =C3+C5+C7 results in the addition of the values in these cell locations. Therefore, any change to a value made in these cell locations causes the answer to change automatically.

  ✓ *NOTE:* *If you are using the number pad and enter the formula (+C3+C5+C7) using a plus sign as the first character, Excel will substitute the equal sign.*

Mathematical Operators

- ■ The standard mathematical operators used in formulas are:

+ Addition	- Subtraction
* Multiplication	/ Division
^ Exponentiation	

- ■ It is important to consider the **order of mathematical operations** when preparing formulas. Operations enclosed in parentheses have the highest priority and are executed first; exponential calculations are executed second.

Multiplication and division operations have the next priority and are completed before any addition and subtraction operations. The order of mathematical operations can be remembered by using the memory aid, "Please Excuse My Dear Aunt Sally," or Parentheses, Exponents, Multiplication, Division, Addition, and Subtraction.

- ■ All operations are executed from left to right in the order of appearance. For example, in the formula =A1*(B1+C1), B1+C1 will be calculated before the multiplication is performed. If the parentheses were omitted, A1*B1 would be calculated first and C1 would be added to that answer. This would result in a different outcome.

- ■ Multiplication and division formulas may result in answers with multiple decimal places. These numbers can be rounded off using a formatting feature. (See Format Data, Exercise 13.)

- ■ When using a **percentage** as a numeric factor in a formula, you can enter it with a decimal or with the percent symbol. For example, you may enter either .45 or 45% to include 45 percent in a formula.

Natural Language Formulas

- ■ Excel allows you to use text labels identifying data instead of cell references in formulas. If the column or data title is a two-line title, use the label closest to the data for the formula reference. Natural language formulas may be used with data identified with column or row labels.

In this exercise, The Novel Tea Bookstore is calculating a sample discount worksheet using formulas with cell and natural language references. **LIST PRICE** refers to the suggested retail price. The **SAVINGS** is a discount off the list price. The **SALES TAX** percentage for this exercise will be 8%. Note the formula used to calculate **SALES TAX**: 8% has been changed to .08.

EXERCISE DIRECTIONS

1. Create the worksheet below.

2. Enter the labels and values in the exact cell locations shown in the illustration.

   ✓ Indent text within cells B2 and B3 as shown.

3. Enter the formula, as shown, to calculate the SALE PRICE.

   ✓ Note that after the formula is entered, the answer appears in the cell and the formula displays on the formula bar.

4. Enter the formula, as shown, to calculate SALES TAX. The 8% tax may be entered as a percent or as a decimal.

5. Enter the natural language formula, as shown, to find the TOTAL.

6. Enter the formulas appropriate for each location to complete the problem. Practice using both types of formulas.

7. Check that answers are reasonable.

   ✓ Excel will not perform a calculation incorrectly, however, you may enter an incorrect formula. It is good practice to check that the answers are reasonable.

8. Save the workbook; name it **SAVINGS**.

9. Close the workbook.

	A	B	C	D	E	F	G	H	I
1		THE NOVEL TEA BOOK STORE							
2		SUMMER SAVINGS SALE							
3		SAMPLE DISCOUNTS							
4									
5			LIST		SALE	SALES			
6	BOOK		PRICE	SAVINGS	PRICE	TAX	TOTAL		
7	Creature Feature		15	4	=C7-D7	=E7*.08	=PRICE+TAX		
8	Public Defender		25	9					
9	Traveling Italy		32	10					
10	Picasso in Blue		86	28					
11									
12									
13									

Formulas using cell addresses

Natural language formula

Enter appropriate formulas here.

KEYSTROKES

ENTER A FORMULA USING CELL REFERENCES

1. Click **cell** .... [↕]
   to receive formula.

2. Press **Equal** .... [=]

3. Type formula using cell references and mathematical operators.

4. Example: =A1*(B2+B10)/2

   ✓ You can select cells instead of typing references to tell Excel which cells you wish the formula to reference.

To insert cell references by selecting cells:

a. Click formula where cell reference will be inserted.

   ✓ If necessary, type preceding operator or parenthesis.

b. Select cell(s) you want the formula to reference.

c. Reference appears in formula.

d. Type desired operator or parenthesis.

e. Repeat steps a–c as needed.

4. Press **Enter** .... [Enter]

ENTER A FORMULA USING NATURAL LANGUAGE

1. Click **cell** .... [↕]
   to receive formula.

2. Press **Equal** .... [=]

3. Type formula using row or column data label and mathematical operators.

   Example: =SALARY-TAX

4. Press **Enter** .... [Enter]

Exercise 12

■ **Open Files** ■ **Save and Save As**
■ **Create Backup Files** ■ **Send Files**

NOTES

Open Files

■ Workbooks that have been saved and closed must be opened using the same drive designation and filename used during the saving process. The **Open dialog box** contains a drop-down list with the drives or folders and a box containing a list of the files in that directory. In addition to opening a previously saved file, you may preview, search for a file and list details on a file from the Open dialog box.

■ When the File menu is accessed, a list of the last four files used is provided. One of these files may be opened by clicking the filename.

■ A newly opened workbook becomes the active workbook and hides any other open workbook. A previously opened workbook will not be closed automatically and can be made the active workbook.

Open Dialog Box

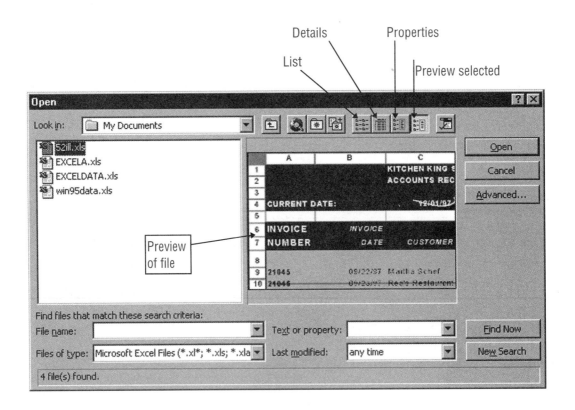

Save and Save As

- When resaving a workbook that contains recent changes, the **Save** option overwrites the previous version. To activate the Save option, click File, Save or press the Save button 📙 on the Standard toolbar.

- The **Save As** option allows for the changing of the filename as well as other save conditions. A new version of a previously saved workbook may be saved under a new name in order to keep both files.

Create Backup Files

- It is also possible to **backup** all workbooks as they are being saved. This setting can be made by selecting the Options button on the Save As dialog box, which brings you into the Save Options dialog box shown below. You can activate **Always create backup**, which will create a copy of your file with a **.BAK** extension.

Options Dialog Box

Save Options	? ✕
☐ Always create backup	OK
File sharing	Cancel
Password to open: [ ]	
Password to modify: [ ]	

Backup feature

Send Files

- Worksheet files may be created in Excel and sent electronically to a mail or routing recipient or to an exchange folder where files can be reviewed or organized by others. These features are usable if you are on a network or on the Internet. Note the Send to options on the File menu below.

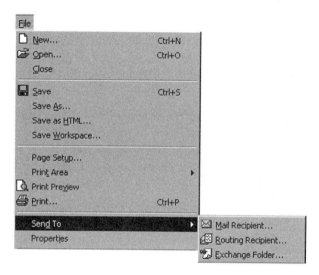

✓ NOTE: Although we will not practice these options, the Mail Recipient option automatically places the active file into an electronic mail document.

In this exercise, you will complete the invoice for Office Barn Supplies Co. by finding the TOTAL PRICE for each item and the TOTAL DUE. The workbook will be saved again, backed up, and then resaved with a new filename.

EXERCISE DIRECTIONS

1. Open ⌨ **INVOICE** or 💾 **12INVOICE**.

2. Enter a formula to multiply QUANTITY by UNIT PRICE to find the TOTAL PRICE for each item.

3. Enter the label TOTAL DUE where indicated.

4. Enter a formula to add the TOTAL PRICE column to find TOTAL DUE.

5. Resave/overwrite the workbook file using the Save command or Save button on the toolbar.
   ✓ *If you used the file created in Exercise 8, resave the file by clicking the Save button or use File, Save. If you are using the data disk, you must use the Save As command to create the INVOICE file.*

6. To create a backup file:
   a. Select File, Save As, Options.
   b. Select Always Create Backup.
   c. Select OK.
   d. Resave the file.

7. Save the workbook as **INV2**.

8. Select File, Open to check for the new files.
   ✓ *You should have INVOICE, INV2, and Backup of INVOICE.*

9. Enable check for viruses:

   Click Tools, click Options, click General tab, select Macro virus protection, click OK.
   ✓ *Hereafter, any files that contain macros will not open unless you disable them or approve the file.*

10. Close the workbook.

	A	B	C	D	E	F	G	H
1				INVOICE				
2		OFFICE BARN SUPPLIES CO.						
3		345 Paperpoint Boulevard						
4		Beverly Hills, CA 90210						
5								
6	SOLD TO:	Barbara Taylor						
7		45 First Street						
8		Beverly Hills, CA 90210						
9								
10	TERMS:	30 days						
11								
12						STOCK	UNIT	TOTAL
13	QUANTITY	UNIT	DESCRIPTION			NUMBER	PRICE	PRICE
14								
15	5	Dozen	Pencils #2			234324	2.47	
16	4	Boxes	Folders - Legal Size			543234	7.86	
17	2	Boxes	Disks - 3.5"			354354	8.21	
18								
19			Total Due					

KEYSTROKES

OPEN A WORKBOOK FILE

1. Click **Open** button .... 📂
   on Standard toolbar.

   OR

   a. Click **File** menu .... `Alt`+`F`

   b. Click **Open**................................. `O`

   To select a drive:

   a. Click **Look in** .... `Alt`+`I`

   b. Select desired drive...... `⬆⬇`, `Enter`

   ✓ *Files in current directory of selected drive appear in File Name list box.*

   To select a folder in the drive:

   Double-click folder name
   in list box .... `⬆⬇`, `Enter`

   ✓ *Files in selected folder appear in File name list box.*

   To list files of a different type:

   a. Click **Files of Type**: .... `Alt`+`T`

   b. Click file type............... `⬆⬇`, `Enter`
      to list.

✓ *Only files of specified type appear in File name list box.*

✓ *Use this option to change the kinds of files displayed in the File name list box. For example, if you want to open a Lotus file into Excel, you would select the Lotus 1-2-3 File item in the drop-down list.*

2. Click file to open in File Name list box.

   OR

   a. Select **File name**
      list box................................ `Alt`+`N`

   b. Type or select file name to open.

3. Click **Open**............................ `Alt`+`O`

RESAVE/OVERWRITE A WORKBOOK FILE

Click **Save** button .... 💾
on Standard toolbar.

OR

1. Click **File** menu .... `Alt`+`F`

2. Click **Save** .... `S`

SAVE AS

Saves and names the active workbook.

1. Click **File** menu..................... `Alt`+`F`

2. Click **Save As**................................ `A`

   To select a drive:

   a. Click **Save in** .... `Alt`+`I`

   b. Select desired drive...... `⬆⬇`, `Enter`

   To select a folder in the drive:

   Double-click folder name
   in list box .... `Tab`, `⬆⬇`, `Enter`

3. Click **File name** .... `Alt`+`N`

4. Type filename.

5. Click **Save**................................ `Enter`

CREATE BACKUP

Sets Excel to always create a backup of previous version when saving.

1. Click **File** menu...................... `Alt`+`F`

2. Click **Save As**................................ `A`

3. Click **Options** button .... `Alt`+`P`

4. Select **Always Create**
   Backup................................. `Alt`+`B`

5. Click **OK** .... `Enter`

6. Click **Save** .... `Enter`

Exercise 13

■ Format Data ■ Use Ranges

Formatting Toolbar

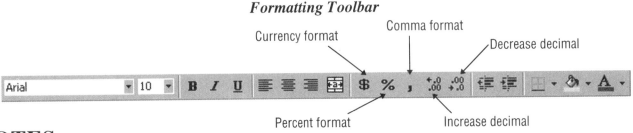

Currency format Comma format Decrease decimal

Percent format Increase decimal

NOTES

Format Data

- You can change the appearance of data to make it more attractive and readable by **formatting** it. Some available number formats are currency, percentage, date, time, and scientific notation.

- The following formats may be used for formatting money values:

  Number Displays number with or without decimal places and commas. Decimal places and 1000 separators or commas may be set.

  Currency Displays number with currency symbols: dollar signs, commas, and decimals.

  ✓ NOTE: *Other formats will be introduced in future exercises.*

- Formats may be set by selecting the data to be formatted and then selecting, **Cells** from the Format menu. The Format Cells dialog box displays, as illustrated on the right, with the Number tab selected.

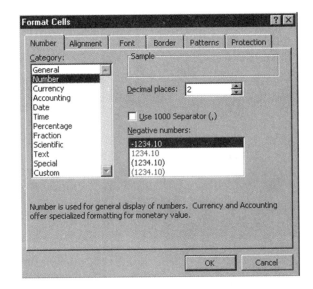

- The **Formatting toolbar** may also be used to set number formats for selected data. The Currency button ⊞ will format numbers for two decimal places and dollar signs.

- The **Increase Decimal** ⊞ and **Decrease Decimal** ⊞ buttons can be used to format data to the desired number of decimal places. Values will be rounded if decimal places are decreased.

Use Ranges

- A **range** is a defined area of a worksheet. For example, if you select the cells F4, F5, and F6, this range of cells can be indicated as F4:F6. You can format data in columns or rows by selecting the range of cells containing the data to format. To select a range of cells with the mouse, point to the first cell until the pointer changes to a plus sign, then drag through the adjacent cells until the range is highlighted.

- A **block of cells** may be defined as a range. For example, A1:G2 includes all the cells in columns A through G in rows one and two. In the illustration on the next page, blocks of cells are indicated with a border around the cells in the range.

- As noted in Exercise 7, label text is left-aligned while values are right-aligned in a cell. The alignment buttons on the Formatting toolbar, or the alignment settings through the menu system, may be used to align a column title in a single cell or all the column titles in a selected range.

- Cell contents may be formatted or aligned before or after data is entered.

In this exercise, you will format money columns and column titles for the SAVINGS worksheet.

EXERCISE DIRECTIONS

1. Open 📇 **SAVINGS** or 💾 **13SAVINGS**.

2. Select the range C5:G6, shown in the illustration, and center all column titles by selecting the center button on the Formatting toolbar.

3. Select the range C7:G10, shown in the illustration, and format data for two decimal places using the Format, Cells commands.

4. Select the data in column G, G7:G10, and format for Currency using the Currency button on the Formatting toolbar.

5. Add the additional data as shown in the illustration.

6. Complete the SALE PRICE, SALES TAX, and TOTAL columns for the new data by entering formulas to calculate the values.

7. Format the new data to match the settings made in steps 3 and 4.

8. Save the workbook file as **SAVINGS**.

9. Close the workbook.

	A	B	C	D	E	F	G	H	I	J
1		THE NOVEL TEA BOOK STORE						Range C5:G6		
2		SUMMER SAVINGS SALE								
3		SAMPLE DISCOUNTS								
4								Range C7:G10		
5			LIST		SALE	SALES				
6	BOOK		PRICE	SAVINGS	PRICE	TAX	TOTAL			
7	Creature Feature		15	4	11	0.88	11.88			
8	Public Defender		25	9	16	1.28	17.28			
9	Traveling Italy		32	10	22	1.76	23.76			
10	Picasso in Blue		86	28	58	4.64	62.64			
11	Vortex Signs		30	10.5						
12	Brown's Tax Guide		35	12.8						
13										

KEYSTROKES

SELECT (HIGHLIGHT) A RANGE OF CELLS USING THE MOUSE

✓ *A range of cells is two or more cells. Cells in a selected range are highlighted and the active cell within the selection is white.*

To select a range of adjacent cells:

1. Point to interior of first cell to select.

    ✓ *Pointer becomes a* ✛ *.*

2. Drag through adjacent cells until desired cells are highlighted.

To select entire row or column:

Click row heading or column heading to select.

To select adjacent rows or columns:

1. Point to first row heading or column heading to select.

    ✓ *Pointer becomes a* ✛ *.*

2. Drag through adjacent headings until desired rows or columns are highlighted.

SELECT (HIGHLIGHT) A RANGE OF CELLS USING THE KEYBOARD

✓ *A range of cells is two or more cells. Cells in a selected range are highlighted and the active cell within the selection is white.*

To select a range of adjacent cells:

1. Press **arrow** keys .... `↑↓` until first cell to select is highlighted.

2. Press **Shift + arrow** keys .... `Shift`+`↑↓`

To select entire row containing active cell:

Press **Shift + Space** .... `Shift`+`Space`

To select entire column containing active cell:

Press **Ctrl + Space** .... `Ctrl`+`Space`

To select adjacent rows:

1. Press **arrow** keys .... `↑↓` until a cell in first row to select is outlined.

2. Press and hold **Shift** .... `Shift` then press **Space** .... `Space` to highlight first row to select.

3. Still pressing **Shift**, press **up** or **down** key .... `↑↓` to highlight adjacent rows to select.

FORMAT NUMBERS USING THE MENU

1. Select cell(s) to format.

2. a. Click **Format** menu .... `Alt`+`O`

    b. Click **Cells**.................................. `E`

    OR

    a. Right-click a selected cell.

    b. Click **Format Cells**..................... `F`

3. Click Number tab .... `Ctrl`+`Tab`

4. Click desired category in Category list .... `Alt`+`C`, `↑↓`

    ✓ *Category list items include: All, Custom, Number, Accounting, Date, Time, Percentage, Fraction, Scientific, Text Currency.*

5. Select option(s) for selected category.................. `Tab`, `↓`

6. Click **OK**.................................... `Enter`

FORMAT NUMBERS USING THE TOOLBAR

Applies commonly used number formats.

Select cell(s) to format.

To apply currency style:

Click **Currency Style** button...................................... `$`

To increase or decrease decimal places:

Click **Increase Decimal** button.............. `←.0\n.00`

OR

Click **Decrease Decimal** button .... `.00\n←.0`

ALIGN (JUSTIFY) LABELS USING THE MENU

Aligns data horizontally or vertically within cells.

1. Select cell(s) containing data to align.

2. a. Click **Format** menu .... `Alt`+`O`

    b. Click **Cells** .... `E`

    OR

    a. Right-click a selected cell.

    b. Click **Format Cells**..................... `F`

3. Click **Alignment** tab.............. `Ctrl`+`Tab`

4. Click **Horizontally**.................. `Alt`+`H`

5. Select horizontal alignment ... `↓` `Enter`

6. Click **Vertical** .... `Alt`+`V`

7. Select vertical alignment .... `↓` `Enter`

8. Click **Indent**..................... `Tab`, `↓` `↑`

9. Select text controls, if desired:

    • **Wrap Text** .... `Alt`+`W`

    • **Shrink to Fit** .... `Alt`+`K`

    • **Merge cells**...................... `Alt`+`M`

10. Click **OK** .... `Enter`

Exercise

14

■ **Copy Data** ■ **Print a Worksheet**

NOTES

Copy Data

■ Once a formula is entered, it may be copied to other rows or columns that need the same formula. Select the item to copy and click Edit, Copy or click the **Copy** button ▣ on the Standard toolbar. Then, you can select the area to receive the copied data and select Edit, Paste, or click the **Paste** button ▣ on the Standard toolbar. Formulas may be copied:

- Horizontally or vertically.

- To another cell or range of cells.

- To another worksheet or workbook.

■ When a formula is copied to a new location, the cell references change relative to their new location. For example, a formula in C1 that reads =A1+B1, will automatically change to =A2+B2 when copied to cell C2.

■ Formulas may be copied down across from a cell location by dragging the fill handle in the bottom right corner of the cell.

Print a Worksheet

■ The workbook, the selected worksheet(s), or the selected range of data may be printed using the Print command. When you select File, Print, Excel allows you to select various print options.

If you use the **Print** button ▣ on the Standard toolbar, the worksheet will be printed on the default printer immediately with default settings. Note the illustration of the Print dialog box that appears when you use the menu.

Print dialog box

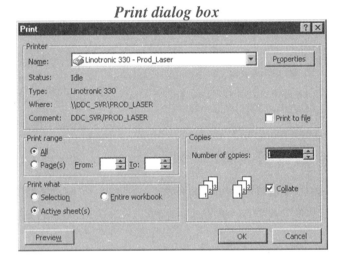

■ Note in the dialog box above that you can preview the print output by selecting the Preview button, or by pressing the **Preview** button ▣ on the Standard toolbar. It is wise to preview your output to check print settings. Also, you may print multiple copies of a report by entering the number in the Copies section of the dialog box.

■ To set print options select File, Page Setup, and a dialog box with four tabs will appear. The page size settings can be accessed by selecting the Page tab. Excel uses the default page size (usually 8 1/2" x 11") of the installed printer. The margin settings for the page can be accessed by selecting the Margins tab. The top and bottom default page margins are set at 1", the right and left default page margins are set at 0.75". As you change the margins, the sample page margins will display the new settings.

Page Setup Dialog Box with the Page Tab Selected

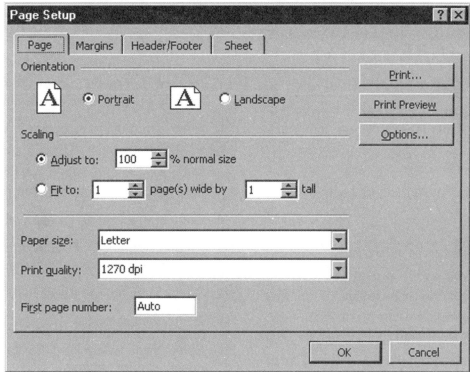

Page Setup Dialog Box with the Margins Tab Selected

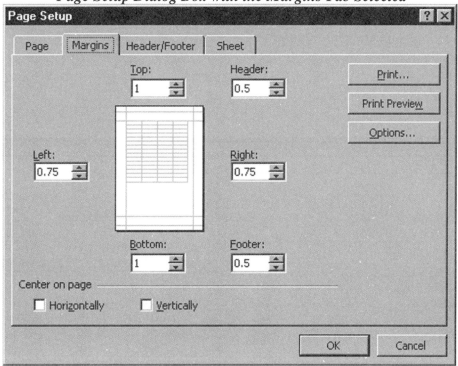

In this exercise, you will prepare and print a payroll where Federal Withholding Tax is calculated using a fixed percentage. NOTE: F.W.T. is actually determined using a table where the tax varies according to your salary and number of exemptions.

EXERCISE DIRECTIONS

1. Open ▦ **PAYROLL** or ▯ **14PAYROLL**.

2. Enter a formula to calculate Gross Pay for the first employee using the hourly rate and hours worked.

   *Hint: Hourly rate * hours worked.*

3. Copy the Gross Pay formula for each employee.

   a. Select cell E7.

   b. Click the Copy button on the toolbar.

   c. Select the range E8:E12.

   d. Click the Paste button on the toolbar.

   e. Check each formula and note that the cell references are appropriate for the location.

4. Enter a formula to compute Social Sec. Tax at 6.2% of Gross Pay.

5. Copy the Social Sec. Tax formula for each employee.

6. Enter a formula to compute Medicare Tax at 1.45% of Gross Pay.

7. Use the Edit menu to copy the Medicare Tax formula for each employee.

8. Enter a formula to calculate F. W. T. at 20% of gross pay.

9. Enter a formula to calculate Net Pay. All the taxes should be subtracted from the Gross Pay.

10. Copy both formulas for each employee.

11. Format columns E, F, G, H, and I for two decimal places using the Number format option.

12. Save the workbook file as **PAYROLL**.

13. Print Preview the file.

14. Select Page Setup from the file menu and check all print settings.

15. Print two copies of the worksheet.

16. Close the workbook without saving the print setting.

	A	B	C	D	E	F	G	H	I
1	FIRST STATE BANK								
2	PAYROLL								
3									
4	Card	Employee	Hourly	Hours	Gross	Social	Medicare		
5	Number	Name	Rate	Worked	Pay	Sec. Tax	Tax	F.W.T.	Net Pay
6									
7	13567	Diaz	5.55	15					
8	13750	Jaffe	7.23	32					
9	13816	Latov	6.18	16					
10	13925	Nestor	4.66	28					
11	14345	Pringle	6.57	12					
12	14715	Wong	8.65	21					

KEYSTROKES

COPY USING THE MENU

Copies the data once and overwrites existing data in the destination cells.

1. Select cell(s) to copy.
2. Click **Copy** button .... 📋
   on Standard toolbar.
   OR
   a. Click **Edit** menu .... Alt + E
   b. Click **Copy** C
   ✓ *A flashing outline surrounds selection.*
3. Select destination cell(s).

   ✓ *Select an area to copy to, or select the upper left cell in the destination cell range. The destination can be in the same worksheet, another sheet, or another workbook.*

4. Click **Paste** button .... 📋
   on Standard toolbar.
   OR
   a. Click **Edit** .... Alt + E
   b. Click **Paste** .... P

PRINT A WORKSHEET

Prints worksheet data using the current page settings.

✓ *When printing a worksheet, Excel will only print the print area, if you defined one.*

1. Click **Print** button .... 🖨
   on Standard Toolbar.
   OR
   a. Click **File** menu .... Alt + F
   b. Click **Print** .... P
2. Select one of the following:
   - **Selection** .... Alt + N
   - **Active sheets** .... Alt + V
   - **Entire Workbook** .... Alt + E
3. Click **OK** .... Enter

Exercise 15

- **Copy Formulas (Absolute and Relative Reference)**
- **Format Data (Bold, Italics and Underline)**

Formatting Toolbar

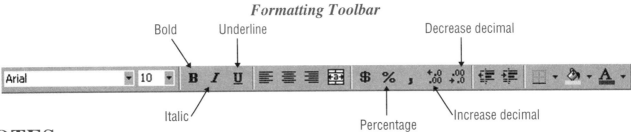

Bold — Underline — Decrease decimal — Italic — Percentage — Increase decimal

NOTES

Copy Formulas (Absolute and Relative Reference)

- When formulas are copied from one cell to another, the cell references change relative to their new location. This is called **relative reference**. If a formula with relative references is copied, a zero appears if the formula is referring to empty cells.

- In some cases, a value in a formula must remain constant when copied to other locations. This is called an **absolute reference**.

- To identify a cell as an absolute value, a dollar sign ($) must precede the column and row references for that cell. For example, in the formula =D7/$D$15, D15 is an absolute reference. When this formula is copied, D15 will remain constant in all formulas. The dollar sign ($) may be typed in the formula in the correct locations or F4 may be used to enter the absolute reference codes.

- In this exercise, we must divide each department's sales by the total to find each department's percentage of total sales. Therefore the formula, =D10/$D$15, represents the sales for PLANTS divided by the TOTAL SALES for the store. D15 is made an absolute reference so that when the formula is copied, the D15 or TOTAL SALES remains constant in every formula. The department sales' cell reference, D10, has no absolute reference code and will change depending on the formula location since it is a relative reference in the formula.

Format Data (Bold, Italic, and Underline)

- Formatting may be used to change decimal answers into a percentage format. The Percentage button on the toolbar formats numbers to percents with no decimal places. If you wish to set decimal places for the percent format, select Cells from the Format menu or use the Increase or Decrease decimal buttons on the Formatting toolbar after using the Percentage button.

- Character formatting options such as **Bold**, *Italic* and Underline may be applied to labels or values to enhance, highlight, or organize your worksheet. The Formatting toolbar contains buttons for each of these options, which are applied by selecting the data and then clicking the appropriate button or buttons. Additional formatting enhancements will be discussed in Lesson 9. The Formatting toolbar buttons are illustrated above.

In this exercise, you will complete the daily sales report for The Veggie Farm by calculating sales, tax and total sales. To analyze departmental sales, the owner requests an analysis showing what percent each department's sales is of the total sales. Labels and values will be bolded, italicized, and underscored.

EXERCISE DIRECTIONS

1. Open 📟 **REGISTER** or 💾 **15REGISTER**.

2. Enter sales data, as shown in italics.

3. Enter a formula to calculate a 5% TAX on Plants in E10.

4. Copy the TAX formula for each department from Plants to Supplies.

5. Enter a formula to determine TOTAL for Fruit.

   Hint: Add Sales and Tax, even though there is no value in the tax column, so that the formula will work for all data.

6. Copy the TOTAL formula for each department.

7. Enter the label TOTAL SALES in cell B15.

8. Enter a formula in cell D15 to calculate TOTAL SALES.

9. Copy the TOTAL SALES formula to cells E15 and F15.

10. Enter the indicated formula using an absolute reference in the % OF SALES column.

11. Copy the % OF SALES formula for each department.

12. Copy the TOTAL SALES formula to find the total of the % OF SALES column and place in G15.

    ✓ *The % OF SALES column should add up to 100% or 1 if not formatted for percents.*

13. Using the Number formatting option, format the money columns (E and F) for two decimal places.

14. Using the Percentage formatting option, format the % OF TOTAL column for percents with two decimal places.

15. Center SALES, TAX, and TOTAL column headings.

16. Bold and underline the two-line title of the worksheet.

17. Bold the Date line. Enter today's date.

18. Bold, underline, and italicize the numbers on the Totals line.

19. Save the workbook file; name it **REGISTER**.

20. Print one copy of the worksheet.

21. Close the workbook.

	A	B	C	D	E	F	G	H
1		THE VEGGIE FARM						
2		DAILY SALES REPORT						
3	DATE:							
4								
5	CODE	DEPARTMENT		SALES	TAX	TOTAL	% OF SALES	
6								
7	A	FRUIT		2342.56			=D7/$D$15	
8	B	VEGETABLES		2854.65				
9	C	DAIRY		643.54				
10	D	PLANTS		965.76				
11	E	BUSHES		854.54				
12	F	FLOWERS		548.78				
13	G	SUPPLIES		1043.54				
14								
15		TOTAL SALES						

KEYSTROKES

ENTER FORMULAS FOR ABSOLUTE CONDITIONS

1. Select cell to receive formula.

2. Press **Equal** .... ⊟

3. Type formula using absolute references and mathematical operators.

   Example of a formula using absolute references: =$A$1*($B$2+$B$10)/2

   ✓ *You can select cells instead of typing absolute references to tell Excel which cells you wish the formula to reference.*

To insert cell references by selecting cells:

1. Click formula where cell reference will be inserted.

   ✓ *If necessary, type preceding operator or parenthesis.*

2. Select cell(s) you want formula to reference.

3. Reference appears in formula.

4. Press **F4** F4

   until absolute reference appears.

5. Type desired operator or parenthesis.

6. Repeat steps 2-5 as needed to complete formula.

7. Press **Enter** .... Enter

FORMAT FOR BOLD, ITALICS, AND UNDERLINE

1. Select data to be formatted.

2. Click one or more of the following Formatting toolbar options:

   • **Bold** .... **B**

   • **Italics** .... *I*

   • **Underline** .... U̲

FORMAT NUMBERS USING THE TOOLBAR

Applies commonly used number formats.

1. Select cell(s) to format.

2. Click one of the following Formatting toolbar options:

   • **Currency Style** .... $

   • **Percent Style** .... %

   • **Comma Style** .... ,

3. To increase or decrease decimal places:

   Increase Decimal .... .00

   OR

   Decrease Decimal .... .00

NEXT EXERCISE

Exercise

16

- ■ **Format Fractions and Mixed Numbers**
- ■ **Spelling** ■ **Look Up Reference**

NOTES

Fractions and Mixed Numbers

- ■ Values can be formatted as fractions or mixed numbers automatically by entering them in a specific way. Values may also be changed to fraction format by selecting **Cells** from the Format menu.

- ■ To enter a value as a **fraction**, which is part of a whole number, type a zero, a space and then type the fraction. For example: 0 1/3.

- ■ To enter a value as a **mixed number**, which is a whole number with a fraction, type the whole number, a space, and then type the fraction. For example: 5 1/3.

- ■ To format a value as a fraction after it has been entered, you must click Format, Cells, the Number tab, and then Fraction from the Category list. If a column contains fractional data, you should format the entire column for fractions to align all the values.

- ■ When you enter or format a value as a fraction, it appears as a decimal (which is also part of a whole number) in the formula bar.

Spelling

- ■ Labels and text entries can be checked for spelling errors by using the Spelling feature. The Spelling button ![ABC] on the Standard toolbar or the Spelling option on the Tools menu, or pressing F7 will access the feature. The words on the worksheet are checked and replacement words are suggested when misspelled words are found.

Look Up Reference

- ■ If you are interested in finding definitions, articles, research, or multimedia related to your worksheet, you can select **Look Up Reference** from the **Tools** menu. The Look Up Reference dialog box, illustrated below, allows you to select Microsoft Bookshelf '95 or Microsoft Bookshelf Basics. Bookshelf Basics is a sample version of the Microsoft Bookshelf '95 reference materials that needs to be installed separately.

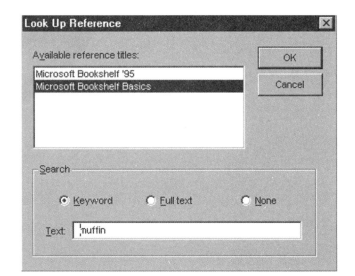

- If you complete the Search text box as shown on the previous page, the reference you select will search for the text, open the reference source, and display the information. Note the illustration of the Microsoft Bookshelf Basics-Dictionary dialog box, along with the desired information and the tabs to access other search areas.

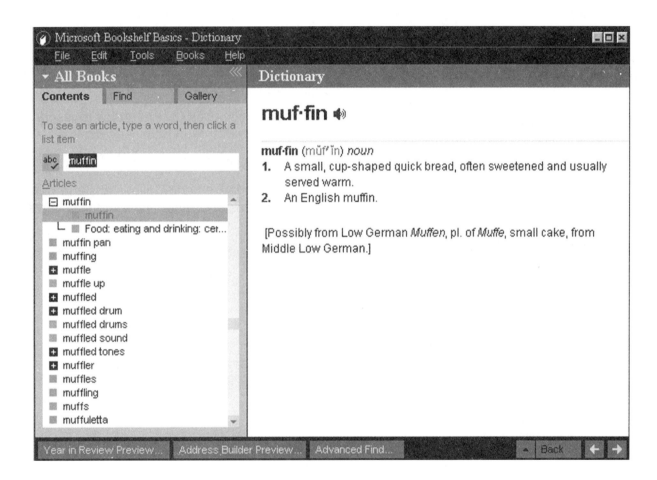

In this exercise, the Old Tyme Bakery wants to computerize their recipes so that they can adjust the amounts of ingredients depending on the desired yield. Fractions and mixed numbers will be used in the recipes.

EXERCISE DIRECTIONS

1. Create the worksheet as illustrated. Bold titles and column headings.

   ✓ *There are spelling errors that will be corrected in Step 9.*

2. Enter the values in the AMT column as shown in the illustration.
   ✓ *Enter fractions or mixed numbers as detailed above.*

3. Format the whole numbers in the AMT column as fractions to align them with the mixed numbers.

4. Center all column headings except for INGREDIENTS as shown.

5. Center the DESIRED YIELD, YIELD, and MEAS. data as shown.

6. In cell A8, enter the formula to find the NEW AMT value for milk as shown in the illustration (AMT/YIELD*DESIRED YIELD—do not use a natural language formula).

   ✓ *In the formula, the YIELD and DESIRED YIELD references must be absolute since they remain constant (=B8/$B$4*$A$4).*

7. Copy the formula to the remaining ingredients.

8. Format the NEW AMT values as fractions using the menu system.

9. Spell check the worksheet.
   ✓ *Ignore abbreviations, such as AMT and tbl. that will appear as misspellings. Along with any errors you might have made, you should find misspellings for vegetable, cinnamon, and whole wheat.*

10. Change the DESIRED YIELD value to 36 and note the changes.

11. Use Tools, Look Up Reference to research muffin in Microsoft Bookshelf Basics.

12. Scroll down the Contents list to view the list.

13. Select the Find and Gallery tabs and view other selections to explore the reference sources.

14. Exit Microsoft Bookshelf Basics by clicking File, Exit, which returns you to the Excel worksheet.

15. Preview and print the worksheet.

16. Save the workbook; name it **BAKERY.**

Enter formula (=B8/$B$4*$A$4).

	A	B	C	D	E	F
1				OLD TYME BAKERY		
2	DESIRED			BASIC MUFFIN RECIPE		
3	YIELD	YIELD				
4	24	12	Muffins			
5						
6	**NEW**					
7	**AMT**	**AMT**	**MEAS.**	**INGREDIENTS**		
8		3/4	cup	milk		
9		3	tbl	vegatable oil		
10		1	large	egg		
11		1 1/4	cups	flour, all-purpose		
12		1/2	cup	flour, whole-wheat		
13		1/4	cup	oats, rolled		
14		1/2	cup	sugar, brown		
15		1/4	cup	sugar, white		
16		1/4	tsp.	salt		
17		2	tsp.	baking powder		
18		1/8	tsp.	cinamon		
19						

Enter amounts as fractions and mixed numbers as shown.

KEYSTROKES

ENTER NUMBERS AS FRACTIONS

1. Select cell to receive number.
2. Press **Zero** .... `0`
3. Press **Space** .... `Space`
4. Type a fraction.
   Example: 0 1/4
5. Press **Enter** .... `Enter`

ENTER MIXED NUMBERS

1. Select cell to receive number.
2. Type a whole number.
3. Press **Space** .... `Space`
4. Type fraction.
   Example: 5 1/4
5. Press **Enter** .... `Enter`

FORMAT NUMBERS FOR FRACTIONS

1. Select cell(s) to format.
2. a. Click **Format** menu .... `Alt`+`O`
   b. Click **Cells** .... `E`
   OR
   a. Right–click a selected cell.
   b. Click **Format Cells**.
3. Click **Number** tab .... `Ctrl`+`Tab`
4. Click **fractions** .... `Alt`+`C`, `↕`
   in **Category** list.
5. Click **Type** and
   select option .... `Alt`+`T`, `↓`
6. Click **OK** .... `Enter`

SPELL CHECK

1. Select any cell.
   ✓ *When one cell is selected for spell checking, Excel prompts you to continue to check all cells, headers, footers, embedded charts, text boxes, cell notes, and text in buttons on the selected sheet. When a selection of text is within one cell, or, when a range of cells is selected, Excel will only spell check that selection.*
   OR
   Select cells to spell check.
   OR
   Select sheets to spell check.
2. Click **Spelling** button .... `ABC✓`
   on Standard Toolbar.
   OR
   a. Click **Tools** menu .... `Alt`+`T`
   b. Click **Spelling** .... `S`

   To replace word not found in dictionary with suggested word:
   a. Type replacement word in
      Change To: [   ]
      OR
      Select word in **Suggestions**
      list box .... `Alt`+`N`, `↕`
   b. Click **Change** .... `Alt`+`C`
      to replace only current instance.
      OR
      Click **Change All** .... `Alt`+`L`
      to replace all instances.

   To undo last change:
   Click **Undo Last** .... `Alt`+`U`

   To skip word not found in dictionary:
   Click **Ignore** .... `Alt`+`I`
   to skip only current instance.
   OR
   Click **Ignore All** .... `Alt`+`G`
   to skip all instances.

   To add word not found to dictionary:
   Click **Add** .... `Alt`+`A`

   To ignore uppercase words:
   Select **Ignore UPPERCASE** .... `Alt`+`R`

   To use words in AutoCorrect Dictionary:
   Select **AutoCorrect** .... `Alt`+`U`

   To end spell checking:
   Click **Cancel** .... `Esc`
   OR
   Click **Close** button .... `Esc`
3. Click **OK** .... `Enter`

USE LOOK UP REFERENCE

1. Click **Tools** .... `Alt`+`T`
2. Click **Look Up Reference** .... `K`
3. Select **Available reference**
   titles .... `Alt`+`V`, `↓`
4. Enter **Search** value .... `Alt`+`S`, *value*
5. Identify value:
   Keyword .... `Alt`+`K`
   OR
   Full Text .... `Alt`+`F`
   OR
   None .... `Alt`+`N`
5. Click **OK** .... `Enter`

Exercise 17

■ Summary

You are employed by **BROWNELL PHARMACEUTICALS** and need to prepare a summary of the number of employees located in plants and offices throughout the United States.

EXERCISE DIRECTIONS

1. Create an appropriate two-line title for your worksheet.

2. Create a listing of each STATE and the number of EMPLOYEES at each location.

Arizona	1060
California	120
Montana	450
New Mexico	695
Oregon	543
South Dakota	267

3. At the bottom of the list, enter a label and find:
   - **Total Employees**

4. Create a new column heading and find for each state:
   - The PERCENT of the firm's employees employed at each location.

     Hint: Use a formula with an absolute reference to the Total Employees.

5. Find the Total of the PERCENT OF EMPLOYEES column.

6. Format PERCENT OF EMPLOYEES column for two-place percents.

7. Right-align all column titles over numeric data.

8. Print one copy of the worksheet.

9. Save the workbook; name it **USEMPS.**

10. Close the workbook.

Exercise 18

■ Summary

You have been asked to set up a worksheet to tally the February sales and compensation for agents in the Spring Car Rental Agency. Each salesperson receives a 2% commission on their car rental sales in addition to their monthly salary.

EXERCISE DIRECTIONS

1. Create an appropriate two-line title for the worksheet in cells C1 and C2.

2. Enter the following information for the sales staff (use columns A and B for AGENT data):

AGENT	SALES	TAX	TOTAL SALES	COMMIS -SION	MONTHLY SALARY	TOTAL
Deb Billings	9567.54				850.00	
Janine Diloren	14356.87				890.00	
Greg Milloy	15321.65				920.00	
Alan Nicks	16754.87				950.00	
Peter Simms	7536.76				820.00	
Kelly Timmer	6675.43				820.00	

3. For each AGENT, find:
   - TAX - sales tax rate is 8%.
   - TOTAL SALES
   - COMMISSION - 2% on pre-tax sales.
   - TOTAL - monthly salary plus commission.

4. Format all money columns for two decimal places.

5. Skip one row and enter a **TOTALS**, label below the worksheet. Find the totals for all money columns.

6. Right-align all column headings for money values.

7. Bold title and total lines.

8. Print one copy of the worksheet.

9. Save the workbook; name it **AGENT**.

10. Close the workbook.

NEXT LESSON

Excel

LESSON 5

FUNCTIONS, FORMATS, FEATURES, AND PRINT OPTIONS

Exercises 19-27

- Use Formulas and Functions
- Formula Bar and Formula Palette
- Paste Function
- AutoCalculate
- Edit
- Copy Part of a Cell's Contents
- Change Column Width
- Create a Series
- Comma Format
- AutoComplete
- Print Options
- Print Preview

- Cell Comments
- AutoSum
- Page Setup (Orientation, Scale, Margins, Header, Footer, etc.)
- Range Entry Using the Collapse Button
- Page Breaks
- Headers and Footers
- Bold Text
- Print Titles

Exercise 19

- **Use Functions** ■ **Formula Bar and Formula Palette**
- **Paste Function**

NOTES

Use Functions

- A **function** is a built-in formula that performs a special calculation automatically. For example, the SUM function can be used with a range of cells to add all values in the range specified. To add the values in A4, A5, and A6, the function appears in the formula as follows: =SUM(A4:A6).

- Functions appear in formulas in the following order: first the *function name* (in either uppercase or lowercase); followed by an *open parenthesis*; then the *number, cell, or range* of cells to be affected; followed by a *closed parenthesis*. You can type or insert functions into formulas. If you are typing a function and you wish to start the formula with a function, first type an equal sign (=).

- A function may be used by itself, or it may be combined with other functions.

- Excel provides functions that are used for statistical and financial analysis or for database operations. Some of the more commonly used functions are:

AVERAGE ()	Averages values in a range of cells.
COUNT()	Counts all the non-blank cells in a range. Cells containing values as well as labels are counted.
MAX ()	Indicates the highest value in a range of cells.
MIN ()	Indicates the lowest value in a range of cells.
SUM	Adds all values in a range of cells.

- The data the functions require you to supply are called **arguments**. For example, in =MAX(A1:A5), the range of cells is the argument.

Formula Bar and Formula Palette

- You can enter or edit a function by using the **Edit Formula button** = (on the formula bar) to access the Formula Palette. The Formula Palette appears with SUM listed in the name box. Click the down arrow to display a list of functions to the left of the formula bar, as illustrated on the next page. You can select the desired function and then enter the arguments using the dialog boxes that appear.

- If you select the AVERAGE function, for example, the dialog box, illustrated on the following page, will display. The Number boxes are for the arguments, formula data, or ranges, to be averaged. At the right of the Number boxes is a **Collapse Dialog Box button** that temporarily collapses the dialog box so you can select the data range for the function. When you finish selecting the range, you can click the button again to redisplay the dialog box.

- The **Formula Palette** is a tool that appears below the formula bar when you click the Edit Formula button. The palette provides information about the selected function in your formula and the result of the function for editing purposes.

Formula Palette

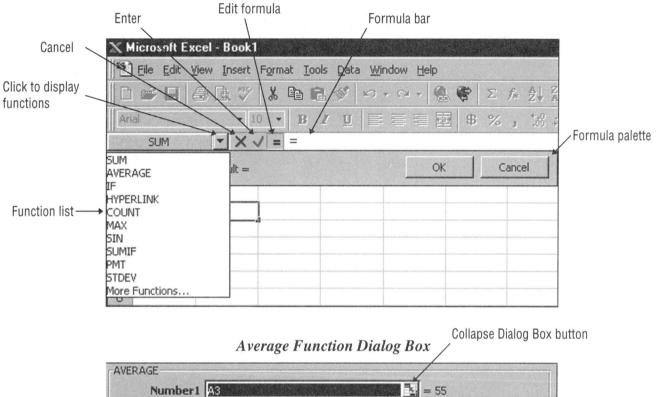

Average Function Dialog Box

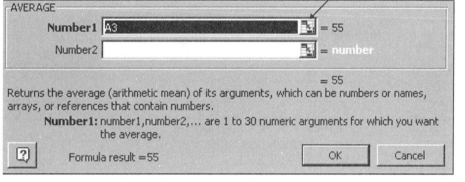

Paste Function

- The **Paste Function** button [fx], located on the Standard toolbar, lets you insert functions into formulas by selecting the function from a list. It provides screens that prompt you for required and optional arguments.

- When you use the **Paste Function** to insert a function at the beginning of a formula, you do not type an equal sign since the Paste Function enters one for you.

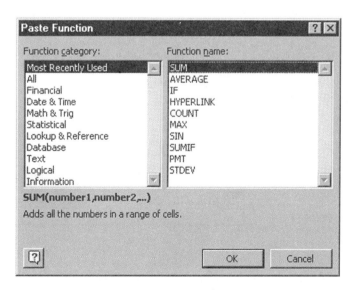

In this exercise, you will enter summary labels and find summary data using the AVERAGE, COUNT, MAX, and MIN functions to complete the SAVINGS worksheet.

NOTE: Only the most commonly used functions are covered in this text. Appendix B (page 393), however, provides the methods to access information on the functions available in Excel.

EXERCISE DIRECTIONS

1. Open [icon] **SAVINGS** or [icon] **19SAVINGS**.

2. Enter new labels in column A, as indicated.

3. Enter the SUM function to total the LIST PRICE column.

4. Copy the formula to the remaining columns.

5. Use the Edit Formula button and Formula Palette to enter the AVERAGE function to average the LIST PRICE column.
   a. Use the collapse dialog box button to select the range C7:C12 for the function range.
   b. Click the button again to redisplay the dialog box.
   c. Click OK to enter the formula.

6. Copy the formula to the remaining columns.

7. Use the Paste Function button and follow the screens to create a function formula for COUNT. Use the range C7:C12 for the function range.

8. Copy the formula to the remaining columns.

9. Enter the MAX and MIN function formulas to complete the worksheet.

10. Copy formulas to the remaining columns.

11. Format summary data money amounts for two decimal places.

12. Save the workbook file; name it **SAVINGS**.

13. Close the workbook.

	A	B	C	D	E	F	G
1		THE NOVEL TEA BOOK STORE					
2		SUMMER SAVINGS SALE					
3		SAMPLE DISCOUNTS					
4							
5			LIST		SALE	SALES	
6	BOOK		PRICE	SAVINGS	PRICE	TAX	TOTAL
7	Creature Feature		15.00	4.00	11.00	0.88	$ 11.88
8	Public Defender		25.00	9.00	16.00	1.28	$ 17.28
9	Traveling Italy		32.00	10.00	22.00	1.76	$ 23.76
10	Picasso in Blue		86.00	28.00	58.00	4.64	$ 62.64
11	Vortex Signs		30.00	10.50	19.50	1.56	$ 21.06
12	Brown's Tax Guide		35.00	12.80	22.20	1.78	$ 23.98
13							
14	TOTALS			⟶			
15	AVERAGE			⟶			
16	COUNT			⟶			
17	MAXIMUM			⟶			
18	MINIMUM			⟶			
19							

KEYSTROKES

INSERT A FUNCTION USING FUNCTION WIZARD

1. Click cell.................................. 🔁
   to contain formula.
   OR
   a. Double-click cell containing
      formula F2
   b. Click formula............................ 🔀
      where function will be inserted.
2. Click **Paste Function**
   button .... *fx*
   OR
   a. Click **Insert** menu.............. Alt + I
   b. Click **Function** .... F
3. Select a
   category...................... Alt + C , 🔁
   in **Function category** list.
4. Select a function .... Alt + N , 🔁
   in **Function name** list.
5. Click **OK** .... Enter
6. Click desired argument box .... Tab
7. Type data.
   *Depending on the function, enter the
   following kinds of data:*
   - **Numbers (constants)**—type
     numbers (integers, fractions, mixed
     numbers, negative numbers) as you
     would in a cell.
   - **References**—type or select cell
     references.

- **Named references or formulas**—
  type or insert named references or
  formulas.
- **Functions**—type a function or click
  Past Function button *fx* (on the
  Standard toolbar) to insert a
  function into an argument
  (nest functions).
  *The Paste Function describes the
  current argument, indicates if
  the argument is required, and shows
  you the result of the values
  you have supplied.*
8. Repeat steps 6 and 7, as needed.
9. Click **OK**.................................... Enter
10. Type or insert remaining parts of
    formula.
    OR
    Press **Enter**................................ Enter

INSERT A FUNCTION IN A FORMULA

1. Select cell to receive formula.
2. Press **Equal**.................................... =
3. Click down arrow in Function name
   box and select function.
   OR
   Click SUM to select that function.
4. Type data range.
   OR
   a. Click collapse button.
   b. Highlight range of data.
   c. Click collapse button again.
5. Click **OK**.................................... Enter

ENTER A FUNCTION USING THE KEYBOARD

1. Select cell to receive formula
2. Press **Equal**.................................. =
3. Type function name.
4. Type open parenthesis .... (
5. Type range or data.
6. Type close parenthesis..................)
7. Press **Enter** .... Enter

EDIT FUNCTIONS USING FORMULA PALETTE

1. Select cell containing formula.
2. In formula bar, click part of formula
   containing function to edit.
3. Click 📋 (Edit Formula button).
   *Formula Palette appears below formula
   bar.*
4. Follow prompts in Formula Palette.

Exercise

20

■ **AutoCalculate** ■ **Edit** ■ **Copy Part of a Cell's Contents**

NOTES

AutoCalculate

- **AutoCalculate** is a new feature that automatically provides the Average, Count, Count Nums, Max, Min, or Sum for a selected range. After selecting the range to be calculated, you can right-click the mouse on the AutoCalculate section of the status bar to get a pop-up list of automatic functions. There is an additional feature called Count Nums. The Count feature will count all entries in a range and the Count Nums will count only the numbers in a range.

- After selecting the desired function, the answer will appear on the status bar as indicated in the illustration below. This result is for your use and cannot be transferred to the worksheet.

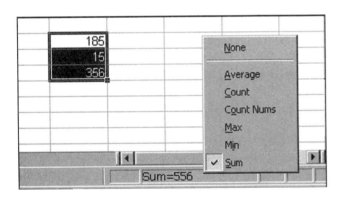

Edit

- Data may be changed either *before* or *after* it has been entered in a cell.

- To clear a cell's content *before* it is entered, you may do any of the following:
    - Press the Backspace key to clear.
    - Press the Escape key.
    - Click the Cancel box on the formula bar.

- To clear a cell's content *after* data is entered, you may do any of the following:
    - Replace the entire entry with new data.
    - Edit part of an entry by **enabling cell editing**.
    - Erase a single cell entry.
    - Erase a range of cell entries.

- Cell editing is enabled by double-clicking on the cell or by pressing F2.

Copy Part of a Cell's Contents

- You can copy part of a cell's contents into another cell by enabling cell editing for the source and destination cells and using copy and paste commands. To copy part of a cell, double-click the cell with data to copy, select the data to copy, click Copy ⌷, double-click the cell to receive the data, click on the insert location, click Paste ⌷, and press Enter.

In this exercise, you will use the AVERAGE, COUNT, MAX and MIN functions to analyze the Cruiser Repair Shop's inventory list. You will use AutoCalculate to preview the answers. In addition, you will find the MARKUP and % MARKUP on each item. Markup is the difference between the selling price and cost of an item. The % markup on cost is determined by dividing the markup by the unit cost.

EXERCISE DIRECTIONS

1. Open ⌨ **INVEN** or 💾 **20INVEN**.

2. Enter new column labels, as indicated below.

3. Enter the first new inventory line for oil filter.

4. To practice copying part of a cell's contents:
   a. Enter the second new item number.
   b. Type only the word **air**, and press Enter.
   c. Enable cell editing in B16 (double-click).
   d. Select the word filter and click the Copy button.
   e. Double-click B17 and select the location after the word **air**.
   f. Click the Paste button.

5. Enter a formula to find MARKUP.

6. Copy the formula to the remaining items.

7. Format all money columns for two decimal places. Enter a formula to find % MARKUP on cost.
   Hint: Markup/Cost

8. Format % MARKUP column for two-place percent.

9. Copy the formula to the remaining items.

10. Enter the AVERAGE function to average the UNIT COST column. Copy the formula to the remaining columns.

11. Preview the answer to the HIGHEST VALUE answer by using AutoCalculate as follows:
    a. Select the values in the UNIT COST column.
    b. Point to the AutoCalculate box on the status bar.
    c. Right-click right mouse to view the pop-up list of functions.
    d. Select MAX.
    e. View the answer on the status bar.

12. Enter the **MAX** function formula to complete the HIGHEST VALUE data. Copy formulas to the remaining columns.

13. Repeat the AutoCalculate process to review the answer for LOWEST VALUE or MIN data.

14. Enter the **MIN** function formula to complete the LOWEST VALUE data. Copy formulas to the remaining columns.

15. Use AutoCalculate and the Count and Count Nums functions on the ITEM and UNIT COST columns to note the difference between these operations.

16. Format summary data, if necessary.

17. Save the workbook file as **INVEN**.

18. Close the workbook.

	A	B	C	D	E	F	G
1		CRUISER REPAIR SHOP					
2		INVENTORY LIST					
3							
4	ITEM			UNIT	SELLING		
5	NUMBER	ITEM		COST	PRICE	MARKUP	MARKUP %
6							
7	142	carburetor		120	168		
8	321	spark plugs		2	3		
9	093	tires		55	77		
10	393	brakes		60	84		
11	659	alarm		125	195		
12	572	mats		45	63		
13	175	battery		45	70		
14	421	radio		185	265		
15	932	fan belt		15	28		
16	*254*	*oil filter*		*18*	*30*		
17	*754*	*air filter*		*23*	*35*		
18	*344*	*antifreeze*		*6*	*10*		
19							
20	AVERAGES						
21	HIGHEST VALUE						
22	LOWEST VALUE						

KEYSTROKES

EDIT CELL CONTENTS AFTER DATA IS ENTERED (ENABLE CELL EDITING)

1. Double-click cell to edit.

   OR

   a. Select cell to edit ....

   b. Press **F2** F2

   An insertion point appears in the active cell and these buttons appear on the formula bar:

    Cancel button–cancels changes made in cell.

    Enter button–accepts changes made in cell.

2. Click desired data position ....
   in cell or in formula bar.

3. Type new data.

   OR

   Press **Backspace**................. Backspace
   to delete character to left of insertion point.

   OR

   Press **Delete** .... Del
   to delete character to right of insertion point.

   To accept changes:

   Press **Enter** .... Enter

   OR

   Click **Enter** button........................... ☑
   on the formula bar.

   To cancel changes:

   Press **Escape** .... Esc

   OR

   Click **Cancel** button...................... ☒
   on the formula bar.

EDIT CELL CONTENTS WHILE TYPING

To delete character to the left of insertion point:

Press **Backspace** .... Backspace

To cancel all characters:

Press **Escape** .... Esc

ERASE CONTENTS OF CELL OR RANGE

1. Select cell or range containing contents to erase.

2. Press **Delete**................................ Del

COPY OR MOVE PART OF A CELL'S CONTENTS

1. Double-click the cell that contains the data to move or copy.

2. In the cell, select the characters to move or copy.

3. To move the selection, click **Cut** ..... ✂
   on the toolbar.

   OR

   To copy the selection, click **Copy**... 📋
   on the toolbar.

4. Double-click the cell to receive the data.

5. In the cell, click where data is to be placed.

6. Click **Paste**.................................... 📋
   on the toolbar.

7. Press **Enter**............................... Enter

AUTOCALCULATE VALUES IN A WORKSHEET

Displays a calculated value for selected cells in a worksheet.

1. Select cells to calculate .... Shift + ↓

2. Right-click on status bar **AutoCalculate** area.

3. Click desired function...............
   Average, Count, Count Nums, Max, Min, Sum

   ✓ *Excel displays result, such as Sum+123, on the AutoCalculate area of the status bar.*

NEXT EXERCISE

Exercise 21

- **Change Column Width** ■ **Create a Series**
- **Comma Format** ■ **AutoComplete**

NOTES

Change Column Width

- All worksheets in a workbook are set for a **standard column width** (default setting is 8.43). This number represents the number of characters displayed in a cell using the standard font.

- When you enter long *labels*, the text flows into the next column if the cell to the right is empty. If the next cell is not empty, text that exceeds the column width is covered by the data in the cell to the right.

- Unlike label text, *numeric data* that exceeds the column width does *not* flow into the next column. If the column is not wide enough to display a numeric value, Excel fills the cell with number signs (######) or displays the number in scientific notation to indicate a need to widen the column.

- Therefore, it is desirable to change (widen or narrow) column widths so text or values can fit or look better. Only the width of an entire column or a group of columns may be changed, not the width of a single cell.

- You can select Format, Column, **AutoFit** to set the column width to fit the longest entry. Or, you can place the mouse on the bar between column letter headings and drag the column to size. Excel will display the width of the column as you drag it to its new size.

- When you select Format, Column, **Width**, you can enter the exact column width you desire.

- To change the width of several columns, select those columns before using any columns width adjustment commands.

Create A Series

- You can use the **Fill**, **Series** option on the Edit menu to quickly enter sequential values in a range of cells. You can enter sequential numbers, dates, or times in any increment (e.g., 2, 4, 6, 8 or 5, 10, 15, 20 or January, February, March, April). As illustrated in the Series dialog box below, you must set the Step value and the Stop value for the series.

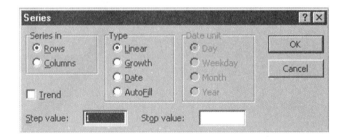

- Another way to fill a range with a series is to drag the **fill handle** of a selection containing the first, or first and second, series values of a range into which you want the series to be entered. Excel completes the series based on the value(s) in the selected cell(s). Note the illustration of the fill handle.

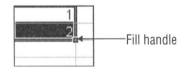

Fill handle

Comma Format

- To make large numbers more readable, formatting may be used to include commas. The **Comma** button ⟦,⟧ on the Formatting toolbar formats data for commas with two decimal places. The number of decimal places to display may also be set within the **Format Cells** dialog box by selecting Format, Cells, the Number tab and then typing the number into the Decimal places text box. Or, you can use the Increase or Decrease Decimal buttons on the Formatting toolbar.

AutoComplete

- **AutoComplete** allows you to enter labels automatically after making repetitive entries. When you enter the first letters of repeated data, Excel will guess or AutoComplete the data from your previously entered data. If the data is correct, press Enter to confirm the AutoComplete entry.

- If labels in a list are repeated randomly, you may also use the quick menu and the Pick from list item, to select the next label from a list.

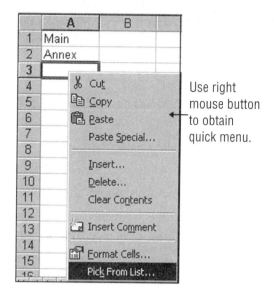

Use right mouse button to obtain quick menu.

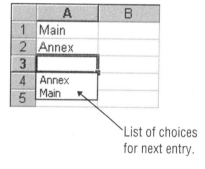

List of choices for next entry.

> *In this exercise, you will create a worksheet for Furniture Showrooms, Inc. showing employees' quarterly SALES and COMMISSION earned. You will use the AutoComplete, AutoCalculate, comma format, and function features. Each employee receives a 5% commission on sales.*

EXERCISE DIRECTIONS

1. Create the worksheet as shown, or open 🖫 **21FURN**.

2. Set column widths as follows:

   Column A: 4   Column B: 18   Column C: 10

   Column E: 12   Column F: 12   Column G: 12

3. Practice using the Fill, Series option as follows:
   a. Place your cursor in A7, type 110 and press Enter.
   b. Select Edit, Fill, Series from the menu bar.
   c. Click Columns in the Series dialog box.
   d. Make sure the Step Value is set to 1.
   e. Set the Stop value at 114.
   f. Click OK.
   g. Delete the employee numbers you just created in column A.

4. Enter 1 and 2 as employee numbers for the first two employees. Select both numbers and use the fill handle to extend the series.

5. Practice using the AutoComplete feature in the BUILDING columns as follows:
   a. Enter Main for Judy Abrams and Annex for Peter Chang.
   b. Place mouse cursor in the next cell (C9) for Kelly Linsey.
   c. Right-click to display a shortcut menu.
   d. Select Pick from list.

   e. Select Main for Kelly Linsey.
   f. Enter Annex for Johnson and Main for Rivera by entering the first letters of the words and confirming the AutoComplete text by pressing the Enter key.

6. Copy the BASE SALARY amount to all remaining employees by using the fill handle.
   ✓ *All employees have the same base salary.*

7. Enter a formula to find COMMISSION for the first employee. The commission rate is 5% of sales. Copy the formula to the remaining employees.

8. Enter a formula to find QUARTERLY SALARY for the first employee by adding BASE SALARY and COMMISSION for the quarter. Copy the formula to the remaining employees.

9. Use AutoCalculate to check the total of the Base Salary column.

10. Enter formulas to find TOTALS, AVERAGES, HIGHEST, and LOWEST values. Copy the formulas to each column.

11. Center column title labels.

12. Format numeric data to include commas and two decimal places.

13. Save the workbook; name it **FURN**.

14. Print one copy.

15. Close the workbook.

	A	B	C	D	E	F	G
1		FURNITURE SHOWROOMS, INC.					
2		QUARTERLY SALES AND SALARY REPORT - JANUARY-MARCH					
3							
4	EMP.			BASE		5%	QUARTERLY
5	NO.	NAME	BUILDING	SALARY	SALES	COMMISSION	SALARY
6							
7		ABRAMS, JUDY		1,500.00	113,456.67		
8		CHANG, PETER			150,654.87		
9		LINSEY, KELLY			234,765.36		
10		JOHNSON, LETOYA			89,765.43		
11		RIVERA, TONY			287,987.76		
12							
13		TOTALS					
14		AVERAGES					
15		HIGHEST					
16		LOWEST					

KEYSTROKES

CHANGE COLUMN WIDTHS USING THE MENU

1. Select any cell(s) in column(s) to change.
2. Click **Format** menu .... `Alt`+`O`
3. Click **Column** .... `C`
4. Click **Width** .... `W`
5. Type number (0-255) in **Column Width** text box.
   - ✓ *Number represents number of characters that can be displayed in cell using the standard font.*
6. Click **OK** .... `Enter`

CHANGE COLUMN WIDTHS USING THE MOUSE

Change one column width:

1. Point to right border of column heading to size.
   - ✓ *Pointer becomes a ↔.*
2. Drag ↔ left or right.
   - ✓ *Excel displays width on left side of formula bar.*

Change several column widths:

1. Select columns to size.
2. Point to right border of any selected column heading.
   - ✓ *Pointer becomes a ↔.*
3. Drag ↔ left or right.
   - ✓ *Excel displays width on left side of formula bar.*

Use right mouse button:

1. Highlight column by clicking on heading label.
2. Right-click mouse.
3. Click **Column Width**.
4. Type desired width.
5. Click **OK** .... `Enter`

SET COLUMN WIDTH TO FIT LONGEST ENTRY

Double-click right border of column heading.

OR

1. Select column to size .... `↔`, `Ctrl`+`Space`
2. Click **Format** menu .... `Alt`+`O`
3. Click **Column** .... `C`
4. Click **AutoFit Selection** .... `A`

SET STANDARD COLUMN WIDTH

Changes column widths that have not been previously adjusted in a worksheet.

1. Click **Format** menu .... `Alt`+`O`
2. Click **Column** .... `C`
3. Click **Standard Width** .... `S`
4. Type new number (0-255) .... *number* in **Standard Column Width** text box.
   - ✓ *Number represents number of characters that can be displayed in the cell using the standard font.*
5. Click **OK** .... `Enter`

RESET COLUMNS TO STANDARD COLUMN WIDTH

1. Select column(s) to format.
2. Click **Format** menu .... `Alt`+`O`
3. Click **Column** .... `C`
4. Click **Standard Width** .... `S`
5. Click **OK** .... `Enter`

CREATE A SERIES OF NUMBERS, DATES, OR TIMES USING THE MENU

1. Enter the first series value in a cell to create a series from a **single value**.
   OR
   Enter first and second series values in consecutive cells to create a series from multiple values.

2. Select cell(s) containing series value(s) and cells to fill.
   - ✓ *Select adjacent cells in rows or columns to fill.*
3. Click **Edit** menu .... `Alt`+`E`
4. Click **Fill** .... `I`
5. Click **Series** .... `S`

   To change proposed step value:
   Type step value in **Step Value** text box.

   To change proposed direction of series:
   Select desired **Series in** option:

   Rows .... `Alt`+`R`
   Columns .... `Alt`+`C`

   To change proposed series type:
   Select desired Type option:

   Linear .... `Alt`+`L`
   to increase/decrease each value in series by number in Step Value text box.

   Growth .... `Alt`+`G`
   to multiply each value in series by number in Step Value text box.

   Date .... `Alt`+`D`
   to set increment by days, weekdays, months, or years.

   AutoFill .... `Alt`+`F`
   to fill cells based on values in selection.

   If Date was selected:
   Select desired **Date Unit** option:

   Day .... `Alt`+`A`
   Weekday .... `Alt`+`W`
   Month .... `Alt`+`M`
   Year .... `Alt`+`Y`

   To set stop value for series:
   - ✓ *Type a stop value if you want series to end at a specific number.*
   a. Click **Stop Value**: .... `Alt`+`O`
   b. Type stop value.
6. Click **OK** .... `Enter`

Exercise

22

■ Print Options ■ Print Preview ■ Cell Comments ■ AutoSum

NOTES

Print Options

- When you select Print from the File menu, Excel allows you to set various print options. You can choose to print a range of cells, one page, or the entire workbook. You can also set print Properties or Preview your settings by using the buttons provided. The properties button accesses settings for Paper, Fonts, Graphics, or Device Options. The Print dialog box can also be accessed by clicking on the Print button on the Standard toolbar.

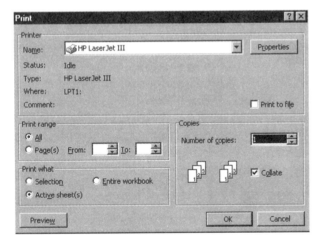

- One of the settings on the Print dialog box is to print the Selection. If you select an area of the worksheet and then activate the Print dialog box, you can choose **Selection** to print only the selected area. Another way to print a specific portion of the worksheet is to make the selection and set the print area by selecting Print Area from the File menu. A dotted line will appear around the selection and will remain until cleared. Making a selection setting on the Print dialog box will override the print area setting.

Print Preview

- In the Print dialog box you can select the Preview button to review, onscreen, the output your settings will yield. The Print Preview dialog box can also be accessed by clicking the Print Preview button on the Standard toolbar. As shown in the illustration below, the preview screen contains a toolbar that provides buttons for Print, Setup, Margins, etc. Setup and Page Break Preview will be discussed later in this lesson.

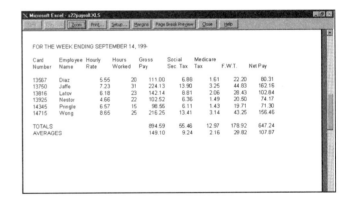

Cell Comments

- It is possible to attach a text **comment** to a cell that displays when the cursor is placed on the cell. This feature is useful to document formulas or assumptions built into the worksheet. Since it is also used to add comments by each user in a shared workbook, Excel 97 enters the name of the user in the Comment box.

- A comment is entered by selecting **Comment** from the Insert menu, typing the comment into the comment box, and then clicking outside of the comment box to close it. A red triangle appears in the corner of the cell to indicate the presence of a cell comment. When the mouse moves over a cell that contains a comment, the comment is automatically displayed. You can size the comment box by using the mouse to move the box to the desired size with its sizing handles. Note the illustration below.

Social	Medicare		
Sec. Tax	Tax	F.W.T.	Ne
	Your Name:		
5.16	Tax calculated at 6.2%.		
14.34			

AutoSum

- The **AutoSum** feature quickly enters the SUM function to total values in a worksheet. Clicking the AutoSum button 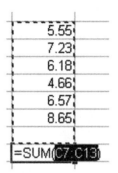 on the Standard toolbar displays a suggestion (with a dotted line) for a range of cells to total. You can accept that range or change it by dragging through the cells you wish to total. The illustration below shows what appears when AutoSum was activated in the cell below the column of data.

5.55
7.23
6.18
4.66
6.57
8.65
=SUM(C7:C13)

In this exercise, you will complete the payroll for the First State Bank for the week ending September 7, 199–. You will then copy the entire worksheet to a new location and edit entries to create another payroll for the week ending September 14, 199–. You will enter cell notes and print the worksheet.

EXERCISE DIRECTIONS

1. Open ⌨ **PAYROLL** or 💾 **22PAYROLL**.

2. Edit the first line of the title, as illustrated.

3. Erase the second line of the title. Replace it, as indicated.

4. Enter the new row labels, as indicated.

5. Find TOTALS for Gross Pay, Soc. Sec. Tax, Medicare Tax, F.W.T. and Net Pay columns by using the AutoSum feature.

6. Find the AVERAGES for the same data.

7. Format TOTALS and AVERAGES for two decimal places.

8. Enter cell comments as follows:

   In F7:   Tax calculated at 6.2%.

   In G7:   Tax calculated at 1.45%.

   In H7:   Tax calculated at 20%.

9. View each cell comment and use the mouse to size the boxes if necessary.

10. Copy the range of data A2: I16 (as shown in the illustration below) to A17.
    - ✓ When copying a range, it is only necessary to specify the first position in the destination range.

11. Make the following edits on the copy or bottom payroll:

    a. Edit the title to read:
    FOR THE WEEK ENDING SEPTEMBER 14, 199-

    b. Edit the HOURS WORKED as follows:
    | Diaz, 20 | Jaffe, 31 | Latov, 23 |
    | Nestor, 22 | Pringle, 15 | Wong, 25 |

12. Preview the printout of this file.

13. Select the September 14th payroll and set the print area.

14. Print one copy of the September 14th payroll.

15. Close and save the workbook, or *save as* **PAYROLL**.

	A	B	C	D	E	F	G	H	I
1	FIRST STATE BANK	PAYROLL							
2	PAYROLL		FOR THE WEEK ENDING SEPTEMBER 7, 199-						
3									
4	Card	Employee	Hourly	Hours	Gross	Social	Medicare		
5	Number	Name	Rate	Worked	Pay	Sec. Tax	Tax	F.W.T.	Net Pay
6									
7	13567	Diaz	5.55	15	83.25	5.16	1.21	16.65	60.23
8	13750	Jaffe	7.23	32	231.36	14.34	3.35	46.27	167.39
9	13816	Latov	6.18	16	98.88	6.13	1.43	19.78	71.54
10	13925	Nestor	4.66	28	130.48	8.09	1.89	26.10	94.40
11	14345	Pringle	6.57	12	78.84	4.89	1.14	15.77	57.04
12	14715	Wong	8.65	21	181.65	11.26	2.63	36.33	131.42
13									
14	TOTALS								
15	AVERAGES								
16									
17					Copy A2:I16				
18	Paste range here.								

KEYSTROKES

CREATE TEXT CELL COMMENTS

1. Select cell to attach note to.
2. Click **Insert** menu .... `Alt`+`I`
3. Click **Comment** .... `M`
4. Type note in box.
5. Click outside of the comment
   box when finished .... `Esc`, `Esc`
   - ✓ *Excel marks each cell containing a note with a note marker (small red triangle).*
   - ✓ *Point to the cell containing the note to view it.*

EDIT CELL COMMENTS

1. Right-click cell with cell comment.
2. Select **Edit comment** .... `Alt`+`E`
3. To size the comment box, use the mouse to drag the handles to the desired size.
4. Edit text as necessary.
5. Click elsewhere on the worksheet.

SET/CLEAR PRINT AREA

1. Select range of cells to print.
2. Click **File** menu .... `Alt`+`F`
3. Click **Print Area** .... `T`
4. Click **Set Print Area** .... `S`
   - ✓ *The print area will have a dotted line border. The Print command must be used to print the area.*

OR

Click **Clear Print Area** .... `C`

PRINT RANGE OF CELLS

Prints data in a selected range using the current page settings.
   - ✓ *This procedure will override a print area if you defined one.*

1. Select range of cells to print.
2. Click **File** menu .... `Alt`+`F`
3. Click **Print** .... `P`
4. Click **Selection** .... `N`
5. Click **OK** .... `Enter`

USE AUTOSUM

1. Select cell(s) to receive formula(s).
   - ✓ *Select blank cell(s) below or to the right of cells containing values to total.*
2. Click **AutoSum** button .... `Σ`
   on Standard toolbar.

OR

Press **Alt + Equal** .... `Alt`+`=`

Excel inserts =SUM( ) function in formula bar, and a flashing outline may surround cells to be totaled.

To change proposed range to total:

Select cells to total.

3. Press **Enter** .... `Enter`

Exercise

23

- ■ **Page Setup (Orientation, Scale, Margins, Header, Footer, Etc.)**
- ■ **Range Entry Using the Collapse Button**

NOTES

Page Setup (Orientation, Scale, Margins, Header, Footer, Etc.)

- ■ Excel 97 uses the default page size (usually 8 1/2" x 11") of the installed printer. To change the page size, click the Page Setup option on the File menu, then select the Page tab.

- ■ The Page Setup dialog box (see below) may be accessed directly from the File menu, or from the Print Preview screen.

- ■ The Page Setup dialog box has several tabs. Each tab contains options that control the print output.

- ■ Page Setup options include:

    Page Tab
    - • **Orientation** The worksheet data may be printed in either **Portrait** (vertical) or **Landscape** (horizontal) paper orientation.

- • **Scaling** The printed worksheet can be enlarged or reduced. The scaling options are: **Adjust to** % of normal size, or **Fit to** pages wide by pages tall. Both scaling options proportionally scale the worksheet.

    ✓ *NOTE: Scaling is often needed when you want a printed worksheet to fit on a specified number of pages. You can use the Print Preview option to check how it will fit before printing.*

- • **Paper Size** The paper size options include: letter, legal and other size options.

Page Setup Dialog Box with Page Tab Selected

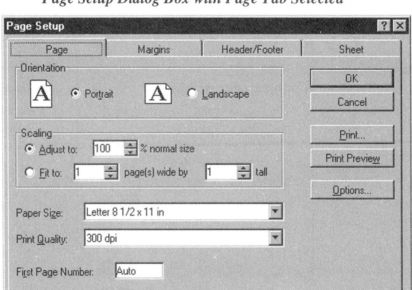

- **Print quality**   The number of dots per inch may be set to increase or decrease print quality.

- **First Page Number**   The starting page number for the pages on the current sheet.

Margins Tab

- **Margins**   The page margins, the distance of the worksheet data from the **Top**, **Bottom**, **Left** or **Right** edge of the page, may be set in inches. The **Header** and **Footer** margins, the distance of the header and footer data from the top and bottom edges of the worksheet, can be set in inches.

- **Center on Page**   The worksheet data can be **Horizontally** and/or **Vertically** centered within the page margins.

Header/Footer Tab

- **Header/Footer**   Left, centered, and right-aligned text may be included above or below the worksheet. This feature may be used to include a title, date, or page number. See **Exercise 24**.

Sheet Tab

- **Print area**   Only define this area if you always want to print the same range of cells when printing a worksheet.

- **Print Titles**   Descriptive information from designated **Rows** that will print on the top of each page and/or **Columns** that will print on the left of each page. *(See **Print Titles**, Exercise 25.)*

- **Print**   Includes the following print options: **Gridlines**, **Comments**, **Draft Quality**, **Black and White**, **Row and Column Headings**.

- **Page Order**   The setting that determines the printed page order: **Down, then Over** or **Over, then Down**.

Range Entry Using Collapse Button

- As in previous versions of Excel, you can type or select cell references in dialog boxes that prompt for cells or ranges. In Excel 97, dialog boxes that prompt for cell references contain a collapse button on the right side of the text box. When you click the collapse button, the dialog box collapses to a smaller size providing access to the worksheet so that the range can be selected. Note the illustration below showing the collapse button on the Sheet tab of the Print Setup dialog box. You can click the dialog box to restore it to full size.

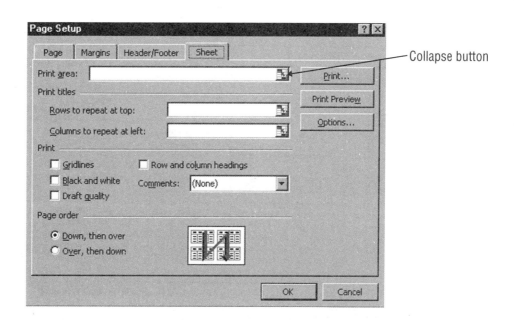

In this exercise, you will open the quarterly sales worksheet for Furniture Showrooms, Inc., expand the worksheet to include quarterly data, and print the worksheet using scaling options, print area, and gridlines settings.

EXERCISE DIRECTIONS

1. Open ⌨ **FURN** or 💾 **23FURN**.

2. Edit the second line of the title. Replace MARCH with JUNE.

3. Replace QUARTERLY with JAN-MAR.

4. Select the column heading and data in the BUILDING column and erase all data.

5. Change column widths as follows:

   Column C: 3
   Columns H, I, J: 12

6. Copy column titles SALES, 5% COMMISSION, and SALARY to columns H, I, and J. Insert the label APR–JUN over SALARY in column J.

7. Center all new labels where necessary.

8. Enter new sales data in column H.

9. Copy the COMMISSION formula for the first employee in column F to column I.

10. Copy the COMMISSION formula down for each employee.

11. Enter a formula in column J to compute BASE SALARY + COMMISSION for the second quarter.

12. Copy the BASE SALARY + COMMISSION formula down for each employee.

13. Find TOTALS, AVERAGES, HIGHEST, and LOWEST for the second quarter. (Copy formulas using one copy command.)

14. Format numeric data for commas and two decimal places.

15. On the Page tab of Page Setup, change the scale setting to fit worksheet on one page.

16. On the Sheet tab Page Setup, set the print area for the entire worksheet using the collapse button.

17. Change the sheet setting to print gridlines.

18. Check your scale setting, using Print Preview.

19. Print one copy.

20. Close and save the workbook; or save as **FURN**.

	A	B	C	D	E	F	G	H ←12→	I ←12→	J ←12→
1		FURNITURE SHOWROOMS, INC.								
2		QUARTERLY SALES AND SALARY REPORT - JANUARY-MARCH →JUNE								
3							JAN-MAR			
4	EMP.			BASE		5%	QUARTERLY			APR-JUN
5	NO.	NAME	BUILDING	SALARY	SALES	COMMISSION	SALARY			
6										
7	1	ABRAMS, JUDY	Main	1,500.00	113,456.67	5,672.83	7,172.83	114342.90		
8	2	CHANG, PETER	Annex	1,500.00	150,654.87	7,532.74	9,032.74	143276.70		
9	3	LINSEY, KELLY	Main	1,500.00	234,765.36	11,738.27	13,238.27	187956.80		
10	4	JOHNSON, LETOYA	Annex	1,500.00	89,765.43	4,488.27	5,988.27	93984.69		
11	5	RIVERA, TONY	Main	1,500.00	287,987.76	14,399.39	15,899.39	254768.60		
12										
13		TOTALS		7,500.00	876,630.09	43,831.50	51,331.50			
14		AVERAGES		1,500.00	175,326.02	8,766.30	10,266.30			
15		HIGHEST		1,500.00	287,987.76	14,399.39	15,899.39			
16		LOWEST		1,500.00	89,765.43	4,488.27	5,988.27			
17										
18			←3→							

KEYSTROKES

SET PRINT OPTIONS FOR WORKSHEET

Sets a print area and shows or hides gridlines on printed sheet.

1. Click **File** menu .... `Alt`+`F`
2. Click **Page Setup** .... `U`
3. Click **Sheet** .... `Ctrl`+`Tab`

   To set a print area:
   ✓ *Use this option to print a specific area of a worksheet each time you print.*

   a. Click in **Print Area**: .... `Alt`+`A`
   b. Click Collapse button .... 🔲

   c. Select range of cells in worksheet to print.
      OR
      Type cell reference(s) of area to print.
      ✓ *To remove a print area, delete the reference.*

   d. Click Collapse button
      on dialog box .... 🔲

   To show or hide gridlines:

   Select or deselect
   Gridlines .... `Alt`+`G`

4. Click **OK** .... `Enter`

CHANGE SCALE OF PRINTED DATA

1. Click **File** menu .... `Alt`+`F`
2. Click **Page Setup** .... `U`
3. Select **Page** .... `Ctrl`+`Tab`

   To reduce or enlarge data on printed sheet:

   a. Click **Adjust to:** .... `Alt`+`A`
   b. Type percentage (10-400)
      ✓ *You can also click the increment box arrows to select a percentage.*

4. Click **OK** .... `Enter`

Exercise 24

■ Page Breaks ■ Headers and Footers ■ Bold Text

NOTES

Page Breaks

- Before printing, you may set page breaks and add headers and footers to a worksheet that requires more than one page. When the **Page Break** option is set, Excel stops printing on the current page and starts printing on the top of a new page.

- Excel inserts automatic page breaks based on the current paper size, scaling, and margin settings. Automatic page breaks appear as dashed lines on the worksheet. To view automatic page breaks, the **Page Breaks** check box must be selected on the View tab in the Options dialog box. You can override the automatic page breaks by inserting **manual page breaks** in your worksheet. Manual page breaks appear as bold dashed lines.

- In Excel 97 a new feature allows you to select **Page Break Preview** from the View menu or, while in Print Preview mode, from the Print Preview toolbar. Page break preview displays the entire worksheet with page break lines and page numbers. Note the illustration of the Page Break Preview screen below:

Headers and Footers

- **Headers and footers** are used when you want to repeat the same information at the top (header) or bottom (footer) of every page.

- With Excel, you can select from built-in headers and footers, or you can customize them. These print enhancements can be set in the Page Setup dialog box from the **Header/Footer** tab.

- Headers and footers are limited to a single line of text and may be formatted as desired. Header/footer text may be separated into segments, as shown in the illustration of a custom header on the next page.

- When you create a custom header, text entered in the left section will be left-justified. Text entered in the middle section will be centered, and text entered in the right section will be right-justified.

- You may insert **codes** to print the current date, time, page number, and/or workbook filename as part of the header/footer text by clicking a code button representing the desired item. Note the illustration of the custom header on the next page.

Bold Text

- To emphasize headings or labels, you may want to bold the text. This can be accomplished by selecting the cell and then clicking the Bold button **B** on the Formatting toolbar, or by selecting the Bold Font Style on the Font tab of the Format, Cells, dialog box. Note the illustration of the Format Cells dialog box on the next page.

Custom Header Window

Total pages

Page number

Date

Time

Font

Filename

Sheet name

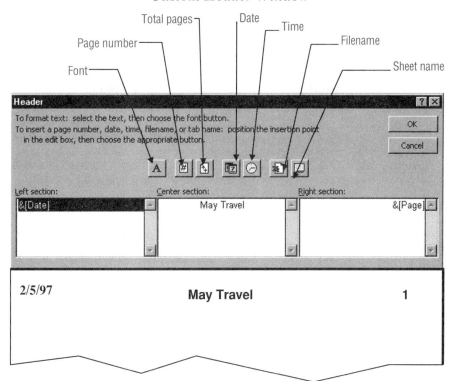

Format Cells Dialog Box with Font Tab Selected

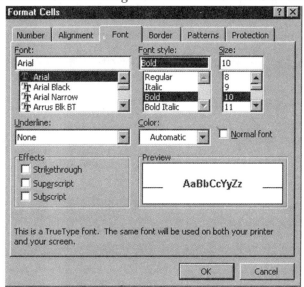

In this exercise, you will create a travel expense report for one of the salespeople at the Papyrus Paper Company. The May travel report will include two trips, each printed on a separate page with a header. The reports will be spell checked.

EXERCISE DIRECTIONS

1. Create the top worksheet shown on the next page, including bold styles, or open 🖫 **24EXPENSE**.

   ✓ *Enter the days of the month as numeric labels.*

2. Set column widths as follows:

   Column A: 15

   Column B: 3

3. Use the Spell Check feature to check your worksheet.

4. Find the following totals for car expenses:
   a. Total Miles (add daily mileage)
   b. Total Travel Expenses (mileage * .29)

5. In the Total Travel Expenses column, find the total for hotel expenses.

6. Copy the formula to each expense item as illustrated.

7. Find:
   a. TOTALS for each day (which include the rows in the TRANSPORTATION section starting at the Car Rental (C15) item).
   b. Total of Total Travel Expenses column (which includes the DAILY EXPENSES and the TRANSPORTATION costs, including car mileage expense).

8. Format all money columns for two decimal places.

9. Center all column titles.

10. Copy the entire worksheet and paste it in cell A33, as illustrated on the next page.

11. Create a page break at cell A32.

12. Edit the DATES, PURPOSE, TRANSPORTATION, and DAILY EXPENSES to display the data for the next trip, as indicated.

13. In the Total Travel Expenses column find:
    a. Total of the Car Rental Expenses
    b. Total of the Air Travel Expenses

14. Use Page Setup to create a custom header that includes a left-justified date, a centered title that reads MAY TRAVEL, and a right-justified page number.

15. Use Print Preview and check the Page Break Preview display.

16. Print the file to fit columns to the page.

17. Save the workbook file; name it **EXPENSE**.

18. Close the workbook.

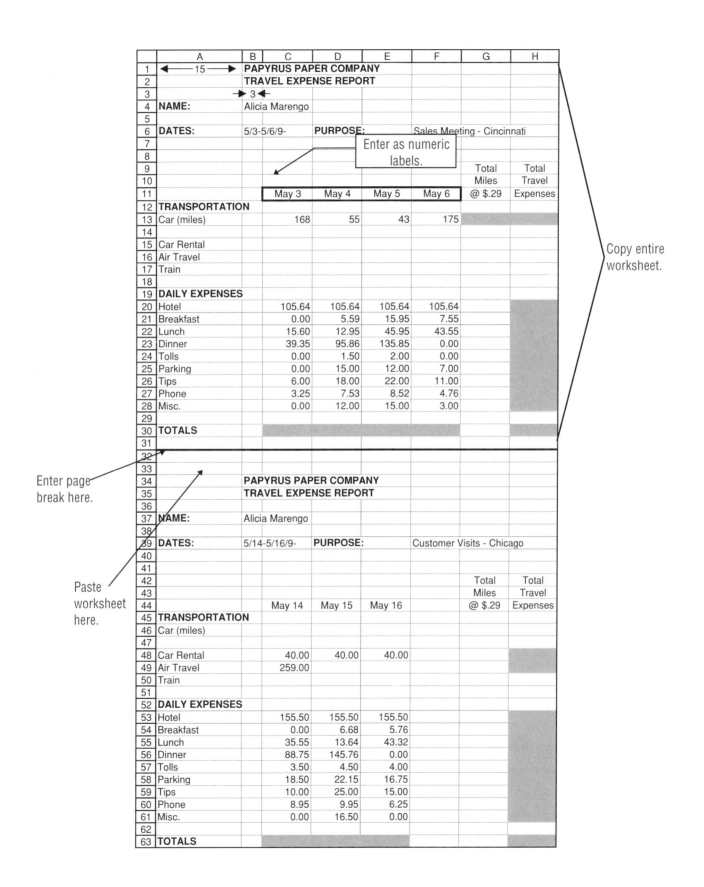

Enter as numeric labels.

Copy entire worksheet.

Enter page break here.

Paste worksheet here.

	A	B	C	D	E	F	G	H
1	◄—15—►		**PAPYRUS PAPER COMPANY**					
2			**TRAVEL EXPENSE REPORT**					
3		► 3 ◄						
4	**NAME:**		Alicia Marengo					
5								
6	**DATES:**		5/3-5/6/9-	**PURPOSE:**		Sales Meeting - Cincinnati		
7								
8								
9							Total	Total
10							Miles	Travel
11			May 3	May 4	May 5	May 6	@ $.29	Expenses
12	**TRANSPORTATION**							
13	Car (miles)		168	55	43	175		
14								
15	Car Rental							
16	Air Travel							
17	Train							
18								
19	**DAILY EXPENSES**							
20	Hotel		105.64	105.64	105.64	105.64		
21	Breakfast		0.00	5.59	15.95	7.55		
22	Lunch		15.60	12.95	45.95	43.55		
23	Dinner		39.35	95.86	135.85	0.00		
24	Tolls		0.00	1.50	2.00	0.00		
25	Parking		0.00	15.00	12.00	7.00		
26	Tips		6.00	18.00	22.00	11.00		
27	Phone		3.25	7.53	8.52	4.76		
28	Misc.		0.00	12.00	15.00	3.00		
29								
30	**TOTALS**							
31								
32								
33								
34			**PAPYRUS PAPER COMPANY**					
35			**TRAVEL EXPENSE REPORT**					
36								
37	**NAME:**		Alicia Marengo					
38								
39	**DATES:**		5/14-5/16/9-	**PURPOSE:**		Customer Visits - Chicago		
40								
41								
42							Total	Total
43							Miles	Travel
44			May 14	May 15	May 16		@ $.29	Expenses
45	**TRANSPORTATION**							
46	Car (miles)							
47								
48	Car Rental		40.00	40.00	40.00			
49	Air Travel		259.00					
50	Train							
51								
52	**DAILY EXPENSES**							
53	Hotel		155.50	155.50	155.50			
54	Breakfast		0.00	6.68	5.76			
55	Lunch		35.55	13.64	43.32			
56	Dinner		88.75	145.76	0.00			
57	Tolls		3.50	4.50	4.00			
58	Parking		18.50	22.15	16.75			
59	Tips		10.00	25.00	15.00			
60	Phone		8.95	9.95	6.25			
61	Misc.		0.00	16.50	0.00			
62								
63	**TOTALS**							

KEYSTROKES

INSERT MANUAL PAGE BREAKS

✓ *After you insert a manual page break, Excel adjusts the automatic page breaks that follow it. To display automatic page breaks see SHOW AUTOMATIC PAGE BREAKS, right.*

Insert a horizontal page break:

1. Select row where new page will start.
2. Click **Insert** menu .... `Alt`+`I`
3. Click **Page Break** .... `B`

Insert a Vertical Page Break:

1. Select column where new page will start.
2. Click **Insert** menu .... `Alt`+`I`
3. Click **Page Break** .... `B`

Insert a Horizontal and Vertical Page Break:

1. Click cell .... `↕↔`
   where new pages will start.
2. Click **Insert** menu .... `Alt`+`I`
3. Click **Page Break** .... `B`

REMOVE MANUAL PAGE BREAKS

✓ *After you remove a manual page break, Excel adjusts the automatic page breaks that follow it. To display automatic page breaks see SHOW AUTOMATIC PAGE BREAKS, right.*

Remove a horizontal page break:

1. Select a cell immediately below page break.
2. Click **Insert** menu .... `Alt`+`I`
3. Click **Remove Page Break** .... `B`

Remove a vertical page break:

1. Select a cell immediately to the right of page break.
2. Click **Insert** menu .... `Alt`+`I`
3. Click **Remove Page Break** .... `B`

Remove all manual page breaks:

1. Click blank button at top left corner of worksheet grid.
2. Click **Insert** menu .... `Alt`+`I`
3. Click **Remove Page Break** .... `B`

Show automatic page breaks

1. Click **Tools** menu .... `Alt`+`T`
2. Click **Options** .... `O`
3. Select **View** tab .... `Ctrl`+`Tab`
4. Click **Page breaks** .... `Alt`+`K`
5. Click **OK** .... `Enter`

BOLD TEXT

1. Select any cell.
2. Click **Bold** button .... **B**
   OR
   Press **Ctrl + B** .... `Ctrl`+`B`

BOLD TEXT USING THE MENU

1. Select any cell.
2. Click **Format** .... `Alt`+`O`
3. Click **Cells** .... `E`
4. Select **Font** tab. .... `Ctrl`+`Tab`
5. Select **Font style** .... `Alt`+`O`
6. Select **Bold** .... `↓`
7. Click **OK** .... `Enter`

SET HEADER AND FOOTER OPTIONS

Adds text or special codes to top or bottom of each page.

1. Click **File** menu .... `Alt`+`F`
2. Click **Page Setup** .... `U`
3. Select **Header/Footer** tab ...... `Ctrl`+`Tab`

To select a built-in header:

a. Click **Header** .... `Alt`+`A`
   drop-down list.
b. Select desired header type .... `↕↔`

To select a built-in footer

a. Click **Footer** .... `Alt`+`F`
   drop-down list.
b. Select desired footer type .... `↕↔`

To customize selected header or footer:

a. Click `Custom Header...` .... `Alt`+`C`
   OR
   Click `Custom Footer...` .... `Alt`+`U`

---

b. Click in section to change:

- **Left** .... `Alt`+`L`
- **Center** .... `Alt`+`C`
- **Right** .... `Alt`+`R`

c. Type or edit text to appear in header or footer section.

To change font of header or footer text:

a. Select text to format.
b. Click **Font** button **A** .... `Tab`+`Enter`
   ✓ *Press Tab until Font button is highlighted.*
c. Select desired font options.
d. Click **OK** .... `Enter`

To insert a header or footer code:

a. Place cursor where code will appear.
b. Click desired code button .... `Tab`+`Enter`

   Code buttons consist of the following:

    Page Number: Inserts page number code.

   Total Pages: Inserts total pages code.

   Date: Inserts current date code.

   Time: Inserts current time code.

   Filename: Inserts filename code.

   Sheet Name: Inserts active sheet name code.

c. Repeat steps a and b for each custom header or footer.
d. Click **OK** .... `Enter`
4. Click **OK** .... `Enter`

PAGE BREAK PREVIEW

1. Click **File** .... `Alt`+`F`
2. Click **Print Preview** .... `V`
3. Click **Page Break Preview** .... `V`

NEXT EXERCISE

NOTES

Print Titles

- As a print option, you may print **column and row titles** which are the column or row labels for data. Column and row titles are set on the Sheet tab of the Page Setup dialog box by selecting the columns or rows for titles using the collapse button. Note the illustration below with a setting for column titles.

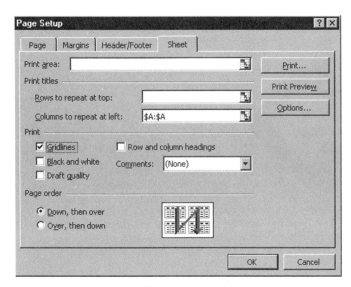

- Column and row titles are used in the following situations.

  - Titles may be useful when printing a range that is too wide or too long to fit on one page. Titles on the second page would clarify the data.

  - You can also print titles when printing a part of a columnar series of data that does not have column or row titles adjacent to the number values.

- The column or row titles you select will repeat at the beginning of the second page when an extra wide or extra long worksheet is set up as the print range.

- If you set column or row titles when printing part of a columnar series of data, you should not include the row or column titles in the print range.

- Note the illustration below. It shows the first and second pages of a worksheet that was too wide for one page, (using 100% sizing). Since column titles were set for column A, both pages show the labels contained in column A.

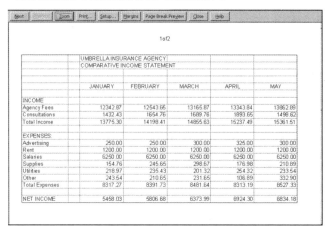

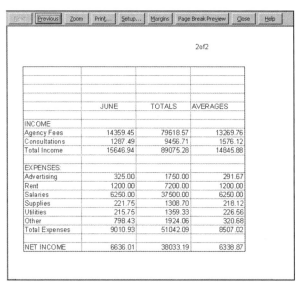

In this exercise, you will create a comparative income statement for the Umbrella Insurance Agency. You will use repeating column titles for labels in the first column to print the worksheet on two pages and to print a section.

EXERCISE DIRECTIONS

1. Create the worksheet as illustrated below, or open 💾 **25INS**.

2. Enter the months by dragging the fill handle to create the series.

3. Set column widths as follows:

   Column A: 15

   Column B: 3

   Column C-J: 12

4. Find for each month:
   - Total Income
   - Total Expenses
   - NET INCOME (Income-Expenses)

5. Find for each item in the worksheet:
   - TOTALS
   - AVERAGE

6. Format all money columns for commas.

7. Center all column titles.

8. Use the collapse button on the Sheet tab of the Page Setup dialog box to select column A as a repeating print title.

9. Create a header that includes the page number and total pages centered on the page.

10. Set the print range for the entire worksheet and be sure that scaling is set to 100% of normal size. Preview both pages of the worksheet.
    - ✓ Page one will show column A with JANUARY through MAY data. Page two will show column A with JUNE through AVERAGES data.

11. Print one copy of the two-page report.

12. Print one copy of the April-June data with column titles:
    a. Select the April-June columns.
    b. Enter commands to print the selection.
    c. Preview the print selection. (The column border was set previously.)
       - ✓ The April-June data will be shown with the column titles in column A.
    d. Print the selection.

13. Change columns C-J back to the standard width.

14. Save the workbook file; name it **INS**.

15. Close the workbook.

	A	B	C	D	E	F	G	H	I	J
1	◄—15—►	►3◄	UMBRELLA INSURANCE AGENCY							
2			COMPARATIVE INCOME STATEMENT							
3										
4										
5			JANUARY	FEBRUARY	MARCH	APRIL	MAY	JUNE	TOTALS	AVERAGES
6										
7	INCOME									
8	Agency Fees		12342.87	12543.65	13165.87	13343.84	13862.89	14359.45		
9	Consultations		1432.43	1654.76	1689.76	1893.65	1498.62	1287.49		
10	Total Income							→	▼	▼
11										
12	EXPENSES:									
13	Advertising		250.00	250.00	300.00	325.00	300.00	325.00		
14	Rent		1200.00	1200.00	1200.00	1200.00	1200.00	1200.00		
15	Salaries		6250.00	6250.00	6250.00	6250.00	6250.00	6250.00		
16	Supplies		154.76	245.65	298.67	176.98	210.89	221.75		
17	Utilities		218.97	235.43	201.32	254.32	233.54	215.75		
18	Other		243.54	210.65	231.65	106.89	332.90	798.43		
19	Total Expenses							→	▼	▼
20										
21	NET INCOME							→	▼	▼

KEYSTROKES

SET REPEATING PRINT TITLES FOR WORKSHEET

Sets titles to print on current and subsequent pages.

1. Click **File** menu...................... `Alt` + `F`

2. Click **Page Setup**... .... `U`

3. Select **Sheet** .... `Ctrl` + `Tab`

   To set columns as repeating print titles:

   a. Click **Columns**
      to Repeat at Left:............. `Alt` + `C`

   b. Select columns in worksheet.
      OR
      Type column reference

      EXAMPLE: The cell reference $A:$A indicates column A.

      ✓ *Columns must be adjacent. To remove print titles, delete the reference.*

   To set rows as repeating print titles:

   a. Click **Rows**
      to Repeat at Top:............. `Alt` + `R`

   b. Select rows in worksheet.
      OR
      Type row reference

      EXAMPLE: The cell reference $1:$4 indicates rows 1 through 4.

      ✓ *Rows must be adjacent. To remove print titles, delete the reference.*

4. Click **OK** .... `Enter`
   to return to the worksheet.
   OR
   Click **Print**............................ `Alt` + `P`
   to print worksheet using current settings.

NEXT EXERCISE

EXCEL Lesson 5: Functions, Formats, Features, and Print Options

Exercise 26

■ Summary

The Music Box store has developed a worksheet comparing the sales for the segments of its product line for the quarters of 1996. They would like to use this worksheet for 1997 data and create a two-page report with footers.

EXERCISE DIRECTIONS

1. Create a worksheet file as illustrated below using fill series to enter the quarter names, or open 🖫26MUSIC.

2. Adjust column width as necessary.

3. Find the TOTAL SALES for each quarter.

4. Using functions and ranges, find for each market segment and for the Total column:
   • TOTAL
   • AVERAGE
   • HIGHEST
   • LOWEST

5. Bold the worksheet titles and column headings.

6. Format all numeric columns for currency with no decimal places.

7. Copy the 1996 worksheet two rows below the existing data.

8. Edit the year and data to create a worksheet for 1997 using the data shown to the right:

1997	CLASSICAL	COUNTRY	JAZZ	ROCK
1st Quarter	5283	6234	5145	6038
2nd Quarter	5521	6843	5863	6254
3rd Quarter	5476	6793	5954	6321
4th Quarter	5843	6932	6043	6278

9. Insert a page break between the two worksheets.

10. Include a footer with the following left-aligned text:

    ANNUAL SALES BY DEPARTMENT

11. Right-align a page number in the footer.

12. Center all column headings.

13. Print Preview the page breaks.

14. Print one copy of the two-page report scaled to 95%.

15. Save the file; name it **MUSIC**.

	A	B	C	D	E	F
1			THE MUSIC BOX			
2			QUARTERLY SALES			
3						
4	1996	CLASSICAL	COUNTRY	JAZZ	ROCK	TOTAL
5	1st Quarter	5573	6934	5454	5978	
6	2nd Quarter	5643	7387	5975	6143	
7	3rd Quarter	5346	7154	5764	6098	
8	4th Quarter	5734	7043	5863	6143	
9						
10	TOTAL					
11	AVERAGE					
12	HIGHEST					
13	LOWEST					

Exercise 27

■ **Summary**

Your teacher, Mr. Victor Tribuzio, has asked you to help him set up a worksheet to organize his grades. He plans to administer three quizzes and three major examinations this term for his Accounting 101 class.

	A	B	C	D	E	F	G
1	ACCOUNTING 101				MR. VICTOR TRIBUZIO		
2	CLASS GRADES						
3							
4	ID#	STUDENT	QUIZ 1	QUIZ 2	QUIZ 3	QUIZ AVG.	
5							
6							

EXERCISE DIRECTIONS

1. Create a worksheet file that summarizes student exam grades. Use a format similar to the illustration above. Provide each student with a consecutive ID number. Begin with the number 1450 for Abbott.

   The students and their quiz grades for Quiz 1, 2, and 3 are:

Abbott, B.	78	96	80
Cruz, M.	71	89	80
Eugenio, M.	67	79	80
Greene, C.	88		80
Ishkowitz, B.	90	70	73
King, M.	76	90	90
Mohad, J.	84	91	75
Oscar, T.	87	68	80
Quercey, K.	98		70
Santos, C.		80	70
Thompson, S.	75	90	93
Wu, J.	75	87	89

A few of the students were absent for some of the quizzes. Leave the cell blank for absentees.

2. Find QUIZ AVERAGE.

3. Adjust column widths to fit the widest entries.

4. Enter these labels below the worksheet and find for each test:
   - No. of Papers
   - Class Average
   - Highest Grade
   - Lowest Grade

5. Format all averages to one decimal place.

6. Center and bold all column titles.

7. Bold the worksheet titles.

8. Print one copy that is 75% of the actual worksheet size. (Your teacher wants to insert the printout into a notebook.)

9. Save the file; name it **GRADES**.

NEXT LESSON

Excel

LESSON 6

WORK WITH WORKBOOKS, WORKSHEETS, AND TEMPLATES

Exercises 28-40

- Insert and Delete Columns and Rows
- Move (Cut/Paste)
- Drag and Drop
- Undo a Command
- Copy and Paste Special
- Transpose Data
- Scroll Tips
- AutoCorrect
- Freeze Titles
- Split Panes
- Copy and Paste Special (Extract Data)
- Create New Workbook
- Arrange Workbooks
- Save Workspace
- Workbook Sheets
- Group Sheets

- Print Workbook
- Named Ranges
- Data Validation
- Format Negative Numbers
- Copy and Paste Special (Add Option)
- Drag and Drop Between Workbooks
- Replace
- Use Templates (Spreadsheet Solutions)
- Original Templates
- Link Workbooks
- 3-D Formulas
- Workbook Sheets
- New (or Duplicate) Workbook Window

Exercise 28

■ **Insert and Delete Columns and Rows** ■ **Move (Cut/Paste)**
■ **Drag and Drop** ■ **Undo a Command**

NOTES

Insert and Delete Columns and Rows

■ It is recommended that you save a workbook before you insert, delete, move, or copy data so you can retrieve the original worksheet in the event of an error.

■ Columns and/or rows may be inserted or deleted to change the structure of a worksheet.

■ When a column or row is inserted, a blank area is created. Existing columns or rows shift to allow for the newly created space. Select the column to the right of the desired new column or the row below the desired new row and then select **Columns** or **Rows** from the **Insert** menu (depending on your selection). If you wish to insert more than one row or column, select that number of rows or columns.

■ When a column or row is **deleted**, all data in that column or row is eliminated. Existing columns or rows shift to fill in the space left by the deletion. Use **Edit, Delete** to delete selected columns or rows. The Delete dialog box, illustrated below, then provides you with delete options.

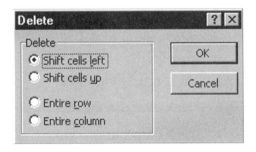

Move (Cut/Paste)

■ To **move** data you remove (cut) the data from one location and reinsert (paste) it into another location. You may choose to overwrite existing data or insert the data and shift existing data.

Drag and Drop

■ Moving data can be accomplished using a combination of cutting and pasting to the paste location or by selecting the range and dragging it to the paste location (known as **drag and drop**).

■ To drag and drop data, select the data to be moved and move the mouse pointer to the edge of the range until it becomes an arrow. Drag the outline of the range to the new location and release the mouse button. As the data is being dragged, the row and column locations display.

■ When data is dragged and dropped, it is cut from the previous location and pasted to the new. If data is dragged to a cell where data already exists, you will be warned that you will overwrite existing data.

■ If you want to insert dragged data between cells or rows without deleting the existing data, you can press Control + Shift and drag the insertion outline onto the row or column insertion point on the gridline. This is essentially a copy, paste procedure.

■ Inserting, deleting, moving, or copying data can affect formulas. Be sure formulas are correct after one of these operations. Data formats will be moved or copied along with the data.

Undo a Command

■ Most editing activity can be reversed by selecting **Undo** from the Edit menu. For example, if you drag and drop data and find it did not move correctly, you could easily undo the activity by using this feature. As shown in the illustration below, the Undo feature specifically names the last edit to be undone.

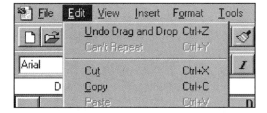

■ The **Undo** and **Redo** buttons on the Standard toolbar serve the same functions and both methods may be used to undo or redo a series of edits.

■ If you wish to undo a series of edits, called a multiple undo, click the down arrow next to the Undo button to display a list of the edits performed. If you select one of the edits, Excel will undo that edit and all edits above the selected edit.

■ Edit activity can also be repeated by selecting Repeat from the Edit menu. As with the Undo feature, the Repeat feature specifically names the last edit to be repeated.

In this exercise, you will insert, delete, and move columns and rows to include additional information in the First State Bank payroll worksheet. In addition, a new payroll worksheet will be created below the existing one for the new pay period.

EXERCISE DIRECTIONS

1. Open 📖 **PAYROLL** or 💾 **28PAYROLL**.

2. Make the following changes on the top payroll as shown in the illustration on the following page:

   a. Insert a new column A.

   b. Move the data in the Employee Name column to column A. (Using drag and drop. Drag the column to its new location after the mouse pointer changes to an arrow.) Use Edit Undo if the move is not correct.) Adjust column width.

   c. Set column width for column C, which is now empty, to 11 and enter the label Social Security No. as the column title.

   d. Enter social security numbers as follows:

Diaz	069-65-4532
Jaffe	123-75-7623
Latov	107-53-6754
Nestor	103-87-5698
Pringle	127-78-0045
Wong	043-67-7600

   e. Copy the social security number column title and data from the September 7 to the September 14 payroll.

   f. Copy the entire September 14 payroll, including the title, to a new location below the existing worksheet.

3. Make the following changes on the bottom payroll:

   a. Edit the title to read:

   FOR THE WEEK ENDING SEPTEMBER 21, 199-

   b. Delete the row containing data for Nestor.

   c. Insert a row where necessary to maintain alphabetical order for a new employee named Franz.

   d. Enter the following information for Franz:

Card Number:	14865
S.S. No.:	146-93-0069
Hourly Rate:	6.25

   e. Edit the HOURS WORKED as follows:

Diaz	22
Franz	33
Jaffe	21
Latov	16
Pringle	18
Wong	28

   f. Copy payroll formulas to complete Franz's data.

4. Format where necessary.

5. Print one copy of all three payrolls to fit on a page.

6. Close and save the workbook file, or save as **PAYROLL.**

	A	B	C	D	E	F	G	H	I
1	FIRST STATE BANK PAYROLL					Insert new column A			
2	FOR THE WEEK ENDING SEPTEMBER 7, 199-								
3									
4	Card	Employee	Hourly	Hours	Gross	Social	Medicare		
5	Number	Move	Rate	Worked	Pay	Sec. Tax	Tax	F.W.T.	Net Pay
6									
7	13567	Diaz	5.55	15	83.25	5.16	1.21	16.65	60.23
8	13750	Jaffe	7.23	32	231.36	14.34	3.35	46.27	167.39
9	13816	Latov	6.18	16	98.88	6.13	1.43	19.78	71.54
10	13925	Nestor	4.66	28	130.48	8.09	1.89	26.10	94.40
11	14345	Pringle	6.57	12	78.84	4.89	1.14	15.77	57.04
12	14715	Wong	8.65	21	181.65	11.26	2.63	36.33	131.42
13									
14	TOTALS				804.46	49.88	11.66	160.89	582.03
15	AVERAGES				134.08	8.31	1.94	26.82	97.00
16									
17	FOR THE WEEK ENDING SEPTEMBER 14, 199-								
18									
19	Card	Employee	Hourly	Hours	Gross	Social	Medicare		
20	Number	Name	Rate	Worked	Pay	Sec. Tax	Tax	F.W.T.	Net Pay
21									
22	13567	Diaz	5.55	20	111.00	6.88	1.61	22.20	80.31
23	13750	Jaffe	7.23	31	224.13	13.90	3.25	44.83	162.16
24	13816	Latov	6.18	23	142.14	8.81	2.06	28.43	102.84
25	13925	Nestor	4.66	22	102.52	6.36	1.49	20.50	74.17
26	14345	Pringle	6.57	15	98.55	6.11	1.43	19.71	71.30
27	14715	Wong	8.65	25	216.25	13.41	3.14	43.25	156.46
28									
29	TOTALS				894.59	55.46	12.97	178.92	647.24
30	AVERAGES				149.10	9.24	2.16	29.82	107.87
31		Copy							
32									

KEYSTROKES

INSERT COLUMNS/ROWS

Inserts blank columns or rows and shifts existing columns or rows to make room for the insertion.

1. Select as many adjacent columns or rows as you want to add to worksheet.
   - ✓ *Click anywhere within column(s) or row(s). New column(s) will be placed to the left of the highlighted column(s). New row(s) will be placed above the highlighted row(s).*
2. Click **I**nsert menu .... `Alt`+`I`
3. Click **C**olumns .... `C`
   OR
   Click **R**ows .... `R`

INSERT COLUMNS/ROWS USING THE MOUSE

Inserts blank columns or rows and shifts existing columns or rows to make room for the insertion.

1. Select as many columns/rows as you want inserted.
2. Right-click any part of selection. (A quick menu appears.)
3. Click **I**nsert .... `I`

DELETE COLUMNS/ROWS

Deletes columns or rows and the data they contain. Existing columns or rows shift to fill in the space left by the deletion.

1. Select column(s) or row(s) to delete.
   - ✓ *Click anywhere within column(s) or row(s). When deleting more than one row or column, select adjacent columns or rows.*
2. Click **E**dit menu .... `Alt`+`E`
3. Click **D**elete .... `D`

MOVE (CUT/PASTE) USING THE MENU

Moves data in a cell or a range of cells to another area.

1. Select cell or range to move.
2. Click **E**dit menu .... `Alt`+`E`
3. Click **C**ut .... `T`
4. Select cell or range to receive data.

- ✓ *You only have to specify the top left cell. The destination range can be in another workbook or worksheet.*

5. a. Click **E**dit menu .... `E`
   b. Click **P**aste .... `P`
   OR
   To move and <u>overwrite</u> existing data in destination cells:
   Press **Enter** .... `Enter`
   OR
   To move and insert between existing cells:
   a. Click **I**nsert menu .... `Alt`+`I`
   b. Click **Cut Ce**lls .... `E`
   c. Select one of the following:
      Shift cells right .... `G`
      Shift cells down .... `D`
      Entire row .... `R`
      Entire column .... `C`
6. Click **OK** .... `Enter`

MOVE (DRAG AND DROP)

Moves data in a cell or range of cells to another area.

1. Select cell or range to cut.
2. Move mouse pointer to edge of range. Pointer becomes a ⬉.
3. To move and overwrite existing data in destination cells:
   a. Drag border outline to new location.
   b. Release mouse button .... `Enter`
   OR
   To move and insert between existing cells:
   a. Press **Shift** and drag .... `Shift`+*drag* insertion outline onto row or column gridline.
      - ✓ *If you drag the insertion outline onto a column gridline, cells are shifted right; if dragged onto a row gridline, cells are shifted down.*
   b. Release the mouse button, then the **Shift** key.

COPY (DRAG AND DROP)

Copies data in a cell or range of cells to another area.

1. Select cell or range to copy.
2. Move mouse pointer to edge of range. Pointer becomes a ⬉.
   To copy and overwrite existing data in destination cells:
   a. Press **Ctrl** and drag .... `Ctrl`+*drag* border outline to new location.
   b. Release the key, then mouse button.
   c. Click **OK** when prompted .... `Enter` to replace contents of destination cells.
   OR
   To copy and insert between existing cells:
   a. Press **Ctrl** + **Shift** and drag insertion outline .... `Ctrl`+`Shift`+*drag* onto row or column gridline.
      - ✓ *If you drag the insertion outline onto a column gridline, cells are shifted right; if dragged onto a row gridline, cells are shifted down.*
   b. Release mouse button, then the key.

UNDO A COMMAND

- ✓ *To successfully undo a command, undo before another command is selected. Not all commands can be undone.*

Click **Undo** button .... ⟲ on Standard toolbar.
OR
Press **Ctrl+Z** .... `Ctrl`+`Z`
OR
1. Click **E**dit menu .... `Alt`+`E`
2. Click **U**ndo .... `U`

To undo multiple edits:

a. Click down arrow to the right of the Undo button.
b. Select edit selection to undo.
   All edits above the selected edit will be undone as well.

Exercise 29

- **Copy and Paste Special** ■ **Transpose Data** ■ **Scroll Tips**
- **AutoCorrect**

NOTES

Copy and Paste Special

- When you use the Copy and Paste features to copy a cell, you are copying the entire contents of that cell. If you wish to copy only specific contents, use the **Paste Special** feature. As shown in the Paste Special dialog box below, the Paste Special command allows you to:

  - Specify which characteristics of the selection should be copied (**Paste** options).

  - Specify how data should be combined when the paste area contains data (**Operation** options).

  - Skip blanks

  - Transpose data

  - Create a Paste Link

Paste Special Dialog Box

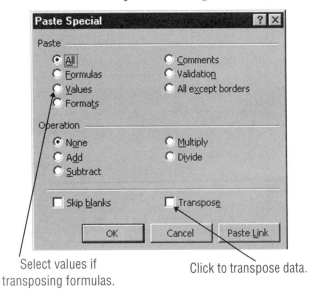

Select values if transposing formulas.

Click to transpose data.

Transpose Data

- You can **transpose data** to copy and rearrange data so data in rows can be copied to columns and vice versa. Note the example below. The labels in column B, when transposed, are copied to row 5.

	A	B	C	D	E	F	G
1							
2							
3		JAN					
4		FEB					
5		MAR		JAN	FEB	MAR	
6							

- When transposing data that includes formulas, select the **Paste Values** option in the Paste Special dialog box. This selection ensures that only the values are copied to the new location, not the formulas. If you do not select the Paste Values option, the formulas will produce unwanted results.

Scroll Tips

- You may move through a large worksheet by moving the scroll box on the horizontal or vertical scroll bars. When you move the scroll box, Excel displays the row or column numbers near the scroll box as you move through the worksheet. Note the illustration below:

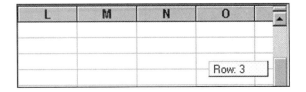

AutoCorrect

- The **AutoCorrect** feature automatically changes text as you type if the word is in the list of commonly misspelled words, or if you, *in advance*, specify the word that you often type incorrectly. This feature also automatically corrects capitalization at the beginning of days of the week and changes the case of incorrectly capitalized letters in the first two positions in a word. Note the illustration of the AutoCorrect dialog box with a new entry being placed into the AutoCorrect replace list.

- The AutoCorrect feature can also be used to speed data entry of a company name or frequently used label by replacing an abbreviation with longer text labels.

AutoCorrect Dialog Box

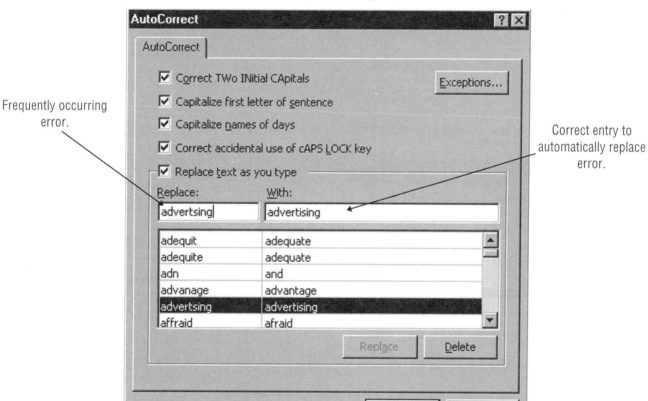

Frequently occurring error.

Correct entry to automatically replace error.

In this exercise, you will insert a new expense item in the worksheet for the Umbrella Insurance Agency Service and practice using the AutoCorrect feature. In addition, you will use transposed data from the income statement to prepare an income statement analysis.

EXERCISE DIRECTIONS

1. Open ⌨ **INS** or 💾 **29INS**.

2. Delete column B.

3. Set column widths for columns B through H to 10.

4. To include a monthly interest expense of $25:
   a. Insert a row between Utilities and Other.
   b. Enter the label: Interest.
   c. Enter $25 for each month.
   d. Copy the TOTALS and AVERAGES formulas to the interest line.
   e. Format the interest line for two decimal places.

5. Practice using the AutoCorrect feature by doing the following:
   a. In cell A24 type saturday. Note the correction to Saturday.
   b. In cell A25 type FRiday. Note the correction to Friday.
   c. In cell A26 type INcome. Note the correction to Income.
   d. Delete data in A24, A25, and A26.

6. Practice entering a word into the AutoCorrect replace list as follows:
   ✓ *If you always type advertising as advertsing, you could place that correction in the automatic replace box.*
   a. Select the AutoCorrect feature from the Tools menu.
   b. In the Replace box enter the misspelled version of the word (advertsing).
   c. In the With box enter the correct version of the word (advertising).
   d. In A13 type Advertising using the incorrect version.
   e. Note the correction to Advertising.

7. Enter T as an abbreviation for TOTAL in the AutoCorrect List.

8. Enter new title and column labels below the existing worksheet, as illustrated. Use T when the word TOTAL should be entered.

9. Center column labels.

10. Transpose the column titles JANUARY through JUNE, including TOTALS, and excluding AVERAGES, to become row titles in column A in the range A31:A37.

11. Transpose Total Income data for JANUARY through JUNE, including TOTALS and excluding AVERAGES, to become row data for column B in the range B31:B37.
    ✓ *Be sure to select the Paste Values option when transposing.*

12. Transpose Total Expenses data for JANUARY through JUNE, including TOTALS, and excluding AVERAGES, to become row data for column D in the range D31:D37.
    ✓ *Be sure to select the Paste Values option when transposing.*

12. Transpose NET INCOME data for JANUARY through JUNE, including TOTALS, and excluding AVERAGES, to become row data for column F in the range F31:F37.
    ✓ *Be sure to select the Paste Values option when transposing.*

13. Enter formulas in the % OF TOTAL columns to find what percent each item is of the six month total.
    Hint: Use absolute reference in the formula.

14. Format % OF TOTAL columns for percentage with one decimal place.

15. Print one copy of the entire worksheet to fit on a page.

16. Close and save the workbook file, or *save as* **INS**.

	A	B	C	D	E	F	G	H	I	J	K	L
1			UMBRELLA INSURANCE AGENCY									
2			COMPARATIVE INCOME STATEMENT									
3	Delete											
4	column B.											
5			JANUARY	FEBRUARY	MARCH	APRIL	MAY	JUNE	TOTALS	AVERAGES		
6												
7	INCOME											
8	Agency Fees		12342.87	12543.65	13165.87	13343.84	13862.89	14359.45	79618.57	13269.76		
9	Consultations		1432.43	1654.76	1689.76	1893.65	1498.62	1287.49	9456.71	1576.12		
10	Total Income		13775.30	14198.41	14855.63	15237.49	15361.51	15646.94	89075.28	14845.88		
11												
12	EXPENSES:											
13	Advertising		250.00	250.00	300.00	325.00	300.00	325.00	1750.00	291.67		
14	Rent		1200.00	1200.00	1200.00	1200.00	1200.00	1200.00	7200.00	1200.00		
15	Salaries		6250.00	6250.00	6250.00	6250.00	6250.00	6250.00	37500.00	6250.00		
16	Supplies		154.76	245.65	298.67	176.98	210.89	221.75	1308.70	218.12		
17	Utilities		218.97	235.43	201.32	254.32	233.54	215.75	1359.33	226.56		
18	Interest		25.00	25.00	25.00	25.00	25.00	25.00	150.00	25.00		
19	Other		243.54	210.65	231.65	106.89	332.90	798.43	1924.06	320.68	Insert row	
20	Total Expenses		8342.27	8416.73	8506.64	8338.19	8552.33	9035.93	51192.09	8532.02	as shown.	
21												
22	NET INCOME		5433.03	5781.68	6348.99	6899.30	6809.18	6611.01	37883.19	6313.87		
23	Transpose											
24												
25			UMBRELLA INSURANCE AGENCY									
26			INCOME STATEMENT ANALYSIS									
27												
28	MONTH		TOTAL	% OF	TOTAL	% OF	NET	% OF				
29			INCOME	TOTAL	EXPENSES	TOTAL	INCOME	TOTAL				
30												
31												
32												
33												
34												
35												
36												
37												

KEYSTROKES

SET AN AUTOCORRECT REPLACEMENT

1. Click **Tools** menu .... Alt + T

2. Click **AutoCorrect** .... A

3. Click **Replace** text box .... R

4. Type abbreviation or commonly misspelled word.

5. Click **With** text box .... W

6. Type replacement text.

7. Click **Add** .... A

8. Click **OK** .... Enter

TRANSPOSE DATA

Copies and transposes data from horizontal to vertical arrangement and vice versa.

1. Select range to transpose.

2. a. Click **Edit** menu .... Alt + E

   b. Click **Copy** C

   OR

   a. Right-click a cell in selection to open shortcut menu.

   b. Click **Copy** C

3. Click upper-left cell .... ↔↕ to receive transposed data.

4. a. Click **Edit** .... Alt + E

   b. Click **Paste Special** .... S

   OR

   a. Right-click destination cell to open shortcut menu.

   b. Click **Paste Special** .... S

5. Click **Transpose** .... E check box.

   To paste transposed data as values, not formulas:

   Click **Values** V

6. Click **OK** .... Enter

7. Press **Escape** .... Esc to end copying mode.

Exercise 30

- Freeze Titles ■ Split Panes
- Copy and Paste Special (Extract Data) ■ Create New Workbook
- Arrange Workbooks Window ■ Save Workspace

NOTES

- Excel provides two methods for working with large worksheets: freezing titles to keep titles in view and splitting the window into two or four panes.

Freeze Titles

- To keep headings or titles in view at the left or top edge of the worksheet when scrolling, it is necessary to hold, or **freeze**, them in place. This is accomplished by selecting the row below or the column to the right of the data to be frozen and then selecting <u>W</u>indow, **Freeze Panes**. To remove the freeze select <u>W</u>indow, **Un<u>f</u>reeze Panes**.

Split Panes

- To view different parts of a large worksheet at one time, the worksheet may be **split** horizontally or vertically so data may be viewed through each of the windows at the same time. To split the worksheet into panes, select <u>W</u>indow, **Split**. To remove the split, select <u>W</u>indow, **Remove <u>S</u>plit**.

- When you split a window *vertically* (by placing the cursor at a location in Row 1) the panes scroll together when you scroll up or down. However, they scroll independently when you scroll left and right.

- When you split a window *horizontally* (by placing the cursor at the split location in column A) the panes scroll together when you scroll left or right. However, they scroll independently when you scroll up and down.

- If you place the cursor in the middle of the worksheet, the worksheet will split into four panes that will scroll like a horizontal split.

- When you freeze a split worksheet, the top and/or left pane locks when you scroll through the worksheet.

Copy and Paste Special (Extract Data)

- You can use the <u>C</u>opy and Paste <u>S</u>pecial commands to copy part of a worksheet into another workbook. Paste Special options allow you to specify the part of the cells you wish to copy.

- Paste options, as shown in the Paste Special dialog box below, include:

<u>A</u>ll	Replaces paste area cells with all formulas, formats, and comments contained in copied cells.
Formulas	Pastes data that exists in formula bar of copied cells (the formulas).
	✓ NOTE: *Relative cell references in formulas will adjust.*
<u>V</u>alues	Pastes data as it appears in copied cells (results of formulas).
Forma<u>t</u>s	Pastes only the formats of cells.
<u>C</u>omments	Pastes only cell comments.
Validatio<u>n</u>	Pastes the validation rules from the copied cells.
All e<u>x</u>cept borders	Pastes cell contents and formats except for borders.

112

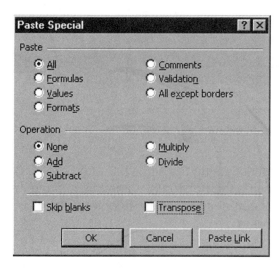

Arrange Workbooks Window

- When working with more than one workbook at a time, you can use the <u>W</u>indow menu to select the desired file from the list of open files or you can arrange them all on the screen at once by using the <u>W</u>indow, **Arrange** command. The Arrange Windows dialog box provides options for the file arrangement.

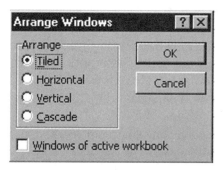

- In the Paste Special dialog box, the **<u>F</u>ormulas** and **<u>V</u>alues** paste options affect the paste result. Select **<u>F</u>ormulas** to extract values, labels, and formulas *exactly as they exist*. Select **<u>V</u>alues** to extract labels, values, *and the results of the formulas*.

  You should select <u>V</u>alues if the range to be extracted contains formulas with references to cells outside that range.

Create New Workbook

- New workbooks can be created to store new or extracted data. You can access a new workbook by selecting the **New Workbook** button ▯ on the Standard toolbar or by selecting **<u>F</u>ile, <u>N</u>ew**.

Save Workspace

- You can save and open a group of arranged workbooks by creating a **workspace** file. The workspace file saves information about the open workbooks, including their locations, window sizes, and screen positions. After you have arranged the workbooks on the screen the way you want them to appear, save the workspace by selecting <u>F</u>ile, **Save <u>W</u>orkspace**. Individual workbooks are saved as usual. When you open the workspace file, your workbooks will open with the saved arrangement of files. The workspace file is saved with .xlw extension.

In this exercise, you will divide the data into quarterly information. To do this, you must insert and delete columns. However, because inserting or deleting columns from the top portion of the worksheet will affect the bottom portion, you will extract the bottom portion of the worksheet, save it to another file, and delete it from the original. The top portion of the worksheet will then be expanded and edited. The workbooks will be arranged and saved as a workspace.

EXERCISE DIRECTIONS

1. Open ⌨ **INS** or 💾 **30INS**.

2. Use the <u>C</u>opy and Paste <u>S</u>pecial commands to extract the Income Statement Analysis portion of the worksheet to a new workbook as indicated in Illustration A; name the new workbook file **ISANA**.

    a. Select and copy the Income Statement Analysis at the bottom of the worksheet.

    b. Open a new workbook.

    c. In A1, select Paste Special, Values option. (The results of the formulas are copied, and not the formulas themselves.)

3. Use the Window menu to switch to the INS workbook. Delete the Income Statement Analysis portion from the **INS** worksheet.

4. Insert a column between MARCH and APRIL and enter the column titles:

    1ST QTR. TOTALS

5. Format the new column for two decimal places.

6. Insert a column between JUNE and TOTALS and enter the column titles:

    2ND QTR. TOTALS

7. Format the new column for two decimal places.

8. Delete the TOTALS and AVERAGES columns.

9. Find 1ST QTR. TOTALS.
    HINT: =January+February+March

10. Copy the formula to the remaining items.

11. Copy the formulas for 1ST QTR. TOTALS to the column for 2ND QTR. TOTALS.

12. Freeze titles in column A.

13. Practice using the scroll bar and ScrollTips by moving the horizontal scroll box to bring the worksheet into position to enter data in column J.

14. Enter the third quarter data, indicated in Illustration B, in the next available column of your worksheet.

15. Copy and edit formulas, where necessary, to complete the worksheet.

16. Find 3RD QTR. TOTALS.

17. Copy the formula to the remaining items.

18. Unfreeze column titles.

19. Test the split panes feature by placing the cursor in F1 and select Window, Split. Use F6 to move between panes. Drag the split bar to the right to adjust the panes. Remove Split.

20. Center column title labels.

21. Format numeric data for two decimal places.

22. Save the file, or *save as* INS.

23. Print one copy of INS to fit on a page.

24. Switch to ISANA workbook.

25. Format and align data as needed.

26. Resave ISANA, then print one copy.

27. Arrange both worksheets on the screen in a tiled arrangement. Adjust the screen so that the INS workbook has more screen space.

28. Save the workspace as **INSANAL**.

29. Close all files.

Illustration A

	A	B	C	D		F	G		J
1		UMBRELLA INSURANCE AGENCY			Insert column 1st Qtr. Totals			Insert column 2ND QTR. Totals	
2		COMPARATIVE INCOME STATEMENT							
3									
4									
5		JANUARY	FEBRUARY	MARCH	APRIL	MAY	JUNE	TOTALS	AVERAGES
6									
7	INCOME								
8	Agency Fees	12342.87	12543.65	13165.87	13343.84	13862.89	14359.45	79618.57	13269.76
9	Consultations	1432.43	1654.76	1689.76	1893.65	1498.62	1287.49	9456.71	1576.12
10	Total Income	13775.30	14198.41	14855.63	15237.49	15361.51	15646.94	89075.28	14845.88
11									
12	EXPENSES:								
13	Advertising	250.00	250.00	300.00	325.00	300.00	325.00	1750.00	291.67
14	Rent	1200.00	1200.00	1200.00	1200.00	1200.00	1200.00	7200.00	1200.00
15	Salaries	6250.00	6250.00	6250.00	6250.00	6250.00	6250.00	37500.00	6250.00
16	Supplies	154.76	245.65	298.67	176.98	210.89	221.75	1308.70	218.12
17	Utilities	218.97	235.43	201.32	254.32	233.54	215.75	1359.33	226.56
18	Interest	25.00	25.00	25.00	25.00	25.00	25.00	150.00	25.00
19	Other	243.54	210.65	231.65	106.89	332.90	798.43	1924.06	320.68
20	Total Expenses	8342.27	8416.73	8506.64	8338.19	8552.33	9035.93	51192.09	8532.02
21									
22	NET INCOME	5433.03	5781.68	6348.99	6899.30	6809.18	6611.01	37883.19	6313.87
23									
24									
25									
26		UMBRELLA INSURANCE AGENCY						Extract to a new workbook and save new workbook as ISANA.	
27		INCOME STATEMENT ANALYSIS							
28									
29	MONTH	TOTAL	% OF	TOTAL	% OF	NET	% OF		
30		INCOME	TOTAL	EXPENSES	TOTAL	INCOME	TOTAL		
31									
32	JANUARY	13775.30	15.5%	8317.27	16.3%	5458.03	14.4%		
33	FEBRUARY	14198.41	15.9%	8391.73	16.4%	5806.68	15.3%		
34	MARCH	14855.63	16.7%	8481.64	16.6%	6373.99	16.8%		
35	APRIL	15237.49	17.1%	8313.19	16.3%	6924.30	18.2%		
36	MAY	15361.51	17.2%	8527.33	16.7%	6834.18	18.0%		
37	JUNE	15646.94	17.6%	9010.93	17.7%	6636.01	17.4%		
38	TOTALS	89075.28	100.0%	51042.09	100.0%	38033.19	100.0%		

Illustration B

	A	J	K	L
1				
2				
3				
4				
5		JULY	AUGUST	SEPT.
6				
7	INCOME			
8	Agency Fees	13976.87	14102.32	14323.32
9	Consultations	1324.54	1243.76	1432.43
10	Total Income			
11				
12	EXPENSES:			
13	Advertising	300.00	275.00	325.00
14	Rent	1200.00	1200.00	1200.00
15	Salaries	6250.00	6250.00	6250.00
16	Supplies	185.43	255.67	231.32
17	Utilities	265.43	275.43	249.76
18	Interest	25.00	25.00	25.00
19	Other	310.32	297.65	542.98
20	Total Expenses			
21				
22	NET INCOME			

KEYSTROKES

COPY AND PASTE SPECIAL (EXTRACT DATA)

Copies a portion of the current worksheet to a new workbook.

1. Copy range to extract to the clipboard:

   a. Select range of worksheet to extract.

   b. Click **Edit** menu .... `Alt`+`E`

   c. Click **Copy** .... `C`

2. Open a new workbook:

   a. Click **File** menu .... `Alt`+`F`

   b. Click **New** .... `N`

   – FROM NEW WORKBOOK –

3. Use Paste Special command:

   a. Click **Edit** menu .... `Alt`+`E`

   b. Click **Paste Special** .... `S`

   c. Click **Values** .... `V`
      to copy data as it appears in cells (results of formulas).
      OR
      Click **Formulas** .... `F`
      to copy data as it exists in formula bar (formulas).
      ✓ *Only relative cell references in formulas will adjust.*

   d. Click **OK** .... `Enter`

4. Save and name the new workbook.

   a. Click **File** menu .... `Alt`+`F`

   b. Click **Save As** .... `A`

   c. Type **File name**
      ✓ *The filename you type replaces default name of the workbook.*

   d. Click **Save** .... `Alt`+`S`

5. Click **OK** .... `Enter`

ARRANGE WORKBOOKS

1. Open the workbooks to be arranged.

2. Click **Window** .... `Alt`+`W`

3. Click **Arrange** .... `A`

---

4. Select arrangement:

   • **Tiled** .... `Alt`+`T`

   • **Horizontal** .... `Alt`+`O`

   • **Vertical** .... `Alt`+`V`

   • **Cascade** .... `Alt`+`C`

5. Click **OK** .... `Enter`

SAVE WORKSPACE

1. Open the workbooks to be opened as a group.

2. Size and position the workbook windows. (see Arrange Workbooks).

3. Click **File** .... `Alt`+`F`

4. Click **Save Workspace** .... `W`

5. Type **File name**

6. Click **Save** .... `Alt`+`S`

CREATE NEW WORKBOOK

Opens a new workbook based on the default template.

Click **New Workbook** button .... `☐`
on Standard toolbar.
OR

1. Click **File** menu .... `Alt`+`F`

2. Click **New** .... `N`

SELECT WORKBOOK

✓ *When more than one workbook is open, the workbook you want may be hidden or reduced to an icon. In order to use the workbook, you need to select the workbook window or open the workbook icon.*

To select a workbook window:

Click anywhere on workbook window.
OR

1. Click **Window** menu .... `Alt`+`W`

2. Select name of workbook.. `↓`, `Enter`
   near the bottom of the menu.

To open a workbook icon:

Double-click workbook icon.
OR

1. Click **Window** menu .... `Alt`+`W`

2. Select name of workbook.. `↓`, `Enter`
   near the bottom of the menu.

SPLIT WORKSHEET INTO PANES USING SPLIT BOXES

Provides simultaneous scrolling of up to four panes. You can freeze panes (see right) to prevent top, left, or both panes from scrolling.

   ✓ *If the scroll bars are not displayed in panes, see **SET VIEW PREFERENCES**, page 194 on scroll bar.*

1. Point to horizontal split box ☐ or vertical split box ☐ on scroll bar

   ✓ *Pointer becomes a ↕ or ↔.*

2. Drag along scroll bar until split bar is in desired position.

SPLIT WORKSHEET INTO PANES USING THE MENU

Provides simultaneous scrolling of up to four panes. You can freeze panes (see right) to prevent top, left, or both panes from scrolling.

1. Select row below where horizontal split will occur.
   OR
   Select column to the right of where vertical split will occur.
   OR
   Select cell below and to the right of where horizontal and vertical splits will occur.

2. Click **Window** menu .... `Alt`+`W`

3. Click **Split** .... `S`

REMOVE SPLIT BARS

Double-click any part of split bar.
OR

1. Click **Window** menu .... `Alt`+`W`

2. Click **Remove Split** .... `S`

ADJUST WORKSHEET PANES

1. Point to horizontal split box ☐ or vertical split box ☐ on scroll bar.

   ✓ *Pointer becomes a ↕ or ↔.*

2. Drag along scroll bar until split bar is in desired position.

MOVE BETWEEN WORKSHEET PANES

Click desired pane.

OR

Press **F6**..[F6]

until active cell is in desired pane.

FREEZE PANES ON A SPLIT WORKSHEET

Locks top and/or left pane when scrolling.

1. Click **Window** menu .... [Alt]+[W]
2. Click **Freeze Panes** .... [F]

UNFREEZE PANES

1. Click **Window** menu .... [Alt]+[W]
2. Click **Unfreeze Panes** .... [F]

FREEZE TITLES

Locks display of title row and/or title column on the screen. This procedure is for a worksheet that has not been split into panes.

1. Select row below horizontal titles to freeze.

   OR

   Select column to right of vertical titles to freeze.

   OR

   Select cell below and to the right of horizontal and vertical titles to freeze.

2. Click **Window** menu............... [Alt]+[W]
3. Click **Freeze Panes** .... [F]

UNFREEZE TITLES

1. Click **Window** menu............... [Alt]+[W]
2. Click **Unfreeze Panes** .... [F]

SCROLL TIPS

1. Click on horizontal or vertical scroll bar.
2. Move bar as desired.
3. Note row or column Scroll Tip.

SET WINDOW OPTIONS

1. Click **Tools** menu .... [Alt]+[T]
2. Click **Options** .... [O]
3. From the **View** tab, select desired option.
4. Click **OK** .... [Enter]

<table>
<tr><td>Exercise
31</td><td>■ **Workbook Sheets** ■ **Group Sheets** ■ **Print Workbook**</td></tr>
</table>

Workbook Sheets

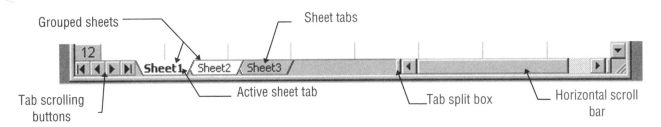

NOTES

Workbook Sheets

- By default, each new workbook contains three worksheets labeled Sheet1 through Sheet3. **Sheet tabs** show the names of each sheet *(see illustration above)*.

- Excel lets you work with sheets in many ways. For example, you can delete, insert, rename, move, copy, and hide sheets. These features let you arrange your workbook to fit your work objectives. You can move sheets by using the drag and drop method and insert sheets by selecting Insert, **Worksheet**. You can also work with sheets by using the menu that appears when a sheet tab is right-clicked, as shown below.

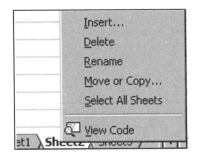

- You can use the **tab scrolling buttons** to scroll a hidden sheet tab into view. If no sheet tabs are visible, you can tell Excel to show them by selecting Tools, Options and selecting the **Show all** and **Sheet tabs** options on the View tab.

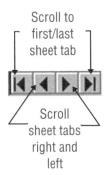

- Excel provides a **tab split box** between the sheet tabs and the horizontal scroll bar. You can drag this split box left or right to show more or fewer sheet tabs.

Group Sheets

- You can select multiple sheets (group sheets) to work on several sheets simultaneously. To group consecutive sheets, select the first and last sheet in the group, pressing Shift between selections. Press Ctrl between sheet selections when selecting non-consecutive sheets for grouping.

- When sheets are grouped, any entries and formats made in the top sheet are simultaneously made in all grouped sheets. In a group selection, selected sheet tabs are white, the active sheet tab is white, and the text is in bold.

Print Workbook

- You can tell Excel onto how many pages you want a worksheet to print. Excel will then automatically scale the worksheet to fit within the specified number of pages.

In this exercise, you will create a payroll template for future use. To do this you will insert and rename sheet tabs and work with grouped sheets to quickly edit data on more than one worksheet at a time.

EXERCISE DIRECTIONS

1. Open ⌨ **PAYROLL** or 💾 **31PAYROLL**.

2. Resave the workbook file as **PAYFORM**.

3. Click sheet tab named Sheet2 to select it.
   - ✓ *Note that Sheet2 is empty.*

4. Select Sheet1.

5. Use tab split box to increase, then decrease, the number of visible sheet tabs.

6. Select Sheet2 through Sheet3. (Sheet1 should not be selected.)
   - ✓ *Note selected sheet tabs are white and [Group] appears on the title bar.*

7. Right-click the grouped sheet tabs and delete the grouped worksheets.
   - ✓ *Note only Sheet1 remains.*

8. Rename Sheet1 to September.

9. Insert a new worksheet; name it October.

10. Insert a new worksheet; name it November.

11. Move the sheets so that they are in chronological order.

12. Select the September sheet and edit the titles in each week's payroll to read:
    FOR THE WEEK ENDING

   - ✓ *Delete the dates.*

13. To make payrolls uniform on the September sheet:
    a. Nestor has left our employment; delete the Nestor rows in the top two payrolls.
    b. Copy the Franz information from the last payroll to the first two payrolls in the correct order.
    c. Copy the third payroll to create a fourth payroll for the month.

14. Select all the data in the September sheet and copy it to the clipboard.
    - ✓ *You can click the Select All button to select the entire worksheet.*

15. Group the October and November sheets.

16. Select the October sheet and select cell A1.

17. Use the Paste command to copy the September worksheet data to the active cell in the grouped sheets (October and November).

18. Click cell A1 to deselect the range.

19. Select the September sheet.

20. Click cell A1 to deselect the range.

21. Select all the sheets in the workbook (September through November)

22. WHILE ALL SHEETS ARE GROUPED:

a. Clear the data in the cells containing the hours worked for each employee in each payroll week. (Do not delete the column.)

b. Jaffe has left our employment; delete the Jaffe row in each payroll week.

c. Set each worksheet to fit on one page when printed.

23. Deselect grouped sheets and check that each sheet contains identical data.

24. Print the entire workbook.

25. Close and save the workbook file.

	A	B	C	D	E	F	G	H	I	J	K	L
1		FIRST STATE BANK PAYROLL										
2		FOR THE WEEK ENDING SEPTEMBER 7, 199-										
3												
4	Employee	Card	Social	Hourly	Hours	Gross	Social	Medicare				
5	Name	Number	Security No.	Rate	Worked	Pay	Sec. Tax	Tax	F.W.T.	Net Pay		
6												
7	Diaz	13567	069-65-4532	5.55	15	83.25	5.16	1.21	16.65	60.23		
8	Jaffe	13750	123-75-7623	7.23	32	231.36	14.34	3.35	46.27	167.39	Delete row	
9	Latov	13816	107-53-6754	6.18	16	98.88	6.13	1.43	19.78	71.54		
10	Nestor	13925	103-87-5698	4.66	28	130.48	8.09	1.89	26.10	94.40	Delete row	
11	Pringle	14345	127-78-0045	6.57	12	78.84	4.89	1.14	15.77	57.04		
12	Wong	14715	043-67-7600	8.65	21	181.65	11.26	2.63	36.33	131.42		
13												
14		TOTALS				804.46	49.88	11.66	160.89	582.03		
15		AVERAGES				134.08	8.31	1.94	26.82	97.00		
16												
17		FOR THE WEEK ENDING SEPTEMBER 14, 199-										
18												
19	Employee	Card	Social	Hourly	Hours	Gross	Social	Medicare				
20	Name	Number	Security No.	Rate	Worked	Pay	Sec. Tax	Tax	F.W.T.	Net Pay		
21												
22	Diaz	13567	069-65-4532	5.55	20	111.00	6.88	1.61	22.20	80.31		
23	Jaffe	13750	123-75-7623	7.23	31	224.13	13.90	3.25	44.83	162.16	Delete row	
24	Latov	13816	107-53-6754	6.18	23	142.14	8.81	2.06	28.43	102.84		
25	Nestor	13925	103-87-5698	4.66	22	102.52	6.36	1.49	20.50	74.17	Delete row	
26	Pringle	14345	127-78-0045	6.57	15	98.55	6.11	1.43	19.71	71.30		
27	Wong	14715	043-67-7600	8.65	25	216.25	13.41	3.14	43.25	156.46		
28												
29		TOTALS				894.59	55.46	12.97	178.92	647.24		
30		AVERAGES				149.10	9.24	2.16	29.82	107.87		
31												
32		FOR THE WEEK ENDING SEPTEMBER 21, 199-										
33												
34	Employee	Card	Social	Hourly	Hours	Gross	Social	Medicare				
35	Name	Number	Security No.	Rate	Worked	Pay	Sec. Tax	Tax	F.W.T.	Net Pay		
36												
37	Diaz	13567	069-65-4532	5.55	22	122.10	7.57	1.77	24.42	88.34		
38	Franz	14865	146-93-0069	6.25	33	206.25	12.79	2.99	41.25	149.22		
39	Jaffe	13750	123-75-7623	7.23	21	151.83	9.41	2.20	30.37	109.85	Delete row	
40	Latov	13816	107-53-6754	6.18	16	98.88	6.13	1.43	19.78	71.54		
41	Pringle	14345	127-78-0045	6.57	18	118.26	7.33	1.71	23.65	85.56		
42	Wong	14715	043-67-7600	8.65	28	242.20	15.02	3.51	48.44	175.23		
43												
44		TOTALS				939.52	58.25	13.62	187.90	679.74		
45		AVERAGES				156.59	9.71	2.27	31.32	113.29		
46												
47												
48												
49												

Copy third payroll to create four payrolls on this worksheet.

KEYSTROKES

USE TAB SPLIT BOX

Lets you show more or fewer tabs.
1. Point to tab split box.
   ✓ *Pointer becomes a ◄║►.*
2. Drag split box left or right.

SELECT SHEETS

Select one sheet:
1. If necessary, click tab .... `|◄ ◄ ► ►|`
   scrolling buttons to scroll a hidden
   sheet tab into view.
2. Click desired sheet tab ...... `＼Sheet #／`

Select all sheets:
1. Right-click any
   sheet tab .... `＼Sheet #／`
2. Click **S**elect All Sheets .... `S`

Select (group) consecutive sheets:
✓ *When you group sheets, entries and*
   formatting applied to one sheet are
   duplicated on all sheets in the group.
1. If necessary, click tab .... `|◄ ◄ ► ►|`
   scrolling buttons to scroll hidden sheet
   tabs into view.
2. Click first sheet tab .... `＼Sheet #／`
3. Press **Shift** and click .... `＼Sheet #／`
   last sheet tab to select.
   [Group] appears in title bar.

Select (group) non-consecutive sheets
✓ *When you group sheets, entries and*
   formatting applied to one sheet are
   duplicated on all sheets in the group.
1. If necessary, click .... `|◄ ◄ ► ►|`
   tab scrolling buttons to scroll hidden
   sheet tabs into view.
2. Click first sheet tab .... `＼Sheet #／`
3. Press **Ctrl** and click .... `＼Sheet #／`
   each sheet tab.
   [Group] appears in title bar.

DESELECT GROUPED SHEETS

Click any sheet tab that is not
in the group........................... `＼Sheet #／`
   OR
1. Right-click....................... `＼Sheet #／`
   any sheet tab in group.
2. Click **U**ngroup Sheets .... `U`

DELETE SHEETS

Delete one sheet:
1. Right-click sheet tab
   to delete........................... `＼Sheet #／`
2. Click **D**elete.............................. `D`
3. Click **OK**.................................. `Enter`

Delete multiple sheets:
1. Select sheet tabs to delete.
2. Right-click any selected
   sheet tab.......................... `＼Sheet #／`
3. Click **D**elete.............................. `D`
4. Click **OK**.................................. `Enter`

RENAME A SHEET

1. Double-click sheet tab
   to rename .... `＼Sheet #／`
   OR
   a. Right-click sheet tab
      to rename .... `＼Sheet #／`
   b. Select **R**ename .... `R`
2. Type new name.
3. Click **OK**.................................. `Enter`

INSERT SHEETS

Insert one worksheet:
1. Right-click sheet tab......... `＼Sheet #／`
   before which new sheet will be
   inserted.
2. Click **I**nsert................................ `I`
3. Select **W**orksheet ....
   on General page.
4. Click **OK**.................................. `Enter`
   Excel inserts sheet and makes the new
   sheet active.

Insert multiple worksheets:
1. Highlight as many sheets as you wish
   to insert.
2. Right-click sheet tab......... `＼Sheet #／`
   before which new sheets will be
   inserted.
3. Click **I**nsert................................ `I`
4. Select **W**orksheet ....
   on General page.
5. Click **OK**.................................. `Enter`
   Excel inserts sheets and
   makes the first new sheet active.

MOVE SHEETS WITHIN A WORKBOOK

Move one sheet:
1. If necessary, click .... `|◄ ◄ ► ►|`
   tab scrolling buttons to
   scroll a hidden sheet tab into view.
2. Drag sheet tab to desired sheet tab position.
   Pointer becomes a ⇖, and black
   triangle indicates point of insertion.

MOVE MULTIPLE SHEETS

1. If necessary, click tab....... `|◄ ◄ ► ►|`
   scrolling buttons to scroll a hidden
   sheet tab into view.
2. Select sheets to move.
3. Drag selected sheet tabs to desired
   sheet tab position.
   Pointer becomes a ⇖, and black
   triangle indicates point of insertion.

PRINT WORKBOOK

Prints worksheet data using the current
page settings.
1. Click **F**ile menu .... `Alt`+`F`
2. Click **P**rint .... `P`
3. Click **E**ntire Workbook .... `Alt`+`E`
4. Click **OK** .... `Enter`

SET WORKSHEET TO PRINT ON SPECIFIED NUMBER OF PAGES

Determines how much to scale printed data
to fit on a specified number of pages.
✓ *Excel ignores manual page breaks when*
   this setting is selected.
1. Click **F**ile menu .... `Alt`+`F`
2. Click **Page Setu**p........................... `U`
3. Select **Page** tab .... `Ctrl`+`Tab`
4. Select **F**it to:.......................... `Alt`+`F`
   To change settings for number
   of pages:
   a. Type number of pages in **page(s)**
      wide.
   b. Type number of pages in **by tall**.
   c. Type number of pages.
5. Click **OK** .... `Enter`

Exercise

32

■ **Named Ranges**

NOTES

Named Ranges

- Excel allows you to assign a **name** to a cell or range of cells rather than use the cell reference for identification.

- Naming ranges makes formulas easy to read and understand and makes printing and combining ranges easier to accomplish. For example, when you define a print area, you can type the name of a range (such as EMPS), rather than type the cell reference (such as A1:D17).

- You should keep range names short and descriptive. Since spaces are not allowed, use an underscore to simulate a space character. Do not use range names that could be interpreted as a number or a cell reference. Range names may contain up to 255 characters and may consist of letters, numbers, underscores (_), backslashes (\), periods (.), and question marks (?).

  • You can define a named range by selecting the range and then selecting Insert, **Name**, **Define commands** or by naming the range in the Name box on the formula bar. The name box [   ] provides a way to view a list of named ranges you have already created and is an easy way to name or select a range.

- A list of the existing named ranges and their locations may be inserted into the worksheet by selecting Insert, Name, **Paste** and clicking the **Paste List** button.

- It is possible to modify a named range by changing the range or the name.

- You can use named ranges in formulas. As discussed in Exercise 11, formulas can contain natural language labels from data column headings. For example, =Sum(SALES) will total the SALES column. If your data does not have labels or if you wish to be certain of the range for a formula, you can create a name that describes the cell or range. You can set label range names by selecting **Insert, Name, Label**.

In this exercise, you will include third-quarter sales commission data and name ranges for printing and for later use in combining files.

EXERCISE DIRECTIONS

1. Open ⌨ **FURN** or 💾 **32FURN**.

2. Edit the title to read:

    QUARTERLY SALES AND SALARY REPORT – JANUARY– SEPTEMBER

3. Insert a row to include a new employee hired on July 1. Employee Number, 6; Name, THOMPSON, JIM; Base Salary, $1500.

    ✓ *Format base salary to be consistent with other formatting.*

4. Freeze columns A-D for vertical titles.

5. Change column widths to 12 for columns K, L, and M.

6. Enter the following data in columns K, L, and M:

	K	L	M
1			
2			
3			
4		5%	JULY-SEPT
5	SALES	COMMISSION	SALARY
6			
7	112469.32		
8	152643.36		
9	215050.16		
10	98463.14		
11	246315.19		
12	76451.13		
13			
14			
15			

7. Format the SALES data for commas.

8. Copy the COMMISSION formulas to the new column.

9. Find JULY-SEPT SALARY using BASE SALARY + COMMISSION.

10. Copy the formula to the remaining employees.

11. Copy the formulas for TOTALS, AVERAGES, HIGHEST, and LOWEST to the new columns. Format answers for numbers with two decimal places.

12. Clear the freeze.

13. Edit the formulas for TOTALS, AVERAGES, HIGHEST, and LOWEST in the BASE SALARY column to include the new employee data.

14. Copy the edited formulas to all columns.

15. Create the following named ranges:

EMPS	A1:D17
JAN_MAR	G1:G17
APR_JUNE	J1:J17
JUL_SEPT	M1:M17

16. Print one copy of the range EMPS.

17. In range beginning at cell B19, insert list of named ranges.

18. Close and save the workbook file, or *save as* **FURN**.

	A	B	C	D	E	F	G	H	I	J	K	L	M
1		FURNITURE SHOWROOMS, INC.											
2		QUARTERLY SALES AND SALARY REPORT - JANUARY-JUNE ⟍					SEPTEMBER						
3											◄──12◄──12◄──12		
4	EMP.			BASE		5%	JAN-MAR		5%	APR-JUN		5%	JULY-SEPT
5	NO.	NAME		SALARY	SALES	COMMISSION	SALARY	SALES	COMMISSION	SALARY	SALES	COMMISSION	SALARY
6													
7	1	ABRAMS, JUDY		1,500.00	113,456.67	5,672.83	7,172.83	114,342.90	5,717.15	7,217.15			
8	2	CHANG, PETER		1,500.00	150,654.87	7,532.74	9,032.74	143,276.70	7,163.84	8,663.84			
9	3	LINSEY, KELLY		1,500.00	234,765.36	11,738.27	13,238.27	187,956.80	9,397.84	10,897.84			
10	4	JOHNSON, LETOYA		1,500.00	89,765.43	4,488.27	5,988.27	93,984.69	4,699.23	6,199.23			
11	5	RIVERA, TONY		1,500.00	287,987.76	14,399.39	15,899.39	254,768.60	12,738.43	14,238.43		Insert row	
12													
13		TOTALS		7,500.00	876,630.09	43,831.50	51,331.50	794,329.69	39,716.48	47,216.48			
14		AVERAGES		1,500.00	175,326.02	8,766.30	10,266.30	158,865.94	7,943.30	9,443.30			
15		HIGHEST		1,500.00	287,987.76	14,399.39	15,899.39	254,768.60	12,738.43	14,238.43			
16		LOWEST		1,500.00	89,765.43	4,488.27	5,988.27	93,984.69	4,699.23	6,199.23			

KEYSTROKES

NAME/MODIFY A RANGE USING THE MENU

1. Click **Insert** menu .... `Alt` + `I`

2. Click **Name** .... `N`

3. Click **Define** .... `D`

   *Active cell reference appears in **Refers to** text box.*

To name a range:

a. Type name for range in **Names in workbook** text box.

b. Click **Add** .... `Alt` + `A`

c. Drag through existing reference .... `Alt` + `R`
   in **Refers to** text box.

d. Select cells in worksheet to name.
   OR
   Type range reference to name.

To delete a name:

a. Click name .... `Tab`, `↕`
   to delete in list box.

b. Click **Delete** .... `Alt` + `D`

To change a name:

a. Click name .... `Tab`, `↕`
   to change in list box.

b. Double-click in .... `Alt` + `W`
   Names in Workbook.

c. Type new name for range.

d. Click **Add** .... `Alt` + `A`

e. Click old name .... `Tab`, `↕`
   to delete in list box.

f. Click **Delete** .... `Alt` + `D`

To change reference a name refers to:

a. Click name .... `Tab`, `↕`
   to edit in list box.

b. Drag through existing reference .... `Alt` + `R`
   in **Refers to** text box.

c. Select cells in worksheet to reference.
   OR
   Type new reference.

4. Click **OK** .... `Enter`

NAME A RANGE USING THE NAME BOX

1. Select range to name.

2. Click in name box on left side of formula bar.

3. Type name of range to create.

4. Press **Enter** .... `Enter`

SELECT A NAMED RANGE

Select a named range using the name box:

1. Click drop-down arrow in name box on left side of formula bar.

2. Click desired named range.

Select a named range using Go To:

1. Press **F5** .... `F5`

2. Type name to select in **Reference** text box.

3. Click **OK** .... `Enter`

INSERT LIST OF NAMED RANGES

Inserts a list of named ranges and their corresponding references in current worksheet.

1. Select upper-left cell in range to receive list.

2. Click **Insert** menu .... `Alt` + `I`

3. Click **Name** .... `N`

4. Click **Paste** .... `P`

5. Click **Paste List** .... `Alt` + `L`

   ✓ *Excel includes sheet names in references.*

6. Press any **arrow** key .... `↕`

SET PRINT AREA FOR A NAMED RANGE

✓ *Use this option only when you want to print a specific area of a worksheet each time you print.*

1. Follow steps to **SET PRINT OPTIONS FOR WORKSHEET**, page 80.

2. When you set the print area, type named range *name* in Print **A**rea text box.

3. Follow steps to **PRINT A WORKSHEET**, page 55.

PRINT A NAMED RANGE

1. Follow steps to **SELECT A NAMED RANGE**, left.

2. Follow steps to **PRINT RANGE OF CELLS**, page 83.

NEXT EXERCISE

Exercise 33

- Data Validation   - Copy and Paste Special
- Format Negative Numbers

NOTES

Data Validation

- **Validation** settings allow you to control data entry in a cell. You can set criteria for the data by creating a list of acceptable entries or by setting limits on the entry. For example, a list of salespeople can be used and only one of those names is valid in the worksheet. Or, you can specify that the value entered must be greater than $100. Note the illustration of the Data Validation dialog box, on the Settings tab, that appears when **Data, Validation** is selected.

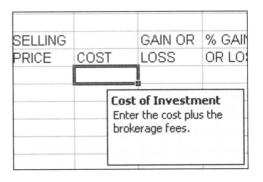

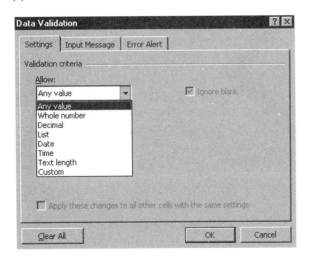

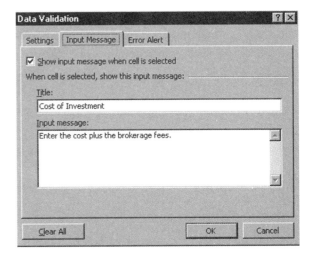

- You can also create input messages that will appear when a cell is selected by using the Input Message tab in the Data Validation dialog box. Warnings, documentation notes or limits for the cell may be included in the message, as shown at top right.

- After you have entered validation settings, any invalid entry will trigger an error message and not allow you to make the entry. You can write a customized error message by using the Error Alert tab in the Data Validation dialog box, as illustrated on the next page.

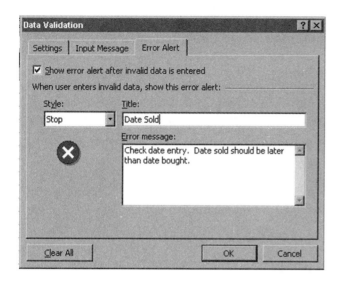

Copy and Paste Special

- When you use the Paste Special dialog box, you can specify which part of the cell contents should be copied. One of the Paste Special options is to paste only the **Validation** rules to the new location. If you select **All** as the Paste Special option, formulas, formats, comments and validation rules are pasted to the new location.

- The **Values** option should be used to paste data as it appears in the cells. This option does not paste formulas, comments or validation rules.

Format Negative Numbers

- In some cases, formulas will result in a negative value. The default format for a negative number is to display the number with a minus sign. You may select the format for negative numbers from a list box as illustrated below. To highlight negative values, select the red number or parentheses format.

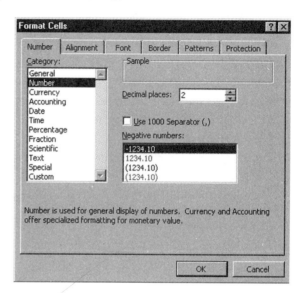

In this exercise, you will create a stock portfolio worksheet prepared to summarize stock transactions for the year. You will enter data validation criteria and use a named range to print the worksheet range. To summarize stock transactions, you will use the Copy and Paste Special commands to combine extracted data in a new worksheet.

EXERCISE DIRECTIONS

1. Create 🖮 the worksheet on the right or open 💾 **33INVEST**.

2. Enter dates in the format illustrated with the current year.

3. Set width of column A to 15.

4. Enter a validation setting in the first cell of the DATE SOLD column (E7) as follows:
   a. Click Data, Validation.
   b. On the Settings tab, click in Allow and select the Date validation criteria setting.
   c. Make the settings below to set DATE SOLD column for a value greater than the DATE BOUGHT column:
      Allow: Date
      Data: greater than
      Start Date: =D7
   d. Click OK.
   e. Test setting by changing the year in cell E7 to 1996.

5. Enter an input message in the first cell of the COST column (G7) as follows:
   a. Click Data, Validation.
   b. Select the Input Message tab.
   c. Enter as a title: Cost of Investment
   d. Enter as a message: Enter the cost plus brokerage fees.
   e. Click OK.
   f. Move out and into the cell to check that the message appears.

6. Enter an input message in the first cell of the SELLING PRICE column (F7) as follows:
   Title: Selling Price
   Message: Enter the sales price less brokerage fees.

7. Use Copy and Paste Special, Validation commands to copy the validation settings from cells E7:G7 to all cells in those columns.

8. Freeze titles in columns A and B.

9. Find GAIN or LOSS (subtract COST from SELLING PRICE).

10. Copy the formula to the remaining stocks.

11. Find TOTAL SELLING PRICE.

12. Copy the total formula to COST and GAIN or LOSS columns; format results for two decimal places.

13. Find % GAIN or LOSS (divide the GAIN or LOSS by the COST) and format the result for a two-place percent.

14. Copy the % GAIN OR LOSS formula to the remaining stocks and to the TOTALS line.

15. Create the following named ranges:
    PRINTALL   A1:I13
    STOCK   A1:B13

16. Use the range name PRINTALL to print one copy to fit on a page.

17. Save the workbook file; name it **INVEST**.

18. Extract the STOCK range from the **INVEST** workbook into a new workbook:
    a. Copy range named STOCK to clipboard.
    b. Create a new workbook.
    c. Use Paste to paste the lables into cell A1 in the new workbook.

19. Set the width of column A to 15.

20. Save the new workbook; name it **INVSUM**.

21. Extract the GAIN or LOSS and % GAIN or LOSS to the INVSUM workbook:
    a. Select the **INVEST** workbook.
    b. Copy the GAIN or LOSS and % GAIN or LOSS columns (H1:I13) to the clipboard.
    c. Select cell D1 in the **INVSUM** workbook and paste the values.
       ✓ *Use the Values paste option from the Paste Special dialog box.*

22. In **INVSUM**, format GAIN OR LOSS numbers to the red parentheses setting to display negative numbers.

23. Enter a worksheet title in **INVSUM** (in cells B1 and B2) that reads:

ROCHELLE MARTLING
INVESTMENT SUMMARY 1997

24. Print one copy of **INVSUM** workbook.
25. Close and save both workbook files.

	A	B	C	D	E	F	G	H	I
1			ROCHELLE MARTLING						
2			INVESTMENT TRANSACTIONS FOR 1997						
3									
4	COMPANY			DATE	DATE	SELLING		GAIN OR	% GAIN
5	NAME	SYMBOL	SHARES	BOUGHT	SOLD	PRICE	COST	LOSS	OR LOSS
6									
7	Focus Motors	FM	100	1/15/96	2/28/97	6950.75	7698.86		
8	General Oil	GNO	200	3/6/96	4/3/97	7656.87	6567.15		
9	IVM	IVM	100	12/18/96	7/31/97	8976.85	9987.08		
10	Microtech	MIC	200	1/5/97	10/3/97	11435.98	8656.45		
11	American Electric	AE	300	3/9/97	11/4/97	5467.43	4132.75		
12									
13	TOTALS								

KEYSTROKES

COPY AND PASTE SPECIAL (COMBINE DATA)

Combines data copied to the paste area in the way you specify.

1. Select range of worksheet to extract.
2. Click **Edit** menu .... Alt+E
3. Click **Copy** C

To change destination workbook or worksheet:

Select workbook and/or sheet to receive data.

4. Select upper-left cell in destination area.
5. Click **Edit** menu .... Alt+E
6. Click **Paste Special** .... S
7. Select **Paste** option:
   - **All** .... A
   - **Formulas** .... F
   - **Values** V
   - **Formats** .... T
   - **Comments** C
   - **Validation** .... N
   - **All except borders** X

To prevent overwriting existing data with blank cells:

Select **Skip blanks** .... B

To change orientation of data in paste area:

Select **Transpose** .... E

8. Click **OK** .... Enter

DATA VALIDATION

1. Select cell to receive validation setting.
2. Click **Data** .... Alt+D
3. Click **Validation** L

To set validation criteria:

a. Select **Allow** to set validation criteria .... Alt+A, ↓
b. Set **Data** operator ...... Alt+D, ↓
c. If applicable, enter or select **Minimum** value .... Alt+M, *value*
d. If applicable, enter or select **Maximum** value .... Alt+X, *value*

To enter an input message:

a. Select Input Message tab .... Ctrl+Tab
b. Enter **Title** .... Alt+T, *title*
c. Enter **Input** message .... Alt+I, *message*

To customize error message:

a. Select Error Alert tab .... Ctrl+Tab
b. Select alert **Style** .... Alt+Y, ↓
c. Enter **Title** .... Alt+T, *title*
d. Enter **Error** message .... Alt+E, *message*

4. Click **OK** .... Enter

FORMAT NEGATIVE VALUES

1. Select cells to be formatted.
2. Click **Format** .... Alt+O
3. Click **Cells** .... E
4. On Number tab, select **Category** and Number.... Alt+C, ↓
5. Select style in **Negative numbers** .... Alt+N, ↓
6. Click **OK** .... Enter

Exercise 34

■ Copy and Paste Special (Add Option)

NOTES

Copy and Paste Special

■ As described in previous exercises, the **Paste Special** command gives you added control on how data is pasted when copied.

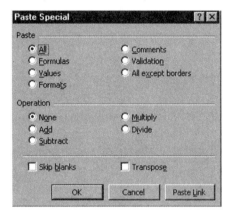

■ The Operation options in the Paste Special dialog box provide a variety of ways to combine data.

None	Replaces paste cells with copied cells (default setting).
Add	Adds numeric data in copied cells to values in paste cells.
Subtract	Subtracts numeric data in copied cells from values in paste cells.
Multiply	Multiplies numeric data in copied cells by values in paste cells.
Divide	Divides numeric data in copied cells by values in paste cells.

■ In this lesson you will use the **Add** operation option in the Paste Special dialog box to copy and paste data to a column in another workbook. The Add option will allow you to add the values from each quarter to obtain a total for all quarters.

> *In this exercise, you will add fourth quarter data to the workbook. Data in named ranges will be extracted to a new file. The Paste Special command will be used to combine (add) the quarterly totals in the new workbook file to create a summary workbook.*

EXERCISE DIRECTIONS

1. Open ⌨ **FURN** or 💾 **34FURN**.

2. Add three additional columns for SALES, 5% COMMISSION, and OCT-DEC SALARY to the worksheet. Column width should be 12.

3. Enter fourth quarter sales data as illustrated on the right, freezing titles in columns A-D to make data entry easier.

4. Enter or copy formulas, as necessary, to complete the worksheet.

5. Change the workbook title to read JANUARY– DECEMBER.

SALES
113,546.32
147,432.54
195,328.76
94,567.32
248,766.55
165,438.77

6. Delete the list of named ranges in B19.
7. Create a named range for OCT_DEC in P1:P17.
8. Beginning at cell B19, insert a list of named ranges.
9. Use the Copy and Paste Special commands to extract the named range EMPS to a cell A1 in a new workbook file using the Formulas option; save and name the new workbook **FURNSUM**.
10. Edit the second line of the FURNSUM workbook title to read:

    COMPENSATION SUMMARY - JANUARY-DECEMBER
11. Select the **FURN** workbook.
12. Use the Copy and Paste Special commands to extract and combine the following named ranges into cell F1 of the FURNSUM workbook.

    JAN_MAR
    APR_JUNE
    JUL_SEPT
    OCT_DEC

✓ *Each time you paste data to cell F1 using the Paste Special command, be sure to set the Paste option to Values and the Operation option to Add. Each quarter's values will be added to the data in the range.*

13. In column F of the **FURNSUM** workbook, enter the column title:

    TOTAL
    COMPENSATION
14. The combined summary data for AVERAGES, HIGHEST and LOWEST is now incorrect.

    To correct this information, copy the formulas for TOTALS, AVERAGES, HIGHEST and LOWEST, from the BASE SALARY column to theTOTAL COMPENSATION column. (*The EMPS range was pasted with a Formulas option, and therefore contains formulas from the original worksheet.*)
15. Format columns D and F for commas.
16. Print one copy of each file.
17. Close and save both workbook files.

	A	B	C	D	E	F	G	H	I	J	K	L	M
1		FURNITURE SHOWROOMS, INC.											
2		QUARTERLY SALES AND SALARY REPORT - JANUARY-SEPTEMBER											
3													
4	EMP.			BASE		5%	JAN-MAR		5%	APR-JUN		5%	JULY-SEPT
5	NO.	NAME		SALARY	SALES	COMMISSION	SALARY	SALES	COMMISSION	SALARY	SALES	COMMISSION	SALARY
6													
7	1	ABRAMS, JUDY		1,500.00	113,456.67	5,672.83	7,172.83	114,342.90	5,717.15	7,217.15	112,469.32	5,623.47	7,123.47
8	2	CHANG, PETER		1,500.00	150,654.87	7,532.74	9,032.74	143,276.70	7,163.84	8,663.84	152,643.36	7,632.17	9,132.17
9	3	LINSEY, KELLY		1,500.00	234,765.36	11,738.27	13,238.27	187,956.80	9,397.84	10,897.84	215,050.16	10,752.51	12,252.51
10	4	JOHNSON, LETOYA		1,500.00	89,765.43	4,488.27	5,988.27	93,984.69	4,699.23	6,199.23	98,463.14	4,923.16	6,423.16
11	5	RIVERA, TONY		1,500.00	287,987.76	14,399.39	15,899.39	254,768.60	12,738.43	14,238.43	246,315.19	12,315.76	13,815.76
12	6	THOMPSON, JIM		1,500.00							76,451.13	3,822.56	5,322.56
13													
14		TOTALS		9,000.00	876,630.09	43,831.50	51,331.50	794,329.69	39,716.48	47,216.48	901,392.30	45,069.62	54,069.62
15		AVERAGES		1,500.00	175,326.02	8,766.30	10,266.30	158,865.94	7,943.30	9,443.30	150,232.05	7,511.60	9,011.60
16		HIGHEST		1,500.00	287,987.76	14,399.39	15,899.39	254,768.60	12,738.43	14,238.43	246,315.19	12,315.76	13,815.76
17		LOWEST		1,500.00	89,765.43	4,488.27	5,988.27	93,984.69	4,699.23	6,199.23	76,451.13	3,822.56	5,322.56
18													
19				EMPS range A1:D17									
20													

KEYSTROKES

COPY AND PASTE SPECIAL (COMBINE DATA)

Combines data copied to the paste area in the way you specify.

1. Select range of worksheet to extract.
2. Click **Edit** menu .... `Alt`+`E`
3. Click **Copy** .... `C`
4. Select workbook and/or sheet to receive data.
5. Select upper-left cell in destination area.
6. Click **Edit** menu .... `Alt`+`E`
7. Click **Paste Special** ... . `S`

8. Select a **Paste** option:
   - **All** .... `A`
   - **Formulas** .... `F`
   - **Values** .... `V`
   - **Formats** .... `T`
   - **Comments** .... `C`
   - **Validation** .... `N`
   - **All except borders** .... `X`

To combine copied data with paste area data:

Select Operation option:
   - **None** .... `O`

   - **Add** .... `D`
   - **Subtract** .... `S`
   - **Multiply** .... `M`
   - **Divide** .... `I`

To prevent overwriting existing data with blank cells:

Select **Skip Blanks** .... `B`

To change orientation of data in paste area:

Select **Transpose** .... `E`

9. Click **OK** .... `Enter`

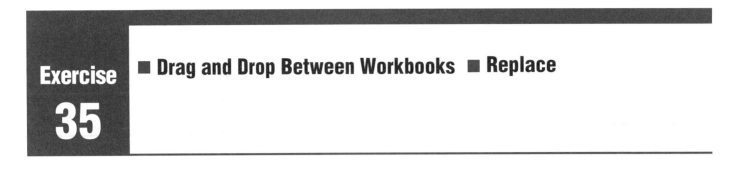

NOTES

Drag and Drop Between Workbooks

- If you have workbooks arranged on the screen, as illustrated below, you can use the drag and drop feature to copy a range from one workbook to another. Select the range, press CTRL and drag the border of the selection to the new workbook.

Replace

- You may find it necessary to change a value or text entry throughout a worksheet. The **Replace** feature can replace all or some of the existing information quickly with another entry.

If you wish to confirm each replacement, you can select the **Find Next** option. Note the Edit, **Replace** dialog box below:

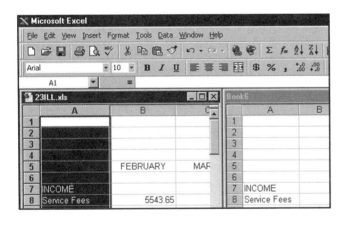

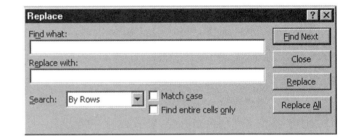

KEYSTROKES

REPLACE

Replaces text in worksheet with specified text.

1. Select any cell to search entire worksheet.
   OR
   Select cells to search.
   OR
   Select sheets to search.
2. Click **Edit** menu .... `Alt`+`E`
3. Click **Replace** .... `E`
4. Click in **Find What** text box .... `Alt`+`N`
5. Type characters to search for.
   ✓ *You may use wildcard characters (* and ?) to represent any character (?) or group of characters (*) in a search. To find data containing wildcard characters, you must type a tilde (~) before the wildcard character.*
6. Click in **Replace with**
   text box .... `Alt`+`E`
7. Type or edit replacement text.

   To set a search direction:

   a. Click **Search** .... `Alt`+`S`
   b. Click desired search
      direction .... `↓` `↑` , `Enter`

      Search options include:
      By Columns, By Rows,
      (All, Down, Up (module sheets only))

   To make search case specific:

   Select **Match case** .... `Alt`+`C`

   To find cells that match exactly:

   Select **Find entire**
   cells only .... `Alt`+`O`

8. Click **Find Next** .... `Alt`+`F`
   Excel selects first cell meeting the search criteria.
9. Select one of the following:

   To globally replace cell contents:

   Click **Replace All** .... `Alt`+`A`
   Excel replaces all matches and returns you to normal operations.

   To selectively replace cell contents:

   a. Click **Replace** .... `Alt`+`R`
      to replace contents of active cell and find next match.
      OR

   Click **Find Next** .... `Alt`+`F`
   to retain contents of active cell and find next match.

   b. Repeat step **a** for each item found.

   c. Click **Close** .... `Esc`
      to close Replace dialog box.

ARRANGE WORKBOOKS

1. Click **Window** .... `Alt`+`W`
2. Click **Arrange** .... `A`
3. Select an arrangement option:
   - **Tiled** .... `Alt`+`T`
   - **Horizontal** .... `Alt`+`O`
   - **Vertical** .... `Alt`+`V`
   - **Cascade** .... `Alt`+`C`
4. Click **OK** .... `Enter`

DRAG AND DROP BETWEEN WORKBOOKS

1. Select range to copy.
2. Press CTRL and drag border of selection to location on new workbook.

> *In this exercise, you will update the Umbrella Insurance Agency worksheet to include fourth-quarter data and replace certain data labels. You will practice using the Replace feature and also create a new worksheet comparing quarterly data using the Copy, Paste Special procedure.*

EXERCISE DIRECTIONS

1. Open ⌨ **INS** or 💾 **35INS**.

2. Enter the following fourth-quarter data beginning in the next available column of your worksheet:

	N	O	P
1			
2			
3			
4			
5	OCT,	NOV.	DEC.
6			
7			
8	13987.65	14323.54	14003.21
9	1342.65	1265.54	1122.32
10			
11			
12			
13	280.00	275.00	275.00
14	1200.00	1200.00	1200.00
15	6250.00	6250.00	6250.00
16	195.34	201.23	195.43
17	224.32	245.34	231.32
18	25.00	25.00	25.00
19	210.50	255.65	275.50

3. Where necessary, copy formulas to complete the worksheet.

4. Find 4TH QTR. TOTALS.

5. Copy the formulas to the remaining items.

6. Center column title labels.

7. Format numeric data for two decimal places.

8. Create the following named ranges (notice underscores) for each quarterly total column:

   _1STQTR
   _2NDQTR
   _3RDQTR
   _4THQTR

   ✓ *Include blank cells in column. For example, E1:E22 for _1STQTR.*

9. Clear the freeze on Column A titles.

10. Save the file, or save as **INS**.

11. Open a new workbook.

12. Use the Window, Arrange commands to arrange the workbooks vertically.

13. Use the drag and drop method to copy column A data, rows 1 through 22, to cell A1 in the new workbook file; save and name the new workbook **INSQTRS**.

14. In **INSQTRS** workbook, adjust column width and enter a worksheet title beginning in cell C1 that reads:

    UMBRELLA INSURANCE AGENCY
    QUARTERLY INCOME STATEMENT
    COMPARISON

15. Select the **INS** workbook.

16. Use the Copy and Paste Special commands to copy the named range _1STQTR to the range beginning in C1 in the **INSQTRS** workbook.

    ✓ *Use the name box to select the named references quickly.*

    IMPORTANT: Set the Paste option to Values, Operation option to None, and select Skip Blanks.

17. Repeat step 16 for the _2NDQTR, _3RDQTR, and _4THQTR named ranges. Paste ranges in **INSQTRS** workbook in columns D1, E1, and F1, respectively.

18. Maximize the **INSQTRS** workbook.

19. Enter title in column G:

    COMBINED
    TOTALS

20. Find the combined total for Agency Fees INCOME.

21. Copy the formula to the remaining items.

22. Practice using the Replace feature as follows:
    a. Select Edit, Replace.
    b. Replace INCOME with REVENUE and check Match Case box.
    c. Click Replace All.
       ✓ *The capitalized "INCOME" words have been replaced.*
    d. Restore the worksheet to its original status by clicking Edit, Undo Replace.

e. Repeat this procedure using the Find Next button. (You may have to move the Replace dialog box so you can see each occurrence.)

f. Replace or skip occurrences using the Find Next button until all are done.

g. Restore the worksheet to its original status by clicking Edit, Undo Replace.

23. Format all numeric values for commas.

24. Save the **INSQTRS** workbook and print one copy.

25. Close all workbook files.

Add 4th Qtr. data

	A	B	C	D	E	F	G	H	I	J	K	L	M	N
1		UMBRELLA INSURANCE AGENCY												
2		COMPARATIVE INCOME STATEMENT												
3														
4					1ST QTR				2ND QTR.				3RD QTR.	
5		JANUARY	FEBRUARY	MARCH	TOTALS	APRIL	MAY	JUNE	TOTALS	JULY	AUGUST	SEPT.	TOTALS	
6														
7	INCOME													
8	Agency Fees	12342.87	12543.65	13165.87	38052.39	13343.84	13862.89	14359.45	41566.18	13976.87	14102.32	14323.32	42402.51	
9	Consultations	1432.43	1654.76	1689.76	4776.95	1893.65	1498.62	1287.49	4679.76	1324.54	1243.76	1432.43	4000.73	
10	Total Income	13775.30	14198.41	14855.63	42829.34	15237.49	15361.51	15646.94	46245.94	15301.41	15346.08	15755.75	46403.24	
11														
12	EXPENSES:													
13	Advertising	250.00	250.00	300.00	800.00	325.00	300.00	325.00	950.00	300.00	275.00	325.00	900.00	
14	Rent	1200.00	1200.00	1200.00	3600.00	1200.00	1200.00	1200.00	3600.00	1200.00	1200.00	1200.00	3600.00	
15	Salaries	6250.00	6250.00	6250.00	18750.00	6250.00	6250.00	6250.00	18750.00	6250.00	6250.00	6250.00	18750.00	
16	Supplies	154.76	245.65	298.67	699.08	176.98	210.89	221.75	609.62	185.43	255.67	231.32	672.42	
17	Utilities	218.97	235.43	201.32	655.72	254.32	233.54	215.75	703.61	265.43	275.43	249.76	790.62	
18	Interest	25.00	25.00	25.00	75.00	25.00	25.00	25.00	75.00	25.00	25.00	25.00	75.00	
19	Other	243.54	210.65	231.65	685.84	106.89	332.90	798.43	1238.22	310.32	297.65	542.98	1150.95	
20	Total Expenses	8342.27	8416.73	8506.64	25265.64	8338.19	8552.33	9035.93	25926.45	8536.18	8578.75	8824.06	25938.99	
21														
22	NET INCOME	5433.03	5781.68	6348.99	17563.70	6899.30	6809.18	6611.01	20319.49	6765.23	6767.33	6931.69	20464.25	

Extract to new file: INSQTRS

Exercise
36

■ Use Templates (Spreadsheet Solutions)

NOTES

- Excel provides **template** spreadsheets (model worksheet designs) for common business tasks. The formulas, formats, print ranges, layout, etc., are pre-set so that you only need to add your own data. If data is added to a template file, the Save As option will be provided when you click Save so that you can name your file.

- You can customize the template for your own purposes and save it as a template file with a new filename. This will enable you to use a customized form that only requires the new variable data. You may also create a template from any standard Excel document by saving it as a template file (see *Original Templates,* **Exercise 37**).

- The template spreadsheet solutions that are available in Excel can be accessed by selecting New from the File menu and clicking the **Spreadsheet Solutions** tab. By default, the **Invoice** and **Village Software** templates are available. Additional templates may be loaded to this directory from the Internet or the CD-ROM that contains your Excel 97 software. Note the illustration of the New dialog box with the Spreadsheet Solutions tab selected.

- The Village Software icon opens an information request screen that links to the Village Software Web site for ordering additional preprogrammed and custom spreadsheet solutions.

- The Invoice spreadsheet solution is a template workbook. It contains a **template worksheet** and a **customize worksheet** with data entry placeholders to customize the form for your use. In addition, a **Template toolbar** appears on screen when the template is opened. Note the illustration of the **Invoice toolbar** with a ToolTip displayed.

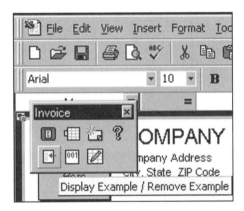

- If you have enabled virus protection in Excel, a warning will display when you open a spreadsheet solution. Since these solutions contain macros, you will have to enable the macros to load the template with all its features.

EXERCISE DIRECTIONS

1. Open a new file.

2. Switch to the Spreadsheet Solutions tab in the New dialog box.

3. Double-click the Invoice template. Enable macros when prompted.

4. Place the mouse pointer under every button on the Invoice toolbar to view the ToolTip.

5. Press the Size to Screen/Return to Size button (top left corner) to view the template. Press the button to return to size.

6. To view a cell tip, place your mouse on the red triangle near **Invoice No.** in the upper right corner of the invoice.

7. Click on the [?] button to view a help screen on the invoice template. After looking at the screen, press the Close button.

8. Close the Invoice toolbar.

9. Switch to the Customize Your Invoice sheet (by clicking the Customize button).

10. Make the entries as shown on the form on the next page.

11. Switch back to the Invoice sheet (by clicking the Invoice tab) and check your input.

12. Click on the **Insert Fine Print Here** location at the bottom of the invoice and insert:

    Please check merchandise carefully upon delivery.

13. Click on the **Insert Farewell Statement Here** location and insert:

    Thank you for your order.

14. Save the file as **ADINV**.

15. Use the **ADINV** worksheet to complete an invoice for Zinno Advertising as follows:

Customer:	Zinno Advertising
	40 Scaran Road
	Peoria, IL 62543
Phone:	402-555-1234

Order No.:	MA25
Invoice Number:	AD456
Rep:	Mary
FOB	Galesburg, IL

QTY	DESCRIPTION	UNIT PRICE
6	Toner Cartridges X-341	69.95
10	Drawing Pads JJ4356	21.95
5	Pencil sets CA65763	5.43

    Payment Details: Check

16. Print a copy of the invoice.

17. Save the invoice as **ZINNO**. *This allows you to reuse **ADINV** as your blank customized invoice.*

18. Close all files.

Customize Your Invoice

CUSTOMIZE YOUR INVOICE

Lock/Save Sheet

Hover Your Pointer
HERE for a Useful Tip!

Type Company Information Here...

Company Name	ART DEPOT
Address	1254 Miller Road
City	Galesburg
State	IL
ZIP Code	61401

Phone 309-555-9000
Fax 309-555-9001

Specify Default Invoice Information Here...

1st Tax Name   IL
Rate   6.00%
☑ Apply tax on local purchases only.

Credit Cards Accepted
Master Plan
Discovery
American Presto

2nd Tax Name
Rate
☐ Apply tax on local purchases only.

7.5
Shipping Charge $7.50

☐ Share invoice numbers on network.   Counter Location

Template Wizard Database   c:\program files\microsoft office\office\library\invdb.xls

Formatted Information

Insert
Logo
Here

ART DEPOT

1254 Miller Road
Galesburg, IL 61401
309-555-9000 fax 309-555-9001

Select Logo

Change Plate Font

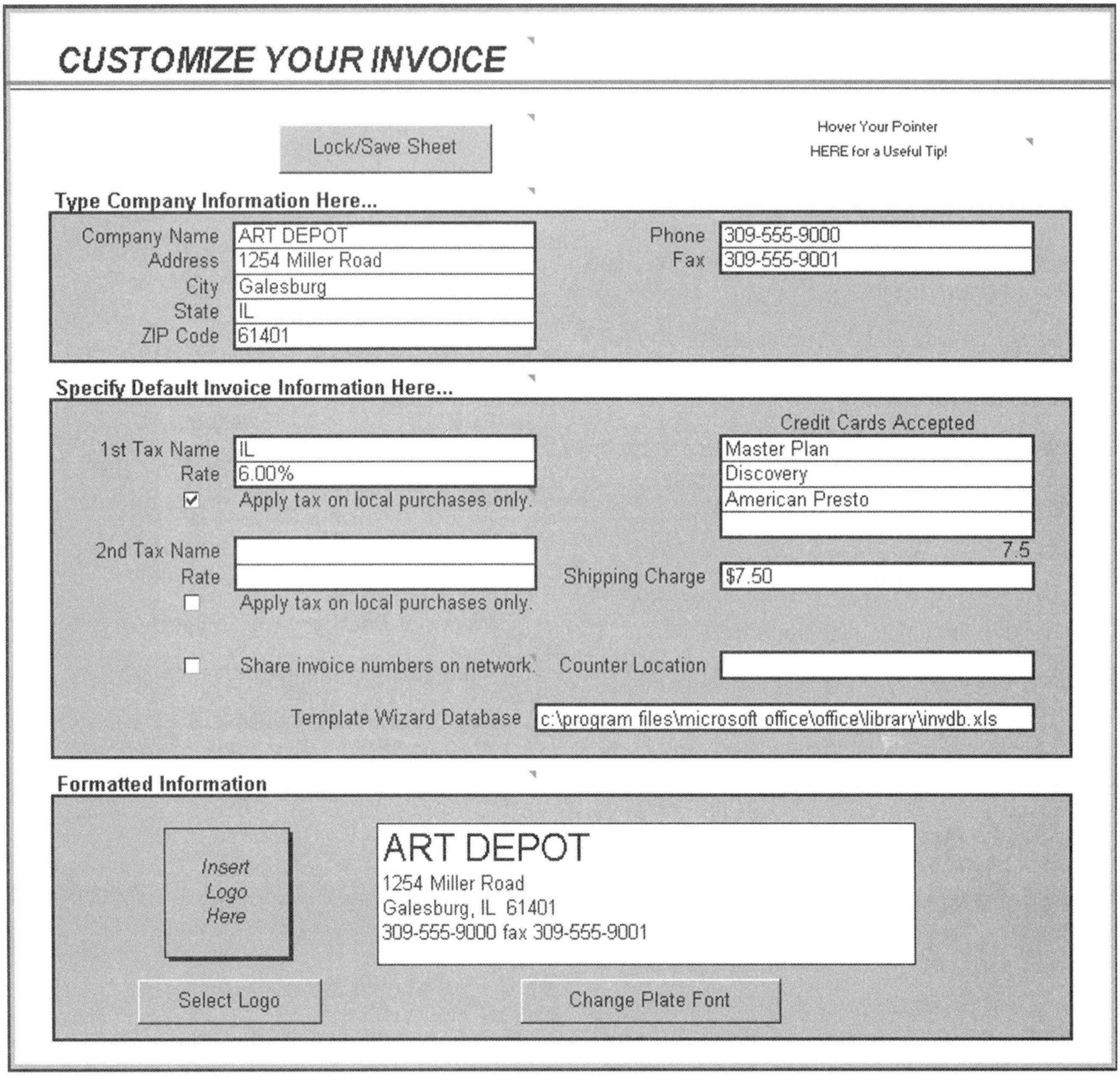

Invoice Template

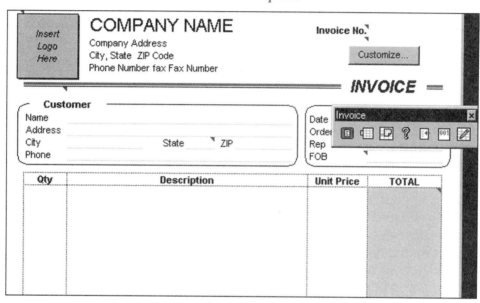

KEYSTROKES

USE AN EXCEL TEMPLATE

1. Click **File** menu..................... `Alt`+`F`
2. Click **New**....................................... `N`
3. Click Spreadsheet Solutions tab.
4. Double-click on desired template.

SAVE A FILE AS A TEMPLATE

1. Click **File** menu .... `Alt`+`F`
2. Click **Save As** .... `A`
   ✓ *If you are saving from an Excel template, a message will be displayed about creating a database record. Click Cancel if the database feature will not be used.*
3. Select drive in **Save in** box..... `Alt`+`I`
4. Double-click folder name in documents list........ `Tab`+`↕`, `Enter`
5. Repeat step 4 until folder to receive template is current.
6. Click in **File name** box .... `Alt`+`N`
7. Enter name of template.
8. Click in **Save as type** box ...... `Alt`+`T`
9. Select **Template** option ...... `↓`, `Enter`
10. Click **Save** .... `Alt`+`S`

OPEN ORIGINAL TEMPLATE FILE

1. Click **Open** button .... `🖿`
   on Standard toolbar.
   OR
   a. Click **File** menu .... `Alt`+`F`
   b. Click **Open**............................... `O`
2. Click in **Files of type** box ...... `Alt`+`T`
3. Select **Templates (*xlt)** ...... `↓`, `Enter`
4. Select folder containing template in **Look in** box............................ `Alt`+`Tab`, `↕`
5. Select template file to open................... `Tab`+`↕`, `Enter`
6. Press **Shift** and click **Open**.

Exercise 37

■ Original Templates ■ Link Workbooks

NOTES

Original Templates

- When you want to create several workbooks containing the same formats, layouts and formulas, you can create a model worksheet and save it as a template. When a file is saved as a template, by default, it is automatically saved to the Templates folder in Microsoft Office. The Templates folder provides several subdirectories you can use. If you save the template in the Other Documents folder, it will appear as an icon on that tab in the new dialog box, as illustrated below.

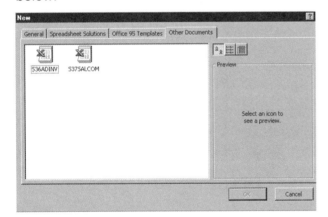

- It is advisable to save a template file as a read-only file so that the format cannot be accidentally changed or overwritten.

  ✓ NOTE: Template files have .XLT filename extensions.

Link Workbooks

- **Linking workbooks** allows you to consolidate and merge data from several workbooks into one summary workbook. Linking allows the summary workbook to be automatically or manually updated when the linked data changes.

- The workbooks that provide the data are referred to as **source workbooks**; the workbook that references the data is referred to as the **dependent workbook**. References to cells in other workbooks are called **external references**.

- By default, links are set to update automatically. Excel updates links when you open the dependent workbook and also when source data is changed while the dependent workbook is open.

- Linking differs from combining data, which usually consists of using Copy and Paste Special commands to copy, add, or subtract data to or from another file. When you combine data, changes in the source workbook are not reflected in the dependent workbook except by repeating the combining procedure.

- There are three ways to link a file:

  - The copied data from the source workbook may be pasted into the dependent workbook as a **pasted link** which automatically creates an external reference that links the workbooks.

    ✓ NOTE: In this exercise, we will use the Paste Link method.

  - An external reference may also be typed in a formula using the following format: **drive:\path\[file.xls]sheetname!reference**

    EXAMPLES:

    =c:\excel\[PAT.xls]Sheet1!A1 creates a link to A1 in the PAT workbook.

    =sum([pat.xls]Sheet1!A1:D1) + B3 finds sum of A1:D1 on Sheet1 of the PAT workbook and adds it to the contents of B3 in the current workbook.

If the source file is in the same directory, you may omit the path.

- An external reference may be included in a formula by selecting cells in the source workbook while editing or creating a formula in the dependent workbook.

■ If you include a cell in an external reference that includes a formula, only the formula result will be brought into the linked workbook.

■ When possible, follow these guidelines for saving linked workbooks:

- Save linked workbooks in the same directory.

- Save the source workbooks before the dependent workbook.

An illustration of the linking process appears below.

Three Source Workbooks

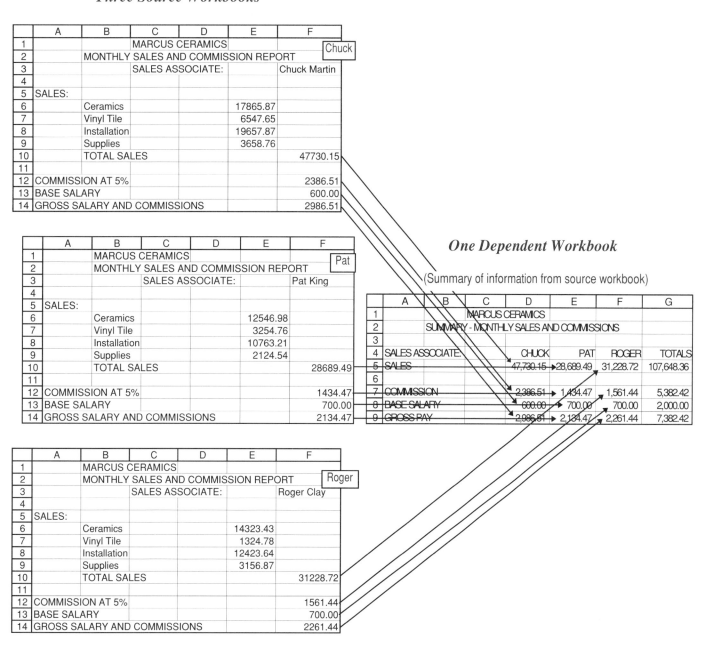

One Dependent Workbook

(Summary of information from source workbook)

In this exercise, the Marcus Ceramics Company creates a monthly sales and salary statement for each sales associate. They would like a summary workbook consolidating the information about the associates' sales performance. Using the Linking feature, the data on the consolidated workbook will automatically update monthly as the associate data changes.

EXERCISE DIRECTIONS

1. Create template Workbook A, as indicated on the right, or open 💾 **37SALCOM**.

2. Add formulas to template to find:
   - TOTAL SALES
   - COMMISSION (5% of Sales)
   - GROSS PAY (Salary +Commission)
   - ✓ *Formulas will result in zero values.*

3. Format all money columns for two decimal places.

4. Save the file as a template; name it **SALCOM**. *Select Template in the Save as type box.*

5. Use the template to create a workbook for each sales consultant using the data below. After each workbook is completed, save and name each workbook file **CHUCK, PAT,** and **ROGER**, respectively. Select Microsoft Excel Workbook as the file type for each file.
   IMPORTANT: Do not close these files after saving.

ASSOCIATE	CHUCK MARTIN	PAT KING	ROGER CLAY
Ceramics	17865.87	12546.98	14323.43
Vinyl Tile	6547.65	3254.76	1324.78
Installation	19657.87	10763.21	12423.64
Supplies	3658.76	2124.54	3156.87
BASE SALARY	600.00	700.00	700.00

6. Open a new workbook and create workbook B (dependent), as indicated on the right; save the workbook; name it **MOSUM** or open 💾 **37MOSUM**.

7. Minimize all workbook windows except **CHUCK** and **MOSUM**; arrange the open workbooks so data in both can be seen.

8. Copy and Paste Link the range including TOTAL SALES, COMMISSION, BASE SALARY, and GROSS PAY in the **CHUCK** workbook to cell D5 in **MOSUM** workbook.
   - ✓ *You can use a multiple selection to do this in one step or link each reference one at a time. Note external reference formula appearing on formula bar for linked data.*

8. Minimize **CHUCK** workbook.

9. Open **PAT** workbook icon; arrange open workbooks.

10. Copy and Paste Link the F10:F14 range in the **PAT** workbook to cell E5 in the **MOSUM** workbook.

11. Minimize **PAT** workbook.

12. Open **ROGER** workbook icon; arrange open workbooks.

13. Copy and Paste Link the F10:F14 range in the **ROGER** workbook to cell E5 in the **MOSUM** workbook.

14. Find all totals in **MOSUM** workbook.

15. Save the **MOSUM** workbook.

16. Print one copy of **MOSUM** workbook.

17. Minimize all windows except **PAT** and **MOSUM** so they are both visible.

18. Select **PAT** workbook and change his Vinyl Tile sales to $8254.76.

19. Note the updated values in the **PAT** column of the **MOSUM** workbook and the updated totals.

20. Close all workbook files, *without* resaving.

	A	B	C	D	E	F	G
1			MARCUS CERAMICS				
2			MONTHLY SALES AND COMMISSION REPORT				
3			SALES ASSOCIATE:				
4							
5	SALES:						
6		Ceramics					
7		Vinyl Tile					
8		Installation					
9		Supplies					
10		TOTAL SALES				0	
11							
12	COMMISSION AT 5%					0	
13	BASE SALARY						
14	GROSS PAY					0	
15							
16		**Workbook A - source template file**					
17							

	A	B	C	D	E	F	G
1			MARCUS CERAMICS				
2		SUMMARY - MONTHLY SALES AND COMMISSIONS					
3							
4	SALES ASSOCIATE:			CHUCK	PAT	ROGER	TOTALS
5	SALES						
6							
7	COMMISSION						
8	BASE SALARY						
9	GROSS PAY						
10							
11		**Workbook B - dependent file**					

KEYSTROKES

CREATE A TEMPLATE WORKBOOK

Saves and names the active workbook as a template file.

1. Click **File** menu .... `Alt`+`F`
2. Click **Save As** .... `A`
3. Click **Save as type** .... `Alt`+`T`
4. Select **Template** file type .. `↑↓`, `Enter`
5. Double-click in **File name** ...... `Alt`+`N`
6. Type filename
7. Click **Save** .... `Enter`

ARRANGE WORKBOOK WINDOWS

1. Click **Window** menu .... `Alt`+`W`
2. Click **Arrange** .... `A`
3. Select desired **Arrange** option:
   - **Tiled** .... `T`
   - **Horizontal** .... `O`
   - **Vertical** .... `V`
   - **Cascade** .... `C`
4. Click **OK** .... `Enter`

LINK WORKBOOKS USING PASTE LINK

1. Open workbooks to link.
2. Arrange workspace so both workbooks are in view.
3. Select cell(s) to reference in source workbook.
4. Click **Edit** menu .... `Alt`+`E`
5. Click **Copy** .... `C`
6. Select cell(s) to receive reference(s) in dependent workbook.
   - ✓ *If referencing more than one cell, select upper-left cell in paste cell range.*
7. Click **Edit** menu .... `Alt`+`E`
8. Click **Paste Special** .... `S`
9. Click **Paste Link** .... `Alt`+`L`
10. Press **Escape** .... `Esc` to end procedure.

SAVE FILE AS A TEMPLATE WITH READ-ONLY RECOMMENDATION

1. Click **File** menu .... `Alt`+`F`
2. Click **Save As** .... `A`
3. Click **Save as type** .... `Alt`+`T`
4. Select **Template** file type . `↑↓`, `Enter`
5. Double-click in **File name** ...... `Alt`+`N`
6. Type filename
7. Click Options .... `Alt`+`P`
8. Click **Read-Only Recommended** .... `Alt`+`R`
9. Click **OK** .... `Enter`
10. Click **Save** .... `Alt`+`S`

Exercise 38

- 3-D Formulas ■ Workbook Sheets
- New (or Duplicate) Workbook Window

NOTES

3-D Formulas

- If you wish to summarize data from several sheets on a totals sheet within the same workbook, you can use **3-D formulas**. The 3-D formulas would be placed on the Totals sheet to summarize all the values in the detail sheets in that workbook. A formula that uses references to values in any sheet or range of sheets in a workbook are often called 3-D references..

- In a 3-D reference:

  - Exclamation points (**!**) separate a sheet name from a cell reference.

  - For example, Sheet3!A2 refers to cell A2 on Sheet 3.

  - Colons (**:**) between worksheet names indicate a range of worksheets. Use quotation marks if the worksheet name contains a space. For example, Sheet3:Sheet5!A1:D1 refers to cells A1 to D1 on Sheet3 through Sheet5.

  - Functions can be combined with 3-D references to create a formula that refers to data on different sheets. You can type a 3-D reference in a formula, or you can insert it by selecting the cells in the worksheet you wish to reference while typing or editing a formula.

  Note the examples that follow and the illustration on the next page:

    =SUM(Sheet1:Sheet3!A1)

    Totals the values in A1 from Sheets 1 to 3.

    =AVERAGE(Sheet3:Sheet5!A1:D4)

    Averages the values in A1:D4 from Sheets 3 to 5.

    =Sheet1!A1+Sheet2!A1

    Adds the values from A1 on Sheets 1 and 2

    ="March Sales"!A5+"April Sales"!A5

    Adds the values from A5 on the March and April Sales sheets.

  - When a formula with a 3-D reference is copied, the cell references will change relative to the new location, but the sheet names will remain constant.

Workbook Sheets

- You can use the sheet tabs or the menu to **copy sheets** and the data they contain. You should copy a sheet when you need to create multiple sheets that contain similar or identical formatting and/or data arrangements.

New (or Duplicate) Workbook Window

- The New Window command on the Windows menu creates a **duplicate workbook** window. When you are working with a workbook with multiple sheets, you can use the duplicate workbook to arrange two sheets on the screen at once.

- Consider the following when working with duplicate workbook windows:

  - Excel places the new workbook window in front of the active workbook window.

    ✓ NOTE: If the active workbook is maximized, you will not be able to see the new workbook.

  - Duplicate workbook windows are noted in the title bar which shows the workbook name followed by a colon and a number. For example, BOOK1**:**1.

- Your system memory determines the number of windows you can have open at one time.

- Closing a duplicate window will not close the workbook.

- You can add or edit data in the original or new window.

3-D Reference Example

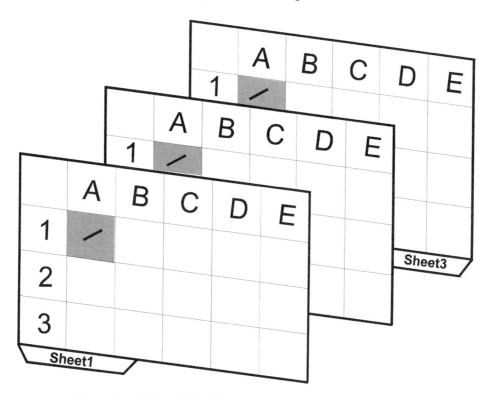

Example: Using 3-D reference to add the values in A1 in a range of sheets.
=SUM(**Sheet1:Sheet3!A1**) or
=Sheet1!A1+Sheet2!A1+Sheet3!A1

> *In this exercise, you will recall the PAYFORM payroll file and add a new worksheet (Totals) to it. In the new worksheet you will enter formulas containing 3-D references to the September, October, and November worksheets. Finally, you will open a new workbook window so you can view the Totals worksheet while you change test values in the September worksheet.*

EXERCISE DIRECTIONS

1. Open ⌨ **PAYFORM** or 💾 **38PAYFORM**.

2. Select and copy the November sheet.

3. Rename November (2) sheet; name it Totals.

4. Move the Totals tab to the right of November.

5. Group the September, October, and November worksheets.

6. Select September and while worksheets are grouped, enter test values in the HOURS WORKED columns for each employee as shown:

   10   for first payroll week

   20   for second payroll week

   30   for third payroll week

   40   for fourth payroll week

7. Deselect grouped sheets and check that test values have been entered on each month's worksheet.

8. Select cell E7 in the TOTALS worksheet and enter a 3-D formula that adds the values in cell E7 in the September, October, and November worksheets.

   HINT: *The completed formula should read:*
   =September!E7+October!E7+November!E7 and 30 (the sum of the test values) should appear in the cell.

9. Repeat step 8 for all employees in each payroll week or copy the formula in E7 to each employee.

10. Open a duplicate workbook window and select the Totals worksheet in the duplicate window.

11. Arrange workbook windows so data in both workbook windows is in view.

12. Select the September worksheet in the original window and change the HOURS WORKED test values in the first payroll week to 50 for each employee.

    ✓ *Note that the Totals worksheet in the duplicate window shows updated values.*

13. Change the HOURS WORKED test values back to 10.

14. Close the duplicate workbook window.

15. Select the Totals worksheet and set it to fit on one page when printed.

16. Print the Totals worksheet.

17. Group the September, October, and November worksheets.

18. Select the September worksheet and delete all test values in HOURS WORKED.

19. Deselect grouped sheets and check that test values have been deleted on each month's worksheet.

20. Select the Totals sheet and check that the formulas are in place in the HOURS WORKED column and that the values are zero.

21. Save **PAYFORM** as a template file.

22. Close the workbook file.

KEYSTROKES

COPY SHEETS WITHIN A WORKBOOK

✓ *Excel will rename sheets that you copy.*

COPY ONE SHEET BY DRAGGING

Press **Ctrl** and drag sheet tab to copy to desired sheet tab position.
Pointer becomes a ⬚ and a black triangle indicates point of insertion.

COPY MULTIPLE SHEETS BY DRAGGING

1. Select sheets to copy.
2. Press **Ctrl** and drag selected sheet tabs to desired sheet tab position.
   Pointer becomes a ⬚ and a black triangle indicates point of insertion.

COPY SHEETS USING THE MENU

1. Select sheets to copy.
2. Click **Edit** menu .... `Alt` + `E`
3. Click **Move or Copy Sheet** .... `M`
4. Click **Before Sheet** .... `Alt` + `B`
5. Select location .... `↓` `↑`
   to insert copied sheet.
6. Click **Create a Copy** .... `Alt` + `C`
7. Click **OK** .... `Enter`

INSERT 3-D REFERENCE IN FORMULA

Using the mouse to select references.

1. Type initial part of formula.
2. Select sheet containing cell(s) to reference.
   ✓ *When you click a sheet tab, its name appears in the formula bar.*
3. Select cell(s) to reference.
   ✓ *When you select the cell(s), the complete 3-D reference appears in the formula bar.*

To reference a range of sheets:

Press **Shift** and click the last worksheet tab to reference.

4. Type or insert remaining parts of formula or repeat steps 2 and 3, if necessary.
5. Press **Enter** .... `Enter`
   ✓ *When you press Enter, Excel returns to the starting worksheet.*

TYPE A 3-D REFERENCE IN FORMULA

1. Type initial part of formula.
2. Place insertion point in formula where reference will be typed.
3. Type the sheet name.
   ✓ *If the sheet name contains a space, type single or double quotes before and after the sheet name.*

To type a 3-D reference for a range of worksheets:

a. Press colon (:) .... `:`
b. Type last sheet name in range.
4. Press exclamation (!) .... `!`
5. Type cell reference or range.
   ✓ *EXAMPLES: Sheet1:Sheet5!A1:A5 'Total Sales'!A1:A5*

OPEN A NEW/DUPLICATE WORKBOOK WINDOW

Creates a new window for active workbook window.

Press **F4** .... `F4`
OR
1. Click **Window** menu .... `Alt` + `W`
2. Click **New Window** .... `N`

CLOSE A DUPLICATE WORKBOOK WINDOW

Double-click workbook window
control menu box ....
OR
1. Select duplicate workbook ..... `Ctrl` + `Tab`
2. Press **Ctrl + F4** .... `Ctrl` + `F4`

Exercise 39

■ Summary

In this exercise, the Old Tyme Bakery wants you to use their Basic Muffin Recipe to create a Low Fat Muffin Recipe and a Low Fat Pumpkin Muffin Recipe. They also want you to use the format to create a new workbook template for a Basic Sweet Dough Recipe. To accomplish this task, the Basic Muffin Recipe must be revised and then saved as a template so that the baker can use it to create other sweet bread recipes.

EXERCISE DIRECTIONS

1. Open ▦ **BAKERY** or 🖫 **39BAKERY**.

2. Rename Sheet1; name it Basic.

3. Copy the Basic sheet twice immediately to the right of the Basic sheet.

4. Rename the new sheets Low Fat and Low Fat Pumpkin.

5. Delete all sheets except Basic, Low Fat, and Low Fat Pumpkin.

6. On the Low Fat sheet, change the title to read: LOW FAT MUFFIN RECIPE

7. On the Low Fat Pumpkin sheet change title to read: LOW FAT PUMPKIN MUFFIN RECIPE

8. Select (group) the Low Fat and Low Fat Pumpkin sheets, then use the Replace feature to change the following ingredients in the selected sheets:

Replace:	With:
milk	skim milk
vegetable oil	apple sauce
egg	egg white

9. Select (group) all sheets and make the following replacements:

Replace:	With:
MEAS.	MEASUREMENT
tbl.	tablespoon
tsp.	teaspoon
AMT	AMOUNT

10. Adjust column widths to fit the longest entry where appropriate.

11. Ungroup the sheets, then make the following changes or additions to the Low Fat Pumpkin Recipe:

    a. Change the skim milk amount to ½ cup.

    b. Add ¾ cup pumpkin, canned.

    c. Add ¼ teaspoon nutmeg.

    d. Add 2 tablespoons walnut pieces.

12. Format the added whole number (2) as a fraction.

13. Copy NEW AMOUNT formula to added ingredients to complete the recipe.

14. Change the DESIRED YIELD value to 48 in all recipes.

15. Save the workbook; or save as **BAKERY**.

16. Print one copy of the workbook.

17. Delete the Low Fat and Low Fat Pumpkin sheets.

18. Delete the data in the AMOUNT, MEASUREMENT, and INGREDIENTS columns.

    ✓ *The formulas in the NEW AMOUNT column will show zeros.*

19. Change the title to read BASIC SWEET DOUGH RECIPE.

    Add amounts and ingredients to the sweet dough recipe as follows:

AMOUNT	MEASUREMENT	INGREDIENTS
¼	ounce	yeast, dry
¼	cup	water (105-115 degrees)
3	large	eggs
½	cup	sweet butter, melted
½	cup	sour cream
½	cup	sugar
1 ½	teaspoon	salt
1	teaspoon	vanilla
4 ½	cups	flour

20. Delete formulas (cells showing zeros) that do not have ingredients.

21. Change the YIELD for the recipe to 2 loaves.

22. Change the DESIRED YIELD to 10.

23. Spell check the worksheet.

24. Save the workbook as a template; name it **BREAD**.

25. Print one copy of the template.

26. Close all workbooks.

Exercise
40

■ Summary

> Mr. Tribuzio administered three additional exams plus a final examination to his class. He needs to revise the worksheet he prepared earlier to include new test data and two new students. In addition, Mr. Tribuzio's supervisor has requested a separate worksheet showing student names and final exam averages.

EXERCISE DIRECTIONS

✓ *Freeze row labels to facilitate data entry.*

1. Open ⌨ **GRADES** or 💾 **40GRADES**.

2. Insert rows in alphabetical sequence for the following two new students: Engler, J., ID# 1472 and Harkins, M., ID# 1475.

3. Enter grades for Quiz 3 for the new students as follows:

   Engler   65

   Harkins   70

4. Copy Quiz Average formula for the new students.

5. Add the new column headings as shown in the illustration on the next page and center all headings.

6. Insert the columns of data, as shown on the right, for TESTS 1, 2, and 3 after the QUIZ AVG. column. Students missing tests earn a zero.

7. Enter a formula to calculate TEST AVG and copy to all students.

8. Enter the FINAL EXAM grades after the TEST AVERAGE column.

9. Find the FINAL AVERAGE for each student. The final exam is worth 1/4, the tests are worth 2/4 or 1/2, and the quizzes are worth ¼ of the final average.

   HINT: (FINAL EXAM+TEST AVERAGE+TEST AVERAGE+QUIZ AVERAGE)/4

10. Format test averages to one decimal place.

11. Check that the summary formulas, at the bottom of the worksheet, include the new students.

12. Extend summary formulas for all new columns.

13. Save the workbook file, or *save as* **GRADES**.

14. Use Copy and Paste to create a separate workbook with student ID numbers and names in column A and B. Adjust column width as necessary.

15. Use Copy and Paste Special (Values) to paste Final Average data from **GRADES** to the new file in column D.

16. Format Final Grades data to one decimal place.

17. Enter MR. VICTOR TRIBUZIO in cell C1.

18. Bold column heading and new title line and center column heading.

19. Save the new file; name it **FINSUM**.

20. Switch to the **GRADES** worksheet. Print one copy of **GRADES** to fit on one sheet.

21. Close the workbook files.

150

	A	B	C	D	E	F	G	H	I	J	K	L
1	ACCOUNTING 101				MR. VICTOR TRIBUZIO							
2	CLASS GRADES											
3											FINAL	FINAL
4	ID#	STUDENT	QUIZ 1	QUIZ 2	QUIZ 3	QUIZ AVG.	TEST 1	TEST 2	TEST 3	TEST AVG.	EXAM	AVERAGE
5	1450	Abbott, B.	78	96	80	84.7	75	0	69		60	
6	1451	Cruz, M.	71	89	80	80.0	85	79	82		85	
7	1472	Engler, J.			65		69	73	79		70	
8	1452	Eugenio, M.	67	79	80	75.3	82	79	85		86	
9	1453	Greene, C.	88		80	84.0	83	84	82		85	
10	1475	Harkins, M.			70		73	79	84		73	
11	1454	Ishkowitz, B.	90	70	73	77.7	72	0	80		70	
12	1455	King, M.	76	90	90	85.3	92	91	95		91	
13	1456	Mohad, J.	84	91	75	83.3	74	73	77		72	
14	1457	Oscar, T.	87	68	80	78.3	85	81	83		89	
15	1458	Quercey, K.	98		70	84.0	72	78	82		75	
16	1459	Santos, C.		80	70	75.0	74	82	83		80	
17	1460	Thompson, S.	75	90	93	86.0	92	91	96		96	
18	1461	Wu, J.	75	87	89	83.7	88	93	95		91	
19												
20		No. of Papers	11	10	14	12						
21		Class Average	80.8	84.0	78.2	81.4						
22		Highest Grade	98	96	93	86						
23		Lowest Grade	67	68	65	75						
24												
25												
26												

NEXT LESSON

Excel

LESSON 7

ADVANCED FEATURES AND FUNCTIONS

Exercises 41-53

- Solve What-If Problems
- Data Tables
- Goal Seek
- Solve What-If Problems (Data Tables)
- PMT Function
- Insert an IF Function
- Paste Function Feature
- Print Compressed Worksheet
- Conditional Sum Wizard
- Audit Formulas
- Enter Dates as Numerical Data
- Format Numerical Dates
- Scenarios
- AutoFormat
- Color Buttons
- Insert Lookup Functions

- Vertical Lookup Function (VLOOKUP)
- Horizontal Lookup Function (HLOOKUP)
- Lock Cells in a Worksheet
- Protect a Sheet
- Hide Data
- Non-Consecutive References in a Function
- Custom Views

Exercise 41

■ Solve What-If Problems ■ Data Tables ■ Goal Seek

NOTES

Solve What-If Problems

■ A **What-if worksheet** is used to answer a question based on one or more factors that might influence the outcome. This exercise contains two methods of solving this type of problem: **data tables** and **Goal Seek**.

Data Tables

■ You can create a **data table** (what-if table) to evaluate a series of possible answers for values you supply in the first row and left-most column of the table. These values are called **substitution values**.

For example, if a company wished to reduce its entire expense budget but was not certain of the effects of each cut, it might test a series of reductions on each of the expense values to allow the manager to decide which reduction was best for the company.

When you select **Table** from the **Data** menu to set up a data table, Excel uses one formula in the upper-left corner of the table to calculate the possible answers using the substitution values. Data tables that require two sets of substitution values (a row and a column) are called **two-input data tables.** Note Illustration A on the following page which shows a two-input data table, the table range, the formula, and the Table dialog box.

■ The format of a two-input data table must meet the following criteria:

- The **column and row input values** that the formula will refer to must be outside the table.

- The **formula** must be in the top-left cell of the table range and must refer to the column and row input values.

- The **substitution values** for the table must be arranged in the first row and column of the table as shown in illustration A.

■ To create the table values, select the **data table range** (which includes the formula), and then select Table from the Data menu and indicate the row and column input cells (the cells that contain the column and row input values) in the Table dialog box.

Illustration A

	A	B	C	D	E	F	G	H	I
1				LITTLE PEOPLE DAYCARE CENTER					
2				EXPENSE REDUCTION ANALYSIS					
3									
4				PRESENT		PERCENTAGE CUT			
5	EXPENSES			BUDGET					
6				47681.136	0.02	0.03	0.04	0.05	
7	Salaries			48654.22					
8	Insurance			7864.54					
9	Utilities			2154.34					
10	Advertising			12437.55					
11	Office expenses			4875.43					
12	Maintenance			5462.33					
13	Other			6409.87					
14									
15	Total			87858.28					
16									
17	row input cell:		2%						
18	column input cell:		48654.22						

Formula in D6 =C18-(C18*C17) refers to input cells below

Data table range D6:H13

Table

Row input cell: $C$17

Column input cell: $C$18

OK   Cancel

Input values

Goal Seek

■ The **Goal Seek** feature, which is accessed from the Tools menu, is another method of answering a what-if question. It will adjust a value in a cell (the changing cell) until a cell containing a formula (the set cell) reaches the value you specify. Illustration B (below) shows the three items to identify for this problem and illustrates the steps in the procedure.

• **Set cell** — Cell reference containing the formula to solve.

• **To value** — Desired outcome or goal for the formula.

• **By changing cell** — The cell that contains a value the Goal Seek command can change to achieve the desired result.

Illustration B

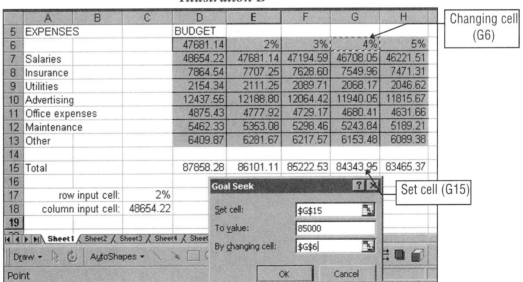

Changing cell (G6)

Set cell (G15)

> *In this exercise, the Little People Daycare Center would like to reduce its budgeted expenses to $85,000. You are to create a data table that will show the effects of 2%, 3%, 4%, and 5% budget cuts and to answer the same question using the Goal Seek method.*

EXERCISE DIRECTIONS

1. Create the worksheet as shown on the following page, or open 🖫 **41REDUCE**.

   Be sure to enter the percentage values as percentages (i.e., 2%, or .02) and to total the Present Budget column for the data in D7:D13.

2. Enter a formula in the top left cell of the table (D6) to calculate the value of an expense after a percent reduction. Use the column and row input values located outside the table that references these values.

   ✓ *The formula must reference the input values in cells C17 and C18. Cell D6 contains the formula =C18-(C18*C17)and displays the answer 47681.14, which is the result for the first calculation. C18 contains the first expense value and C17 contains the first percentage value from the table.*

3. Do the following:
   a. Format entire table and cells that will contain totals for two decimal places.
   b. Format percentage values as percentages with two decimal places.

4. Follow the procedure to create a two-input data table as follows:
   a. Select the data table range, D6:H13.
   b. Click Data.
   c. Click Table.
   d. Enter or select Row input cell, C17.
   e. Enter or select Column input cell, C18.
   f. Click OK.

5. Copy Total formula to each column of values to complete the worksheet.

6. Save the workbook file; name it **REDUCE**.

7. Print one copy.

8. Based on the data in the table, which estimated budget cuts would result in expenses not exceeding $85,000?

9. Format the cells containing the percentage row substitution values to show two decimal places.

10. Use Goal Seek to determine the *exact* percentage cut that would result in a total expense budget of $85,000.
    a. Click Tools, Goal Seek.
    b. Set cell: $G$15 (click on G15)
    c. To value: 85000
    d. By changing cell: $G$6 (click on G6)
    ✓ *The percent in the G6 location will change to the exact % cut necessary to achieve a $85,000 total expense figure.*

11. Based on the Goal Seek procedure, what is the exact percentage cut that will result in expenses of $85,000?

12. Close the workbook file *without* saving the Goal Seek results.

EXCEL **Lesson 7:** Advanced Features and Functions

	A	B	C	D	E	F	G	H	I
1				LITTLE PEOPLE DAYCARE CENTER					
2				EXPENSE REDUCTION ANALYSIS					
3									
4				PRESENT		PERCENTAGE CUT		Row substitution values	
5	EXPENSES		Formula in D6	BUDGET					
6			=C18-(C18*C17) refers to input cells below.	47681.136	0.02	0.03	0.04	0.05	
7	Salaries			48654.22					
8	Insurance			7864.54					
9	Utilities			2154.34					Data table range D6:H13
10	Advertising			12437.55					
11	Office expenses			4875.43					
12	Maintenance			5462.33					
13	Other		Column substitution values.	6409.87					
14									
15	Total			87858.28					
16									
17		row input cell:	2%						
18		column input cell:	48654.22						

KEYSTROKES

TWO-INPUT DATA TABLES (WHAT-IF TABLES)

Data tables generate values that change from one or two values in a formula. For example, a two-input table displays results of changing two values in a formula.

*The **row input cell** is used to indicate an initial input value that the formula will reference.*

*The **column input cell** is used to indicate an initial input value that the formula will also reference.*

✓ *Because Excel uses a table function to generate answers for each pair of substitution values, you cannot edit or delete any single value in the answer set. However, you can delete **all the answers** in the generated data table.*

Although instructions listed below are for a two-input data table, you could also create a one-input data table that would find answers for a single row or column of substitution values.

CREATE A TWO-INPUT DATA TABLE

1. Enter initial value in row input cell.
2. Enter initial value in column input cell.
3. Enter series of substitution values in a column.

4. Enter series of substitution values in a row.
   ✓ *The first value in row and column will contain a single formula.*
5. Click upper-left cell ....
   in table.
6. Type formula
   ✓ *Formula must refer to row and column input cells.*
7. Select all cells in data table range.
   ✓ *Select cells containing formula, substitution values, and cells where results will be displayed.*
8. Click **Data** menu .... Alt + D
9. Click **Table** .... T
10. Click **Row input cell**
    text box .... Alt + R
11. Click row input cell in worksheet.
    OR
    Type reference of input cell.
12. Click **Column Input Cell:** .... Alt + C
13. Click cell in worksheet containing column input data.
    OR
    Type reference of column input cell.
14. Click **OK** .... Enter

FIND A SPECIFIC SOLUTION TO A FORMULA (GOAL SEEK)

1. Enter formula and dependent values in cells.
2. Click **Tools** menu .... Alt + T
3. Click **Goal Seek** .... G
4. Click **Set cell** .... Alt + S
5. Click cell in worksheet containing formula.
   OR
   Type reference of cell containing formula
6. Click **To value** .... Alt + V
7. Type desired formula result value.
8. Click **By changing cell** .... Alt + C
9. Select cell in worksheet containing value to change.
   OR
   Type reference of cell containing value to change.
10. Click **OK** .... Enter
    Excel displays status of goal seeking.

■ Solve What-If Problems (Data Tables) ■ PMT Function

Exercise 42

NOTES

Data Tables

■ The data table created in a what-if problem is used to evaluate different situations based on certain variables, and enables you to find the best solution. For example, if you want to purchase a home and can only afford to spend $1,000 per month on your mortgage payment, you might want to determine the maximum mortgage amount you can afford to borrow and the number of years for which you should apply. A data table should be created showing the mortgage payments for various loan amounts and loan payment periods. Then you can determine what you can afford.

PMT Function

■ Excel provides many built-in functions that make calculations easier. (See Appendix B for a full list of functions.) One of the Financial functions is the **PMT** (payment) **function** that is used to calculate a loan payment when constant payments and interest rates are defined. Therefore, you need the principal (amount of the loan), interest rate and number of payment periods to determine a loan payment. This function can be used to determine your monthly mortgage payment when borrowing money over 30 years at a specified rate of interest. The PMT function uses the following format and contains three required arguments, which are defined on the right.

The arguments for the PMT function and examples for monthly payments are:

=PMT (rate,nper,pv)

rate Interest rate per period (for example, interest/12).

nper Number of payment periods (for example, term*12).

pv Present value—total amount that a series of future payments is worth now (for example, the principal).

✓ *NOTE: The rate and the number of payment periods (nper) must be expressed in the same manner. For example, if you are calculating a monthly payment at a an 8% rate of interest for 25 years, and the interest is expressed as an annual rate, you must enter .08/12 as the monthly rate; and if the term is expressed in years, you must enter 25*12 to get the number of monthly payment periods (nper).*

In this exercise, you will create a mortgage payment table to determine payment amounts at 8% for various principal amounts and for various numbers of years.

EXERCISE DIRECTIONS

1. Create the worksheet below, or open 💾 **42LOAN**.

2. Enter a formula in B4, to find the monthly mortgage payment for $100,000 at 8% for 15 years using the input cell data as follows: column: 100000 (B15)   row: 15 (B16)

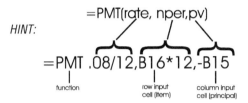

HINT:

=PMT(rate, nper,pv)

=PMT .08/12,B16*12,-B15

function | row input cell (item) | column input cell (principal)

   ✓ *If you type a minus sign before the principal, Excel finds a positive number as the monthly mortgage payment; otherwise, the result will be a negative number.*

3. Format answer for two decimal places.

4. Create a two variable data table by completing the Table dialog box.

5. Save the file; name it **LOAN**.

6. Print one copy.

   ❷ Based on the data in the table, what would be the highest principal you can borrow, with a payment of approximately $950 a month?

7. Use Goal Seek to determine the *exact* mortgage amount you could afford assuming a $950 monthly payment, an 8% interest rate and a 30-year term.

   a. Place cursor on the mortgage payment in the 30-year column closest to but less than $950. (917.21)

   b. Click Tools, Goal Seek.

   c. Set cell: $F$10

   d. To value: 950

   e. By changing cell: Click on Mortgage amount. $B$10.

      ✓ *The mortgage in the B10 location will change to the exact loan available with a $950 payment at 8% interest.*

   ❷ Based on the Goal Seek procedure, what is the exact mortgage loan available for a $950 mortgage payment on a 30-year, 8% mortgage?

8. Close the file *without* saving.

	A	B	C	D	E	F
1	MORTGAGE PAYMENT TABLE AT 8%					
2						
3				TERM IN YEARS		
4			15	20	25	30
5	PRINCIPAL	100000				
6		105000				
7		110000				
8		115000				
9		120000				
10		125000				
11		130000				
12		135000				
13						
14	Input cells					
15	column:	100000				
16	row:	15				

KEYSTROKES

USE THE PMT FUNCTION

Applies the PMT function to find the monthly payment for a principal for a specific number of years.

1. Click cell .... ⬛
   where answer should appear.

2. Press **Equal** .... ⬛

3. Type *PMT* .... 🄿🄼🅃

4. Press **(** (open parenthesis).............. ⬛

5. Type rate */12*............... *rate* 🄸🄸🄸

   ✓ The **rate** is a percentage. You can type the percentage or type the cell reference containing the percentage.

6. Press **,** (comma)............................. ⬛

7. Type term **12* .... *term* 🄸🄸🄸

   ✓ The **term** is the number of years. You can type the number or type the cell reference containing the number.

8. Press **,** (comma)............................. ⬛

9. Type principal.

   ✓ The **principal** is the amount of the loan. You can type the amount or type the cell reference containing the amount. If you want the answer expressed as a positive number, type a minus sign before the principal.

10. Press **)** (close parenthesis).............. ⬛

    EXAMPLES: =PMT(.08/12,20*12,-100000)

    =PMT(A1/12,A2*12,-A3)

11. Press **Enter**............................... Enter

160

NEXT EXERCISE

Exercise

43

■ **Insert an IF Function** ■ **Paste Function Feature**

NOTES

Insert an IF Function

■ An **IF statement** is a logical function that uses a conditional statement to test data. The results of the statement are determined by the truth or falsity of the condition.

■ The format for an IF statement is:

=IF(CONDITION,X,Y)

If the condition is true, the function results in X; if the condition is false, the function results in Y.

■ In this exercise, the teacher uses an IF statement to determine the final grade based on the final average. The passing grade is 65. Therefore, an IF statement is used to test whether the final average is greater than 64.9. If the condition is true, the average is greater than 64.9, the student passes and the word PASS is entered in the function location. If the condition is false, the word FAIL is entered in the function location.

Note the analysis of one of the IF statement formulas used in this problem:

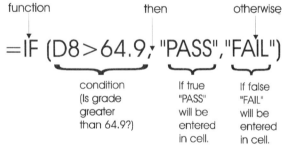

function   then   otherwise

$$=IF (D8>64.9, \text{"PASS"},\text{"FAIL"})$$

| condition (Is grade greater than 64.9?) | If true "PASS" will be entered in cell. | If false "FAIL" will be entered in cell. |

✓ *NOTE: Since PASS and FAIL are labels, you must enclose them in quotation marks (").*

■ IF statements may use the following conditional operators to state the conditional question:

=	Equals	<=	.... Less than or equal to
>	Greater than	>=	....Greater than or equal to
<	Less than	&	...........Used for linking text
<>	Not equal to		

✓ *NOTE: IF statements may be used in combination with OR, AND, and NOT statements to evaluate complex conditions.*

Paste Function Feature

■ The IF function may be entered using the keyboard or by using the Paste Function feature. Press the **Paste Function** button f_x on the Standard toolbar to view the list of functions available in Excel. Select the IF function and complete the dialog box illustrated below. The first section is used to enter the condition or logical test. The second line is for the value or action to be executed if the test is true. The third line is for the value or action to be executed if the test is false. Each line has a collapse box at the end so that ranges can be selected from the workbook.

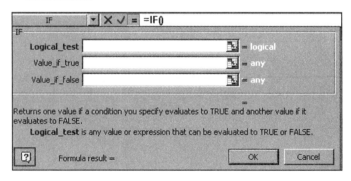

162

In this exercise, you will calculate the FINAL GRADE and CREDITS GRANTED for Victor Tribuzio's class—based on a 65% passing grade—by using IF statements.

EXERCISE DIRECTIONS

1. Open ⌨ FINSUM or 💾 43FINSUM.

2. Insert the following column headings after FINAL AVERAGE:

FINAL   CREDITS
GRADE   GRANTED   NOTE

3. Center the new column headings.

4. Enter an IF statement for the first student in the FINAL GRADE column that will produce the word PASS if the final average is greater than 64.9, and FAIL if it is not.

   Hint: See notes on previous page.

5. Copy the formula to the other students.

6. Use the Paste Function button to enter an IF statement for the first student in the CREDITS GRANTED column that will produce the number three, for three credits, if the final average is greater than 64.9, and zero if it is not.

Hint: *Logical_test: D6>64.9*

Value_if_true: 3

Value_if_false: 0

7. Copy the formula to the other students.

8. Center the new entries in the FINAL GRADE and CREDITS GRANTED columns.

9. Enter an if statement using either method in the NOTE column to enter "Register for Accounting 120," for those who passed the course and "See Dr. Roberts," for those who failed.

10. Delete the row containing Number of Papers.

11. Print one copy of the worksheet

12. Close and save the workbook file; name it **FINSUM**.

	A	B	C	D	E	F	G
1	ACCOUNTING 101		MR. VICTOR TRIBUZIO				
2	CLASS GRADES						
3				FINAL	FINAL	CREDITS	
4	ID#	STUDENT		AVERAGE	GRADE	GRANTED	NOTE
5	1450	Abbott, B.		60.2			
6	1451	Cruz, M.		82.3			
7	1472	Engler, J.		70.6			
8	1452	Eugenio, M.		81.3			
9	1453	Greene, C.		83.8			
10	1475	Harkins, M.		75.1			
11	1454	Ishkowitz, B.		62.3			
12	1455	King, M.		90.4			
13	1456	Mohad, J.		76.2			
14	1457	Oscar, T.		83.3			
15	1458	Quercey, K.		78.4			
16	1459	Santos, C.		78.6			
17	1460	Thompson, S.		92.0			
18	1461	Wu, J.		89.7			
19							
20		No. of Papers		14			
21		Class Average		78.9			
22		Highest Grade		92			
23		Lowest Grade		60.2			

KEYSTROKES

INSERT AN IF FUNCTION USING PASTE FUNCTION

✓ *You can also type a function to insert it.*

1. Click cell .... 〔↕↔〕
   to receive function.

2. Click **Paste Function** button .... 〔*fx*〕
   on Standard toolbar.

3. Select **Logical**................................. 〔↕↓〕
   in **Function category** list.

4. Select **IF** function......... 〔Alt〕+〔N〕, 〔↕↓〕
   in **Function name** list.

5. Click **OK**.................................... 〔Enter〕

6. Type condition in **Logical test** box.

   ✓ *You can click cells in worksheet to insert cell references.*

7. Click **Value_if_true** box.................. 〔Tab〕

8. Type the argument if condition is true.

9. Click **Value_if_false** box .... 〔Tab〕

10. Type the argument if condition is false.

11. Click **OK**................................... 〔Enter〕

INSERT IF FUNCTION USING KEYBOARD AND MOUSE

1. Click cell to receive function........... 〔↕↔〕

2. Type =**IF** .... 〔=〕〔I〕〔F〕

3. Press **(** (open parenthesis) .... 〔(〕

4. Type condition.

5. Press **,** (comma) .... 〔,〕

6. Type action if condition is true.

7. Press **,** (comma) .... 〔,〕

8. Type action if condition is false.

9. Press **)** (close parenthesis) .... 〔)〕

10. Press **Enter**................................ 〔Enter〕

NEXT EXERCISE

Exercise

44

- ■ IF Function ■ Print Compressed Worksheet
- ■ Conditional Sum Wizard

NOTES

IF Function

- An IF statement may be created to perform one calculation if the condition is true, and perform another or no calculation if the condition is false. For example, to find a bonus, if sales are $500,000 or more, multiply the sales by a bonus of .5% otherwise, no bonus.

- When creating a condition using the **greater than** operator (>), care must be taken to use the correct value. For example, when testing if sales are over $500,000, it is necessary to use >499,999 or >=500,000 in the formula so that a value of 500,000 is interpreted as a true condition.

Print Compressed Worksheet

- The **Scaling** option which is available on the Page tab of the Page Setup dialog box, is used to print a worksheet larger or smaller than its actual size. Note the illustration of the scaling option below:

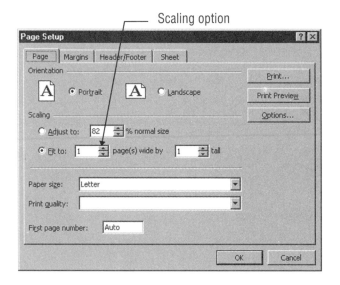

Scaling option

Conditional Sum Wizard

- You can summarize values in a list that meet specific conditions by using the **Conditional Sum Wizard.** The Conditional Sum Wizard is an add-in program that should be on the Tools, Wizard submenu. If Conditional Sum Wizard is not there, you need to install and load it.

- If you have data that is labeled in an adjacent column, such as COMPENSATION and LOCATION in this exercise, you can create formulas that calculate the total compensation for each location.

- To use the Conditional Sum Wizard:

  - Select the range that includes the data, the labels, and column headings, F5:G18 in this exercise.

  - Select Tools, Wizards, Conditional Sum Wizard and accept the data selection screen, Step 1.

  - On the Step 2 screen, as illustrated on the right, select the LOCATION column and the first value Phoenix, and Add Condition.

  - On the Step 3 screen, select Copy just the formula to a single cell.

  - On the Step 4 screen, select the cell to receive the formula.

  - Repeat this procedure for each total you require. Excel will find the values for the location specified, sum the values, and place the result in the location specified. You can also have Excel place the name of the location on the worksheet if desired.

Conditional Sum Wizard—Step 2 of 4

```
┌─────────────────────────────────────────────────────────────┐
│ Conditional Sum Wizard - Step 2 of 4                     [X] │
├─────────────────────────────────────────────────────────────┤
│ Which column contains the values to sum? Select the column   │
│ label.                                                        │
│                                                               │
│ Column to sum:        ┌──────────────────────────┬──┐        │
│                       │ COMPENSATION             │▼ │        │
│                       └──────────────────────────┴──┘        │
│                                                               │
│ Next, select a column you want to evaluate, and then type or  │
│ select a value to compare with data in that column.           │
│                                                               │
│ Column:               Is:          This value:               │
│ ┌────────────────┬─┐  ┌───┬─┐      ┌──────────────────┬─┐    │
│ │ LOCATION       │▼│  │ = │▼│      │ Phoenix          │▼│    │
│ └────────────────┴─┘  └───┴─┘      └──────────────────┴─┘    │
│                                                               │
│        ┌──────────────────────┐  ┌──────────────────────┐    │
│        │    Add Condition     │  │   Remove Condition    │    │
│        └──────────────────────┘  └──────────────────────┘    │
│ ┌───────────────────────────────────────────────────────┐    │
│ │ LOCATION=Phoenix                                       │    │
│ │                                                        │    │
│ │                                                        │    │
│ └───────────────────────────────────────────────────────┘    │
│                                                               │
│ [?]    ┌────────┐  ┌────────┐  ┌────────┐  ┌────────┐        │
│        │ Cancel │  │ < Back │  │ Next > │  │ Finish │        │
│        └────────┘  └────────┘  └────────┘  └────────┘        │
└─────────────────────────────────────────────────────────────┘
```

> *In this exercise, you will find the commission on sales for sales personnel working at AutoMart Used Cars. AutoMart gives a .5% (half of one percent) bonus to agents whose sales are $500,000 or more.*

EXERCISE DIRECTIONS

1. Create the worksheet on the following page or open 💾 **44AUTO**. Set column widths for A-B to AutoFit.

2. Find COMM. (commission).

3. Copy the formula to the remaining employees.

4. Using an IF statement, find the BONUS for those agents whose sales are $500,000 or more.

   HINT: If SALES are greater than or equal to $500,000, compute a .5% bonus on SALES; otherwise, enter zero.

5. Find TOTAL COMPENSATION.

6. Copy the formula to the remaining employees.

7. Format all money columns for currency with no decimal places.

8. Total all money columns.

9. Set column widths, as necessary.

10. Use the Conditional Sum Wizard to determine the Total Compensation for Phoenix.

a. Select the range that includes the COMPENSATION and LOCATION data, and column headings, F5:G18.

b. Select Tools, Wizards, Conditional Sum Wizard and accept the data selection screen on the Step 1 screen. Click Next.

c. On the Step 2 screen, select the LOCATION column as the column to evaluate, =, and the first value Phoenix. Click Add Condition and Next.

d. On the Step 3 screen, select Copy just the formula to a single cell. Click Next.

e. On the Step 4 screen, select the cell to receive the formula by using the collapse button or by entering F22. Click Finish.

11. Repeat this procedure for Tempe and Tuscon, placing the sum in the locations provided on the worksheet.

12. Print one copy compressed to 50% of its actual size.

13. Close and save the workbook file; name it **AUTO**.

	A	B	C	D	E	F	G
1			AUTOMART USED CARS				
2			SEMI-ANNUAL COMMISSION REPORT FOR SALES PERSONNEL				
3							
4			COMM.			TOTAL	
5	NAME	SALES	RATE	COMM.	BONUS	COMPENSATION	LOCATION
6							
7	R. Buick	$640,000	4.00%				Phoenix
8	M. Caddy	$450,000	3.00%				Tempe
9	J. Dodge	$125,000	3.00%				Phoenix
10	O. Ford	$745,000	4.00%				Tucson
11	W. Honda	$0	3.00%				Phoenix
12	V. Jaguar	$550,000	4.00%				Tucson
13	A. Lexus	$210,000	3.00%				Tempe
14	E. Lincoln	$435,000	4.00%				Phoenix
15	B. Nissan	$745,000	4.00%				Tucson
16	C. Pontiac	$532,543	4.00%				Tempe
17	J. Subaru	$334,654	3.00%				Phoenix
18	V. Jeep	$445,875	4.00%				Tucson
19							
20	TOTALS						
21							
22							Phoenix
23							Tempe
24							Tucson

KEYSTROKES

CHANGE SCALE OF PRINTED DATA

1. Click **File** menu .... [Alt]+[F]

2. Click **Page Setup** .... [U]

3. Click **Page** tab .... [Ctrl]+[Tab]

   To reduce or enlarge data on printed sheet:

   a. Click Adjust **to** .... [Alt]+[A]

   b. Type percentage (10-400)

      of **normal size** .... [↓][↑]

4. Click **OK** .... [Enter]

CONDITIONAL SUM WIZARD

1. Select range of data to be summed, range of data labels and column headings.

2. Click **Tools** .... [Alt]+[T]

3. Click **Wizard** .... [W]

4. Click **Conditional Sum** .... [C]

5. Step 1: Click **Next** .... [Enter]

6. Step 2: Select **Column to sum**, if not already displayed. .... [Alt]+[S], [↓]

7. Select **Column** to be checked for conditional values. .... [Alt]+[C], [↓]

8. Select **Is** condition operator .... [Alt]+[I], [↓]

9. Select **This value** label... [Alt]+[T], [↓]

10. Click **Add condition** .... [Alt]+[A]

11. Click **Next** .... [Enter]

12. Step 3: **Select Copy just the formula to single cell** .... [Alt]+[C]

13. Click **Next** .... [Enter]

14. Step 4: Enter cell location for formula in **Type or select a cell and then click Finish** box.......... [Alt]+[T], *cell location*

    OR

    use collapse button to select cell.

15. Click **Finish** .... [Enter]

Exercise 45

■ Audit Formulas

Auditing Toolbar

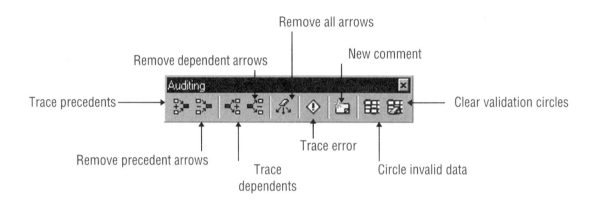

NOTES

Audit Formulas

- If you are using a worksheet created by another person or if you have an error in a formula, you may wish to audit or trace the formulas. When the **Auditing** feature is selected on the **Tools** menu, a list of options appears along with the option to Show the Auditing Toolbar. The toolbar, as shown above, contains icons to trace the **precedents** or **dependents** of a cell in a formula.

- The **precedents** are the cells that are referred to by the formula in the cell you wish to audit. For example, if you select a formula cell and click Trace Precedents, arrows will appear showing the cells used in the formula.

- The **dependents** are the cells that contain formulas that refer to the cell you wish to audit. For example, if you select a cell that is used in a formula and click Trace Dependents, arrows will appear showing the cell with the formula that refers to that active cell.

- In order for the **Trace Error** button to work, the selected cells must contain an error.

- The **New Comment** button provides another way to access the Cell Comments feature discussed in an earlier exercise. Once a cell comment is entered, it can be viewed by moving into the cell.

- The **Circle Invalid Data** and **Clear Validation Circles** buttons can be used to quickly note errors and to clear the error circles from a worksheet.

EMPLOYEE	YEARS OF SENIORITY	SALARY 1996	SALARY 1997	RAISE 1997	1997% INCREASE
Abrahams, Larry	15	45,500.00	49,000.00	3,500.00	7.69%
Barrow, Wilson	11	32,300.00	35,000.00	2,700.00	8.36%
Barrow, Wilson	5	16,500.00	17,500.00	1,000.00	6.06%

Trace Precedents of formula

EMPLOYEE	YEARS OF SENIORITY	SALARY 1996	SALARY 1997	RAISE 1997	1997% INCREASE
Abrahams, Larry	15	45,500.00	49,000.00	3,500.00	7.69%
Barrow, Wilson	11	32,300.00	35,000.00	2,700.00	8.36%
Barrow, Wilson	5	16,500.00	17,500.00	1,000.00	6.06%
D'Agostino, Joe	3	18,500.00	20,000.00	1,500.00	8.11%
Harrison, Reggie	7	21,000.00	23,000.00	2,000.00	9.52%
Ingold, Terry	4	25,600.00	27,000.00	1,400.00	5.47%
Nunez, Maria	8	28,500.00	30,000.00	1,500.00	5.26%
Presser, Carol	9	33,000.00	35,000.00	2,000.00	6.06%
Tse, Sandra	6	25,400.00	27,000.00	1,600.00	6.30%
Wingate, George	10	38,000.00	41,500.00	3,500.00	9.21%
TOTALS		284,300.00	305,000.00	20,700.00	

Trace Dependents of formula

KEYSTROKES

AUDIT WORKSHEET

These audit tools can be used to debug worksheet formulas. Tracer arrows are not saved with the workbook.

SHOW AUDITING TOOLBAR

1. Click **Tools** menu .... Alt + T
2. Click **Auditing** .... U
3. Click **Show Auditing Toolbar** .... S

TRACE DEPENDENT FORMULAS

1. Select cell containing data used by a formula.
2. Click **Trace Dependents** button ...... on Auditing toolbar.
   ✓ *If tracer arrows do not appear, deselect the Hide All option on the View sheet in the Tools, Options dialog box.*

REMOVE DEPENDENT TRACER ARROWS

1. Select cell containing data used by a formula.
2. Click **Remove Dependent Arrows** button .... on Auditing Toolbar.

TRACE PRECEDENT DATA AND FORMULAS

1. Select cell containing formula.
2. Click **Trace Precedents** button .... on Auditing toolbar.

REMOVE PRECEDENT TRACER ARROWS

1. Select cell containing formula.
2. Click **Remove Precedent Arrows** button .... on Auditing toolbar.

REMOVE ALL TRACER ARROWS

Click **Remove All Arrows** button .... on Auditing toolbar.

ATTACH COMMENT TO A FORMULA

1. Select cell to receive comment.
2. Click **New Comment** button .... on Auditing toolbar.
3. Enter comment.
4. Click **OK** .... Enter

The Claudine Manufacturing Company is changing their policy on salary increases to one based on seniority. Employees who have more than five years of service will receive a 7.25% raise; otherwise, they will receive a 4.5% raise.

In this exercise, you will do a salary analysis by comparing the amount of SALARY and % INCREASE each employee received this year over last year and then compute the new raise and salary. Auditing will be used to check formulas.

EXERCISE DIRECTIONS

1. Create the worksheet on the right exactly as shown or open 🖫 **45RAISE**.

2. Freeze titles vertically at column E.

3. Find:
   - RAISE 1997 (from 1996 to 1997)
   - 1997% INCREASE (based on 1996 salary)

4. Copy the formula to the remaining employees.

5. Using YEARS OF SENIORITY as a condition, create an IF statement to enter the percent of the raise (7.25% or 4.5%) in the 1998% INCREASE column.

   HINT: If YEARS OF SENIORITY is greater than five, .0725; otherwise, .045.

6. Find RAISE 1998 by using the 1998% INCREASE and SALARY 1997.

7. Format all money columns for two decimal places and all percent columns for two-place percents.

8. Find SALARY 1998.

   HINT: 1997 salary + 1998 raise

9. Copy the formula to the remaining employees.

10. Total all money columns.

11. Set column widths, as necessary.

12. Clear the freeze.

13. Select Tools, Auditing and show the Auditing Toolbar.

14. Select the Raise 1997 formula in F8 and Trace Precedents.

    ✓   *Arrows to the cells referenced in the formula display.*

15. Remove the precedent arrows.

16. Select the Salary 1997 figure in E8 and Trace Dependents.

    ✓   *Arrows to the formula cells that use E8 display.*

17. Remove the dependent arrows.

18. Select several other formula or data locations and trace precedents or dependents.

19. Remove all arrows.

20. Select the Raise 1998 formula in I8 and attach the following New Comment:

    Raise is computed at 7.25% for employees with more than five years of service.

    Employees with less than five years receive a 4.5% raise.

21. Format all money columns for commas.

22. Print one copy to fit on a page.

23. Save and close the file; name it **RAISE**.

	A	B	C	D	E	F	G	H	I	J
1				CLAUDINE MANUFACTURING COMPANY						
2				ANALYSIS OF SALARY INCREASES						
3										
4										
5			YEARS OF	SALARY	SALARY	RAISE	1997%	1998%	RAISE	SALARY
6	EMPLOYEE		SENIORITY	1996	1997	1997	INCREASE	INCREASE	1998	1998
7										
8	Abrahams, Larry		15	45500.00	49000.00					
9	Barrow, Wilson		11	32300.00	35000.00					
10	Barrow, Wilson		5	16500.00	17500.00					
11	D'Agostino, Joe		3	18500.00	20000.00					
12	Harrison, Reggie		7	21000.00	23000.00					
13	Ingold, Terry		4	25600.00	27000.00					
14	Nunez, Maria		8	28500.00	30000.00					
15	Presser, Carol		9	33000.00	35000.00					
16	Tse, Sandra		6	25400.00	27000.00					
17	Wingate, George		10	38000.00	41500.00					
18										
19	TOTALS									

Exercise 46

■ Enter Dates as Numerical Data ■ Format Numerical Dates

NOTES

Enter Dates as Numerical Data

■ Excel recognizes the number format you desire based on your data entry. For example, if you enter 25%, the entry is recognized as a value with a percent format. Similarly, if you enter 12/24/97 without a label prefix, the entry is recognized as numerical data in date format.

■ Dates can be entered as label data by using a label prefix. However, when there is a need to add or subtract dates, they must be entered without label prefixes as standard numerical data.

■ Dates entered in one of the standard formats are automatically recognized as dates and assigned a **serial value**. The serial value is the number of days the date represents counting from January 1, 1900. Therefore, 1/1/1900, is given a serial value of 1 and 1/30/1900 is given a serial value of 30. This system allows you to add or subtract dates and obtain the correct valuation.

■ The current date can be entered on any worksheet by pressing Ctrl+; (semicolon).

Format Numerical Dates

■ Once you enter a date as a numerical value, you may change the date format, to any of those below. Select Format, Cells and the Number tab. Then select Date from the Category list and the desired date format from the Type list. Excel 97 uses March 4, 1997 to illustrate date formats.

Standard Date Formats

3/4	4-MAR	3/4/97 1:30 PM
3/4/97	4-MAR-97	3/4/97 13:30
03/04/97	04-MAR-97	M
	MAR-97	M-97
	March-97	
	March 4, 1997	

■ As you will note in the illustration below, your date entry, the formula bar entry, and the format may all be different. If you enter a date without the year, the current year is assumed for numerical purposes. If you enter a month and year and no date, the first of the month is assumed for numerical purposes. Excel 97 assumes the year 2000 if you enter 00. Therefore, if you intend to enter 1900, you must enter the full year.

■ To view a serial value for a date, you can format the date as a number.

Your Entry	Formula Bar	Format	Displays	Numerical Value
January 1, 1900	1/1/1900	March 4, 1997	January 1, 1900	1
12/24/00	12/24/2000	03/4/97	12/24/00	36884
5/98	5/1/1998	MAR-97	MAY-98	35916
12/30	12/30/1997	4-MAR	30-DEC	35794

KEYSTROKES

ENTER A DATE AS NUMERICAL DATA

   ✓ *Dates, entered as numerical data, are right–aligned and can be calculated.*

1. Select cell to receive date.

   To enter current date:

   Press **Ctrl + ;** (semicolon) ...... `Ctrl`+`;`

   To enter a specific date:

   Type date in valid format.

   You may use the following formats:

   m/d/yy .... *(e.g. 6/24/96)*

   d-mmm .... *(e.g. 24-Jun)*

   d-mmm-yy .... *(e.g. 24-Jun-96)*

   mmm-yy .... *(e.g. Jun-96)*

2. Press **Enter** .... `Enter`

   ✓ *If Excel displays number signs (######), the column is not wide enough to display the date. To see the entry, double–click the right border of the column heading.*

FORMAT NUMERICAL DATES

1. Select cells containing numerical dates to format.

2. a. Click **Format** menu............ `Alt`+`O`

   b. Click **Cells**................................ `E`

   OR

   a. Right–click any selected cell.

   b. Click **Format Cells** .... `F`

3. Click **Number** tab.................. `Ctrl`+`Tab`

4. Select **Date** .... `Alt`+`C`, `↕` in **Category** list.

5. Select desired format.................. `↕`

6. Click **OK** .... `Enter`

In this exercise, you will modify the stock analysis worksheet to find how many days each stock was held, and to determine the annual rate of return. In addition, you will modify the named range, PRINTALL, to include the larger worksheet and use the Auditing feature to check formulas.

EXERCISE DIRECTIONS

1. Open ⌨ **INVEST** or open 💾 **46INVEST**.

2. Center all column headings and bold titles and column headings.

3. When the dates were entered they were automatically recognized as numerical dates.

   To view the serial values:

   Format the DATE BOUGHT dates to numbers using Format, Cells, Number, Number.

   To format dates:

   Select dates in DATE BOUGHT and DATE SOLD columns. Format dates to 4-MAR-1997 format using Format, Cells, Number, Date.

4. Insert a column entitled DAYS HELD between DATE SOLD and SELLING PRICE columns.

5. Use the Data, Validation commands to clear all settings for the DAYS HELD column by allowing any value to be entered in the cell.

6. Find DAYS HELD.
   HINT: DATE SOLD-DATE BOUGHT
   *   (Format column F to General number format.)*

7. Copy the formula to the remaining companies.

8. Add a column, entitled ANNUAL YIELD, after the % GAIN OR LOSS column.

9. Based on a 365-day year, find the ANNUAL YIELD.
   HINT: (%GAIN OR LOSS/DAYS HELD)*365

10. Format the ANNUAL YIELD for a two-place percent.

11. Copy the formula to the remaining companies and to the TOTALS line.

12. An error message should appear in the TOTALS line for ANNUAL YIELD. Use the Tools, Auditing commands to trace the precedents of the formula. Note that the formula refers to the total of DAYS HELD which has not been calculated.

13. Add the AVERAGES line to the worksheet under the TOTALS line.

14. Find the AVERAGES of the DAYS HELD to GAIN OR LOSS columns.

15. Edit the formula for the TOTAL of the ANNUAL YIELD column to reference the average of the DAYS HELD column.

16. Edit the named range PRINTALL to include the entire worksheet.

17. Save the file; name it **INVEST**.

18. Print one copy to fit on a page using the range PRINTALL.

19. Close the workbook file.

	A	B	C	D	E	F	G	H	I	J	K
1				ROCHELLE MARTLING							
2				INVESTMENT TRANSACTIONS FOR 1997							
3											
4	COMPANY			DATE	DATE	DAYS	SELLING		GAIN OR	% GAIN	ANNUAL
5	NAME	SYMBOL	SHARES	BOUGHT	SOLD	HELD	PRICE	COST	LOSS	OR LOSS	YIELD
6											
7	Focus Motors	FM	100	15-Jan-96	28-Feb-97		6950.75	7698.86	-748.11	-9.72%	
8	General Oil	GNO	200	06-Mar-96	03-Apr-97		7656.87	6567.15	1089.72	16.59%	
9	IVM	IVM	100	18-Dec-96	31-Jul-97		8976.85	9987.08	-1010.23	-10.12%	
10	Microtech	MIC	200	05-Jan-97	03-Oct-97		11435.98	8656.45	2779.53	32.11%	
11	American Electric	AE	300	09-Mar-97	04-Nov-97		5467.43	4132.75	1334.68	32.30%	
12											
13	TOTALS						40487.88	37042.29	3445.59	9.30%	
14	AVERAGES										
15											
16											

Format dates to display as illustrated

Exercise

47

■ **Scenarios**
■ **AutoFormat** ■ **Color Buttons**

NOTES

Scenarios

■ We used Data tables and Goal Seek in Exercises 41 and 42 to perform a what-if analysis. Another tool provided by Excel for forecasting various outcomes is the **scenario** feature. You can create and save different groups of values that represent different results due to factors that are yet unknown. For example, you can use scenarios to set up worst case, average case, and best case results for a company's income statement. All the scenarios can be summarized, printed, and compared in a summary worksheet.

■ To create a scenario, select **Scenarios** from the Tools menu, click Add, name the scenario, set the Changing cells, and click OK to add it to the list. You can delete, edit, merge, or summarize scenarios from the Scenario Manager dialog box as illustrated below.

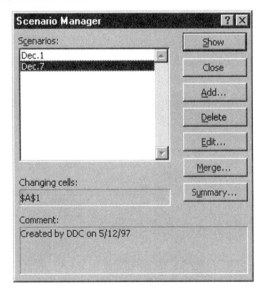

■ A summary of the results of all the scenarios for a range of data can be automatically prepared by using the Summary option. The summary is created on a new sheet in the workbook.

AutoFormat

■ Excel provides built-in formats that can be applied to a range of data. These formats, **AutoFormats**, include number formatting, fonts, borders, patterns, colors, alignments, row heights, and column widths. AutoFormats can give the worksheet a professional, organized appearance.

■ The AutoFormat dialog box provides a selection of table formats that may be applied to a range of data. (See illustration on the next page.) Any of the AutoFormats may be customized through the Options dialog box.

Color Buttons

■ The **Color buttons** on the Formatting toolbar provide a palette of colors that can be used to set the Fill Color or the Font Color in a selected cell or range of cells. (See the illustrations below.)

■ If you are not connected to a color printer, your AutoFormat or color settings may not print properly.

Fill Color button   *Font Color button*

AutoFormat Dialog Box

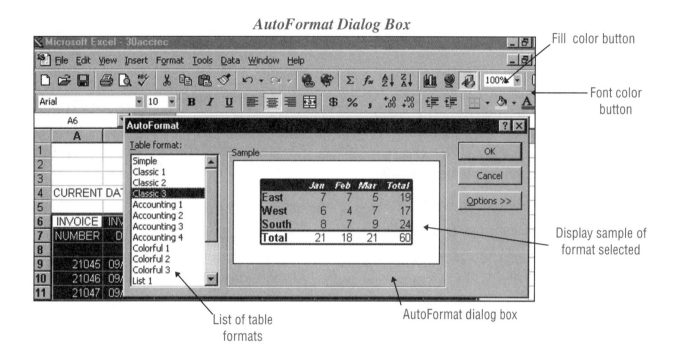

Fill color button

Font color button

Display sample of format selected

AutoFormat dialog box

List of table formats

In this exercise, Kitchen King Stores wants to determine how many days, as of today (December 1, 1997), the accounts receivable invoices have been unpaid. A late fee of 1% is to be calculated on accounts unpaid for 50 days or more. A scenario will be created to determine the changes in late fees if the bills are sent out on December 7. The worksheet will be formatted using AutoFormat and Color buttons.

Note: Accounts Receivable are records for customers who owe money to a company. Aging of accounts receivable is done to determine how many days a payment is overdue.

EXERCISE DIRECTIONS

1. Create the worksheet on the following page, or open 🖫 **47AR**.

2. Find the DAYS UNPAID.
   HINT: DAYS UNPAID = CURRENT DATE-INVOICE DATE
   ✓ *The reference to the current date should be an absolute reference.*

3. Use an IF statement to find a 1% LATE FEE only if the days unpaid are greater than 49.

4. Copy the formula to the remaining invoices.

5. Find AMOUNT DUE and copy to all invoices.

6. Total all money columns. Set money columns to two decimal places.

7. Add the current scenario to the Scenario Manager by doing the following:
   a. Click Tools, Scenarios.
   b. Click Add.
   c. Enter Dec 1 as the Scenario name.
   d. Set C4 as the changing cell. Click OK.
   e. Click OK to accept 12/1/97 as the Scenario Value.

8. Click Add to create a new scenario for Dec 7, using C4 as the changing cell and 12/7/97 as the Scenario Value. Close the Scenario Manager.

9. Note the total of the LATE FEE column.

10. Open the Scenario Manager, select the Dec 7 scenario and click Show. Note the total of the LATE FEE column.

11. To create a summary of the scenarios:
    a. Click Tools, Scenarios.
    b. Click Summary.
    c. With the Scenario Summary selected, select the LATE FEE column G9:G19 as the result cells. Click OK.
    The result cells are the cells you wish to see summarized in the scenario summary. A new sheet will appear summarizing the values for the scenarios.

12. Switch to Sheet1.

13. To AutoFormat the worksheet:
    a. Select column D and delete the column.
    b. Select the column headings and data, in the range A6:G21.
    c. Click Format, AutoFormat.
    d. Select each format to view the available formats.
    e. Select the Classic 3 format.
    f. Click OK.

14. Select the heading range A1 to G4 and do the following:
    a. Format the text for bold type.
    b. Change the background color to dark blue.
    c. Change the text color to white.

15. Print one copy of Sheet1 on one page.

16. Print one copy of the Scenario Summary.

17. Save and close the workbook file; name it **AR**.

	A	B	C	D	E	F	G	H
1			KITCHEN KING STORES					
2			ACCOUNTS RECEIVABLE AGING REPORT					
3								
4	CURRENT DATE:		12/01/97					
5								
6	INVOICE	INVOICE			DAYS			AMOUNT
7	NUMBER	DATE	CUSTOMER		UNPAID	AMOUNT	LATE FEE	DUE
8								
9	21045	09/22/97	Martha Schef			475.43		
10	21046	09/23/97	Red's Restaurant			321.43		
11	21047	09/24/97	Martha Schef			543.98		
12	21049	10/02/97	Kay's Inn			32.45		
13	21050	10/03/97	Marvin Diamant			1324.32		
14	21052	10/06/97	Red's Restaurant			124.98		
15	21054	10/15/97	George Lopez			564.12		
16	21056	10/18/97	Kay's Inn			187.65		
17	21062	10/28/97	Marvin Diamant			454.56		
18	21079	11/05/97	Sam Hopkins			308.21		
19	21087	11/20/97	Red's Restaurant			163.28		
20								
21	TOTALS							

KEYSTROKES

APPLY AUTOFORMAT

1. Select range of data to be formatted.
2. Click **Format** menu .... `Alt`+`O`
3. Click **AutoFormat** .... `A`
4. Select desired format.
5. Click **OK** .... `Enter`

APPLY COLOR TO FILL CELL

1. Select object or range of cells.
2a. Click **Fill Color** button arrow .... `🎨·`
   on Formatting toolbar
 b. Select color .... `↕·`
   OR
 a. Click **Format** menu .... `Alt`+`O`
 b. Click **Cells** .... `E`
 c. Select **Patterns** tab .... `Ctrl`+`Tab`
 d. Click **Color** .... `Alt`+`C`
 e. Select color .... `↓``↑`
3. Click **OK** .... `Enter`

APPLY COLOR TO CELL FONT

1. Select range of data.
2. a. Click on **Font Color** button
      arrow .... `A·`
   b. Select color .... `↕·`
   OR
   a. Click **Format** menu .... `Alt`+`O`
   b. Click **Cells** .... `E`
   c. Select **Font** tab .... `↤↦`
   d. Click **Color** .... `Alt`+`C`
   e. Select color .... `↕·`
3. Click **OK** .... `Enter`

CREATE A SCENARIO

1. Click **Tools** .... `Alt`+`T`
2. Click **Scenarios** .... `E`
3. Click **Add** .... `A`
4. In **Scenario name** box, enter name.
5. In **Changing cells** box, select or enter
   cell references .... `Alt`+`C`, *cells*

6. Click **OK** .... `Enter`
7. In **Scenario Values** dialog box, enter
   values for changing cell(s).
8. Click **OK** .... `Enter`

TO VIEW A SCENARIO

1. Click **Tools** .... `Alt`+`T`
2. Click **Scenarios** .... `E`
3. Select a scenario .... `↓``↑`
4. Click **Show** .... `Alt`+`S`

TO CREATE A SCENARIO SUMMARY

1. Click **Tools** .... `Alt`+`T`
2. Click **Scenarios** .... `E`
3. Click **Summary** .... `Alt`+`U`
4. With **Scenario Summary** selected,
   select the range of result cells.
5. Click **OK** .... `Enter`

Exercise 48

■ Insert Lookup Functions

NOTES

Insert Lookup Functions

■ The **lookup functions** (VLOOKUP and HLOOKUP) select an appropriate value from a table and enter it into a location on the worksheet. For example, the VLOOKUP function may be used to look up taxes on a tax table to create a payroll, or to look up postage rates to complete a bill of sale.

■ The table containing the data to be looked up must be created in a separate location on the worksheet. The mortgage payment table, which was created in Exercise 42 (illustrated below), may be used as the table for a lookup function.

■ As with all formulas, the lookup function is entered in the location on the worksheet that requires an answer from a table.

■ There are two ways to look up data, depending on the way the data is arranged: **vertically** or **horizontally**.

• **VLOOKUP** (vertical lookup) looks up data in a particular *column* in the table, while

• **HLOOKUP** (horizontal lookup) looks up data in a particular *row* in the table.

■ The VLOOKUP function uses the following format and contains three arguments (parts), defined below:

=VLOOKUP(*lookup_value,table-range,column-position*)

• **Lookup_Value** is text, a value, or a cell reference of the item you are looking for (*search item*) and should be in the first column of the VLOOKUP table. Numerical search items should be listed in ascending order.

	A	B	C	D	E	F	G	H
1	MORTGAGE PAYMENT TABLE AT 8%							
2								
3				TERM IN YEARS				
4			15	20	25	30		
5	PRINCIPAL	100000	955.65	836.44	771.82	733.76		
6		105000	1003.43	878.26	810.41	770.45		
7		110000	1051.22	920.08	849.00	807.14		Table range B5:F12
8		115000	1099.00	961.91	887.59	843.83		
9		120000	1146.78	1003.73	926.18	880.52		
10		125000	1194.57	1045.55	964.77	917.21		
11		130000	1242.35	1087.37	1003.36	953.89		
12		135000	1290.13	1129.19	1041.95	990.58		
13		1	2	3	4	5		Column positions
14								

- **TABLE-RANGE** is the range reference or range name of the lookup table in which the search is to be made. If the lookup function is to be copied, the range should be expressed as an absolute reference.

- **COLUMN-POSITION** is the column number in the table from which the matching value should be returned. The far left column has a position number of one; the second column has a position number of two, etc.

  ✓ *NOTE:* *Column positions are counted from the left column in the range, not from the left column of the worksheet.*

■ For example, note the outlined lookup table on the left. To look up the mortgage payment for a mortgage amount of $105,000 for 25 years at 8%, a lookup formula would be created as follows:

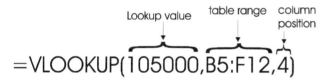

■ In looking up numeric data, the lookup function returns to the formula location:

- The value from the table (in this case 810.41), or

- The largest value less than or equal to the search item.

■ When looking up more than one item or copying the lookup formula, make sure the formula uses the cell reference, not the value, as the search item. In addition, the range should be absolute so that the table range remains constant.

EXAMPLE:

In this exercise, you will retrieve the mortgage table created earlier and develop a worksheet for the Dream Home Realty Company that calculates the mortgage amount and the customer's monthly mortgage payment for 25 or 30 years. Use the VLOOKUP function to enter mortgage payments depending on the mortgage amount.

EXERCISE DIRECTIONS

1. Open ⌨ **LOAN** or 💾 **48LOAN**.

   REMINDER: The values in cells B4, B15, and B16 are needed to compute those in the table. Do not delete or change these values.

2. Create the DREAM HOME REALTY COMPANY worksheet below the MORTGAGE PAYMENT TABLE, as illustrated on the next page.

3. Center all column titles and set column widths to AutoFit.

4. Find MORTGAGE AMOUNT by subtracting the DOWN PAYMENT from the CONTRACT PRICE.

5. Copy the formula to the remaining customers.

6. Using the VLOOKUP function, find the monthly payment for the first customer (for 25 years) based on the amount to be mortgaged.

   ✓ *Note the outlined range and column positions in the illustration.*

7. Format the result for two decimal places.

8. Copy the formula to the remaining customers.

9. Using the VLOOKUP function, find the monthly payment for the first customer (for 30 years) based on the amount to be mortgaged.

   ✓ *Note the range and column position illustrated.*

10. Format the result for two decimal places.

11. Copy the formula to the remaining customers.

12. Select the Dream Home Realty Company title and column headings. Do the following:
    a. Set the color to yellow.
    b. Set the font color to black.
    c. Bold the text.

13. Select the DREAM HOME REALTY COMPANY portion of the worksheet.

14. Print one copy of the selection to fit on one page.

15. Close and save the file; name it **DREAM**.

	A	B	C	D	E	F	G	H	I
1		MORTGAGE PAYMENT TABLE AT 8%							
2									
3				TERM IN YEARS					
4		955.65	15	20	25	30			
5	PRINCIPAL	100000	955.65	836.44	771.82	733.76	← Table range		
6		105000	1003.43	878.26	810.41	770.45	B5:F12		
7		110000	1051.22	920.08	849.00	807.14			
8		115000	1099.00	961.91	887.59	843.83			
9		120000	1146.78	1003.73	926.18	880.52			
10		125000	1194.57	1045.55	964.77	917.21			
11		130000	1242.35	1087.37	1003.36	953.89			
12		135000	1290.13	1129.19	1041.95	990.58			
13		1	2	3	4	5	← Column positions		
14	Input cells								
15	column:	100000							
16	row:	15			Lookup values				
17									
18		DREAM HOME REALTY COMPANY					VLOOKUP functions		
19							MONTHLY	MONTHLY	
20			CONTRACT	DOWN	MORTGAGE		PAYMENT	PAYMENT	
21	CUSTOMER		PRICE	PAYMENT	AMOUNT		25 YEARS	30 YEARS	
22									
23	Roberts, John		185000	80000					
24	Crimmins, Barbara		255000	120000					
25	Sloan, Greg		320000	200000					
26	Chang, Charles		195000	80000					
27	Panetta, Anthony		215000	105000					

KEYSTROKES

INSERT A VLOOKUP OR HLOOKUP FUNCTION USING FUNCTION WIZARD

✓ You can also type a function to insert it.

1. Click cell............................ [✛]
   to receive function.

2. Click **Function Wizard** button .... [fx]
   on Standard toolbar.

3. Select **Lookup & Reference** .... Alt + C , [↕]
   in **Function Category** list.

4. Select **VLOOKUP** or **HLOOKUP** .... Alt + N , [↕]
   in **Function Name** list.

5. Click **OK** .... Enter

6. Type item in **lookup_value** box.
   ✓ Item can be an actual column item or a reference to a cell containing the column item. You can click cell in worksheet to insert cell reference.

7. Click **table_array** box .... Tab

8. Type reference to table range.
   ✓ You can select range in worksheet to insert cell references.

9. Click **col_index_num** box .... Tab

10. Type the column position.

11. Click **OK** .... Enter

Exercise 49

■ Vertical Lookup Function (VLOOKUP)

NOTES

Vertical Lookup Function (VLOOKUP)

■ In Exercise 48, you created lookup formulas using the cell references of the table range. It is possible to use a named range rather than the cell reference of the table. When you copy a formula containing a named range, the reference will not change, and will always refer to the original table location. An absolute reference is not required if a named range is used in a lookup formula.

■ When the items in a lookup table are not in ascending order (A-Z), you must add the FALSE argument to the VLOOKUP function. Otherwise, VLOOKUP may return inaccurate results.

Lookup value   table range   column position

=Example: VLOOKUP(A1,Table,2,FALSE)

The FALSE argument requires VLOOKUP to find an exact match in the first column of the lookup table. If an exact match is not found, VLOOKUP returns the #VALUE! error message.

In this exercise, you will create an inventory valuation for Cruiser Repair Shop. On March 1, Cruiser did an inventory of the parts they had on hand by item number. Use the VLOOKUP function to find the item name and unit cost using a table created from a previously saved worksheet. Use either a named table range or a range reference with absolute references in your formula.

EXERCISE DIRECTIONS

1. Open ⌨ **INVEN** or 💾 **49INVEN**.

2. Edit the title as shown.

3. Create the top shaded portion of the worksheet as illustrated by inserting rows to accommodate the new data.
   ✓ *Item numbers should be entered as label data in both parts of the worksheet.*

4. Center all column titles appropriately.

5. Name the range A22:G33, ITEM.

6. Using the VLOOKUP function and the range name ITEM, find the ITEM NAME based on the item number.
   ✓ *Since the item numbers in the ITEM table are not in ascending order, you must include the FALSE argument in each VLOOKUP function. See Notes above.*

7. Copy the formula to the remaining items.

8. Using the VLOOKUP function, find the UNIT COST based on the item number.

9. Copy the formula to the remaining items.

10. Find:
    - VALUE (COST*QUAN) and copy the formula to the remaining items.
    - TOTAL of the VALUE column (format for two decimal places).

11. Select the top portion of the worksheet and copy it to a new worksheet using the Paste Special, Values option.

12. In the new worksheet, select the three-line title and column headings and set to bold.

13. Right-align the Unit Cost, Quan, and Value column headings.

14. Since formats do not copy with the Paste Values option, format the UNIT COST and VALUE columns for two decimal places.

15. Save the workbook file, name it **VALUE**.

16. Print one copy of **VALUE**.

17. Close the workbook file.

18. Close **INVEN** without saving the file.

	A	B	C	D	E	F	G
1		CRUISER REPAIR SHOP					
2		INVENTORY VALUATION					
3		MARCH 1, 199-					
4							
5	ITEM	ITEM		UNIT			
6	NUMBER	NAME		COST	QUAN	VALUE	
7							
8	142				8		
9	175				12		
10	421				4		
11	572				4		
12	659				6		
13	932				25		
14							
15	TOTAL						
16							
17							
18							
19	ITEM			UNIT	SELLING		
20	NUMBER	ITEM		COST	PRICE	MARKUP	MARKUP %
21							
22	142	carburetor		120.00	168.00	48.00	40.00%
23	321	spark plugs		2.00	3.00	1.00	50.00%
24	093	tires		55.00	77.00	22.00	40.00%
25	393	brakes		60.00	84.00	24.00	40.00%
26	659	alarm		125.00	195.00	70.00	56.00%
27	572	mats		45.00	63.00	18.00	40.00%
28	175	battery		45.00	70.00	25.00	55.56%
29	421	radio		185.00	265.00	80.00	43.24%
30	932	fan belt		15.00	28.00	13.00	86.67%
31	254	oil filter		18.00	30.00	12.00	66.67%
32	754	air filter		23.00	35.00	12.00	52.17%
33	344	antifreeze		6.00	10.00	4.00	66.67%
34	1	2	3	4	5	6	0
35	AVERAGES			58.25	85.67	27.42	53.08%
36	HIGHEST VALUE			185.00	265.00	80.00	86.67%
37	LOWEST VALUE			2.00	3.00	1.00	40.00%

Exercise 50

- **■ Horizontal Lookup Function (HLOOKUP)**
- **■ Lock Cells in a Worksheet**
- **■ Protect a Worksheet**

NOTES

Horizontal Lookup Function (HLOOKUP)

- While VLOOKUP looks up data in a particular *column* in the table, HLOOKUP looks up data in a particular *row* in the table.

- The HLOOKUP function uses the same format and contains the same three arguments (parts) as VLOOKUP.

  =HLOOKUP(item,table-range,row-position)

  - **ITEM** is text, a value, or a cell reference of the item you are looking for (**search item)** and should be in the first row of the (HLOOKUP) table. Numerical search items should be listed in ascending order.

  - **TABLE-RANGE** is the range reference or range name of the lookup table in which the search is made.

  - **ROW-POSITION** is the row number in the table from which the matching value should be returned. The top row has a position number of one; the second row has a position number of two, and so forth.

Lock Cells in a Worksheet

- It is possible to **protect**, or **lock**, an entire worksheet, individual cells, or a range of cells from accidental changes or unauthorized use. The protection feature locks the cells so that they cannot be changed.

- By default, all cells are locked in a worksheet. The locked status, however, only becomes enabled when you protect the worksheet. Therefore, if you need to keep certain cells accessible in a protected worksheet, these cells must be unlocked *before* the worksheet is protected. To lock or unlock cells in a worksheet, select the cell range then select **Cells** from the <u>F</u>ormat menu, and click the Protection tab.

Protect a Worksheet

- A worksheet is protected by selecting <u>T</u>ools, **Protection**, **Protect Sheet**. The Protect sheet dialog box, illustrated below, allows you to protect the contents (of cells), objects, (text boxes and graphic objects), or scenarios (defined variations of the worksheet discussed in the last exercise), and to set a password.

- When a worksheet is protected, the following message will appear when you try to change the contents of protected cells: "The cell or chart you are trying to change is protected and therefore read-only." When protection is enabled, Excel will let you copy, but not move, locked cells to an unlocked area of the worksheet. Locked cells cannot receive moved or copied cells.

✓ *IMPORTANT: If you set a password when protecting a worksheet and you forget the password, you will not be able to make changes in the worksheet. However, you can usually access most protected data by copying it and then pasting it into a new sheet.*

In this exercise, you will create a worksheet listing daily sales for a mail order firm. As an employee of the J.J. Carrot Company, you are to compute the sales tax and shipping charges for all orders. Using HLOOKUP, you will compute the postage and sales tax required, depending on the zone to which the package is being shipped.

EXERCISE DIRECTIONS

1. Create the worksheet as shown on the next page, or open 🖫 **50MAIL**.

2. Create a series to enter the order numbers.

3. Name the postage rates range, C23:H25, RATES.

4. Using HLOOKUP, find TAX RATE (based on the zones.) *Be sure to use the name RATES in the function and 3 for the row number.*

5. Copy the function to the remaining items.

6. Find SALES TAX. Format for two decimal places and copy formula to the remaining items.

7. Using HLOOKUP, find POSTAGE (based on the zone.) *Be sure to use the name RATES in the function and 2 for the row number.*

8. Copy the function to the remaining items.

9. Find TOTAL SALE (including postage and sales tax). Format for two decimal places. Copy formula to the remaining items.

10. Bold worksheet titles.

11. Select the column headings and the data without the lookup table. Use AutoFormat to apply the Colorful 2 format.

12. Change the background color and font color of the title range A1:G3 to match the column headings.

13. To protect the lookup table:
    - Unlock the range A1:G20. (To keep this part of the worksheet unprotected.)
    - Protect the worksheet; do not set a password.

14. To test protection:
    - Try to edit an entry in the rate table.
    - Try to copy a value to the rate table.
    - Try to edit an entry in the PRICE column.
        - ✓ *Since the price column was unlocked the edit should have been successful. Undo the last edit.*

15. Unprotect the worksheet and add a new zone to the worksheet. Zone 7, Postage 7.00, Sales Tax Rate .05.

16. Edit the named range RATES to include the new zone.

17. Protect the lookup table again.

18. Print one copy of the top portion of the worksheet.

19. Close and save the workbook file; name it **MAIL**.

	A	B	C	D	E	F	G	H	I
1			J. J. CARROT COMPANY						
2			JUNE 29, 199-						
3									
4				TAX	SALES		TOTAL		
5	ORDER NO.	PRICE	ZONE	RATE	TAX	POSTAGE	SALE		
6									
7	C54363	59.95	1						
8	C54364	65.49	3						
9	C54365	32.54	2						
10	C54366	43.98	4						
11	C54367	16.89	5						
12	C54368	98.78	6						
13	C54369	35.89	5						
14	C54370	54.99	3						
15	C54371	36.76	6						
16	C54372	89.67	1						
17	C54373	29.95	4						
18	C54374	43.65	3						
19	C54375	41.99	6						
20	C54376	18.50	4						
21									
22			POSTAGE AND SALES TAX RATE						
23	ZONE		1	2	3	4	5	6	**Row 1**
24	POSTAGE		4	4.5	5	5.5	6	6.5	**Row 2**
25	SALES TAX RATE		0.08	0.06	0	0.04	0.05	0.07	**Row 3**
26				C23:H25 Rates					
27									

KEYSTROKES

PROTECT A SHEET

Prevents changes to locked cells, graphic objects, embedded charts in a worksheet or chart items in a chart sheet.

1. Lock or unlock cells as desired.
   - ✓ *By default, all cells and objects in a worksheet are locked.*
2. Click **Tools** menu .... `Alt`+`T`
3. Click **Protection** .... `P`
4. Click **Protect Sheet** .... `P`

   To password protect sheet:

   Type a password in **Password (optional)** text box.

   To protect cell contents and chart items:

   Select **Contents** .... `Alt`+`C`

   To protect graphic objects:

   Select **Objects** .... `Alt`+`O`

   To protect scenarios:

   Select **Scenarios** .... `Alt`+`S`

5. Click **OK** .... `Enter`

   If a password was typed:

   a. Retype password in text box.

   b. Click **OK** .... `Enter`

UNPROTECT A SHEET

1. Click **Tools** menu .... `Alt`+`T`
2. Click **Protection** .... `P`
3. Click **Unprotect Sheet** .... `P`

   If sheet is password protected:

   a. Type password in **Password** text box.

   b. Click **OK** .... `Enter`

LOCK/UNLOCK CELLS IN A WORKSHEET

Locks or unlocks specific cells. By default, all cells in a worksheet are locked when a worksheet is protected.

1. If necessary, unprotect worksheet.
   - ✓ *You cannot lock or unlock cells if the worksheet is protected.*
2. Select cell(s) to unlock or lock.
3. Click **Format** menu .... `Alt`+`O`
4. Click **Cells** .... `E`
   - ✓ *Press **Ctrl + 1** to access **Format** options quickly.*
5. Click **Protection** tab .... `Ctrl`+`Tab`
6. Deselect or select **Locked** ...... `Alt`+`L`
   - ✓ *A gray check box indicates the current cell selection contains mixed (locked/unlocked) settings.*
7. Click **OK** .... `Enter`
8. Repeat steps for each cell or object to lock or unlock.
9. Protect worksheet to enable locking.(See **PROTECT A SHEET** above.)

Exercise 51

■ Hide Data ■ Non-Consecutive References in a Function
■ Custom Views

NOTES

Hide Data

■ There are two ways to hide data in a worksheet, **Hide Cell Contents** and **Hide Columns**.

■ **Hide Cell Contents**

• You may hide data to make a cell or a range appear blank.

• When you make a hidden cell active or edit the cell's contents, the data it contains appears in the formula bar.

• If hidden cell data is moved or copied, it remains hidden in the new location.

■ **Hide Columns**

• You may hide one or more columns to make them disappear from the display. The contents of hidden cells do not print. Therefore, this feature may be used to print *selected, non-consecutive columns* of data in a worksheet.

• To hide columns, select the columns you wish to hide and then click Format, **Column, Hide**. You can also drag the border of a column heading to the left to hide the column.

• Hidden columns may be redisplayed at any time. A column must first be **unhidden** in order to view or edit the hidden data.

• The worksheet border does not display the column letters of hidden columns. To unhide a column, use the menu or point to the right of the column heading border and drag right.

Non-Consecutive References in a Function

■ When using functions whose arguments (parts) are from *non-consecutive columns*, you cannot use a range in your formula. Instead, you must specify the individual cells to be calculated using commas (,) to separate the cells.

EXAMPLE: =SUM(E7,H7,K7,N7)

Custom Views

■ In Excel 97, you can save the current appearance of a workbook so that you don't have to change the settings every time you view or print the workbook using the **custom views** option. This is useful if you hide cells or columns and wish to have both views available.

■ Before you create a view, set up the workbook and print settings exactly as you want them to appear. Select **Custom Views** from the View menu, click **Add**, and then name the view. You can include options at this time as well. If you have multiple sheets, it may be wise to use the sheet name as the view name.

■ To view a custom view, select View, Custom Views, click on the view to be displayed, and then click **Show**.

In this exercise, Furniture Showrooms, Inc. would like a simplified report showing only quarterly sales of employees. To accomplish this, you will hide columns, find total sales for January through December, and print desired data. Custom views will be created for the worksheet.

EXERCISE DIRECTIONS

1. Open ▦ **FURN** or 🖫 **51FURN**.

2. Create a custom view of the present settings of the worksheet.
   a. Click View, Custom Views.
   b. Click Add.
   c. Enter name: Full View.
   d. Leave default settings.
   e. Click OK.

3. Hide columns C, D, F, G, I, J, L, M, O, and P.

4. Edit the second title to read:
   QUARTERLY SALES SUMMARY- JANUARY-DECEMBER

5. Add the quarterly labels to the SALES headings as follows:
   column E: JAN-MAR
   column H: APR-JUNE
   column K: JULY-SEPT
   column N: OCT-DEC.

6. Insert a new, centered column title in column Q:
   JAN-DEC
   SALES

7. In column Q, find total JAN-DEC SALES using the non-consecutive columns format in your formula.

8. Copy formula for the remaining employees.

9. Copy formulas for TOTALS, AVERAGES, HIGHEST, and LOWEST to column Q.

10. Format columns for two decimal places with commas.

11. Reset column width, as necessary.

12. Select the range A1:Q17 and print the selection.

13. Create a custom view of this worksheet, name it Sales View, leaving the default settings.

14. Use the custom views dialog box to show the Full View setting.

   ✓ Note that the new column is in the full view and the worksheet heading remains edited.

15. Re-edit the second title to read:
   QUARTERLY SALES REPORT- JANUARY-DECEMBER

16. Close and save the workbook; name it **FURN**.

	A	B	C	D	E	F	G	H	I	J	K	L	M	N	O	P
1		FURNITURE SHOWROOMS, INC.														
2		QUARTERLY SALES AND SALARY REPORT - JANUARY-SEPTEMBER														
3																
4	EMP.			BASE			5%	JAN-MAR			5%	APR-JUN			5%	JULY-SEPT
5	NO.	NAME		SALARY	SALES	COMMISSION	SALARY	SALES	COMMISSION	SALARY	SALES	COMMISSION	SALARY	SALES	COMMISSION	SALARY
6																
7	1	ABRAMS, JUDY		1500.00	113,456.67	5,672.83	7,172.83	114,342.90	5,717.15	7,217.15	112,469.32	5,623.47	7,123.47	113,546.32	5,677.32	7,177.32
8	2	CHANG, PETER		1500.00	150,654.87	7,532.74	9,032.74	143,276.70	7,163.84	8,663.84	152,643.36	7,632.17	9,132.17	147,432.54	7,371.63	8,871.63
9	3	LINSEY, KELLY		1500.00	234,765.36	11,738.27	13,238.27	187,956.80	9,397.84	10,897.84	215,050.16	10,752.51	12,252.51	195,328.76	9,766.44	11,266.44
10	4	JOHNSON, LETOYA		1500.00	89,765.43	4,488.27	5,988.27	93,984.69	4,699.23	6,199.23	98,463.14	4,923.16	6,423.16	94,567.32	4,728.37	6,228.37
11	5	RIVERA, TONY		1500.00	287,987.76	14,399.39	15,899.39	254,768.60	12,738.43	14,238.43	246,315.19	12,315.76	13,815.76	248,766.55	12,438.33	13,938.33
12	6	THOMPSON, JIM		1500.00							76,451.13	3,822.56	5,322.56	165,438.77	8,271.94	9,771.94
13																
14		TOTALS		9000.00	876,630.09	43,831.50	51,331.50	794,329.69	39,716.48	47,216.48	901,392.30	45,069.62	54,069.62	965,080.26	48,254.01	57,254.01
15		AVERAGES		1500.00	175,326.02	8,766.30	10,266.30	158,865.94	7,943.30	9,443.30	150,232.05	7,511.60	9,011.60	160,846.71	8,042.34	9,542.34
16		HIGHEST		1500.00	287,987.76	14,399.39	15,899.39	254,768.60	12,738.43	14,238.43	246,315.19	12,315.76	13,815.76	248,766.55	12,438.33	13,938.33
17		LOWEST		1500.00	89,765.43	4,488.27	5,988.27	93,984.69	4,699.23	6,199.23	76,451.13	3,822.56	5,322.56	94,567.32	4,728.37	6,228.37
18																
19																
20																
21				hide			hide			hide			hide			hide
22																
23																

KEYSTROKES

HIDE CONTENTS OF CELL

1. Select cells containing data to hide.
2. a. Click **F**ormat menu .... `Alt`+`O`

   b. Click **C**ells .... `E`
   OR
   a. Right-click selection.

   b. Click **F**ormat Cells...................... `F`
3. Click **Number** tab .... `Ctrl`+`Tab`
4. Click the **C**ategory
   list box .... `Alt`+`C`
5. Select **Custom** .... `↑/↓`
   in **C**ategory list box.
6. Click the **T**ype:
   text box .... `Alt`+`T`
7. Type **;;;** (three
   semicolons) .... `;` `;` `;`
8. Click **OK**.................................... `Enter`

REDISPLAY HIDDEN CELL

1. Repeat steps 1-4 in **HIDE CONTENTS OF CELL**.
2. Select desired format .... `↑/↓`
3. Click **OK**.................................... `Enter`

HIDE COLUMNS USING THE MENU

1. Select any cells in column(s) to hide.
2. Click **F**ormat menu .... `Alt`+`O`
3. Click **C**olumn .... `C`
4. Click **H**ide..................................... `H`
   ✓ *A bold column heading border
   appears where a column is hidden.*

HIDE COLUMNS BY DRAGGING

Hide one column:

1. Point to the right border of column heading.

   Pointer becomes a ↔.
2. Drag ↔ left to column's left border.

   *Excel displays a bold column heading
   border where a column is hidden.*

Hide multiple columns:

1. Select columns.
2. Point to the right border of any selected column heading.

   Pointer becomes a ↔.
3. Drag ↔ left to column's left border.

   *Excel displays a bold column heading
   border where a column is hidden.*

SHOW HIDDEN COLUMNS BY DRAGGING

1. Point just right of bold column heading border.

   Pointer becomes a ↔.
2. Drag ↔ right.

SHOW HIDDEN COLUMNS USING THE MENU

1. Select surrounding columns.
2. Click **F**ormat menu .... `Alt`+`O`
3. Click **C**olumn .... `C`
4. Click **U**nhide .... `U`

CREATE CUSTOM VIEWS

1. Make all settings, including print settings, as you wish to view it.
2. Click **V**iew menu..................... `Alt`+`V`
3. Click **Custom Views** .... `V`
4. Click **A**dd .... `Alt`+`A`
5. Enter name of view.
6. Change options, if desired.
7. Click **OK**.................................... `Enter`

VIEW CUSTOM VIEWS

1. Click **V**iew menu..................... `Alt`+`V`
2. Click **Custom Views** .... `V`
3. Select view to display.
4. Click **S**how............................. `Alt`+`S`

NEXT EXERCISE

Exercise 52

■ Summary

Kitchen King is updating its accounts receivable aging report as of 2/1/98. Paid invoices will be deleted from this new report, and other invoices that have not been paid will be added. In addition, Kitchen King has changed its late fee policy. It will now determine late fees based on the number of days the account is unpaid. The late fee will be determined by using a Lookup formula.

EXERCISE DIRECTIONS

1. Open ⌨ **AR** or 💾 **52AR**.

2. Delete rows for paid invoices shown in the illustration on the right.

3. Insert rows below remaining invoices and enter the following new unpaid invoices:

	A	B	C	D	E
1	INVOICE	INVOICE		DAYS	
2	NUMBER	DATE	CUSTOMER	UNPAID	AMOUNT
3					
4	21093	12/10/97	Jim Barkowski		168.42
5	21106	12/16/97	Kay's Inn		396.16
6	21142	12/29/97	Red's Restaurant		84.96
7	21179	1/4/98	CyberCafe		1490.14
8	21205	1/10/98	George Lopez		354.75
9	21246	1/25/98	Kay's Inn		742.15

4. Change the CURRENT DATE to: 2/1/98

5. Copy the DAYS UNPAID formula for the new data.

6. Create the LATE FEE TABLE below the worksheet.

7. Name the range in LATE FEE TABLE containing days and interest values LATETABLE.

8. Insert a column between AMOUNT and LATE FEE, and enter the label INTEREST RATE.

9. Delete values in the LATE FEE and AMOUNT DUE columns.

10. Format INTEREST RATE column for three decimal places.

11. Protect the LATE FEE TABLE:
    a. Unlock cells in the entire worksheet.
    b. Select cells in LATE FEE TABLE and lock them.
    c. Turn worksheet protection on.

12. Using VLOOKUP, find INTEREST RATE (based on the days unpaid).

13. Copy the function to the remaining items.
    ✓ *If you did not use the LATETABLE range name in the function, you must set the table range to absolute before copying.*

14. Find:
    • LATE FEE
    • AMOUNT DUE

15. Copy formulas to the remaining items.

16. Disable worksheet protection.

17. Format all remaining money columns for two decimal places.

18. Center column titles.

19. Edit the TOTAL formulas.

20. Change the interest rate for one unpaid day to be 0.005.

21. Protect the worksheet.

22. Print one copy of the top portion of the worksheet.

23. Add Feb 1 as a new scenario, with C4 as the changing cell.

24. Resave the workbook file.

25. Save and close the file; name it **AR**.

	A	B	C	D	E	F	G	H
1			KITCHEN KING STORES					
2			ACCOUNTS RECEIVABLE AGING REPORT					
3								
4	CURRENT DATE:		12/01/97 2/1/98					
5								
6	INVOICE	INVOICE			DAYS		AMOUNT	
7	NUMBER	DATE	CUSTOMER		UNPAID	AMOUNT	LATE FEE	DUE
8								
9	21045	09/22/97	Martha Schef		70	475.43	4.75	480.18
10	21046	09/23/97	Red's Restaurant		69	321.43	3.21	324.64
11	21047	09/24/97	Martha Schef		68	543.90	5.44	549.42
12	21049	10/02/97	Kay's Inn		60	32.45	0.32	32.77
13	21050	10/03/97	Marvin Diamant		59	1324.32	13.24	1337.56
14	21052	10/06/97	Red's Restaurant		56	124.98	1.25	126.23
15	21054	10/15/97	George Lopez		47	564.12	0.00	564.12
16	21056	10/18/97	Kay's Inn		44	187.65	0.00	187.65
17	21062	10/28/97	Marvin Diamant		34	454.56	0.00	454.56
18	21079	11/05/97	Sam Hopkins		26	308.21	0.00	308.21
19	21087	11/20/97	Red's Restaurant		11	163.28	0.00	163.28
20								
21	TOTALS					4500.41	28.28	4528.64
22								
23								
24	LATE FEE TABLE							
25								
26	UNPAID	INTEREST						
27	DAYS	RATE						
28	1	0.000						
29	30	0.010						
30	60	0.015						
31	90	0.020						
32	120	0.025						
33	150	0.030						
34								

Insert INTEREST RATE column.

Name range LATETABLE.

Exercise

53

■ **Summary**

As the manager of the Seas of Grain Export Company, you are responsible for determining the foreign price per bushel and the currency type, for our exports. You will use a lookup table, AutoFormat, and scenarios to complete this problem.

EXERCISE DIRECTIONS

1. Create the worksheet and table on the next page or open 💾 **53GRAIN**.

2. Format the worksheet to set column width at 12.

3. Right-align column titles.

4. Using VLOOKUP, find the CURRENCY each country uses.

5. Using VLOOKUP, find the CONVERSION FACTOR by using the FOREIGN UNITS THAT EQUAL ONE DOLLAR data for each country.

6. Format Conversion Factor to four decimal places.

7. Find FOREIGN PRICE PER BUSHEL.

8. Format for two decimal places.

9. Copy all formulas for each country.

10. Use Scenario Manager to add a scenario named Wheat, with E2:E3 as the changing cells.

11. Use Scenario Manager to add two additional scenarios as follows:

    Name: Soybeans

    Values Changing Cells: SOYBEANS $8.92

    Name: Corn

    Values Changing Cells: CORN $3.35

12. Use the Show button in Scenario Manager to see each of the scenarios.

13. Use the Summary button in Scenario Manager and the E9:E14 range to summarize the scenarios.

14. Save the workbook file; name it **GRAIN**.

15. Use the Copy, Paste Special feature to copy the top portion of this worksheet to a new workbook.

16. Format the Conversion factor to a four-place decimal.

17. Format Foreign Price to two-place decimals.

18. Use the AutoFormat feature and select a style for the worksheet.

19. Adjust column widths, if necessary.

20. Save the workbook file; name it **BPRICE**.

21. Print one copy of **BPRICE**.

22. Close all workbooks.

	A	B	C	D	E
1		SEAS OF GRAIN EXPORT CO.			
2		ITEM:			**WHEAT**
3		CURRENT PRICE PER BUSHEL		$	3.93
4					
5					FOREIGN
6				CONVERSION	PRICE
7	COUNTRY		CURRENCY	FACTOR	PER BUSHEL
8					
9	BRAZIL				
10	CHINA				
11	EGYPT				
12	ITALY				
13	RUSSIA				
14	POLAND				
15					
16	.				
17					
18	CONVERSION TABLE FOR FOREIGN CURRENCY				
19			DOLLAR	FOREIGN	
20			VALUE OF	UNITS THAT	
21			ONE FOR'N	EQUAL ONE	
22	COUNTRY	CURRENCY	UNIT	DOLLAR	
23					
24	AUSTRALIA	DOLLARS	0.7795	1.2829	
25	BRAZIL	REAL	0.9448	1.0584	
26	BRITAIN	POUNDS	1.6234	0.6160	
27	CANADA	DOLLARS	0.7177	1.3934	
28	CHINA	YUAN	0.1201	8.3265	
29	FRANCE	FRANCS	0.1731	5.7785	
30	EGYPT	POUNDS	0.2944	3.3962	
31	GERMANY	MARKS	0.5821	1.7178	
32	INDIA	RUPEES	0.0279	35.8250	
33	ITALY	LIRA	0.0006	1695.7500	
34	JAPAN	YEN	0.0080	125.6500	
35	RUSSIA	RUBLE	0.0002	5732.5000	

NEXT LESSON

Excel

LESSON 8

CHART AND MAP DATA

Exercises 54-64

- Chart Basics
- Create and Edit Charts
  Pie
  Column
  Stacked Bar
  Line
  Area
  Line-Column Chart
  Stock Charts
  3-D Charts
- Chart Toolbar
- Select Chart Data
- Chart Elements
- Chart Types and Subtypes
- Select, Size and Edit Embedded Charts
- Custom Chart Types

- Chart Sheets and Embedded Charts
- Print Charts
- Change Data Orientation
- Chart Options
- Change Colors and Patterns
- Format Chart Data
- Edit Linked Text
- Use Map Feature
- Edit Maps
- Map Toolbar

Exercise 54

■ **Chart Basics** ■ **Select Chart Data** ■ **Chart Elements**
■ **Create Column, Line, and Pie Charts** ■ **Chart Types**
■ **Select, Size, and Edit Embedded Chart** ■ **Enable Chart Editing**

NOTES

Chart Basics

■ **Charts** provide a way of presenting and comparing data in a graphic format.

■ You can create **embedded charts** or **chart sheets**.

  • When you create an **embedded chart** the chart exists as an *object* in the worksheet alongside the data.

  • When you create a **chart sheet** the chart exists on a separate sheet within the workbook. Excel names chart sheets Chart1, Chart2, etc. You can change these sheet names to better describe the chart.

■ All charts are linked to the data that they plot. When you change data in the plotted area of the worksheet, the chart also changes.

Select Chart Data

■ To create a chart, you must first select the data to plot. Here are some guidelines for selecting data to chart:

  • The selection should be rectangular.

  • The selection should not contain blank columns or rows.

  • A **non-adjacent selection** is used to plot data separated by other data or blank columns or rows.

  • Hide columns you do not wish to plot.

  • The blank cell in the upper-left corner of a selection tells Excel the data below and to the right of the blank cell, contains labels for the values to plot.

  • The selection determines the orientation (in columns or rows) of the data series. However, orientation may be changed as desired.

■ Illustration A (on the next page) shows two selections that would result in the same displayed chart. Both selections are rectangular and contain a blank cell (outlined) in the upper-left corner. The second selection (B) contains non-adjacent ranges that are required because of the blank column between the data. Select non-adjacent columns by holding down the Control key while selecting the columns.

■ Typically, the selection of worksheet data will include the following:

data series   Values the chart represents (Sales values).

series labels   Labels identifying the charted values. These labels appear in the chart **legend** that identify each data series in the chart. (Label for 1997.)

category labels   Labels identifying each data series shown on the horizontal or x-axis (products labels).

  ✓ NOTE: *Note Illustrations A and B on the next page that identify the chart elements.*

Illustration A

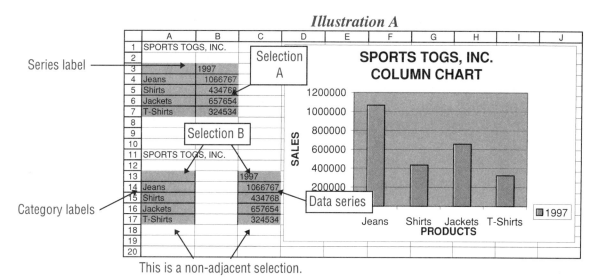

Series label

Selection A

Category labels

Selection B

Data series

This is a non-adjacent selection.

Illustration B

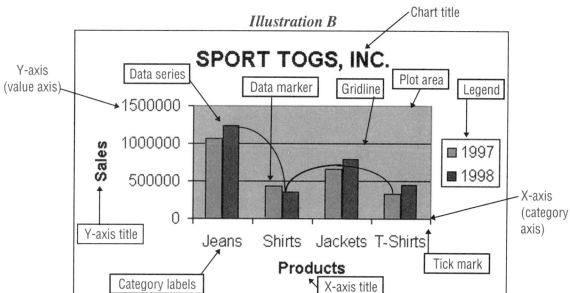

Chart title

Y-axis (value axis)

Data series

Data marker

Gridline

Plot area

Legend

Y-axis title

Category labels

Products

X-axis title

Tick mark

X-axis (category axis)

Chart Elements

- The elements of a column chart are labeled in the Illustration B above. In Excel 97, as you move your mouse over each chart element, the name of the element is displayed.

- For charts that use axes (all except pie charts):

  - The **y-axis** typically represents the vertical scale. The scale values are entered automatically, based on the values being charted (see illustration above).

  - The **y-axis title** describes the y-axis (vertical) data, (*Sales* in the illustration).

  - The **x-axis** is the horizontal scale and typically represents the data series categories.

  - The **x-axis title** describes the x-axis (horizontal) data, (*Products* in the illustration).

Create Column, Line, and Pie Charts

- The basic steps for creating a chart are:

  1. Select the worksheet data to chart.

  2. Select the Chart Wizard Button.

  3. Follow the Chart Wizard Prompts:

     Step 1: Select Chart Type.

     Step 2: Check Chart Source Data Range.

     Step 3: Select Chart Options.

     Step 4: Select Chart Location.

     ✓ NOTE: Charts may be placed on a separate chart sheet, if desired.

■ In Excel 97, Chart Wizard contains tabbed dialog boxes that allow you to select and format chart types and elements with greater control and ease. As you make selections, Chart Wizard shows you exactly how the chart will look. Thus you can select the format best suited to presenting your data.

Chart Types

■ Excel provides many chart types. In this exercise we will discuss and explore three of them (illustrated below):

- **Column charts** which compare individual or sets of values. The height of each bar is proportional to its corresponding value in the worksheet.

- **Pie charts** which are circular graphs used to show the relationship of each value in a data range to the entire data range. The size of each wedge represents the percentage each value contributes to the total.

♦ Only one numerical data range may be used in a pie chart to indicate the values to be represented as pie slices.

♦ Pie charts may be formatted to indicate the percentage each piece of the pie represents of the whole.

- **Line charts** which are another way of presenting data graphically. Line charts are especially useful when plotting trends because lines connect points of data and show changes over time effectively.

■ Charts can be copied and then edited to produce a different chart that uses the same worksheet data.

✓ NOTE: The contents of the clipboard remain unchanged until another item is copied. Therefore, you can paste a copied object more than once.

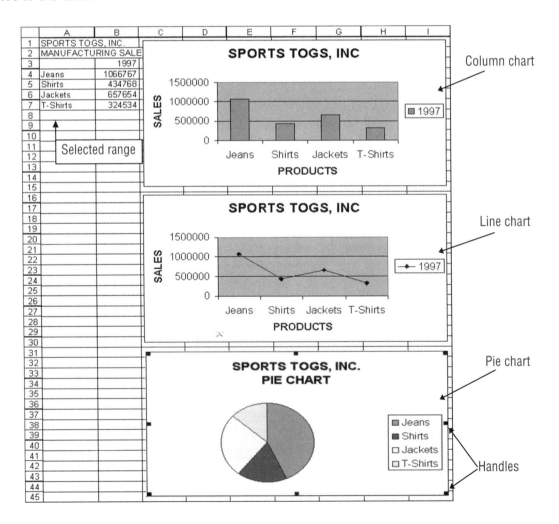

Select, Size, and Edit Embedded Charts

- You can click an embedded chart once to select it or to enable chart editing. Once you click it, handles (see illustration on previous page) appear around its border. When a chart is selected this way, it can be sized, edited, moved, and copied.

Enable Chart Editing

- As discussed above, clicking a chart once enables editing. To edit a chart sheet, just click the sheet tab of the chart you want to change.

- All chart elements, such as legends and data markers, can be changed and enhanced by clicking the item and making the edit. When you right-click chart items, Excel displays a shortcut menu containing relevant commands.

- To edit a chart, Excel provides the following features:

  - **Menu bar options**

    Excel modifies the menu bar so that options specific to the chart type and selected chart item are available. For example:

    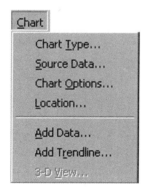

- **Shortcut menu options**

  When you right-click an element within a chart, Excel displays a shortcut menu that is appropriate to the element selected. The illustration below shows the menu that appears when a data series is right-clicked.

- **Name box**

  The Name box on the formula bar displays the selected chart element.

  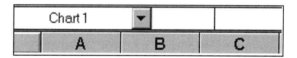

- **Chart toolbar**

  The Chart toolbar appears onscreen when an Embedded Chart is selected or a Chart Sheet is opened. The toolbar will be discussed in the next exercise.

In this exercise, you will create a column chart, a line chart, and a pie chart with labels showing manufacturing sales for Sports Togs, Inc.

EXERCISE DIRECTIONS

1. Create the worksheet as shown below, or open 🖫 **54SPORTS**.

2. Create an embedded chart to show the 1997 sales for each product:
   a. Select the non-adjacent ranges indicated by the shaded cells in the worksheet, using Ctrl between selections.
   b. Follow the Chart Wizard steps and make the following selections:
      Step 1: Note chart type selections. Since the Column type is the default, click Next.
      Step 2: Check the data range, note the illustration of the data range selected, and click Next.
      Step 3: On the Titles tab, enter the following titles:
      SPORT TOGS, INC.   Chart title
      PRODUCTS   Category X axis
      SALES   Category Y axis
      Click Next
      Step 4: Place the chart as an object on Sheet1. Click Finish.

3. Size and move the chart, if necessary, so that the chart appears in D1:J15.

4. Copy the embedded chart to the worksheet range beginning at D16.

5. Enable chart editing for the copied chart and change the chart type to a line chart.

6. Reselect the worksheet data making the following selections in Chart Wizard:
      Step 1: Select Pie Chart type. Click Next.
      Step 2: Note the selection.
      Step 3: Enter SPORT TOGS INC. as the title.
      Step 4: Place the chart as a new sheet on Chart1.

7. Select Chart1 sheet and edit the chart title to add a second line:
   MANUFACTURING SALES

8. Preview the pie chart on the chart sheet.
   ✓ *Note the chart will print on its own sheet.*

9. Select Sheet1 and deselect the worksheet data.

10. Preview Sheet1.
    ✓ *Note the column and line charts will print with the worksheet data.*

11. Save the workbook file; name it **SPORTS**.

12. Close the workbook file.

	A	B	C
1	SPORTS TOGS, INC.		
2	MANUFACTURING SALES		
3			1997
4	Jeans		1066767
5	Shirts		434768
6	Jackets		657654
7	T-Shirts		324534

KEYSTROKES

SELECT NON-ADJACENT CELLS USING THE MOUSE

1. Click first cell.
2. Press **Ctrl** and click each additional cell.

SELECT NON-ADJACENT RANGES

1. Click first cell.
2. Press **Shift** and drag through cells until desired cell ranges are highlighted.
3. Click **Ctrl** at the end of first range.
4. Click **Shift** again at beginning of new range and drag through cells to highlight.

SELECT NON-ADJACENT CELLS USING THE KEYBOARD

1. Select first cell in range .... `↔↕`
2. Select first range of cells ..... `Shift` + `↔↕`
3. Press **Shift + F8** .... `Shift` + `F8`
   to begin ADD mode.
4. Move active cell .... `↔↕`
   to first cell in next range to select.
5. Select cells in range .... `Shift` + `↔↕`
6. Repeat steps 2-4 for each additional range to select.

CREATE A CHART FROM WORKSHEET DATA

1. Select cells containing data to plot.
2. a. Click **Insert** .... `Alt` + `I`
   b. Click **Chart** .... `H`
   ✓ This brings you into Chart Wizard. (See below.)

CREATE CHART WITH CHART WIZARD

1. Select data to chart.
2. Click **Chart Wizard** button
   on Standard toolbar. .... `⬚`
3. **CHART WIZARD STEP 1 OF 4**
   Select a chart type:

To select a standard chart type:

a. Click **Standard** types tab .. `Alt` + `Tab`
b. Select a
   Chart type .... `Alt` + `C`, `↗↙`
c. Select **Chart sub-type** .... `Alt` + `T`

d. If desired, select the
   Press and hold to view
   sample command .... `Alt` + `V`
   OR

To select a custom chart type:

a. Click **Custom Types** tab .... `Alt` + `Tab`
b. Click **User defined** .... `Alt` + `U`
   OR
   Click **Built-in** .... `Alt` + `B`
c. Select desired custom
   chart in **Chart type** list ...... `Alt` + `C`
4. Click **Next** .... `Enter`
5. **CHART WIZARD STEP 2 OF 4**
   If desired, change data range options:
   Click **Data Range** tab .... `Ctrl` + `Tab`

To change data range:

Type or select new worksheet range in
Data range text box. .... `Alt` + `D`

To change orientation of data series:

Click **Series in Rows** .... `Alt` + `R`
OR
Click **Series in Columns** .... `Alt` + `L`
6. If desired, click **Series**
   tab to change series options . `Ctrl` + `Tab`

To add a series:

a. Click **Add** button .... `Alt` + `A`
   Excel adds a series to Series list.
b. Type new name for series
   in **Name** text box .... `Alt` + `N`
c. Type or select range
   for new series (just the
   data) in **Values** text box .... `Alt` + `V`

To remove a series:

a. Select series to remove
   in **Series** list .... `Alt` + `S`, `↗↙`
b. Click **Remove** .... `Alt` + `R`

To change range containing category labels:

Type or select range containing
labels in **Category X axis**
labels text box .... `Alt` + `T`
7. Click **Next >** .... `Enter`
8. **CHART WIZARD STEP 3 OF 4**
   If desired, from **Titles** tab, type title text:
   a. Type chart title in
      Chart Title text box .... `Alt` + `T`
   b. Type labels for category, series, and value axis.
      (Axis label options will vary.)
9. If desired, click **Axes** tab
   to set axis options: .... `Ctrl` + `Tab`

To set axis display options:

Select category, series. and value axis
display options.
(Axis display options will vary.)
10. a. If desired, click **Gridlines** tab
       to set gridline options .... `Ctrl` + `Tab`
    b. Select category, series, value, 2-D, and 3-D gridline options, etc.
       (Gridline options will vary.)
11. If desired, click **Legend** tab
    to set legend options .... `Ctrl` + `Tab`
    a. Select **Show legend** .... `Alt` + `S`
    b. Select one placement option:
       • **Bottom** .... `Alt` + `M`
       • **Corner** .... `Alt` + `O`
       • **Top** .... `Alt` + `T`
       • **Right** .... `Alt` + `R`
       • **Left** .... `Alt` + `L`
12. If desired, click **Data Labels** tab to
    set data label options .... `Ctrl` + `Tab`

To set display of data labels:

a. Select desired data label display option:

- **N**one .... Alt + N
- Show **v**alue .... Alt + V
- Show **p**ercent .... Alt + P
- Show **l**abel .... Alt + L
- Show label **a**nd percent .... Alt + A
- Show **b**ubble sizes .... Alt + U

b. Select on deselect **Legend k**ey next to labels .... Alt + K

(Option selection may vary.)

13. If desired, click **Data Table** tab to set data table options ... Alt + Ctrl + Tab

To show data table:

Click **Show d**ata table .... Alt + D

To show legend keys:

Select **Show l**egend keys ...... Alt + L

14. Click **Next** .... Enter

15. **CHART WIZARD STEP 4 OF 4**
Place chart:

To place chart as a new sheet:

a. Select **As new s**heet .... Alt + S

b. Type name for sheet in As new s**heet** text box.

OR

To place chart as an object in sheet:

a. Select **As o**bject in .... Alt + O

b. Type name for sheet in As o**bject in** text box.

16. Click **F**inish .... Alt + F

ENABLE CHART EDITING

Embedded Chart:

Click embedded chart.
A border with handles surrounds the chart or, if the entire chart was not displayed on the sheet, the chart appears in a window.

Chart Sheet:

Select chart sheet.

DISABLE CHART EDITING

Embedded Chart:

Click any cell in worksheet.

Chart Sheet:

Click another sheet tab .

SIZE EMBEDDED CHARTS

1. Select chart.

2. Point to handle on side of border to size.

3. Pointer becomes a ↔ when positioned correctly.

   ✓ *To size object proportionally, point to corner handle.*

4. **To size object without constraints:**
Drag border outline until desired size is obtained.
OR

To size object and align to gridlines:

Press **Alt** and drag border outline until desired size is obtained.

CHANGE CHART TYPE FOR ENTIRE CHART

1. Select chart object or chart sheet.

2. Click Chart Type button on Chart toolbar and select Type
OR

1. Click **C**hart menu .... Alt + C

2. Click Chart **T**ype .... T

3. Select a chart type:

   See Create Chart with Chart Wizard, step 3 above.

To set current chart type as default:

Click S**e**t as default chart ...... Alt + E

5. Click **OK** .... Enter

EDIT CHART TEXT IN CHART

Edits unlinked chart text (such as axis and chart titles, text boxes, and trend line labels) and some linked text (data labels and tick mark labels).

✓ *When you edit linked text in a chart, Excel removes the link to the worksheet data.*

1. Enable chart editing.

2. Double-click chart item containing text.

3. To replace existing text with new text:

   a. Type desired text.
   (*Text appears in formula bar.*)

   b. Press **Enter** .... Enter

To edit existing text:

1. Click desired character position in chart text.

2. Insert and delete characters as desired.

   ✓ *To insert a line break, press* ***Enter****.*

3. Click anywhere outside of chart text.

NEXT EXERCISE

Exercise 55

■ **Chart Types and Subtypes** ■ **Custom Chart Types**
■ **Select Chart Items** ■ **Change Legend Position**
■ **Chart Toolbar** ■ **Edit Chart in its Own Window**

NOTES

Chart Types and Subtypes

■ When you create a chart, you select a chart type and format that best presents the worksheet data. Worksheet data may be charted using one of fourteen chart types: area, bar, column, line, pie, doughnut, radar, xy (scatter), surface, bubble, stock, cylinder, cone, or pyramid.

■ Excel also provides chart subtypes or formats that are variations on the selected chart type. Each chart type has at least two chart subtypes. Note the illustration below of the chart subtypes for the column chart. After you select the chart type, you can then select the subtype you desire.

Chart Type Dialog Box

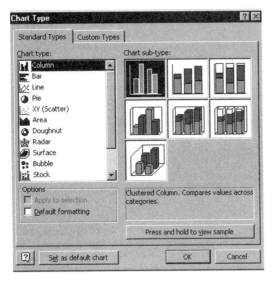

■ The stacked column chart, shown in the second and third column subtypes illustrated in the Chart Type dialog box to the left, is one example of a chart subtype. This chart subtype is often used to show the total effect of several sets of data. Each bar consists of sections representing values in a range.   For example, in the illustration below, each bar contains two sections representing 1997 and 1998 sales values.

Stacked Column Chart

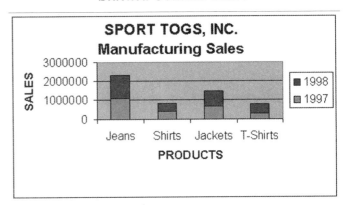

Custom Chart Types

■ You can select customized chart types by selecting the Custom Types tab on the Chart Types dialog box. When each chart type is selected, Excel will plot your data with the customized type selection.

■ The combination chart is a custom chart type that lets you plot each data series as a different chart type. For example, in the illustration of the line-column chart on the next page, the line chart type is used to plot the 1998 data and the column chart type issued to plot the 1997 data.

Chart Toolbar

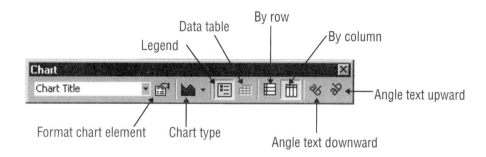

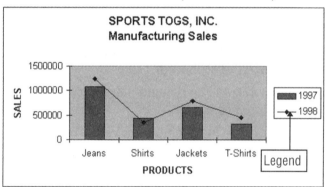

Combination Chart (Line-Column)

Select Chart Items

■ Any item in a chart may be selected and changed when chart editing is enabled. Selected items are marked with squares, and the name of the selected item is displayed in the name box.

Change Legend Position

■ A chart legend is usually created automatically when the data is charted. Legend placement and labels may be changed or edited by clicking on the legend in chart edit mode, right-clicking the mouse, and selecting Format Legend.

Chart Toolbar

■ You can display the Chart toolbar, illustrated above, by selecting View, Toolbars, Chart.

■ The Chart toolbar provides the following tools:

Chart Element Box	displays the selected chart element and allows you to select chart elements.
Format Chart Element	formats chart area (borders and background colors).
Chart Type	provides list of chart types from which you can select.
Legend	hides or displays the chart legend.
Data Table	hides or displays data table in the chart.
By Rows	changes orientation of data series to rows.
By Column	changes orientation of data series to columns.
Angle Text Downward	angles selected text downward.
Angle Text Upward	angles selected text upward.

Edit Chart in its Own Window

■ You can open an embedded chart in its own window so that you can edit it independent of the worksheet. After selecting the chart, click View, Chart Window to open a chart window. Sizing or moving the window will change the appearance of the chart on the sheet after you close the window.

In this exercise, you will retrieve the Sports Togs, Inc. statistics, include additional data, delete charts, and prepare several new charts. The owner wants to compare the sales in 1997 with 1998.

EXERCISE DIRECTIONS

1. Open 🖮 **SPORTS** or 💾 **55SPORTS**.

2. Delete all embedded charts in Sheet1.

3. Enter new data in column D, as shown below. Enter 1998 as a numeric label.

	A	B	C	D
1	SPORTS TOGS, INC.			
2	MANUFACTURING SALES			
3			1997	1998
4	Jeans		1066767	1235467
5	Shirts		434768	354245
6	Jackets		657654	789643
7	T-Shirts		324534	453234

4. Rename Sheet1; name it **DATA**.

5. To create an embedded column chart showing 1997 and 1998 sales in the **DATA** sheet:

    a. Select the non-adjacent ranges indicated by the shaded cells in the worksheet.

    ### *FROM CHART WIZARD:*

    b. Select the default chart type (Column)

    c. Add the chart title: SPORT TOGS, INC.

    d. Create axis titles as follows:

    Category (X):   PRODUCTS

    Value (Y):   SALES

6. Size the chart and place it in the range B10:G24.

7. Select and set the legend placement to the bottom of the chart.

8. Edit the chart in a Chart Window and add a second line to the chart title:

    Manufacturing Sales

9. Close the chart window. Select the chart and cut it to the clipboard.

10. In Sheet2, select cell A1 and paste the chart stored in the clipboard.

11. Select cell A17 and paste the chart stored in the clipboard again.

12. Display the Chart toolbar by View, Toolbars, Chart.

13. Use the Chart Type button to change the chart in cell A17 to a line chart.

14. In Sheet2, select cell A33 and paste the chart stored in the clipboard.

15. Use the shortcut menu to change the subtype of this chart to stacked column (second chart pictured in the column Subtype group).

16. Place legend on right side of chart.

17. Select the column chart (first chart in Sheet2) and copy it to the clipboard.

18. In Sheet2, select cell A49 and paste the column chart stored in the clipboard.

19. Change the new chart to a combination chart:

    a. Right-click the chart.

    b. Select Chart Type on the shortcut menu.

    c. Select the Custom Types tab.

    d. Select the Lines-Column selection.

    ✓ *Your data will be displayed. Make other selections to test the custom feature.*

20. Rename Sheet2; name it **EMBEDDED CHARTS**.

21. Rename Chart1 sheet; name it **PIE CHART**.
    To preview the embedded charts:
    a. Select **EMBEDDED CHARTS** sheet.
    b. Set it to print on one page.
    c. Preview the worksheet.

22. Select the **DATA** sheet.
23. Close and save the workbook file, or save as **SPORTS**.

KEYSTROKES

DELETE AN EMBEDDED CHART

1. Select embedded chart as an object.
2. Press **Delete** .... `Del`

CHANGE CHART SUBTYPE

1. Enable chart editing.
2. Click **Chart Menu** .... `Alt`+`C`
3. Click **Chart Type** .... `Alt`+`T`
4. Click **Standard
   Types** tab .... `Ctrl`+`Tab`
5. Select type from
   Chart type list .... `Alt`+`C`, `↕`
6. Select Subtype from
   Chart subtype list .... `Alt`+`T`, `↕`
7. Click **OK** .... `Enter`

CREATE A LINE-COLUMN CHART

1. Enable chart editing.
2. Select data series for which a new chart type will be selected.
3. Click **Chart Menu** .... `Alt`+`C`
4. Click **Chart Type** .... `Alt`+`T`
5. Click **Custom Types** tab .... `Ctrl`+`Tab`
6. Select **Line-Column**
   from **Chart type** list........ `Alt`+`C`, `↓`
7. Click **OK** .... `Enter`

POSITION LEGEND IN CHART

1. Enable chart editing.
2. Right-click legend.
3. Select **Format Legend**........... `Alt`+`O`
4. Select **Placement** .... `Ctrl`+`Tab`
5. Select desired position:
   - **Bottom** .... `Alt`+`B`
   - **Corner** .... `Alt`+`C`
   - **Top** .... `Alt`+`T`
   - **Right** .... `Alt`+`R`
   - **Left**.................................. `Alt`+`L`
6. Click **OK** .... `Enter`

SELECT CHART ELEMENTS

Select chart elements (such as the legend or a data series) prior to selecting commands to change the item in some way.

✓ *Excel marks the currently selected chart elements with squares, and displays its name in the name box.*

Enable chart editing, then perform desired options below.

- **To select next or previous class of chart elements:**

  Press up or down .... `↕`
- **To select next or previous elements for selected chart class:**

  Press left or right.......................... `↔`
- **To select specific elements with the mouse:**

  Click chart element.
- **To select a data series:**

  Click any data marker in data series.

- **To select a data marker:**
  a. Click any data marker in data series.
  b. Click data marker in selected series.
- **To select the chart area:**

  Click any blank area outside plot area.
- **To select the plot area:**

  Click any blank area inside plot area.
- **To select the legend or legend component:**

  ✓ *Legend items are the legend entry and key.*
  a. Click legend.
  b. Click item in legend.
- **To deselect a selected chart element:**

  Press **Escape** .... `Esc`

OPEN EMBEDDED CHART IN A WINDOW

1. Click chart to select it.
2. Click **View** menu.................... `Alt`+`V`
3. Click **Chart Window**......................... `A`

   To return to normal editing:

   Click Close button ☒ on window.
   To size window:
   Drag border of window to increase or decrease size.
   To move window:
   Drag window title bar.

Exercise 56

- **Edit Linked Chart Text** ■ **Edit Titles and Axis Labels**
- **Series Labels for Pie Charts** ■ **Move Embedded Charts**
- **Change Chart Colors and Patterns**

NOTES

Edit Linked Chart Text

- Chart text or labels linked to the worksheet, such as category labels and legend entries, are automatically created from the data in the worksheet selection.

  If you edit linked chart text in the worksheet, Excel automatically updates the chart.

Edit Chart Titles and Axis Labels

- Chart titles and axis labels are not linked to the worksheet. You can add unlinked text (such as a chart subtitle) at any time by clicking on the text until the text box displays, then adding the desired text.

- You can also change the font type, size, style, or color of chart text by selecting the text and using the format dialog box. To display the Format dialog box, use Ctrl + 1; select Format and the name of the item to be formatted; or select Format from the shortcut menu; or double-click the item to be formatted.

Series Labels for Pie Charts

- In a **pie** chart, all the wedges make up the data series and each wedge represents a data point in the series. To identify the wedges in the pie chart, a label range should be selected as series labels. See the selection for pie chart data on the next page.

Move Embedded Charts

- You can move an embedded chart when chart editing is enabled.

Change Chart Colors and Patterns

- Charts may be customized by changing the colors or patterns that automatically appear to differentiate data markers. A different pattern and/or color (area format) may be specified for data. For example, you may wish to change the color of the bars or lines for a color presentation, or change the colors to a black and white pattern for a crisper printout from a black and white printer.

- To change colors or patterns on a data series:

  a. Select the chart item while chart editing is enabled.

  b. Press **Ctrl+1**
     or
     Right-click and select **Format Data Series**
     or
     Click Format, **Selected Data Series**
     or
     Double click on the **Data Series**.

  - Make the changes in the Format Data Series dialog box, or if patterns are desired select Fill Effects and then select the Pattern tab.

- The Format Data Series dialog box, as shown on the next page, contains six tabs including the Patterns tab (illustrated). Colors can be changed using this dialog box.

- When you select the Fill Effects button on the Patterns tab, a Fill Effects dialog box with four tabs appears on screen. Excel 97 provides fill effects for patterns, textures, gradients, and pictures.

Format Data Series Dialog Box

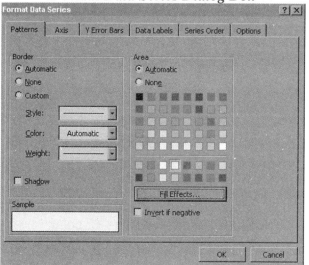

Fill Effects Dialog Box

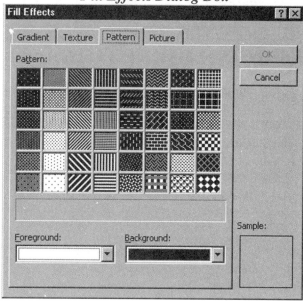

Pie Chart Selection

	A	B	C	D	E	F	G
2			QUARTERLY INCOME STATEMENT				
3							
4			1ST QTR	2ND QTR.	3RD QTR.	4TH QTR.	COMBINED
5			TOTALS	TOTALS	TOTALS	TOTALS	TOTALS
6							
7	INCOME						
8	Agency Fees		38,052.39	41,566.18	42,402.51	42,314.40	164,335.48
9	Consultations		4,776.95	4,679.76	4,000.73	3,730.51	17,187.95
10	Total Income		42,829.34	46,245.94	46,403.24	46,044.91	181,523.43
11							
12	EXPENSES:						
13	Advertising		800.00	950.00	900.00	830.00	3,480.00
14	Rent		3,600.00	3,600.00	3,600.00	3,600.00	14,400.00
15	Salaries		18,750.00	18,750.00	18,750.00	18,750.00	75,000.00
16	Supplies		699.08	609.62	672.42	592.00	2,573.12
17	Utilities		655.72	703.61	790.62	700.98	2,850.93
18	Interest		75.00	75.00	75.00	75.00	300.00
19	Other		685.84	1,238.22	1,150.95	741.65	3,816.66
20	Total Expenses		25,265.64	25,926.45	25,938.99	25,289.63	102,420.71
21							
22	NET INCOME		17563.7	20319.49	20464.25	20755.28	79102.72

Column Chart Selection

	A	B	C	D	E	F	G
1			UMBRELLA INSURANCE AGENCY				
2			QUARTERLY INCOME STATEMENT				
3							
4			1ST QTR	2ND QTR.	3RD QTR.	4TH QTR.	COMBINED
5			TOTALS	TOTALS	TOTALS	TOTALS	TOTALS
6							
7	INCOME						
8	Agency Fees		38,052.39	41,566.18	42,402.51	42,314.40	164,335.48
9	Consultations		4,776.95	4,679.76	4,000.73	3,730.51	17,187.95
10	Total Income		42,829.34	46,245.94	46,403.24	46,044.91	181,523.43
11							
12	EXPENSES:						
13	Advertising		800.00	950.00	900.00	830.00	3,480.00
14	Rent		3,600.00	3,600.00	3,600.00	3,600.00	14,400.00
15	Salaries		18,750.00	18,750.00	18,750.00	18,750.00	75,000.00
16	Supplies		699.08	609.62	672.42	592.00	2,573.12
17	Utilities		655.72	703.61	790.62	700.98	2,850.93
18	Interest		75.00	75.00	75.00	75.00	300.00
19	Other		685.84	1,238.22	1,150.95	741.65	3,816.66
20	Total Expenses		25,265.64	25,926.45	25,938.99	25,289.63	102,420.71
21							
22	NET INCOME		17563.7	20319.49	20464.25	20755.28	79102.72

In this exercise, you will retrieve the Umbrella Insurance Agency's quarterly income statement comparison worksheet and prepare and modify several charts to present the data graphically.

EXERCISE DIRECTIONS

1. Open 💾 **INSQTRS** or 🖥 **56INSQTRS**.

2. Create an embedded pie chart, comparing 1ST, 2ND, 3RD, and 4TH QUARTER NET INCOME:

   a. Make a non-adjacent selection that includes a blank cell. Hold the Ctrl key between selections.

      ✔ When selecting worksheet data to chart, the selection area must be rectangular and a blank cell should be included in the selection. Note the illustrations on the previous page of the non-adjacent selections (shaded) that include a blank cell. The selection of a blank cell helps Excel correctly identify the labels for the data series.

   b. Select Chart Wizard.

   c. Select **pie** chart type.

   d. Accept the chart range and note the non-adjacent selection.

   e. Enter a chart title: UMBRELLA INSURANGE AGENCY.

   f. Place the chart as an object on Sheet1.

   g. Place the chart in the range C24:G37.

3. Edit the pie chart and insert a chart subtitle.

   a. Double-click title until a text box appears around the title.

   b. Move to the end of the text, return and enter the subtitle: Quarterly Net Income.

4. In the worksheet, change labels for 1ST QTR., 2ND QTR, etc. to read: JAN-MAR, APR-JUNE, JULY-SEPT, OCT-DEC.

   ✔ Linked text changes in chart legend.

5. Select the APR-JUNE pie slice and change the color using the Format Data Point dialog box.

   ✔ Click on the pie, then click to select the desired pie slice. Excel 97 will display the name of the selected chart element.

6. Create an embedded column chart comparing EXPENSES for the four quarters:

   a. Use the selection illustrated on the previous page. Do not include TOTAL EXPENSES column or TOTALS row.

   b. Select Chart Wizard.

   c. Select default chart type and format.

   d. Data series should be in columns.

   e. Enter titles as follows:

Title:	UMBRELLA INSURANCE AGENCY
X-AXIS:	Expenses
Y-AXIS:	Dollars

   f. Place the chart as an object on Sheet1.

   g. Move the chart to the range A39:G60.

7. Select each chart text area, including the title, x-axis title, y-axis title, series labels, category labels, and change the font to 12 point.

8. Select the legend and change the font to 10 point.

9. Move the legend to the best position for viewing all the data.

10. Using the same data and titles as those for the column chart, create a stacked column chart. Use the third subtype that shows data based on 100% for each column.

11. Place the stacked column chart in the range A62:G83.

12. Select each of the quarterly data series items and change the format so that the columns use different patterns instead of colors. *Use Ctrl+1 and the Format dialog box, Patterns tab, Fill Effects button, and Pattern tab.*

13. Using the same data and titles as those for the **column** chart, create a **line** chart.

14. Place the line chart in the range A85:G107.

15. Note that the line chart is not a good way to display the data. Change the chart type to a bar chart type, default type.

16. Format alignment of access labels appropriately. If necessary, move and size charts to align them.

17. Set worksheet to print on one page.

18. Use Print Preview to view your work.

19. Save and close the workbook file; name it **INSQTRS**.

	A	B	C	D	E	F	G
1			UMBRELLA INSURANCE AGENCY				
2			QUARTERLY INCOME STATEMENT				
3							
4			1ST QTR	2ND QTR.	3RD QTR.	4TH QTR.	COMBINED
5			TOTALS	TOTALS	TOTALS	TOTALS	TOTALS
6							
7	INCOME						
8	Agency Fees		38,052.39	41,566.18	42,402.51	42,314.40	164,335.48
9	Consultations		4,776.95	4,679.76	4,000.73	3,730.51	17,187.95
10	Total Income		42,829.34	46,245.94	46,403.24	46,044.91	181,523.43
11							
12	EXPENSES:						
13	Advertising		800.00	950.00	900.00	830.00	3,480.00
14	Rent		3,600.00	3,600.00	3,600.00	3,600.00	14,400.00
15	Salaries		18,750.00	18,750.00	18,750.00	18,750.00	75,000.00
16	Supplies		699.08	609.62	672.42	592.00	2,573.12
17	Utilities		655.72	703.61	790.62	700.98	2,850.93
18	Interest		75.00	75.00	75.00	75.00	300.00
19	Other		685.84	1,238.22	1,150.95	741.65	3,816.66
20	Total Expenses		25,265.64	25,926.45	25,938.99	25,289.63	102,420.71
21							
22	NET INCOME		17,563.70	20,319.49	20,464.25	20,755.28	79,102.72

KEYSTROKES

EDIT LINKED CHART TEXT IN WORKSHEET

When you edit linked text (legend entries, data labels [values or text], and tick mark labels) in the worksheet, Excel automatically updates the chart.

1. Select worksheet containing chart data to edit.
2. Edit cell containing data label or value.

MOVE AN EMBEDDED CHART

1. Select chart.
2. Point to chart border.

   Pointer becomes a ⬉ when positioned correctly.

3. Drag border outline to desired position.
   OR
   Press **Alt** and drag border outline to align object to gridlines.

EDIT CHART TEXT

1. Enable chart editing.
2. Click on chart text until text box appears.
   a. Right-click.
   b. Select **Format** .... `O`
   c. Change font size and style, as desired.
3. Click **OK** .... `Enter`
   ✓ *Chart titles and axis labels are not linked to worksheet data, and they can be edited in the chart.*

FORMAT DATA SERIES

1. Enable chart editing.
2. Select data series to format.
3. Press **Ctrl+1** .... `Ctrl`+`1`
   OR
   a. Click **Format** .... `Alt`+`O`

b. Click **Selected Data Series** .... `E`
   OR
   a. Right-click.
   b. Select **Format Data**
      Series .... `Alt`+`O`
4. Select desired tab and formats.
   To select patterns:
   a. Click **Pattern**
      tab .... `Alt`+`Ctrl`+`Tab`
   b. Click **Fill Effects**
      tab .... `Alt`+`I`
   c. Select **Pattern**
      tab .... `Alt`+`Ctrl`+`Tab`
   d. Select **Pattern** .... `Alt`+`T`, `↕`
      ✓ *For a pie chart, Format Data Point replaces data series options above.*
5. Click **OK** .... `Enter`

Exercise 57

■ Print Charts ■ Print Preview Charts ■ Print Embedded Charts
■ Black and White Printers ■ Add Data to a Chart

NOTES

Print Charts

- Charts can be printed with the worksheet or as separate sheets. If you select an embedded chart to print apart from the worksheet, it will print to fit one page.

Print Preview Charts

- You can use Print Preview mode to see how a worksheet or chart will print. Note the illustration of the Print Preview screen and toolbar below.

- From Print Preview mode, you can also:

  - View the **Previous** or **Next** page when more than one page will be printed.

  - Change the page margins by dragging the handles that appear when you select the **Margins** button.

  - Click the **Setup** button to access the Page Setup dialog box from which you can change many page print settings such as scaling.

  - Print the chart or worksheet.

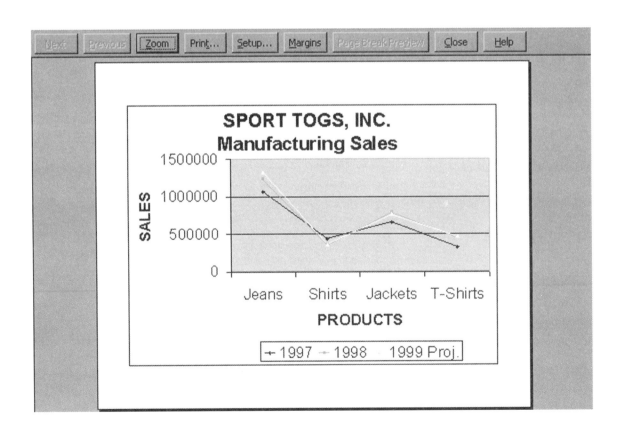

Print Embedded Charts

■ An embedded chart may be printed as part of the worksheet or, if it is selected, as a separate chart. When printing a selected embedded chart or a chart sheet:

- Excel selects the page orientation (**Portrait** or **Landscape**) that best matches the shape of the chart. You can change the page orientation from the Page tab in the Page Setup dialog box.

- The Sheet tab is replaced by the Chart tab, as shown in the illustration below, in the Page Setup dialog box. You can set chart print options such as **Printing Quality** and **Printed Chart Size** from the Chart tab.

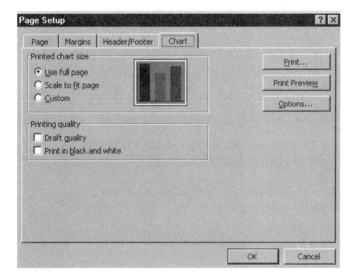

Black and White Printers

■ If your computer equipment includes a color monitor, the data markers will be shown in different colors. When you print colored charts using a black and white printer, colored text and lines are printed in black, colored areas are printed in shades of gray, and background colors are ignored.

Add Data to a Chart

■ You may need to add an additional series of data to a chart to update the information. For example, you may want to add information about another division or add another year's information. To add data to an embedded chart on the same worksheet, select the new data and drag it onto the chart. On a chart sheet or separate worksheet, use the Copy and Paste options commands to add the information to a selected chart and plot area.

In this exercise, you will add information for projected data for 1999 and print the charts you created for SPORTS TOGS, INC.

EXERCISE DIRECTIONS

1. Open ⌨ **SPORTS** or 💾 **57SPORTS.**

2. Enter the new information for the 1999 Proj. column in the worksheet as shown on the next page.

3. Copy the new column, select EMBEDDED CHARTS sheet, select the column chart and each plot area and paste the data.

4. Repeat this process for all charts on the worksheet.

5. Adjust font size and location of chart elements on the stacked bar chart to view all data. Make any other edits as necessary.

6. Print Preview the Embedded Charts sheet in the worksheet.

7. From the Print Preview window, select the Setup button.

8. From Page Setup dialog box:
   a. Select the Sheet tab, and turn printing of gridlines off.
   b. Select the Page tab, and set worksheet scale to one page wide by one page tall.

9. Return to the Preview screen and print the worksheet.

10. Enable chart editing for the line chart, then select Print Preview.
    ✓ *Only the line chart appears.*

11. Select the Setup button.

12. Select the Chart tab, and set the Printed Chart Size to Scale to Fit the Page; set print quality to draft.

13. Return to Print Preview and print the chart.

14. Select the PIE CHART sheet.

15. Preview the chart sheet and note the page orientation.

16. Click the Setup button and change the orientation of the page (Landscape or Portrait).

17. Close the dialog box and preview the chart sheet.

18. If the page orientation is set to portrait, change it back to landscape.

19. Print the chart sheet from the Print Preview window.

20. Save and close the workbook file; name it **SPORTS**.

Sports Workbook With Data Sheet Selected

	A	B	C	D	E
1	SPORTS TOGS, INC.				
2	MANUFACTURING SALES				
3			1997	1998	1999 Proj.
4	Jeans		1066767	1235467	1324555
5	Shirts		434768	354245	363456
6	Jackets		657654	789643	765655
7	T-Shirts		324534	453234	465788
8					
9					
10					
11					
12					
13					
14					
15					

PIE CHART \ **DATA** / EMBEDDED CHARTS / Sheet3 /

KEYSTROKES

PRINT CHARTS

Prints chart sheet or embedded chart as part of the worksheet.

1. Select worksheet or chart sheet containing chart to print.
2. Follow steps to **PRINT A WORKSHEET**, Keystrokes section, Exercise 14.

PRINT EMBEDDED CHART SEPARATELY

1. Enable chart editing for chart to print.
2. Follow steps to **PRINT A WORKSHEET**, page 57.

SET CHART PRINT OPTIONS

1. **FROM PRINT PREVIEW:**

   Click **Setup** .... [Alt]+[S]

   OR

   FROM WORKSHEET OR CHART SHEET:

   a. Click **File** menu .... [Alt]+[F]

   b. Click **Page Setup** .... [U]

2. Click **Chart tab** .... [Ctrl]+[Tab]

   ✓ *Available options depend upon the currently selected printer.*

3. **To set printed chart size:**

   Select desired Printed Chart Size option:

   • **Use full page** .... [Alt]+[U]

   • **Scale to fit page** .... [Alt]+[F]

   • **Custom** .... [Alt]+[C]

   ✓ *With Custom selected, you can center the chart on the page from the Margins tab.*

4. **To set print quality of chart:**

   Select **draft quality** .... [Alt]+[Q]

5. To print chart in black and white:

   Select **Print in black and white** .... [Alt]+[B]

6. Click **OK** .... [Enter]
   to return to sheet or Print Preview.

SET PAGE ORIENTATION OF PRINTED PAGE

1. **FROM PRINT PREVIEW:**

   Click **Setup** .... [Alt]+[S]

   OR

   FROM WORKSHEET OR CHART SHEET:

   a. Click **File** menu .... [Alt]+[F]

   b. Click **Page Setup** .... [U]

2. Click **Page tab** .... [Ctrl]+[Tab]

3. Select **Portrait** .... [Alt]+[T]

   OR

   Select **Landscape** .... [Alt]+[L]

4. Click **OK** .... [Enter]
   to return to sheet or Print Preview.

ADD DATA SERIES TO A CHART

1. Select column or row of data.
2. Click **Edit** menu .... [Alt]+[E]
3. Click **Copy** .... [C]
4. Select chart to receive data.
5. Click **Edit** menu .... [Alt]+[E]
6. Click **Paste** .... [P]

Exercise 58

- ■ **Change Location of Charts**
- ■ **Change Orientation of Data Series**
- ■ **Change Orientation of Chart Text** ■ **Chart Options**

NOTES

Change Location of Charts

- ■ We have seen charts on chart sheets or embedded into the worksheet. You can easily change the location of a chart by using the Chart, **Location** options to move an embedded chart to a chart sheet or to place a chart from a chart sheet as an object on a worksheet.

Change Orientation of Data Series

- ■ For charts that use axes (all except pie charts), Excel automatically determines if the selected data range(s) will be **plotted by row** or **by column** layout. When you are creating a chart, Chart Wizard proposes the orientation of the data series and allows you to make a change. You can also change the orientation of the data series *after* creating the chart, by enabling chart editing and selecting **Source Data** from the **Chart** menu to access the Chart Wizard settings screen. Note the change to the orientation of data in the illustration on the next page.

- ■ Chart Wizard proposes how to plot the data series based on your selection.

If selection contains more columns than rows:

- • Chart Wizard proposes to plot the data series in rows.
- • Column labels are used as x-axis labels.
- • Row labels are used as legend labels.

If selection contains more rows than columns:

- • Chart Wizard proposes to plot the data series in columns.
- • Row labels are used as x-axis labels.
- • Column labels are used as legend labels.

If selection contains an equal number of rows and columns:

- • Chart Wizard proposes to plot the data series in rows.

Change Orientation of Chart Text

- ■ Chart text, such as axis labels or titles, can be arranged vertically, rotated to any angle, or arranged horizontally. The axis text should be selected while in chart edit mode then formatted by selecting **Selected text** from the Format menu and clicking the Alignment tab.

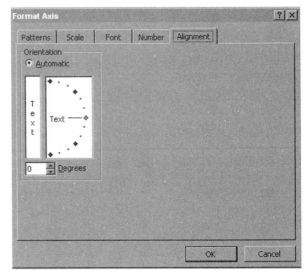

Chart Options

■ All the settings you make in Chart Wizard can be changed or enhanced by selecting **Chart Options** from the Chart menu. When you select a chart and open the options dialog box, you will see your chart, which will change as you make setting changes. You can make or change settings for Titles, Axes, Gridlines, Legend, Data Labels, and Data Table for this column chart. Note the illustration of the Chart Options dialog box to the right.

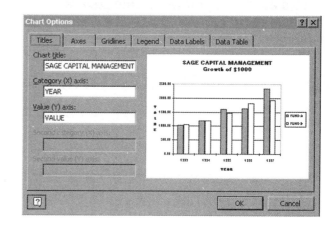

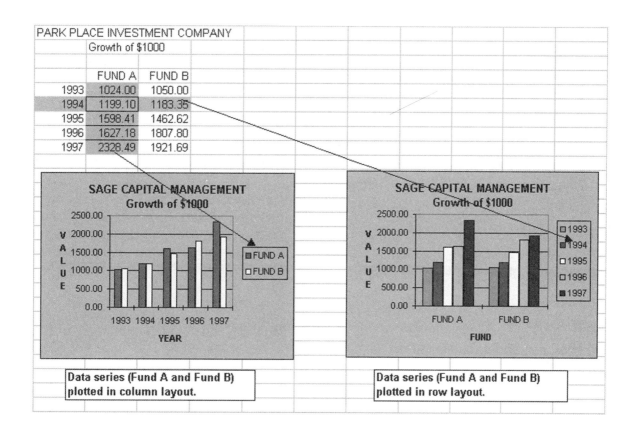

Data series (Fund A and Fund B) plotted in column layout.

Data series (Fund A and Fund B) plotted in row layout.

> *In this exercise, you will create several charts comparing the growth and performance of an investment in Fund A to one in Fund B over a five year period for Park Place Investments Company.*

EXERCISE DIRECTIONS

1. Create the worksheet as shown below, or open 🖫 **58GROW.**

   ✓ *The row labels (years) should be formatted as label data.*

	A	B	C	D
1	PARK PLACE INVESTMENT COMPANY			
2		Growth of $1000		
3				
4		FUND A	FUND B	
5	1993	1024.00	1050.00	
6	1994	1199.10	1183.35	
7	1995	1598.41	1462.62	
8	1996	1627.18	1807.80	
9	1997	2328.49	1921.69	

2. Create an embedded column chart to compare Fund A to Fund B for 1993-1997, by using the Chart Wizard button.

   a. Select the default format for the column chart.

   ChartWizard (step 2) proposes to plot the data series in columns. Accept the default setting.

   b. Add the following titles:

Chart Title:	PARK PLACE INVESTMENT COMPANY
Category (X):	YEAR
Value (Y):	VALUE

   c. Place the chart as an object on Sheet1.

   d. Place the chart in the range A11:F25.

3. Edit the chart and add a subtitle to the chart title:

   Growth of $1000

4. Copy the column chart to the clipboard, then paste it to the range starting at G11.

5. Change the plot orientation to rows by enabling chart editing and selecting Source Data from the Chart or shortcut menu.

   ✓ *Note changes to the legend entries and x-axis labels.*

6. Edit the x-axis title to FUND.

7. Edit both column charts and change the alignment of the y-axis title to vertical orientation (one letter under the other).

   Hint: Right-click the y-axis label, select Format Axis Title and the Alignment tab. Then select the vertical textbox in the Orientation section.

8. Place another copy of the column chart in the range starting at A27.

9. Change the chart type to a bar chart.

10. Create an embedded pie chart that shows the values of Fund A for 1993-1997.

    a. Use the default format for the **pie** chart type.

    b. Add chart title:

    c. PARK PLACE INVESTMENT COMPANY.

    d. Place the chart on Sheet1.

    e. Place it in the range G27:L41.

11. Edit the pie chart and add a second line to the chart title that reads:

    Growth of $1000 in Fund A

12. Use the Chart, Chart Options commands to change the Data Labels settings. Check each setting to view the effect of each change. Set the data labels to Show label and percent. Change size of chart to accommodate new labels.

13. Use the Chart Options dialog box to set the legend position to the bottom of the chart.

14. Change Zoom percentage on the View menu, to view entire worksheet.

15. Align charts (size and move them) as needed.

16. Change colors of bars in the column and bar charts so that each chart is different.

17. Print Preview the sheet.

18. Print the worksheet so that the data and charts fit on one page.

19. Save and close the workbook file; name it **GROW.**

KEYSTROKES

CHANGE ORIENTATION OF DATA SERIES

1. Enable chart editing.
2. Click **Chart** .... `Alt`+`C`
3. Click **Source Data** .... `S`
4. Select **Rows** or...................... `Alt`+`R`

   Columns .... `Alt`+`L`

CHANGE ORIENTATION OF CHART TEXT

✓ *You cannot change orientation of text in a legend.*

1. Enable chart editing.
2. Double-click chart text.
   OR
   a. Click text to change.
   b. Click **Format** menu .... `Alt`+`O`
   c. Click **Selected Axis Title** .... `E`
   OR
   a. Click text to change.
   b. Click **Ctrl+1** .... `Ctrl`+`1`
3. Click **Alignment** tab .... `Ctrl`+`Tab`
4. Click desired text alignment:
   •Horizontal .... `Alt`+`H`, `↕`
   •Vertical...................... `Alt`+`V`, `↕`
5. Type **Degrees** if
   desired .... `Alt`+`D`, *degrees*
6. Click **OK**................................... `Enter`

CHANGE CHART OPTIONS

1. Enable chart editing.
2. Click **Chart** .... `Alt`+`C`
3. Click **Chart Options** .... `O`
4. Select desired tab:
   • **Titles**
   • **Legend**
   • **Data Labels**
5. Make desired settings
6. Click **OK** .... `Enter`

Exercise 59

- ■ **Create Stock Charts**
- ■ **Format Data Markers** ■ **Set Scale of Value Axis**
- ■ **Charts with Two Value Axes**

NOTES

Create Stock Charts

- ■ Excel 97 provides four chart subtypes for **stock market** and **price analysis**, as illustrated below. High-Low-Close, Open-High-Low-Close, Volume-High-Low-Close, and Volume-Open-High-Low-Close charts are used to track changes in stock data during a particular time period.

- ■ The Volume refers to the sales volume for the stock for the day. The Open value refers to the opening price of the stock for the day. The High and Low values refer to the highest and lowest prices for the day. The closing price of the stock is the close value. On the Open-High-Low-Close chart the white bars indicate a close up in price and a black bar indicates a close down in price.

Format Data Markers

- ■ The values on line or stock charts for different data series are indicated by unique **data markers**. Excel lets you format the shape and color of the data markers by selecting the marker and pressing Ctrl+1 to display the Format Data Series dialog box below. You can choose a custom shape, set its size and color and set a shadow, if desired.

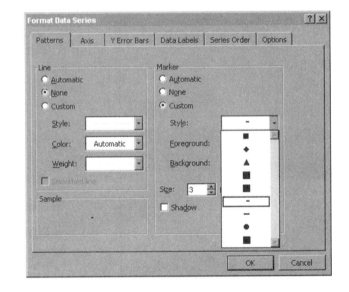

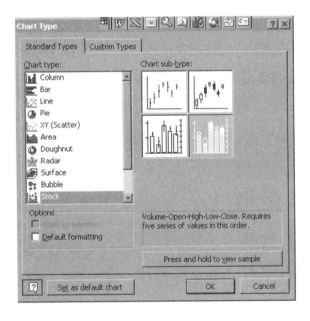

Set Scale of Value Axis

■ Excel automatically determines the scale used on the **value axis** from the range of data plotted. This scale can be changed. For example, you can select the value axis, press Ctrl+1, and set the display of the minimum and maximum values and the major and minor units of values on the y-axis.

> ✓ NOTE: *When selecting chart elements such as a data series or y-axis, check that the correct element has been selected before formatting.*

Charts With Two Value Axes

■ If you are charting data series, like stock volume and stock prices, which are related but not in numeric value, Excel will create a chart with **two value axes**. The volume will be charted on the left value axis and the stock prices will be charted on the right value axis. Note the example shown below.

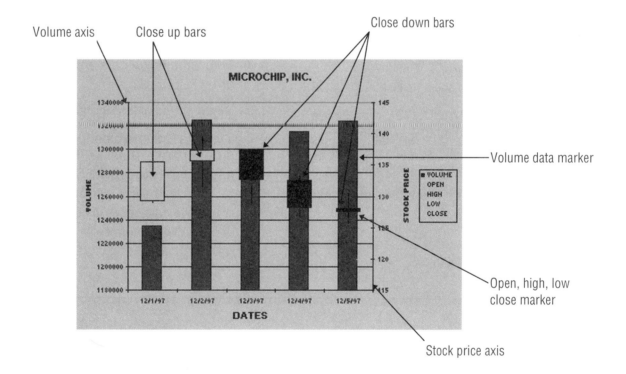

> *In this exercise, you will prepare several stock analysis charts for Alan Tracey. He is considering the sale of his MicroChip Inc. stock and wants to evaluate the stock's performance for the week.*

EXERCISE DIRECTIONS

1. Create the worksheet as shown on the next page, or open 🖫 **59STOCK.**
   - ✓ *Enter the values as mixed numbers.*

2. Create a High-Low-Close chart on a separate sheet using Chart Wizard.
   a. Select the non-adjacent selection including the DATE, HIGH, LOW and CLOSE columns.
   b. Select the first Stock chart subtype.
   c. Chart titles should be as follows:
Chart Title:	MICROCHIP, INC.
Category (X):	DATE
Value (Y):	PRICE

   d. Name the new chart sheet, HIGH-LOW-CLOSE.

3. Select the chart and the CLOSE data series, which is the tick mark on the vertical line.
   - Format the data marker for a custom, solid square marker, and change the size to 4 points.

4. Select the y value axis chart item and format its scale as follows:
Minimum:	120
Maximum:	145
Major Unit:	5
Minor Unit:	1
Cross x-axis at:	120

   Since we changed only the first and last settings, leave the Auto check mark off for those two custom settings.

5. Check the new value axis settings.

6. Rename the Sheet1 sheet, DATA.

7. Create an Open-High-Low-Close chart on a separate sheet using Chart Wizard.
   a. Select the non-adjacent selection including the DATE, OPEN, HIGH, LOW, and CLOSE columns.
   b. Select the top right (2nd) Stock chart subtype.
   c. Chart titles should be as follows:
Chart Title:	MICROCHIP, INC.
Category (X):	DATE
Value (Y):	PRICE

   d. Name the new chart sheet, OPEN-HIGH-LOW-CLOSE.

8. Select the down bars and set format color to red.

9. Select the up bars and set format color to blue.

10. Create a Volume-Open-High-Low-Close chart on a separate sheet using Chart Wizard.
   a. Select all data columns.
   b. Select the bottom right (4th) Stock chart subtype.
   c. Arrange data series in columns.
   d. Chart titles should be as follows:
Chart Title:	MICROCHIP, INC.
Category (X):	DATE
Value (Y):	VOLUME
Second Value (Y):	STOCK PRICE

   e. Name the new chart sheet, VOLUME-OPEN-HIGH-LOW-CLOSE.

11. Print the VOLUME-OPEN-HIGH-LOW-CLOSE sheet.

12. Close and save the workbook file; name it **STOCK.**

	A	B	C	D	E	F
1			ALAN TRACEY			
2			MICROCHIP, INC.			
3			FOR THE WEEK ENDING 12/5/97			
4	DATE	VOLUME	OPEN	HIGH	LOW	CLOSE
5	12/01/97	1234543	129 1/8	138 1/8	128 7/8	135 1/2
6	12/02/97	1325434	135 1/2	139 5/8	131 1/2	137 3/8
7	12/03/97	1287634	137 3/8	137 3/8	128 5/8	132 1/2
8	12/04/97	1315434	132 1/2	133 3/8	126 5/8	128 1/8
9	12/05/97	1324320	128 1/8	130 3/8	125 5/8	127 3/8

KEYSTROKES

SET SCALE OF VALUE AXIS

1. Enable chart editing.
2. Double-click value axis to format.
   OR
   a. Right-click value axis.
   b. Click **Format Axis**........................ `O`
3. Click **Scale** tab .... `Ctrl`+`Tab`
4. a. Select scale options to change:
   - **Minimum** .... `Alt`+`N`
   - **Maximum** .... `Alt`+`X`
   - **Major Unit** .... `Alt`+`A`
   - **Minor Unit** .... `Alt`+`I`
   - **Category (X) Axis Crosses at**........................ `Alt`+`C`
   b. Type desired value number for selected item in text box.
5. Repeat Step 4 for each scale option to change.
6. Click **OK** .... `Enter`

FORMAT DATA MARKERS IN A LINE CHART

1. Enable chart editing.
2. Double-click any data marker in series to format.
   OR
   a. Select data series to format.
   b. Click **Format** menu .... `Alt`+`O`
   c. Click **Selected Data Series**........ `E`
3. Click **Patterns** tab .... `Ctrl`+`Tab`
4. Select desired options:
   - **Line**
     Click **Automatic** .... `Alt`+`A`
     OR
     Click **None** .... `Alt`+`N`
     OR
     a. Click **Custom**........................ `↗↓`
     b. Click **Style**........... `Alt`+`S`, `↗↓`
     c. Click **Color** .... `Alt`+`C`, `↕↕`
     d. Click **Weight** .... `Alt`+`W`, `↗↓`
     e. Click **Smoothed Line** .... `Alt`+`M`

   - **Marker**
     Click **Automatic**................ `Alt`+`U`
     OR
     Click **None**........................ `Alt`+`O`
     OR
     a. Click **Custom** .... `↗↓`
     b. Click **Style** .... `Alt`+`L`
     c. Click **Foreground** `Alt`+`F`, `↕↕`
     d. Click **Background** `Alt`+`B`, `↕↕`
     e. Click **Size**........... `Alt`+`Z`, `↗↓`
     f. Click **Shadow**................ `Alt`+`D`
5. Click **OK** .... `Enter`

Exercise 60

- ■ **Create an Exploded Pie Chart**
- ■ **Size Plot Area or Legend in a Chart**
- ■ **Create an Area Chart**

NOTES

Create an Exploded Pie Chart

- ■ An **exploded pie chart** has one or more wedges of the pie separated from the circle for emphasis. To create an exploded chart effect, click twice on the wedge and move any selected wedge (data point) by dragging it away from the center of the pie.

    ✓ *NOTE: When you drag a slice, the associated labels move with it.*

Size Plot Area or Legend in a Chart

- ■ After adding data labels to a chart, you may want to move or size the plot area of the chart. When you do this, the data labels adjust with the plot area. When the plot area is selected, "Plot Area" appears in the name box. Note the illustration of a pie chart with plot area selected below.

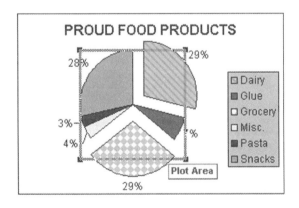

Create an Area Chart

- ■ A **two-dimensional area chart** can be described as a stacked bar and line chart combined. The data series are stacked, but a trend line is drawn between the data points. An illustration of an area chart is shown below.

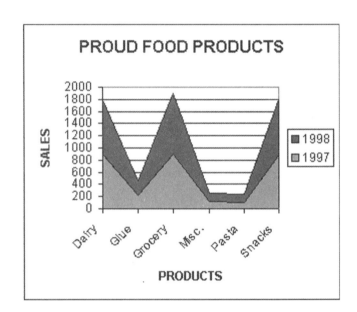

230

In this exercise, you will create a worksheet for Proud Food Products, a diversified food products company. They want to compare sales for all products for each year by creating separate pie charts and then compare both years by creating an area chart.

EXERCISE DIRECTIONS

1. Create the worksheet as shown below, or open 🖫**60PROD**.

	A	B	C	D
1		PROUD FOOD PRODUCTS		
2		PRODUCT SALES		
3				
4		1997	1998	
5	Dairy	906	895	
6	Glue	215	250	
7	Grocery	901	1003	
8	Misc.	122	125	
9	Pasta	94	135	
10	Snacks	888	912	

2. Create an embedded pie chart illustrating 1997 sales, using ChartWizard.
   a. Accept default pie chart format.
   b. Show the percent values for each wedge.
   c. Add the chart title to read:
      PROUD FOOD PRODUCTS
   d. Place the chart on the sheet in the range A11:G27.

3. Edit the chart title to add a subtitle: 1997 Sales.

4. Change the font size of the titles to 14 point.

5. Select the plot area of chart, (click the outer area around the pie until the plot area displays) then size and move it as desired. Try to enlarge the pie portion of the chart.

6. Explode the pie sections for Dairy and Grocery by clicking twice on each data point and dragging it away from the center of the pie. Be sure the correct data point is selected. If you move the wrong item, select Undo from the Edit menu.

7. Format the Dairy wedge area for yellow with a pattern and the Grocery wedge area for blue with a pattern.

8. Create an embedded pie chart illustrating 1998 sales using ChartWizard and a nonadjacent selection of data:
   a. Accept default pie chart format.
   b. Show the percent values for each wedge.
   c. Add the chart title to read:
   d. PROUD FOOD PRODUCTS
   e. Place the chart on the sheet in the range H11:N27.

9. Edit the chart and add a subtitle: 1998 –Sales

10. Repeat the same edits as in steps 5, 6, and 7 to make the charts uniform.

11. Create an embedded area chart illustrating 1997 and 1998 sales, including the year labels in your selection.
    a. Select an area chart and the second subtype showing the stacked areas.
    b. Add titles as follows:
    | Chart title: | PROUD FOOD PRODUCTS |
    | X-Axis title: | PRODUCTS |
    | Y-Axis title: | SALES |

12. Edit the chart and add a second line to chart title to read:
    PRODUCT SALES - 1997-1998

13. Format the data series colors to Blue for 1998 and Yellow for 1997.

14. With the worksheet selected, set entire worksheet to print on one page.

15. Save and close the workbook file; name it **PROD**.

KEYSTROKES

SIZE PLOT AREA OR LEGEND IN A CHART

1. Enable chart editing.
2. Select plot area or legend.

   Handles appear on border of item.

3. Point to handle on side of item to size. ↗↑↖

   Pointer becomes a ↔ .

4. Drag item outline in direction to size.

MOVE CHART ELEMENT— EXPLODE A PIE SECTION

✓ *You can move the plot area, legend, chart title, data labels, pie slices and axes labels.*

1. Enable chart editing.
2. Click twice on the chart item to move.
3. Drag chart item outline to desired position.

CHANGE AREA FORMAT OF A DATA SERIES OR DATA POINT

1. Enable chart editing.
2. Select appropriate chart element:

   To format a specific series:

   a. Select desired series.

   b. Click **Format** menu .... Alt + O

   c. Click **Selected Data Series** .... E

   To format a specific data point:

   a. Select desired data marker.

   b. Click **Format** menu .... Alt + O

   c. Click **Selected Data Point** .... E

   ✓ *The name box displays currently selected chart item.*

3. Click **Patterns** tab .... Ctrl + Tab

4. Select desired options:

   • **Border**

      Click **Automatic** .... Alt + A

      OR

      Click **None** .... Alt + N

   OR

   a. Click **Custom** .... ↕

   b. Click **Style** .... Alt + S , ↕

   c. Click **Color** .... Alt + C

   d. Click **Weight** .... Alt + W

   e. Click **Shadow** .... Alt + D

   • **Area**

      Click **Automatic** .... Alt + U

      OR

      Click **None** .... Alt + E

      OR

   a. Select a color .... Tab , ↕↔

   b. Click **Fill Effects** I

   c. Click **Pattern** tab . Alt + Ctrl + Tab

   d. Select desired pattern .... ↕↔ , Enter

5. Click **OK** .... Enter

UNDO LAST CHANGE

1. Click **Edit** menu .... Alt + E

2. Click **Undo** .... U

   ✓ *Complete name of Undo menu item depends on last action performed.*

NEXT EXERCISE

Exercise 61

- ■ **Enter Line Breaks in a Cell Entry**
- ■ **Add Gridlines and Data Labels**
- ■ **Create a 3-D Chart**

NOTES

Enter Line Breaks in a Cell Entry

- ■ When you select worksheet text to chart, Excel uses the labels in individual cells to identify markers and sometimes axes within a chart.

- ■ If your worksheet labels are in more than one row, you should combine the text from both cells so that it is contained in a single cell, as shown below. Use F2 to edit the cell and press Alt+Enter, if necessary, to insert a line break in the contents of the cell. The row height adjusts automatically to show multiple lines of text.

	A	B	C	D	E	F
1			ROCHELLE MARTLING			
2			INVESTMENT TRANSACTIONS FOR 1997			
3						
4	COMPANY NAME	SYMBOL	SHARES	DATE BOUGHT		

Add Gridlines or Data Labels

- ■ You can add **gridlines** to some charts to further clarify where data points fall on the chart. These lines may be added to or removed from any axis by selecting Chart Options from the Chart Menu and clicking the **Gridlines** tab. The Gridlines tab will also appear as a Chart Options tab in step 3 of the Chart Wizard. This option, however, is not available for chart types such as pie, doughnut, bubble, and radar.

- ■ **Data labels** are labels on the columns or bars in a chart that display the actual value of the series item. Labels are added by using the Data Labels tab on the Chart and Options dialog box, which may be accessed from Step 3 of the Chart wizard. It can also can be accessed by enabling Chart Editing and then selecting Chart Options from the Chart menu. Data Labels that represent values, text, or percentages may be added to a chart.

Create a 3-D Chart

- ■ You can select a **3-D Chart** format to add interest and emphasize the data you want to compare. Changing a 2-D chart to 3-D adds a **z-axis**, which then becomes the value axis.

You may change the view of a 3-D chart by using the following 3-D format options:

- • increase or decrease elevation
- • rotate chart left or right
- • lock axes at right angles

Note the illustration of the Format 3-D View dialog box:

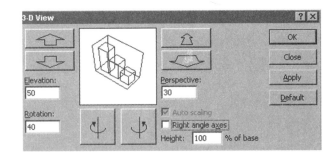

234

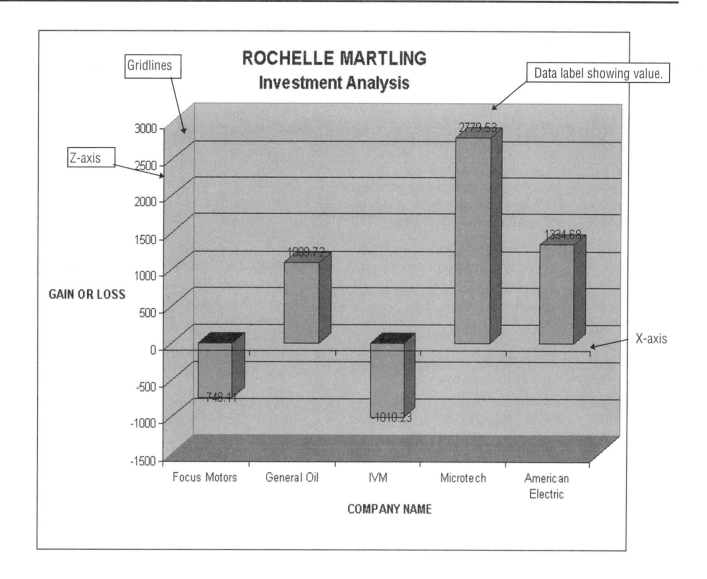

ROCHELLE MARTLING
Investment Analysis

- Gridlines
- Z-axis
- Data label showing value.
- GAIN OR LOSS
- X-axis

3000
2500
2000
1500
1000
500
0
-500
-1000
-1500

2779.53
1009.72
1334.68
748.11
-1010.23

Focus Motors   General Oil   IVM   Microtech   American Electric

COMPANY NAME

In this exercise, you will retrieve Rochelle Martling's stock analysis data and create enhanced charts to present her gain and loss for the year. In addition, using a 3-D pie chart, you will chart the percentage that each stock's selling price represents of her total portfolio sales.

EXERCISE DIRECTIONS

1. Open ⌨ **INVEST** or 💾 **61INVEST**.

2. Use the Window command to unfreeze panes, if necessary.

3. Edit row four so each cell contains the text now found in rows four and five. Most cells will then contain two lines of text.

   For example, cell A4 should contain the label:

   COMPANY

   NAME

4. After editing row four, delete row five.

5. Create an embedded 3-D column chart showing COMPANY NAME of stocks and the GAIN OR LOSS on each stock:
   a. Select the Clustered column with 3-D visual effect. (First chart in second row.)
   b. Accept the data range.
   c. Set Chart Options as follows:
      Titles Tab:
      Chart: ROCHELLE MARTLING
      Category (X): COMPANY NAME
      Category (Z): GAIN OR LOSS
      Legend Tab: Remove the legend

Gridlines Tab: Major Gridlines on Z axis

Data Labels Tab: Show value

d. Chart location on Sheet1.

e. Place the chart in A16:K48.

6. Edit text items (axis labels, data labels, category labels) and change font size to 10 points.

7. Edit the chart, change chart title to 16 point size and add a second line to the chart title: Gain or Loss—1997. Set subtitle to 14 point size.

8. Enable chart editing, select the data area, and format the 3-D view using the following controls in the Format, 3-D View dialog box:

a. Change the elevation.

b. Change the rotation of the chart.

c. Click OK to view the chart.

d. Re-select the data and 3-D View dialog box.

e. Deselect the Right Angle Axes box.

f. Change the perspective.

g. Move dialog box so chart is visible.

h. Click Default to return to default settings.

9. Create a 3-D pie chart showing COMPANY NAME and SELLING PRICE data:

a. Select the Exploded pie with 3-D visual effect chart type. Chart sub-type(5)

b. Select chart options that include data labels showing percentages.

c. Add chart title: Rochelle Martling

d. Place the chart on Sheet1 in the range A50:J71.

10. Edit the chart and add a second line to the chart title:

Stock Portfolio Sales—1997

11. Change the elevation and rotation of the pie chart using the 3-D View dialog box.

12. Create a 3-D bar chart using the COMPANY NAME and ANNUAL YIELD data

a. Select the Clustered Bar with 3-D Visual Effect chart type. Chart sub-type(4)

b. Chart the series data in rows.

c. Select chart options that include data labels showing values.

d. Add chart title: Rochelle Martling

e. Place the chart on Sheet1 in the range K50:U71.

13. Edit the chart and add second line to chart title: Annual Yield—1997

14. Select the worksheet and set it to print on one page.

15. Print the worksheet.

16. Close and save the workbook; name it **INVEST**.

	A	B	C	D	E	F	G	H	I	J	K
1			ROCHELLE MARTLING								
2			INVESTMENT TRANSACTIONS FOR 1997								
3											
4	COMPANY NAME	SYMBOL	SHARES	DATE BOUGHT	DATE SOLD	DAYS HELD	SELLING PRICE	COST	GAIN OR LOSS	% GAIN OR LOSS	ANNUAL YIELD
5	NAME	SYMBOL	SHARES	BOUGHT	SOLD	HELD	PRICE	COST	LOSS	OR LOSS	YIELD
6											
7	Focus Motors	FM	100	15-Jan-96	28-Feb-97	410	6950.75	7698.86	-748.11	-9.72%	-8.65%
8	General Oil	GNO	200	06-Mar-96	03-Apr-97	393	7656.87	6567.15	1089.72	16.59%	15.41%
9	IVM	IVM	100	18-Dec-96	31-Jul-97	225	8976.85	9987.08	-1010.23	-10.12%	-16.41%
10	Microtech	MIC	200	05-Jan-97	03-Oct-97	271	11435.98	8656.45	2779.53	32.11%	43.25%
11	American Electric	AE	300	09-Mar-97	04-Nov-97	240	5467.43	4132.75	1334.68	32.30%	49.12%
12											
13	TOTALS						40487.88	37042.29	3445.59	9.30%	11.03%
14	AVERAGES					308	8097.58	7408.46	689.12		
15											

KEYSTROKES

ENTER LINE BREAKS IN A CELL ENTRY

1. Double–click cell to edit.
   OR
   a. Select cell to edit.
   b. Press **F2** .... `F2`
2. Place insertion point .... `⇥` where line break will be inserted.
3. Press **Alt + Enter** .... `Alt`+`Enter`
4. Type text as needed.

INSERT OR REMOVE GRIDLINES

1. Enable chart editing.
2. Click **Chart** menu .... `Alt`+`C`
3. Click **Chart Options** .... `O`
4. Select **Gridlines** tab .... `Ctrl`+`Tab`
5. Select or deselect (X/Y/Z) axis options:
   ✓ *Available options depend upon selected chart type.*
   • Major Gridlines.
   • Minor Gridlines.
6. Click **OK** .... `Enter`

ENTER DATA LABELS

1. Enable chart editing.
2. Click **Chart** menu .... `Alt`+`C`
3. Click **Chart Options** .... `O`
4. Click **Data Labels** tab.
5. Select display option:
   • **None** .... `Alt`+`O`
   • **Show value** .... `Alt`+`V`
   • **Show percent** .... `Alt`+`P`
   • **Show label** .... `Alt`+`L`
   • **Show label and percent** ... `Alt`+`A`
   • **Show bubble sizes** .... `Alt`+`B`

   ✓ *Only the options that apply to the chart type will display.*

6. Click **OK** .... `Enter`

SET VIEW OPTIONS FOR A 3-D CHART (CHANGE ROTATION AND ELEVATION)

1. Enable chart editing.
2. Click **Chart** menu .... `Alt`+`C`
3. Click **3-D View** .... `V`
4. Set the following options:

   To increase or decrease elevation:
   Click **Elevation**
   button .... `⬆` or `⬇`
   OR
   a. Select desired **Elevation** button .... `Tab`
   b. Press **Space** .... `Space` until desired elevation is obtained.
   OR
   a. Click **Elevation** text box ..... `Alt`+`E`
   b. Type desired elevation number.

   To rotate chart left or right:
   Click **Rotation**
   button .... `⟲` or `⟳`
   OR
   a. Select desired **Rotation** button .... `Tab`
   b. Press **Space** .... `Space` until desired rotation is obtained.
   OR
   a. Click **Rotation** text box ...... `Alt`+`R`
   b. Type desired Rotation number.

To increase or decrease perspective:

✓ *This option is not available if **Right Angle Axes** is selected.*

Click **Perspective**
button .... `⬎` or `⬏`

OR
a. Select desired **Perspective** button .... `Tab`
b. Press **Space** .... `Space` until desired perspective is obtained.
OR
a. Click **Perspective** text box .... `Alt`+`P`
b. Type desired perspective number.

To lock axes at right angles:

Click **Right Angle Axes** .... `Alt`+`X`

To scale chart to fill window:

✓ *This option is available if **Right Angle Axes** is selected.*

Select **Auto Scaling** .... `Alt`+`S`

To set height in relation to base of chart:

a. Click **Height of Base** text box .... `Alt`+`I`
b. Type number (5-500).

To preview chart in sheet with current settings:

a. Move dialog box so chart is visible.
b. Click **Apply** .... `Alt`+`A`

To return chart to default settings:

Click **Default** .... `Alt`+`D`

5. Click **OK** .... `Enter`

Exercise

62

■ **Use Map Feature** ■ **Edit Maps**
■ **Map Toolbar**

NOTES

Use Map Feature

■ Excel 97 has a **map feature** that displays geographic data, such as information about countries or states, on the appropriate map. To use the map feature, select the range of cells to be mapped including the geographic data, and click the Map button 🌐 on the Standard toolbar. The cross hair ✛ mouse symbol will then appear on screen so you can drag to create and size the map. Excel automatically assigns the map that best relates to the data selected. (If you do not have the Map button on your toolbar, rerun the Setup program to install the mapping feature.)

■ This exercise will demonstrate several of the many options in the data mapping feature.

Edit Maps

■ As with charts, in order to edit the map while in worksheet mode, you must click on the displayed map. When the map is first created, you are automatically in edit mode. Edit mode is indicated by the presence of a border around the map, the Map Control dialog box, a menu bar that includes mapping commands, and the Map that toolbar replaces the Standard and Formatting toolbars. Note the illustration below of the Mapping menus, toolbar, and dialog box.

■ The **Map Control** dialog box may be hidden or displayed. It is displayed when the map is created and may be used to format items on the map. The format buttons may be dragged onto the box area to change the format of the map. The Map Control dialog box may be closed with the Close button ☒ or by clicking the **Show/hide Microsoft Map Control** button on the Map toolbar.

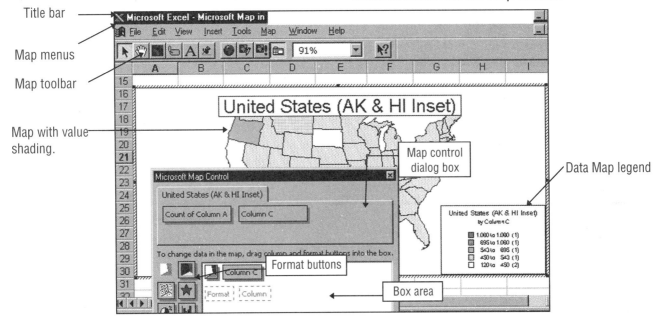

Map Toolbar

- The Map toolbar, which appears when you enable editing for a map, contains buttons that let you edit the map and change map views. Note the illustration of the Map toolbar below:

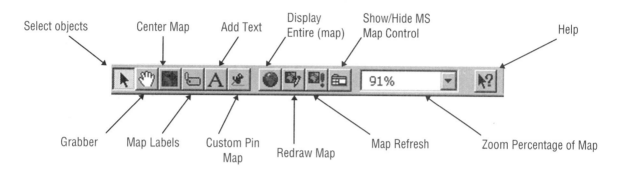

In this exercise, you will use Brownell Pharmaceuticals' worksheet to apply the map feature. The map and the legend will be edited, data labels added, and the map sized and moved for better appearance. Use the illustration of the solution on the next page to assist you in creating the desired result.

EXERCISE DIRECTIONS

1. Open 📠USEMPS or 💾62USEMPS.

2. Select the range to map, including the state names and the number of employees.

3. Click the Map button 🌐 on the Standard toolbar.

4. Place the map in the range A16:I30.

5. Select the United States (AK and HI insert) map from the Multiple Maps Available box.

   The default map will appear along with a legend, the Map Control dialog box, map menus and the Map toolbar.

6. Explore the Map Control dialog box by moving the pointer over the format buttons to see the ToolTips.

   ✓ *Note that the chart is using Value Shading.*

7. Change the chart to Category Shading by clicking and dragging the Category Shading button into the box.

   ✓ *Note that the shading changes to colors.*

8. Close the Map Control dialog box.

9. Double-click the map to change to edit map mode.

10. To hide the United States heading:
    a. Click on the United States (AK & HI inset) title box.
    b. Right-click and select Hide from the shortcut menu.

11. To edit the legend:
    a. Click on the legend box.
    b. Right-click and select Edit from the shortcut menu.
    c. Check that Use Compact Format is deselected and that Show Legend is selected.
    d. Change the titles and fonts as follows:
       Title: Brownell Pharmaceuticals. (Bookman Old Style, 11 pt.)
       Subtitle: Employees by State (Bookman Old Style, 9 pt.)
    e. Close the dialog box and reposition the legend, if necessary.

12. To label the map with state names and data:
    a. Click the Map Labels button on the Map toolbar (in edit mode).
    b. In the Map Labels dialog box, select Map Feature Names for state labels.

label in the topmost position within each state. Click to insert the label. Right-click to clear unwanted labels.

d. Click the Map Labels button on the Map toolbar.

e. In the Map Labels dialog box, select the Values from option and note that Column C or the column with the values is selected. Close the dialog box.

f. Point to each state and click to enter the value below the state name.

13. To change colors of the states:

a. Select the Map, Category Shading Options from the map menu bar

b. Go to the values for Arizona (120 - Red) and change it to White.

c. Go to the values for Montana (543 - Blue) and change it to Light Gray.

14. To move the map into view:

a. Change the Zoom % to 100% to bring the map closer for easier viewing.

b. Use the Grabber icon to move the map to the left of the map area.

c. Move the legend box to the bottom right corner of the map.

(Use the illustration of the solution as a guide for moving the elements of the map.).

15. Print a copy of the worksheet.

16. Close and save the workbook file, or save as **USEMPS**.

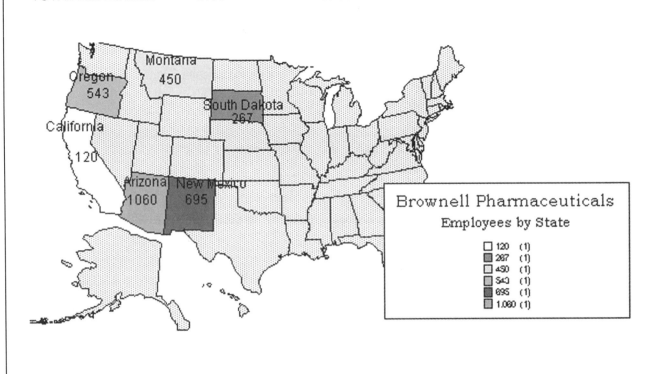

BROWNELL PHARMACEUTICALS BRANCH EMPLOYEES

STATE	EMPLOYEES	% OF TOTAL
Arizona	1060	33.81%
California	120	3.83%
Montana	450	14.35%
New Mexico	695	22.17%
Oregon	543	17.32%
South Dakota	267	8.52%
TOTAL EMPLOYEES	3135	100.00%

KEYSTROKES

INSERT AND USE A DATA MAP

1. Select cells containing geographic data.

2. Click **Map** button on standard toolbar... 🌐

   OR

   a. Click **Insert** .... [Alt]+[I]

   b. Click **Map** .... [A]

      Pointer becomes a ╋.

3. Drag rectangle to define map area.

4. a. If prompted, select desired map in list.

   b. Click **OK**................................[Enter]

ENABLE MAP EDITING

Double-Click data map.
The Data Map Control window opens and the Data Map toolbar appears below the menu bar.

CHANGE CATEGORY SHADING

1. Select **Map** ....[Alt]+[M]

2. Select **Category Shading Options** tab...................................[T]

3. Select **Category** ....[C]

4. Select category ....[↓]

5. Select **Color**...................................[O]

6. Select new color ....[↓]

7. Click **OK**...................................[Enter]

Exercise

63

■ **Summary**

The Music Box store will be adding projected 1998 data to its worksheet and would like you to prepare charts to compare sales information for 1996-1998.

EXERCISE DIRECTIONS

	A	B	C	D	E	F
34	**1998P**	**CLASSICAL**	**COUNTRY**	**JAZZ**	**ROCK**	**1998P**
35	1st Quarter	$ 5,400	$ 6,400	$ 5,300	$ 6,200	$ 23,300
36	2nd Quarter	$ 5,500	$ 6,900	$ 5,700	$ 6,400	$ 24,500
37	3rd Quarter	$ 5,700	$ 7,000	$ 6,100	$ 6,500	$ 25,300
38	4th Quarter	$ 5,900	$ 7,100	$ 6,200	$ 6,700	$ 25,900
39						

1. Open ⌨MUSIC or 🖫63MUSIC.

2. Copy the 1997 worksheet to A31.

3. Edit the copied data to enter projected 1998 data as shown above.

4. Change the heading of the TOTAL columns to 1996 and 1997 for the two worksheets above the projected data, and as shown in the illustration.

5. Rename Sheet1 to Data.

6. Create a 3-D embedded column chart on Sheet2 comparing total sales for each quarter for 1996, 1997, and 1998P.
   Use a non-adjacent selection as illustrated with the shaded data areas on the next page. Select the Quarters Labels and the total sales for 1996, 1997, and 1998.
   a. Include appropriate titles, a legend, and horizontal gridlines.
   b. Place the chart in the range A1:H18 on Sheet2.
   c. Change the font size of category labels and value axis labels to 12 points.
   d. Add a subtitle to the chart: Quarterly Sales.
   e. Change the font size of the title and subtitle to 14 points.

7. Copy the 3-D column chart to A20 and change its type to a Line chart.

8. Copy the Line chart to A39 and change its type to a custom Line-Column chart, showing the projected sales as a line and the actual sales as columns.

9. Rename Sheet2 to Quarterly Sales Charts.

10. Create a Custom Chart type (columns with depth) comparing total sales for each department for 1996, 1997, and 1998P.
    Use a non-adjacent selection as illustrated with the lightly shaded data areas. Select department labels and the total sales rows for each year, as shown in the illustration.
    a. Chart the data by columns.
    b. Include appropriate titles, a legend, and horizontal gridlines.
    c. Place the chart in the range A1:H22 on Sheet3.
    d. Change the font size of category labels and value axis labels to 12 points.
    e. Add a subtitle to the chart: Departmental Sales.
    f. Change the font size of the title and subtitle to 16 points.
    g. Format the Country data series for a pattern design.

11. Copy the custom chart to A24 and change its type to a Stacked column chart with 3-D visual effect.

12. Rename Sheet3 to Departmental Sales Charts.

13. Print a copy of each of the sheets containing charts.

14. Close and save the workbook; name it **MUSIC**.

	A	B	C	D	E	F	G	H
1			THE MUSIC BOX					
2			QUARTERLY SALES					
3						1996		
4	**1996**	**CLASSICAL**	**COUNTRY**	**JAZZ**	**ROCK**	TOTALS		
5	1st Quarter	$ 5,573	$ 6,934	$ 5,454	$ 5,978	$ 23,939		
6	2nd Quarter	$ 5,643	$ 7,387	$ 5,975	$ 6,143	$ 25,148		Include 1998P data in shaded selection for quarterly sales.
7	3rd Quarter	$ 5,346	$ 7,154	$ 5,764	$ 6,098	$ 24,362		
8	4th Quarter	$ 5,734	$ 7,043	$ 5,863	$ 6,143	$ 24,783		
9								
10	TOTAL	22,296	28,518	23,056	24,362	$ 98,232		
11	AVERAGE	$ 5,574	$ 7,130	$ 5,764	$ 6,091	$ 24,558		
12	HIGHEST	$ 5,734	$ 7,387	$ 5,975	$ 6,143	$ 25,148		
13	LOWEST	$ 5,346	$ 6,934	$ 5,454	$ 5,978	$ 23,939		
14								
15								
16			THE MUSIC BOX					
17			QUARTERLY SALES					
18						1997		
19	**1997**	**CLASSICAL**	**COUNTRY**	**JAZZ**	**ROCK**	TOTALS		
20	1st Quarter	$ 5,283	$ 6,234	$ 5,145	$ 6,038	$ 22,700		
21	2nd Quarter	$ 5,521	$ 6,843	$ 5,863	$ 6,254	$ 24,481		
22	3rd Quarter	$ 5,476	$ 6,793	$ 5,954	$ 6,321	$ 24,544		Include 1998P data in dotted selection for departmental data.
23	4th Quarter	$ 5,843	$ 6,932	$ 6,043	$ 6,278	$ 25,096		
24								
25	TOTAL	22,123	26,802	23,005	24,891	$ 96,821		
26	AVERAGE	$ 5,531	$ 6,701	$ 5,751	$ 6,223	$ 24,205		
27	HIGHEST	$ 5,843	$ 6,932	$ 6,043	$ 6,321	$ 25,096		
28	LOWEST	$ 5,283	$ 6,234	$ 5,145	$ 6,038	$ 22,700		
29								
30					Copy to A31.			
31								

Exercise

64

■ **Summary**

As an employee of the Furniture Showrooms, Inc., you have been asked to chart sales and commission data for the four quarters of the year from a previously saved worksheet.

EXERCISE DIRECTIONS

1. Open ⌨ **FURN** or 💾 **64FURN**.

2. Unhide all hidden columns.

3. Use a non-adjacent selection to create an embedded 3-D column chart comparing quarterly salary data for each employee. Select NAME column data and each quarterly salary column.

   a. Plot the data in rows.
   b. Include appropriate titles, a legend, and horizontal gridlines.
   c. Place the chart below the worksheet and size it appropriately.
   d. Edit the heading to add an appropriate subtitle.
   e. Change the y-axis title to vertical alignment.
   f. Change the font sizes for titles, the legend, and axis labels, if necessary.

4. Use a non-adjacent selection to create an embedded Line chart with markers (format 4) comparing quarterly sales data for each employee. Select NAME column data and each quarterly sales column.

   a. Plot the data in rows.
   b. Include appropriate titles, a legend, and horizontal gridlines.
   c. Place the chart to the right of the first chart and size it appropriately.
   d. Edit the heading to add an appropriate subtitle.
   e. Change the font sizes for titles, the legend, and axis labels, if necessary.

5. Using the same data, titles and enhancements as in the line chart, create an embedded 3-D stacked column chart below the first chart.

6. Create a 3-D pie chart displaying JAN-DEC sales for each employee. Use a non-adjacent selection of the NAME and JAN-DEC SALES columns.

   a. Use an appropriate two-line title.
   b. Place the chart to the right of the last chart.
   c. Adjust the size of the chart, plot area, and font settings as necessary.
   d. Use a pattern on the section of the pie representing the highest compensation.
   e. Enter data labels on the pie sections showing the percents.
   f. Explode the largest section.

7. Print a copy of only the pie chart.

8. Print a copy of the entire worksheet on one page.

9. Close and save the workbook file; name it **FURN**.

Excel

LESSON 9

ENHANCING THE WORKSHEET

Exercises 65-73

- Change Font and Font Size
- Change Font Style
- RotateText
- Change Cell Colors and Patterns
- Hide Worksheet Gridlines
- Format Painter
- Set Styles
- Format Sheet Backgrounds
- Change Cell Borders
- Insert AutoShapes
- Page Setup Options
- Center Titles Over Selected Range

- Edit Cell Formats
- Use WordArt Feature
- Enlarge the Printout
- Insert and Size Pictures
- Download Clip Art from the Internet
- Use Drawing Toolbar
- Insert Objects
- Format Graphic Objects
- Adjust Row Height
- Enhance a Worksheet and Chart
- Add and Format a Text Box
- Add Callouts

Exercise
65

- ■ **Change Font and Font Size**
- ■ **Change Font Style (Bold, Italic, and Underline)**
- ■ **Rotate Text**

NOTES

- ■ Excel lets you apply desktop publishing features to create a more attractive screen view and printout. In Exercise 47, a worksheet was formatted using AutoFormat, a feature that provides sets of styles to enhance your worksheet. In this lesson, customized styles and enhancements are discussed so that you can create any format you wish. To view or print a color worksheet, you must have access to a color monitor and/or printer.

Change Font and Font Size

- ■ Worksheet enhancements, such as changing the font and font size, can be accomplished by using the appropriate toolbar buttons.

- ■ A **font** is a set of characters that share a design and name. Since Windows TrueType fonts are scalable, a single TrueType font can be set to a variety of sizes. The current font name (usually Arial) is displayed in the Font box and the current font size is displayed in the Font Size box.

- ■ You can change the default or standard font that Excel uses. To do this, select <u>T</u>ools, <u>O</u>ptions, and click the General tab. You can then adjust the St<u>a</u>ndard font and font Siz<u>e</u> options.

- ■ The **font size** is an attribute that sets the height of characters in a scalable font. This size is measured in **points**. A point is $1/72$ of an inch. When the size of a font is changed, Excel automatically adjusts the row height but does not adjust the column width.

- ■ The easiest way to apply a new font or font size is to select the cells to format, then select the font or font size in the **Font** or **Font Size box** on the Formatting toolbar. (See the illustration below.) When a font and font size are selected, Excel immediately formats the text in the selected cells.

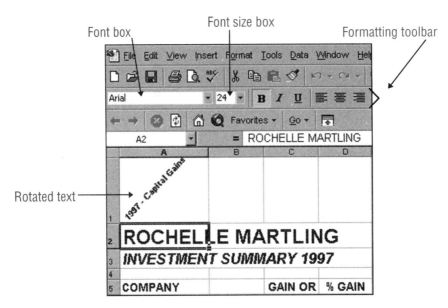

246

- Another way to apply new fonts or font sizes is to select Cells from the Format menu, which then displays the **Format Cells** dialog box. The illustration below shows the Font tab of the format cells dialog box.

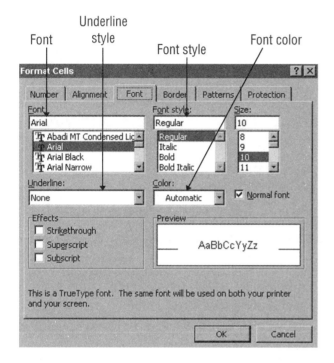

Change Font Style (Bold, Italic, Underline)

- The Bold, Italics, and Underline styles were discussed in Exercise 15 and may be used with font and font size changes to further enhance the worksheet. These attributes may be set by using the Formatting toolbar, as shown earlier, or by using the settings in the Format Cells, **Font** tab dialog box as shown above.

Rotate Text

- Text can be aligned by using the Formatting toolbar alignment buttons or by using the Alignment tab in the Format Cells dialog box, as illustrated below. The Orientation option provides the ability to set text rotation for a selected cell by moving the pointer or setting the degrees of rotation. A positive number in the degree box rotates the text from lower left to upper right in the cell. A negative number in the degree box, rotates the text from upper left to lower right in the cell.

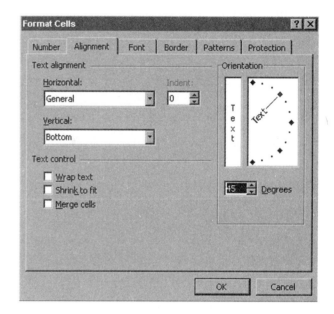

In this exercise, you will enhance the INVSUM worksheet by changing fonts, font sizes, and text style for selected parts.

EXERCISE DIRECTIONS

1. Open ⌨ **INVSUM** or 💾 **65INVSUM**.
   - Using the illustration below, compare **INVSUM** with the enhanced version on the next page.

2. Move, cut, and paste the main title and subtitle to column A.

3. Make the font changes indicated below using the Format Cells dialog box:
   a. Main title: Arial 22 point, Bold Italic
   b. Secondary titles: Arial 16 point, Bold
   c. Column titles: Arial 14 point, Italic
   d. Data in rows 7–11: MS Serif 10 point
   e. TOTALS row: Arial 12 point, Bold
   ✓ *If your system does not have these fonts, choose a font that best matches the illustration on the next page.*

4. Delete column C.

5. Change alignment of data and column headings in the SYMBOL column to center all text.

6. Bold the company names.

7. Adjust column widths to view complete labels and values in each column.

8. Make the font changes indicated below using the Formatting toolbar:
   a. Main title: Arial 24 point, Bold
   b. Secondary titles: Arial 18 point, Bold Italics
   c. Column titles: Arial 14 point, Bold
   d. Data in rows 7–11: MS Sans Serif 12 point
   e. TOTALS row: Arial 12 point, Bold, Underline

9. Adjust column widths to view complete labels and values in each column.

10. Insert a row at the top of the worksheet.

11. Enter 1997—Capital Gains in cell A1.

12. Use Format, Cells, and Alignment tab to set a text rotation of 45 degrees. Try using the line and the degrees box to make the settings. Test various settings to note the effect of text rotation.

13. Preview the worksheet.

14. Print one copy of the worksheet.

15. Save and close the workbook file; name it **INVSUM**.

	A	B	C	D	E
1		ROCHELLE MARTLING			
2		INVESTMENT SUMMARY 1997			
3					
4	COMPANY			GAIN OR	% GAIN
5	NAME	SYMBOL		LOSS	OR LOSS
6					
7	Focus Motors	FM		(748.11)	-9.72%
8	General Oil	GNO		1089.72	16.59%
9	IVM	IVM		(1010.23)	-10.12%
10	Microtech	MIC		2779.53	32.11%
11	American Electric	AE		1334.68	32.30%
12					
13	TOTALS			3445.59	9.30%

	A	B	C	D
1	*1997 - Capital Gains*			
2	**ROCHELLE MARTLING**			
3	*INVESTMENT SUMMARY 1997*			
4				
5	**COMPANY**		**GAIN OR**	**% GAIN**
6	**NAME**	**SYMBOL**	**LOSS**	**OR LOSS**
7				
8	**Focus Motors**	FM	(748.11)	-9.72%
9	**General Oil**	GNO	1089.72	16.59%
10	**IVM**	IVM	(1010.23)	-10.12%
11	**Microtech**	MIC	2779.53	32.11%
12	**American Electric**	AE	1334.68	32.30%
13				
14	**TOTALS**		**3445.59**	**9.30%**
15				

KEYSTROKES

CHANGE FONT USING THE FONT BOX

1. Select cells (or characters in a cell) to format.
2. Click **Font** box drop-down arrow on Formatting toolbar .... `Arial ▼`
3. Select desired font .... , `Enter`

CHANGE FONT SIZE USING THE FONT SIZE BOX

1. Select cells (or characters in a cell) to format.
2. a. Click **Font Size** box drop-down arrow on Formatting toolbar.............................. `10 ▼`
   b. Select a number in list.. `↑↓`, `Enter`
   OR
   a. Click **Font Size** box on Formatting toolbar .... `10 ▼`
   b. Enter desired number and press Enter .... `Enter`

CHANGE FONT, FONT SIZE, AND FONT STYLE USING THE MENU

Ctrl+1

1. Select cells (or characters in a cell) to format.
2. Click **Format** menu .... `Alt`+`O`
3. Click **Cells** .... `E`
4. Select **Font** tab .... `Ctrl`+`Tab`

To set font:

a. Click **Font**........................... `Alt`+`F`
b. Select desired font .... `↑↓`

To set font style:

a. Click **Font** Style .... `Alt`+`O`
b. Select desired style .... `↑↓`

To set font size:

a. Click **Size**........................ `Alt`+`S`
b. Select desired font size .... `↑↓`

To set underline:

Click **Underline** .... `Alt`+`U`

ROTATE TEXT

Ctrl+1

1. Select cells to format.
2. Click **Format** menu................. `Alt`+`O`
3. Click **Cells**..................................... `E`
4. Select **Alignment** tab .... `Ctrl`+`Tab`
5. Select **Degrees** .... `Alt`+`D`
6. Enter degrees of rotation.
   OR
   Use the mouse to move the pointer to the rotation setting.
7. Click **OK** .... `Enter`

Exercise 66

- ■ **Change Cell Colors and Patterns** ■ **Hide Worksheet Gridlines**
- ■ **Format Painter** ■ **Set Styles**
- ■ **Format Sheet Backgrounds**

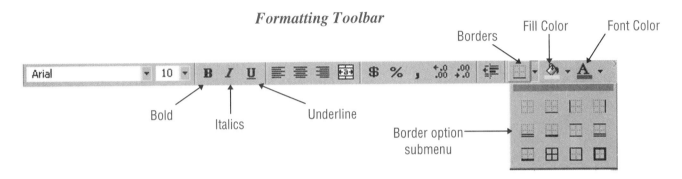

Formatting Toolbar

Borders · Fill Color · Font Color

Bold · Italics · Underline

Border option submenu

NOTES

Change Cell Colors and Patterns

- ■ Cells in a worksheet may be filled with a **pattern** and/or **color**. The color buttons on the Formatting toolbar were discussed in Exercise 47. In addition, however, you may make color and pattern settings by using the Format cells dialog box, as shown on the Patterns tab sheet in the illustration below. The settings on the Patterns sheet affect the cell background.

- ■ Font color may also be set from the Format Cells dialog box by clicking on the Font sheet. It is more efficient, however, to use the Font Color button on the Formatting toolbar.

- ■ It is possible to display and print data in white against a black (or color) background. This is sometimes called **reverse type**.

Select the Patterns tab to set cell color.

Cell background patterns

Cell background colors

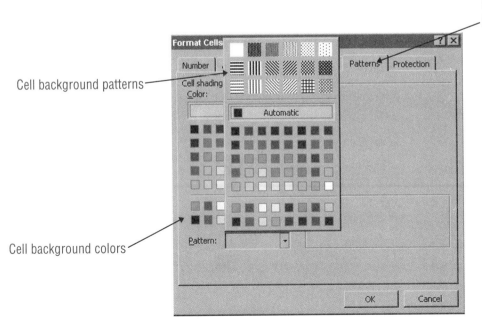

Hide Worksheet Gridlines

■ You can further enhance a worksheet by adding or removing the gridlines. For printing purposes, the gridlines can be added or removed using the File, Page Setup, Sheet tab. The default setting is for hidden gridlines. For display purposes, gridlines may be removed using the Tools, Options, View tab window options.

Format Painter

■ Once you make a series of settings, you may need to reproduce them for other data on the worksheet. Custom formats can be reused with Format Painter or by defining the settings as a style.

■ The **Format Painter** button on the Standard toolbar allows you to copy all the formats from one cell to another in one step. By clicking the cell that contains the desired format, clicking the Format Painter button and then the cell to be formatted, all formatting is copied to the new location. If you wish to use the Format Painter function on several different cells, you should double-click the Format Painter to enable it for multiple applications. Select the Format Painter button again to turn off multiple formatting.

Set Styles

■ The second method of reusing formats is to set and name a style that can be invoked when needed. This is useful, for example, if your company uses the same formats for headings or totals for all reports. To set a style, select the cell with your custom formatting, then use the Format, Style commands to give the style a name. Once the style has a name, it can be applied to any cell using the same menu commands to select the style name. Templates can be created with styles that could be repeated for all worksheets.

Format Sheet Background

■ Microsoft Office 97 software contains a directory of Background files that can be used to apply a graphic image as a background to an entire worksheet. If the image is small, it will take on a wallpaper effect and be repeated throughout the worksheet. Select **Format**, **Sheet**, **Background** to open the Backgrounds directory from the Microsoft Office 97 CD-ROM or installation disks. When you select one of the backgrounds, such as clouds, coins, sand, etc., the design will appear as the cell background for all cells that have no fill setting.

✓ NOTE: *You may import any graphic file as a worksheet background. You are not limited to using only those images provided with your software.*

Excel ■ Lesson 9 ■ Exercise 66   251

In this exercise, you will enhance the salary report for the Claudine Manufacturing Company using Format Painter, colors, patterns, backgrounds, and styles.

EXERCISE DIRECTIONS

1. Open ▦ **RAISE** or ▯ **66RAISE**.

   - Use the illustration on the right to compare **RAISE** with the enhanced version below it.

2. Change the worksheet so it looks like the enhanced version: *(If you do not have the fonts listed, use a similar font from your font list.)*

   a. Main title: Bazooka 18 point bold.

   b. Subtitle: Bazooka 14 point bold.

   c. Main and Subtitle area (A1:J3): Color background to Yellow (Row 4, Box 3), cell borders to underline.

      ✓ *Row and box numbers refer to location of color in color palette.*

   d. Column titles: Bold and color background to Sky Blue (Row 4, Box 6).

   e. Use Format Painter to copy format from column titles to TOTALS line.

   f. SALARY 1996 column data: Color to gray-25% (Row 4, Box 8).

   g. RAISE 1997: Use Format Painter to copy color format from SALARY 1996.

   h. SALARY 1997: Font color White and cell color black for reverse type.

   i. EMPLOYEE, YEARS OF SENIORITY column data: color to color scheme (Row 5, Box 2)

   j. Use Format Painter to copy data format from columns A:C to data in columns G:J.

   k. TOTALS data: Select numbers and set underline for Double Accounting style and number format to commas using the Format cells dialog box.

3. Turn gridlines off for worksheet.

4. Preview the worksheet.

5. To set a style for total numbers:

   a. Select the numbers on the TOTALS line.

   b. Click Format, Style, then and name the style Total Numbers.

6. To test and apply the style:

   a. Select Joe D'Agostino's salary for 1996.

   b. Click Format, Style and use the Style Name list box to select Total Numbers. Click OK.

      ✓ *The number will take on the Total Num style.*

   c. Use Format Painter to return the salary number to its original style.

7. Format the sheet for a background if your installation software is available or if you have another graphic file in your system that you wish to use.

   a. Click Format, Sheet, Background.

   b. Select the Clip Art/Photos/Background folder. Or, select the folder that contains the graphic you wish to use.

   c. Select the Washers background. Or, select any desired graphic file.

8. Set the worksheet to print on one page, then print the worksheet.

9. Save the workbook file; name it **RAISE**.

	A	B	C	D	E	F	G	H	I	J
1				CLAUDINE MANUFACTURING COMPANY						
2				ANALYSIS OF SALARY INCREASES						
3										
4										
5			YEARS OF	SALARY	SALARY	RAISE	1997%	1998%	RAISE	SALARY
6	EMPLOYEE		SENIORITY	1996	1997	1997	INCREASE	INCREASE	1998	1998
7										
8	Abrahams, Larry		15	45,500.00	49,000.00	3,500.00	7.69%	7.25%	3,552.50	52,552.50
9	Barrow, Wilson		11	32,300.00	35,000.00	2,700.00	8.36%	7.25%	2,537.50	37,537.50
10	Barrow, Wilson		5	16,500.00	17,500.00	1,000.00	6.06%	4.50%	787.50	18,287.50
11	D'Agostino, Joe		3	18,500.00	20,000.00	1,500.00	8.11%	4.50%	900.00	20,900.00
12	Harrison, Reggie		7	21,000.00	23,000.00	2,000.00	9.52%	7.25%	1,667.50	24,667.50
13	Ingold, Terry		4	25,600.00	27,000.00	1,400.00	5.47%	4.50%	1,215.00	28,215.00
14	Nunez, Maria		8	28,500.00	30,000.00	1,500.00	5.26%	7.25%	2,175.00	32,175.00
15	Presser, Carol		9	33,000.00	35,000.00	2,000.00	6.06%	7.25%	2,537.50	37,537.50
16	Tse, Sandra		6	25,400.00	27,000.00	1,600.00	6.30%	7.25%	1,957.50	28,957.50
17	Wingate, George		10	38,000.00	41,500.00	3,500.00	9.21%	7.25%	3,008.75	44,508.75
18										
19	TOTALS			284,300.00	305,000.00	20,700.00			20,338.75	325,338.75

CLAUDINE MANUFACTURING COMPANY
ANALYSIS OF SALARY INCREASES

EMPLOYEE	YEARS OF SENIORITY	SALARY 1996	SALARY 1997	RAISE 1997	1997% INCREASE	1998% INCREASE	RAISE 1998	SALARY 1998
Abrahams, Larry	15	45,500.00	49,000.00	3,500.00	7.69%	7.25%	3,552.50	52,552.50
Barrow, Wilson	11	32,300.00	35,000.00	2,700.00	8.36%	7.25%	2,537.50	37,537.50
Barrow, Wilson	5	16,500.00	17,500.00	1,000.00	6.06%	4.50%	787.50	18,287.50
D'Agostino, Joe	3	18,500.00	20,000.00	1,500.00	8.11%	4.50%	900.00	20,900.00
Harrison, Reggie	7	21,000.00	23,000.00	2,000.00	9.52%	7.25%	1,667.50	24,667.50
Ingold, Terry	4	25,600.00	27,000.00	1,400.00	5.47%	4.50%	1,215.00	28,215.00
Nunez, Maria	8	28,500.00	30,000.00	1,500.00	5.26%	7.25%	2,175.00	32,175.00
Presser, Carol	9	33,000.00	35,000.00	2,000.00	6.06%	7.25%	2,537.50	37,537.50
Tse, Sandra	6	25,400.00	27,000.00	1,600.00	6.30%	7.25%	1,957.50	28,957.50
Wingate, George	10	38,000.00	41,500.00	3,500.00	9.21%	7.25%	3,008.75	44,508.75
TOTALS		284,300.00	305,000.00	20,700.00			20,338.75	325,338.75

KEYSTROKES

BOLD, ITALICIZE, OR UNDERLINE DATA USING THE TOOLBAR

1. Select cells or characters in cells to format.

2. Click **Bold** button............................
   on Formatting toolbar.
   AND/OR

   Click **Italic** button...........................
   on Formatting toolbar.
   AND/OR

   Click **Underline** button ....
   on Formatting toolbar.

   To remove font style:

   Click format button again.

CHANGE FONT COLOR USING THE TOOLBAR

1. Select cells or characters in cells to format.

2. Click color option on

   Font Color button.........................
   to apply it to selection.
   OR

   a. Click **Font Color** button

      drop-down arrow..................

   Excel displays a color palette.

   ✓ *To apply several colors, drag color palette off the toolbar to keep the color palette open.*

   b. Click desired color on palette.

HIDE WORKSHEET GRIDLINES

   (*See **SET VIEW PREFERENCES**, Keystrokes section, Exercise 2.*)

   (*See **SET PRINT OPTIONS FOR WORKSHEETS**, Keystrokes section, Exercise 23.*)

COPY FORMATS USING FORMAT PAINTER

Select cell(s) containing formats to copy.

   To copy formats only once:

   a. Click **Format Painter** button ....
      on Standard toolbar.

   Pointer changes to a .

   b. Select cell or range of cells where you want to apply the formats.

   To copy formats several times:

   a. Double-click **Format Painter** .....
      button on Standard toolbar.

   Pointer changes to a ⊹🖌.

   b. Select destination cell(s).

   c. Repeat Step b for as many cells as desired.

   d. Click **Format Painter** button ....
      to end copying.

SET FONT AND FONT ATTRIBUTES USING THE MENU

Changes font, font attributes, size and color. Underlines and sets special effects for data in cells.

1. Select cells or characters in cells to format.

2. Click **Format** menu.................

3. Click **Cells** ....
   OR

   a. Right-click any selected cell.

   b. Click **Format Cells**.....................

4. Click **Font** tab ....

   To change font:

   Select a font name
   in **Font** list box ....

   To change font style:

   Select a font style in
   Font Style list box. ....

To change font size:

Select a point size.........
in **Size** list box.

To select underline style:

a. Click **Underline**.................

b. Select an underline
   style............................

To apply effects:

Select desired **Effects** options:

Strikethrough ....

Superscript ....

Subscript ....

To set font to normal font style:

Select **Normal Font** ....
(Arial, Regular 10pt.)

To set font color:

a. Click **Color**........................

b. Select a color...............

5. Click **OK**..............................

CHANGE COLOR OF CELLS USING THE TOOLBAR

1. Select cell(s) to format.

2. Click color option on

   Color button..............................
   to apply it to selection.
   OR

   a. Click **Color** button

      drop-down arrow..................

   Excel displays a color palette.

   ✓ *To apply several colors, drag color palette off the toolbar to keep the color palette open.*

   b. Click desired color on palette.

FORMAT SHEET BACKGROUND

1. Click **F**ormat .... `Alt`+`O`
2. Click **Sh**eet....................................... `H`
3. Click **Ba**ckground........................... `B`
4. Locate directory with Background files.
5. Select background.
6. Click **O**pen .... `Enter`

CHANGE COLOR AND/OR PATTERN OF CELLS USING THE MENU

1. Select cell(s) to format.
2. Click **F**ormat menu .... `Alt`+`O`
3. Click **C**ells..................................... `E`
   OR
   a. Right-click any selected cell.
   b. Click **F**ormat Cells. .... `F`
4. Click **P**atterns tab................. `Ctrl`+`Tab`

   To select a color for cells:

   Click desired color .... `Alt`+`C`, `↕↔`
   in **C**olor palette.

   To select a pattern for cells:

   a. Click **P**attern .... `Alt`+`P`
   b. Select a pattern .... `↕↔`
   c. Click **P**attern again .... `Alt`+`P`

      Select a pattern color .... `↕↔`
5. Click **OK** .... `Enter`

SET STYLES BY EXAMPLE

1. Select cell containing desired formats.
2. Click **F**ormat menu .... `Alt`+`O`
3. Click **S**tyle....................................... `S`
4. Type **Style Name** in text box.

   Excel displays the style's formats in Style Includes box.
5. Click **OK**. .... `Enter`

   To exclude format categories from style:

   Deselect desired **Style Includes** options.
5. Click **OK** .... `Enter`

APPLY STYLES

1. Select cell to be formatted.
2. Click **F**ormat .... `Alt`+`O`
3. Click **S**tyle....................................... `S`
4. Select desired **Style Name**.... `S`, `↕↓`
5. Click **OK** .... `Enter`

Exercise

67

■ **Change Cell Borders**
■ **Insert AutoShapes**

NOTES

Change Cell Borders

■ To outline or separate data, you can include a variety of line styles that **border** the edge of a cell or range of cells. You can add, remove, or change lines to the left, right, top, or bottom of any cell or range of cells. Borders can be set by accessing the **Border** tab of the Format Cells dialog box or by using the **Borders** button on the Formatting toolbar.

Borders button

■ The Format Cells Borders tab contains three preset border formats, in addition to other border styles illustrated around the sample box. The Line Style and Color boxes allow you to set these features for the selected border style. Your settings will be illustrated within the sample box in the center of the Border tab.

■ When you clear cell contents, the border format does not change; therefore, the border must be cleared separately. Excel provides a keyboard shortcut (**Ctrl** + **Shift** + **-**) that quickly removes all borders from selected cells.

Format Cells Dialog Box with Border Tab Selected

Sample of settings display here.

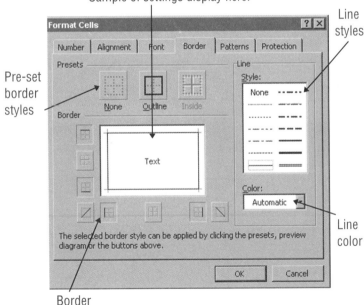

Borders Button Options Available on the Formatting Toolbar

Insert AutoShapes

- Excel 97 provides an **AutoShapes** feature on the Drawing toolbar. The Drawing toolbar can be displayed by clicking View, Toolbars, and then selecting **Drawing** from the list. The AutoShapes button, as illustrated below, provides a list of shapes that you can use to enhance your worksheets. To use an AutoShape, click the **AutoShapes** button on the Drawing toolbar, select from the shape submenu (as illustrated below), select the desired shape, and then use the mouse to place and size the shape.

- The AutoShape may be formatted for fill color, line properties, and arrow settings. Select the shape and click Format, AutoShape or right-click and select Format AutoShape. The dialog box that appears is illustrated below.

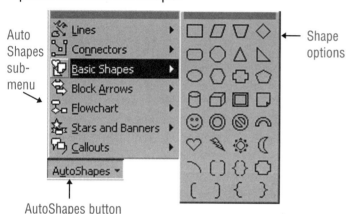

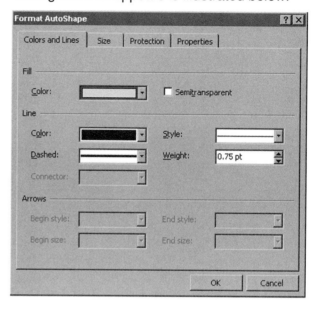

In this exercise, you will enhance the AutoMart Used Cars commission report so your supervisor can present it at the next staff meeting. AutoShapes will be added to the worksheet and formatted for color.

EXERCISE DIRECTIONS

1. Open ⌨ **AUTO** or 💾 **67AUTO**.
    - Use the illustration on the next page to compare **AUTO** with the enhanced version below it.

2. Make the changes to your worksheet as indicated below:
    a. Insert a row above the titles.
    b. Titles: Move both worksheet titles to column A.
    c. Edit subtitle to: COMMISSION REPORT – JANUARY-JUNE 199-
    d. Set both titles to a decorative 16-point bold font.
    e. Title and subtitle: Outline—use the Border button.
    f. Column titles: Arial Black, 12 point.
    g. Column title cells: Thick top and bottom borders. Set the top and bottom borders separately using the Format Cells dialog box, the sample line styles, and the line style settings.

    h. Titles and column titles: Color cell Light Green (Row 5, Box 4).
    i. Column A , B, and F data: light Green Color (Row 5, Box 4).
    j. Column E data: light Yellow Color (Row 5, Box 3).
    k. Column B data: Medium width line to right side of cells.
    l. Last row of data: Medium width line to bottom of cells.
    m. TOTALS data: Double-line across bottom of all cells.
    n. TOTALS lines: Pale Green Color (Row 5, Box 4).

3. Add an AutoShape to the top of the worksheet:
    a. Display the Drawing toolbar. (see notes.)
    b. Click AutoShapes, and Stars and Banners.
    c. Select the star in Row 1, Box 4.
    d. Place the star, as shown, in G1:G3.

e. Size appropriately.

f. Format the AutoShape for Yellow (Row 4, Box 3) fill color.

4. Insert two rows at F21.

5. Insert an AutoShape arrow from the Block Arrows menu in cells F22:F24, as illustrated. Use Format Painter to format it to Yellow fill color.

6. Set worksheet to print on one page and preview the worksheet.

7. Print the worksheet.

8. Close and save the workbook file; name it **AUTO**.

	A	B	C	D	E	F	G
1			AUTOMART USED CARS				
2			SEMI-ANNUAL COMMISSION REPORT FOR SALES PERSONNEL				
3							
4			COMM.			TOTAL	
5	NAME	SALES	RATE	COMM.	BONUS	COMPENSATION	LOCATION
6							
7	R. Buick	$640,000	4.00%	$25,600	$ 3,200	$28,800	Phoenix
8	M. Caddy	$450,000	3.00%	$13,500	$ -	$13,500	Tempe
9	J. Dodge	$125,000	3.00%	$3,750	$ -	$3,750	Phoenix
10	O. Ford	$745,000	4.00%	$29,800	$ 3,725	$33,525	Tucson
11	W. Honda	$0	3.00%	$0	$ -	$0	Phoenix
12	V. Jaguar	$550,000	4.00%	$22,000	$ 2,750	$24,750	Tucson
13	A. Lexus	$210,000	3.00%	$6,300	$ -	$6,300	Tempe
14	E. Lincoln	$435,000	4.00%	$17,400	$ -	$17,400	Phoenix
15	B. Nissan	$745,000	4.00%	$29,800	$ 3,725	$33,525	Tucson
16	C. Pontiac	$532,543	4.00%	$21,302	$ 2,663	$23,964	Tempe
17	J. Subaru	$334,654	3.00%	$10,040	$ -	$10,040	Phoenix
18	V. Jeep	$445,875	4.00%	$17,835	$ -	$17,835	Tucson
19							
20	TOTALS	$5,213,072		$197,326	$16,063	$213,389	
21							
22						$ 59,990	Phoenix
23						$ 43,764	Tempe
24						$ 109,635	Tucson

AUTOMART USED CARS						
COMMISSION REPORT - JANUARY-JUNE 199-						
NAME	SALES	COMM. RATE	COMM.	BONUS	TOTAL COMM.	LOCATION
R. Buick	$640,000	4.00%	$25,600	$ 3,200	$28,800	Phoenix
M. Caddy	$450,000	3.00%	$13,500	$ -	$13,500	Tempe
J. Dodge	$125,000	3.00%	$3,750	$ -	$3,750	Phoenix
O. Ford	$745,000	4.00%	$29,800	$ 3,725	$33,525	Tucson
W. Honda	$0	3.00%	$0	$ -	$0	Phoenix
V. Jaguar	$550,000	4.00%	$22,000	$ 2,750	$24,750	Tucson
A. Lexus	$210,000	3.00%	$6,300	$ -	$6,300	Tempe
E. Lincoln	$435,000	4.00%	$17,400	$ -	$17,400	Phoenix
B. Nissan	$745,000	4.00%	$29,800	$ 3,725	$33,525	Tucson
C. Pontiac	$532,543	4.00%	$21,302	$ 2,663	$23,964	Tempe
J. Subaru	$334,654	3.00%	$10,040	$ -	$10,040	Phoenix
V. Jeep	$445,875	4.00%	$17,835	$ -	$17,835	Tucson
TOTALS	$5,213,072		$197,326	$16,063	$213,389	
					$ 59,990	Phoenix
					$ 43,764	Tempe
					$ 109,635	Tucson

KEYSTROKES

CHANGE CELL BORDERS USING THE TOOLBAR

1. Select cell(s) to format.
2. Click border option on

   Borders button........................... [⊞▾]

   to apply it to selected cells.

   OR

   a. Click **Borders** button

      drop-down arrow .... [⊞▾]

      Excel displays a border palette.

      ✓ *To apply several border styles,
         drag border palette
         off the toolbar to keep the border
         palette open.*

   b. Click desired border on palette.. [⬍⬌]

ADD CUSTOM BORDERS TO CELLS

Applies or removes borders from cells.

1. Select cell(s) to format.
2. Click **Format** menu .... [Alt]+[O]
3. Click **Cells**............................... [E]

   OR

   a. Right-click any selected cell.

   b. Click **Format Cells**. .... [F]

4. Click **Border** tab .... [Ctrl]+[Tab]
5. Select a border settings:

   From Pre-sets:

   • **None** .... [Alt]+[N]

   • **Outline**............................ [Alt]+[O]

   • **Inside**............................. [Alt]+[I]

   OR

   • Select an additional

      border choice: .... [⬍⬌]

• **Top**............................ [⬚]
• **Center, Horizontal** .... [⬚]
• **Bottom** .... [⬚]
• **Diagonal Up**............................. [◿]
• **Left** .... [⬚]
• **Right** .... [⬚]
• **Diagonal Down** .... [◺]

6. Click **Line Style**..................... [Alt]+[S]
7. Select a style option .... [⬍⬌], [Enter]
8. Repeat steps 5 and 6 for each border.

   a. Click **OK** .... [Enter]

   To change border color:

   a. Click **Color:** .... [Alt]+[C]

   b. Select desired color...... [⬍⬌], [Enter]

   To remove border:

   Follow steps to apply border again.

REMOVE ALL BORDERS FROM CELLS

1. Select cells with borders to remove.
2. Press **Ctrl + Shift + -** .... [Ctrl]+[Shift]+[-]

DISPLAY DRAWING TOOLBAR

1. Click **View** .... [Alt]+[V]
2. Click **Toolbars**............................. [T]
3. Select **Drawing** .... [↓]

USE AUTO SHAPES

1. Display Drawing toolbar.
2. Click **AutoShapes** button. ...... [Alt]+[U]
3. Select submenu:

   • **Lines**................................. [L]

   • **Connectors** .... [N]

   • **Basic Shapes**....................... [B]

   • **Block Arrows**....................... [A]

   • **Flowchart**............................ [F]

   • **Stars and Banners**................... [S]

   • **Callouts** .... [C]

4. Select **AutoShape** .... [⬍⬌]
5. Use mouse to place and size the shape.

FORMAT AUTO SHAPE

1. Select AutoShape to format.
2. Right-click and select **Format
   AutoShape**....................................... [O]

   OR

   a. Click **Format** .... [Alt]+[O]

   b. Click **Format AutoShape**............. [O]

3. Use Colors and Lines, Size, Protection,
   and Properties tabs to format
   AutoShape.
4. Click **OK**. .... [Enter]

Exercise

68

■ Page Setup Options ■ Center Titles Over Selected Range
■ Edit Cell Formats ■ Use WordArt Feature

NOTES

Page Setup Options

■ You can set a variety of print options from the tabs in the Page Setup dialog box.

Page tab:

- Page orientation.
- Reduce or enlarge data on printed sheet.
- Paper size.
- Print quality.
- Fit a sheet to a specific number of pages.
- First page number.

Margins tab:

- Page margins.
- Header and footer margins.
- How data is aligned on page.

Header/Footer tab:

- Select a built-in header.
- Select a built-in footer.
- Customize header or footer.

Sheet tab:

- Print area.
- Rows as repeating print titles.
- Columns as repeating print titles.
- Printing of gridlines.
- Printing of row and column headings.
- Printing to black and white.
- Printing to draft quality.

- Printing of comments.
- Page order when printing.

OR

Chart tab:

- Printed chart size.
- Printed quality of chart.
- Printing to black and white printer.

■ You can access the Page Setup dialog by:

- Selecting Page Setup from the File menu.
- Clicking the Setup button in the Print Preview window.

■ Excel lets you set print margins in two ways:

- By dragging margin handles to approximate positions in the Print Preview window.

  OR

- By indicating exact margins in inches using the Margins tab in the Page Setup dialog box.

■ As with charts, a worksheet can be printed with either a **portrait** (vertical) or **landscape** (horizontal) paper orientation. Landscape orientation must be supported by the available printer. Note examples below.

WordArt Toolbar

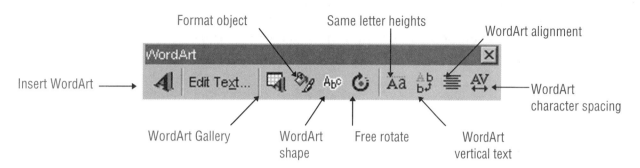

Insert WordArt → **Format object** · **Same letter heights** · **WordArt alignment** · **WordArt Gallery** · **WordArt shape** · **Free rotate** · **WordArt vertical text** · **WordArt character spacing**

Center Titles Over Selected Range

- A title can be realigned so that it is centered over a range of cells. You can do this by selecting the title and extending the selection to include the cells in which the title should be centered across. Excel will center the title when you click the **Merge and Center** button 🔲 on the Formatting toolbar.

- Centering across columns changes where data appears on a worksheet—it does not change the original cell location of the data. For example, text may be located in cell A1 but appears centered between columns A and I.

Edit Cell Formats

- Cell formats may be cleared or reset using the Format Cells dialog box. Formats that have been set using the Font tab, such as underline, must be cleared in the dialog box.

- If you are uncertain as to which color or pattern you had previously set, you may select one of the cells in question and check the Patterns tab in the Format Cells dialog box.

Use WordArt Feature

- You can add special effects to text by using the **WordArt** button 🔲 on the Drawing toolbar.

- The **WordArt Gallery**, illustrated on the right, appears when the WordArt button is clicked. Text can be shadowed, rotated, stretched, and displayed within a predefined shape. Add a special effect to text by selecting the WordArt button and then selecting the desired effect from the WordArt Gallery dialog box.

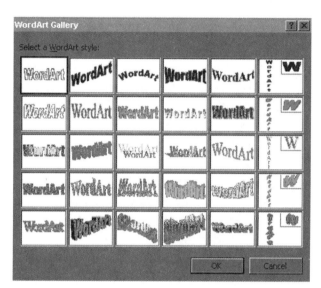

- After you select an effect from the WordArt Gallery, the Edit WordArt text dialog box will appear, as illustrated below, where you can insert your text.

- The WordArt text you create displays with handles and may be moved, sized, and placed as an object. The WordArt toolbar will appear when the text object displays. The WordArt toolbar, illustrated at the top of the page, can also be displayed by selecting View, Toolbars, and then WordArt. It provides tools to edit and format WordArt objects.

In this exercise, you will edit a worksheet for presentation. After making changes to the worksheet, including creating a WordArt title and centering the subtitle, you will test the effectiveness of the presentation by printing the worksheet in portrait orientation using the default margin settings and comparing it to a second printing in landscape orientation with wider margins.

EXERCISE DIRECTIONS

1. Open ⌨ **RAISE** or 💾 **68RAISE**.
   - Use the illustration on the right to compare **RAISE** with the enhanced version below it.

2. Make the changes to your worksheet indicated below:
   a. Remove cell borders from rows 1 and 2.
   b. Insert two rows at the top of the worksheet.
   c. Delete main title.
   d. Insert WordArt title:
      - Display Drawing toolbar.
      - Click WordArt button.
      - Select Row 4, Box 4 style.
      - Edit text to Claudine Manufacturing Company.
      - Click OK.
      - Place text in rows 1-3.
   e. Move subtitle to Column A.
   f. Center subtitle over columns A-J.
   g. Columns A-C: Color same as column heading area, Sky Blue.
   h. Column C: Center data. Cell border at the right of the cells.
   i. Row 19: Bottom border across worksheet.
   j. Columns D-F: Color to Tan (Row 5, Box 2).
   k. Column E: Text color, black.
   l. Column J: Font black, background sky blue, cell border at the left.
   m. TOTALS rows 20 and 21: Color Pale Blue.
   n. Row 21: Remove font format for double accounting underline. Insert cell border for double lines across bottom of worksheet.
   o. Format money columns for commas.
   p. Adjust column widths, if necessary.

3. Set worksheet to fit on one page.

4. Preview the worksheet.

5. Print one copy of the worksheet with portrait orientation.

6. Change top, bottom, right, and left margins to 1".

7. Print one copy of the worksheet.

8. Change the page orientation to landscape.

9. Preview the worksheet.

10. In Print Preview, adjust margins as desired.

11. Print two copies of the worksheet.

12. Save and close the workbook file; name it **RAISE**.

13. Decide which worksheet would be better for the presentation.

CLAUDINE MANUFACTURING COMPANY
ANALYSIS OF SALARY INCREASES

EMPLOYEE	YEARS OF SENIORITY	SALARY 1996	SALARY 1997	RAISE 1997	1997% INCREASE	1998% INCREASE	RAISE 1998	SALARY 1998
Abrahams, Larry	15	45,500.00	49,000.00	3,500.00	7.69%	7.25%	3,552.50	52,552.50
Barrow, Wilson	11	32,300.00	35,000.00	2,700.00	8.36%	7.25%	2,537.50	37,537.50
Barrow, Wilson	5	16,500.00	17,500.00	1,000.00	6.06%	4.50%	787.50	18,287.50
D'Agostino, Joe	3	18,500.00	20,000.00	1,500.00	8.11%	4.50%	900.00	20,900.00
Harrison, Reggie	7	21,000.00	23,000.00	2,000.00	9.52%	7.25%	1,667.50	24,667.50
Ingold, Terry	4	25,600.00	27,000.00	1,400.00	5.47%	4.50%	1,215.00	28,215.00
Nunez, Maria	8	28,500.00	30,000.00	1,500.00	5.26%	7.25%	2,175.00	32,175.00
Presser, Carol	9	33,000.00	35,000.00	2,000.00	6.06%	7.25%	2,537.50	37,537.50
Tse, Sandra	6	25,400.00	27,000.00	1,600.00	6.30%	7.25%	1,957.50	28,957.50
Wingate, George	10	38,000.00	41,500.00	3,500.00	9.21%	7.25%	3,008.75	44,508.75
TOTALS		284,300.00	305,000.00	20,700.00			20,338.75	325,338.75

Claudine Manufacturing Company
ANALYSIS OF SALARY INCREASES

EMPLOYEE	YEARS OF SENIORITY	SALARY 1996	SALARY 1997	RAISE 1997	1997% INCREASE	1998% INCREASE	RAISE 1998	SALARY 1998
Abrahams, Larry	15	45,500.00	49,000.00	3,500.00	7.69%	7.25%	3,552.50	52,552.50
Barrow, Wilson	11	32,300.00	35,000.00	2,700.00	8.36%	7.25%	2,537.50	37,537.50
Barrow, Wilson	5	16,500.00	17,500.00	1,000.00	6.06%	4.50%	787.50	18,287.50
D'Agostino, Joe	3	18,500.00	20,000.00	1,500.00	8.11%	4.50%	900.00	20,900.00
Harrison, Reggie	7	21,000.00	23,000.00	2,000.00	9.52%	7.25%	1,667.50	24,667.50
Ingold, Terry	4	25,600.00	27,000.00	1,400.00	5.47%	4.50%	1,215.00	28,215.00
Nunez, Maria	8	28,500.00	30,000.00	1,500.00	5.26%	7.25%	2,175.00	32,175.00
Presser, Carol	9	33,000.00	35,000.00	2,000.00	6.06%	7.25%	2,537.50	37,537.50
Tse, Sandra	6	25,400.00	27,000.00	1,600.00	6.30%	7.25%	1,957.50	28,957.50
Wingate, George	10	38,000.00	41,500.00	3,500.00	9.21%	7.25%	3,008.75	44,508.75
TOTALS		284,300.00	305,000.00	20,700.00			20,338.75	325,338.75

KEYSTROKES

CHANGE PRINT MARGINS

1. **FROM PRINT PREVIEW:**

Click **Setup** button.................. [Alt]+[S]
OR
FROM WORKSHEET OR CHART SHEET:

a. Click **File** menu .... [Alt]+[F]

b. Click **Page Setup** .... [U]

2. Click **Margins** tab .... [Ctrl]+[Tab]

To set page margins:

a. Select margin to change:

* **Top** .... [Alt]+[T]

* **Bottom** .... [Alt]+[B]

* **Left**................................. [Alt]+[L]

* **Right** .... [Alt]+[R]

b. Type or select number in margin increment box.

c. Repeat steps a. and b. as needed.

To set header and footer margins:

✓ *To prevent data from overlapping, these settings should be less than the top and bottom margin settings.*

a. Select margin to change:

* **Header** .... [Alt]+[A]

* **Footer**............................... [Alt]+[F]

b. Type or select number in margin increment box.

c. Repeat steps a. and b. as needed.

To center data within margins:

Select **Horizontally**................ [Alt]+[Z]
AND/OR

Select **Vertically**.................... [Alt]+[V]

✓ *For chart sheets, you must first select **Custom** from the Chart tab to enable these options.*

3. Click **OK**.................................. [Enter]
to return to sheet or Print Preview.

CHANGE PRINT MARGINS BY DRAGGING MARGIN HANDLES

FROM PRINT PREVIEW:

1. Click **Margins** button.............. [Alt]+[M]

Excel displays margin and column handles.

2. Drag margin handle to desired position.

✓ *Status bar displays size as you drag handle.*

CHANGE PAGE ORIENTATION

1. Click **File** menu .... [Alt]+[F]

2. Click **Page Setup**........................... [U]

3. Click **Page** tab .... [Ctrl]+[Tab]

4. Select **Portrait** .... [Alt]+[T]
OR

Select **Landscape**.................. [Alt]+[L]

5. Click **OK**..................................... [Enter]

SPECIFY NUMBER OF COPIES TO PRINT

Prints worksheet data using the current page settings a specified number of times.

1. Click **File** menu .... [Alt]+[F]

2. Click **Print**.................................... [P]

3. Click **Number of copies**
text box: .... [Alt]+[C]

4. Type numbers of copies.

5. Select desired **Print What** option:

Selection .... [Alt]+[N]

Active Sheet(s) .... [Alt]+[V]

Entire Workbook................... [Alt]+[E]

6. Click **OK**.................................... [Enter]

CENTER TITLES OVER SELECTED RANGE

1. Select cells across which data will be centered.

2. Click **Merge and Center** button ...... [icon]
on Formatting toolbar.
OR

a. Click **Format** menu .... [Alt]+[O]

b. Click **Cells** .... [E]

c. Click **Alignment**............... [Ctrl]+[Tab]

d. Click **Horizontal**................. [Alt]+[H]

e. Select **Center across selection** .. [↓]

USE WORD ART FEATURE

1. Click **WordArt** button on the Drawing

toolbar... [icon]

2. Select a **WordArt** style .. [Alt]+[W], [↕]

3. Click **OK**.................................... [Enter]

4. Select **Font** .... [Alt]+[F], [↕]

5. Select **Size** .... [Alt]+[S], [↕]

6. Type desired text.

7. Click **OK**.................................... [Enter]

8. Use mouse to size and place text.

NEXT EXERCISE

Exercise 69

- **Enlarge the Printout** ■ **Insert and Size Pictures**
- **Download Clip Art from the Internet**

NOTES

Enlarge the Printout

- In the last exercise, the worksheet was reduced so that a large print range would fit on one page. It is possible, however, to expand a small worksheet printout to fill the page, thus enlarging the worksheet data. Use the scaling feature in Page Setup to set worksheets to print to a size greater than 100%.

Insert and Size Pictures

- You may insert pictures into your worksheet to enhance its appearance. When **Insert, Picture** is selected, your choices include Clip Art, pictures from a file, AutoShapes, Organization chart or WordArt, as illustrated below.

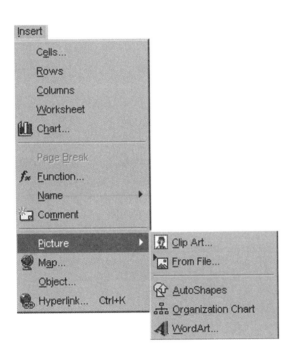

- When Clip Art is selected, the Microsoft Clip Gallery will display. You may encounter an error message if your ClipGallery is empty. Clip art can be added to your gallery by using the Import Clips button. The Add clip art to Clip Gallery dialog box appears where you can select the desired files from your software disk or CD-ROM drive (or other folder or drive that contains clip art you wish to use). The Office directory from the Microsoft Office 97 installation CD-ROM is illustrated below. You can select files from a variety of clip art categories and styles to add to your gallery.

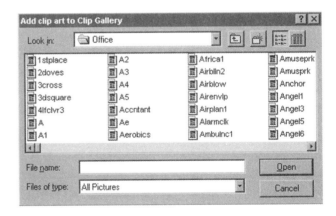

- Once clip art is added to your gallery, you can select it from the sample images in the gallery as illustrated on the next page and insert it into your worksheet. You may also import clip art directly from other files; by selecting Insert, Picture, From File. This option does not add the sample to your gallery. If you frequently use specific picture files, it would be better to add them to your gallery.

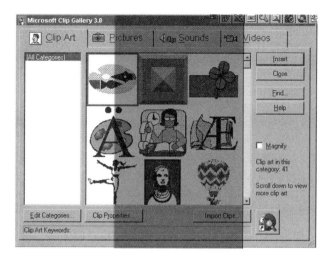

- When an object is inserted into a worksheet, it may have to be sized or moved for proper placement. Selecting the object creates a frame and a set of handles that are used to move and size the object, just as you moved and sized various chart objects.

Download Clip Art from the Internet

Internet Symbol

- You will note the Internet symbol at the bottom right of the Microsoft Clip Gallery dialog box. This is a shortcut to the Microsoft Clip Gallery Live Internet Web site. If you have established an Internet connection and have a Web browser currently running, you will be automatically connected to the Clip Gallery Browse feature once you click the Internet button. You can select a clip art category, view the samples, and download the file to disk or to your hard drive. Generally, it is advisable to download to disk, but the files on this Web site work best when downloaded directly to your Clip Gallery.

- You can also access the Clip Gallery Live Web site while connected to the Web by typing the following URL address: http://www.Microsoft.com/clipgallerylive

---

In this exercise, The Music Box wants you to enhance its quarterly sales report by adding clip art, inserting and deleting rows, using WordArt for the title, and then expanding the size and centering the print range for the report.

EXERCISE DIRECTIONS

1. Open 📠 **MUSIC** or 💾 **69MUSIC**
   - Use the illustration on page 269 to compare **MUSIC** with the enhanced version next to it.

2. Make the changes to your worksheet indicated below:

   Titles:
   a. Move title and subtitle to column A.
   b. Insert two rows under the subtitle and two rows above the title.
   c. Add a second subtitle: Beginning in A5: 1996, 1997, AND PROJECTED 1998 SALES.
   d. Center each of the subtitles separately over the column range A:F and delete THE MUSIC BOX title.
   e. Insert WordArt, select the style as illustrated, use the Impact font, 24 points, and edit the text to THE MUSIC BOX.
   f. Place the title in rows 1 to 3 centered over the worksheet.
   g. Set the fill color for rows 1 to 5 to Light Green, Row 5, Box 4.

   Year Titles:
   a. Delete the blank row above the titles as well as the title and subtitles from the second and third worksheets.
   b. Move the years from the top left corners of the worksheets from 1996, 1997, and 1998P to one row above the existing location. For example, move 1996 from A8 to A7.
   c. Center 1996 over the column range A:F, bold the year, and change font size to 14.
   d. Format year line for a border on all 4 sides.
   e. Change fill color to Light Green, Row 5, Box 4.
   f. Use Format Painter to format 1997 and 1998P lines with the same settings.

   Column headings:
   - Change fill color to Light Turquoise, Row 5, Box 5.

   Data:
   - Change fill color to Light Turquoise, Row 5, Box 5 for the summary data on all worksheets.

3. Insert a clip art file at the top of the worksheet:
   a. Click Insert, Picture, Clip Art

b. If your Clip Gallery displays, locate the Music notes (as shown in the illustration on the next page) and click Insert. **Proceed to step 4**.

c. If you get an error message that Clip Art is not installed, and you have the Office CD-ROM in the machine, click OK and Import Clips.

d. Select the CD drive, the Clip Art folder, and then the Office folder.

e. Use the Ctrl key to select the four music clip art files. Click Open.

f. Click Add all clips to the selected categories.

g. Select category from the list or add a New Category. Click OK.

h. Select the music notes from the Clip Art Gallery and click Insert.

4. Size and move the object into place as per the illustration.

5. Copy the illustration to the other side of the title.

6. Right-click the clip art image and format the fill color to Light Green, Row 5, Box 4, and the line color to no line.

7. Use Format Painter to format the other music image with the same settings.

8. Use the Internet or the **Excel Internet Simulation CD-ROM** to insert additional Microsoft clip art at the bottom of the worksheet.
   See page vi in the Introduction if you need help installing the Excel Internet Simulation.

   a. Sign on to your Internet service provider and select your Web browser.
   OR
   To use the Excel Internet Simulation:
   - Click **Go**, **Open** on the Web toolbar.
   - Type **C:\DDCPUB\EX97INT.IMR**
   - *If the Excel Simulation has been installed on another drive, replace C: with the accurate letter representing the drive.*
   - Click **OK** to launch the simulation.
   - Select **Exercise 69: Clip Art**.
     You will enter a simulated Excel document.

   b. Click Insert menu, Picture, Clip Art.

   c. If you receive a message regarding additional Clip Art, click OK. Then, click the Internet shortcut button.

   d. If you receive a message about connecting to the Web, read it and click OK. You will be automatically connected to the Microsoft Clip Gallery Live Web Page.

   e. Read and accept the license agreement.

f. The Browse Clip Art icon is selected by default. From the Select a Category pull-down menu, select Music and click Go.

g. Click once on the filename for the music sheet graphic link (**ENTE001748-X5.WMF**).
   Depending on which Web browser you use, a dialog box may appear prompting you to save the file to disk or to import it directly to your Clip Gallery. Make a selection and click OK.

9. Exit from your browser and disconnect from your Internet service provider, or exit the Excel Internet Simulation.

10. **IF YOU USED THE INTERNET:**
    The clip art file was either:
    a. downloaded directly to your Clip Gallery. In which case, **proceed to step 11**.
    OR
    b. saved to a hard drive or removable disk. In which case, you must import the file to your Clip Gallery:
    - Click Insert, Picture, Clip Art and then the Import Clips button.
    - Select the appropriate drive and folder in the Look in folder.
    - Double-click on the file: **ENTE0017.WMF**, select Music from the Categories list, and click OK.

    IF YOU USED THE EXCEL INTERNET SIMULATION:
    Step 8 only simulated the download process. The actual clip art file has been provided for you in the **Clip Art** folder on the CD-ROM that accompanied this book. To import the clip art file to your Clip Gallery:
    - Insert the CD in your CD-ROM drive.
    - Follow the three bulleted steps above.

11. Return to Excel, select the graphic from your Clip Gallery, and insert the new clip art file at the bottom of your worksheet.

12. Size and adjust the image to fit.

13. Format the image so that the fill color is Light Turquoise, Row 5, Box 5, and there is no line.

14. Change the page setup to scale the output to 110%. From the Margins tab, center the page between margins horizontally and vertically.

15. Preview the worksheet. It should fit on one page in portrait orientation.

16. Print one copy with this setting.

17. Save and close the workbook file; name it **MUSIC**.

	A	B	C	D	E	F
1			THE MUSIC BOX			
2			QUARTERLY SALES			
3						
4	1996	CLASSICAL	COUNTRY	JAZZ	ROCK	1996
5	1st Quarter	$ 5,573	$ 6,934	$ 5,454	$ 5,978	$ 23,939
6	2nd Quarter	$ 5,643	$ 7,387	$ 5,975	$ 6,143	$ 25,148
7	3rd Quarter	$ 5,346	$ 7,154	$ 5,764	$ 6,098	$ 24,362
8	4th Quarter	$ 5,734	$ 7,043	$ 5,863	$ 6,143	$ 24,783
9						
10	TOTAL	$ 22,296	$ 28,518	$ 23,056	$ 24,362	$ 98,232
11	AVERAGE	$ 5,574	$ 7,130	$ 5,764	$ 6,091	$ 24,558
12	HIGHEST	$ 5,734	$ 7,387	$ 5,975	$ 6,143	$ 25,148
13	LOWEST	$ 5,346	$ 6,934	$ 5,454	$ 5,978	$ 23,939
14						
15						
16			THE MUSIC BOX			
17			QUARTERLY SALES			
18						
19	1997	CLASSICAL	COUNTRY	JAZZ	ROCK	1997
20	1st Quarter	$ 5,283	$ 6,234	$ 5,145	$ 6,038	$ 22,700
21	2nd Quarter	$ 5,521	$ 6,843	$ 5,863	$ 6,254	$ 24,481
22	3rd Quarter	$ 5,476	$ 6,793	$ 5,954	$ 6,321	$ 24,544
23	4th Quarter	$ 5,843	$ 6,932	$ 6,043	$ 6,278	$ 25,096
24						
25	TOTAL	$ 22,123	$ 26,802	$ 23,005	$ 24,891	$ 96,821
26	AVERAGE	$ 5,531	$ 6,701	$ 5,751	$ 6,223	$ 24,205
27	HIGHEST	$ 5,843	$ 6,932	$ 6,043	$ 6,321	$ 25,096
28	LOWEST	$ 5,283	$ 6,234	$ 5,145	$ 6,038	$ 22,700
29						
30						
31			THE MUSIC BOX			
32			QUARTERLY SALES			
33						
34	1998P	CLASSICAL	COUNTRY	JAZZ	ROCK	1998P
35	1st Quarter	$ 5,400	$ 6,400	$ 5,300	$ 6,200	$ 23,300
36	2nd Quarter	$ 5,500	$ 6,900	$ 5,700	$ 6,400	$ 24,500
37	3rd Quarter	$ 5,700	$ 7,000	$ 6,100	$ 6,500	$ 25,300
38	4th Quarter	$ 5,900	$ 7,100	$ 6,200	$ 6,700	$ 25,900
39						
40	TOTAL	$ 22,500	$ 27,400	$ 23,300	$ 25,800	$ 99,000
41	AVERAGE	$ 5,625	$ 6,850	$ 5,825	$ 6,450	$ 24,750
42	HIGHEST	$ 5,900	$ 7,100	$ 6,200	$ 6,700	$ 25,900
43	LOWEST	$ 5,400	$ 6,400	$ 5,300	$ 6,200	$ 23,300

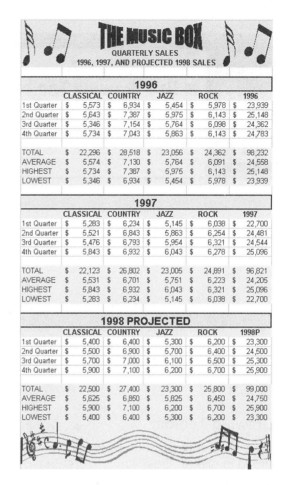

KEYSTROKES

INSERT CLIP ART OBJECT INTO WORKSHEET

1. Select cell where object will be inserted.
2. Click **Insert** menu .... Alt + I
3. Click **Picture** .... P
4. Click **Clip Art** C
5. Select category .... ↓
6. Select clip art image .... Tab, ↕
7. Select **Insert** .... Alt + I

SIZE AND MOVE CLIP ART OBJECTS

1. Click on object.
2. To size object:
   a. Select object border.
      Handles appear on the item's border.
   b. Point to handle on side of item to size.
   c. Drag item outline in direction to size.
3. To move object:
   Drag object item outline.

IMPORT CLIP ART FROM OFFICE SOFTWARE

1. Select cell where object will be inserted.
2. Click **Insert** menu .... Alt + I
3. Click **Picture** .... P
4. Click **Clip Art** C
5. Click **Import clips** .... Alt + T
6. Select drive and folder for clip art.
   Use Office CD, select Clipart, Office Folders.
7. Select clip art file.
8. Click **Open** .... Alt + O

To select categories:
1. Click appropriate categories.
   OR
   Click **New Category**
2. Enter Name
3. Click **OK** .... Enter

CHANGE SCALE OF PRINTED DATA

1. Click **File** menu .... Alt + F
2. Click **Page Setup** .... U
3. Click **Page** tab .... Ctrl + Tab
4. Double-click **% normal size** textbox .... Alt + A
5. Type percentage (10-400).
   ✓ *You can also click the increment box arrows to select a percentage.*
6. Click **OK** .... Enter

Exercise 70

■ Use Drawing Toolbar ■ Insert Objects ■ Format Graphic Objects ■ Adjust Row Height

Drawing Toolbar

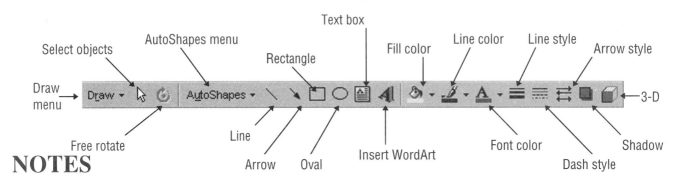

NOTES

Use Drawing Toolbar

■ If you wish to add **graphic objects** that are not provided in clip art files, you can create a customized object by using the tools available on the **Drawing toolbar**. You can draw lines, arcs, arrows, rectangles, ellipses, polygons, or freehand graphics on any area of a worksheet or chart. Select View, Toolbars, **Drawing** to display the Drawing toolbar. The Drawing toolbar, which may be docked anywhere on the screen, is illustrated above.

■ Select the desired button to draw or format an object. The line, arrow, rectangle, text box, and oval buttons will enable the mouse to draw objects that may be dragged to the required size.

Insert Objects

■ In the previous exercise, you inserted pictures into a worksheet by selecting Picture from the Insert menu. You can insert pictures, as well as other types of objects you create in other software applications, by selecting **Object** from the Insert menu. An object is embedded on the sheet unless the Link to File box is checked, in which case it becomes a linked object.

■ Click **Insert**, **Object** to view the Object dialog box, as illustrated below. Select the object type, on the Create New tab, if you are creating a new file to insert. You can use this procedure if, for example, you are creating a Microsoft Word object in the worksheet. If you have a file saved that you wish to insert, use the Create from File tab. You can enter or browse for the filename and link the file, if desired. On both tabs you can select Display as icon to display the object as an icon within your document.

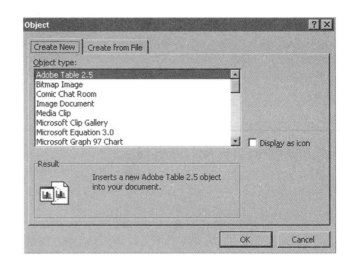

Format Graphic Objects

■ Graphic objects can be rotated, sized, moved, copied, and deleted. They can also have various background and border attributes. When a transparent (default) background is selected, the underlying data will not be obscured. Object borders or fill patterns, including shadows and rounded corners, may be formatted by selecting the object and then using the formatting tools available on the Drawing toolbar. You can also click Format, Object, or press Ctrl+1, and the Format Auto Shape dialog box will appear.

Adjust Row Height

■ **Row height** is determined (by default) by the point size of the typeface used. However, you may increase or decrease the row height, as desired, by selecting **Format, Row, Height.** If you increase the row height, you may then select the alignment of the text within the row, just as you would column data. For example, text may be placed at the top, center or bottom (default) of a row that has been increased in height.

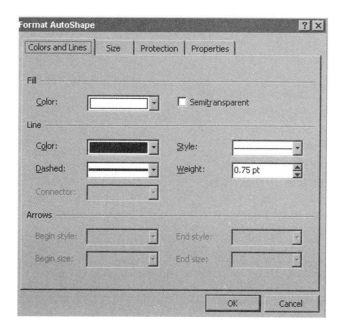

In this exercise, The Novel Tea Bookstore would like to include a logo on its report by using the Drawing toolbar and a clip art object. The worksheet will be enhanced by increasing the row height and by using other previously learned techniques.

EXERCISE DIRECTIONS

1. Open ⌨ **SAVINGS** or 💾 **70SAVINGS**.
   - Use the illustration to compare **SAVINGS** with the enhanced version on the next page.
2. Make the changes to your worksheet as indicated:
   a. Insert a row above the titles.
   b. Main title: Move to C2, Book Antiqua, 18 pt., bold. (If you do not have this font, use a serif, or fancy font.) Format row height to 30 pt.
   c. Subtitles: Move to column C, Book Antiqua, 12 pt., bold.
   d. Change fill color of A1:H7 to Light Green, Row 5, Box 4.
3. Make the Drawing toolbar active and do the following:
   a. Use the Oval drawing tool to draw the saucer of the tea cup to the right of the titles.
   b. Select the oval and use the Shadow button on the toolbar to set a shadow. (Row 4, Box 2)
   c. Format oval to Light Yellow color, Row 5, Box 3.
   d. Use the Can shape from the AutoShapes, Basic Shapes menu, Row 4, Box 1, to create the cup. Adjust placement and size as illustrated.
   e. Format the cup color to Sea Green, Row 3, Box 4.
   f. Select the Shadow button to apply the Row 4, Box 2 shadow.
   g. Use the Block Arc shape from the AutoShapes, Basic Shapes menu, Row 5, Box 4, to create the cup handle.
   h. Select the AutoShape and use the Format AutoShapes dialog box and the Size tab to set the rotation of the object at 90 degrees.
   i. Size and place the shape to create the handle of the cup.
   j. Format the cup handle to Sea Green.
   k. Use the Scribble line from the AutoShapes, Lines menu to draw two lines representing the steam from the tea.

4. Use Insert, Object, Microsoft Office Clip Gallery to display the Clip Gallery. Using the method discussed in Exercise 69, import all clip art files from the CD-ROM that relate to books.
5. Insert object from the MS Clip Gallery, representing books, in the location shown in the illustration.
6. Format the clip art fill color to Light Green and the line to no line.
7. Format cell borders, as illustrated, above and below the column heading rows.
8. Format the column headings for Book Antiqua, 12 pt., bold. Right-align column headings for all money columns.
9. Format the remaining data for Book Antiqua, 10 pt.
10. Change the color fill for the data section to Light Yellow, Row 5, Box 3.
11. Change the color fill for the summary section to Light Green, Row 5, Box 4.
12. Format cell borders, as illustrated, above and below the summary rows.
13. Format a cell border for the average savings value.
14. Select the arrow from the Drawing toolbar and point out the average book price, as illustrated.
15. Preview the worksheet.
16. If necessary, turn printing of gridlines off.
17. Save and close the file; name it **SAVINGS**.

	A	B	C	D	E	F	G
1		THE NOVEL TEA BOOKSTORE					
2		SUMMER SAVINGS SALE					
3		SAMPLE DISCOUNTS					
4							
5			LIST		SALE	SALES	
6	BOOK		PRICE	SAVINGS	PRICE	TAX	TOTAL
7	Creature Feature		15.00	4.00	11.00	0.88	$ 11.88
8	Public Defender		25.00	9.00	16.00	1.28	$ 17.28
9	Traveling Italy		32.00	10.00	22.00	1.76	$ 23.76
10	Picasso in Blue		86.00	28.00	58.00	4.64	$ 62.64
11	Vortex Signs		30.00	10.50	19.50	1.56	$ 21.06
12	Brown's Tax Guide		35.00	12.80	22.20	1.78	$ 23.98
13							
14	TOTALS		223.00	74.30	148.70	11.90	160.60
15	AVERAGE		37.17	12.38	24.78	1.98	26.77
16	COUNT		6	6	6	6	6
17	MAXIMUM		86.00	28.00	58.00	4.64	62.64
18	MINIMUM		15.00	4.00	11.00	0.88	11.88

THE NOVEL TEA BOOKSTORE
SUMMER SAVINGS SALE
SAMPLE DISCOUNTS

BOOK	LIST PRICE	SAVINGS	SALE PRICE	SALES TAX	TOTAL	
Creature Feature	15.00	4.00	11.00	0.88	$ 11.88	
Public Defender	25.00	9.00	16.00	1.28	$ 17.28	
Traveling Italy	32.00	10.00	22.00	1.76	$ 23.76	
Picasso in Blue	86.00	28.00	58.00	4.64	$ 62.64	
Vortex Signs	30.00	10.50	19.50	1.56	$ 21.06	
Brown's Tax Guide	35.00	12.80	22.20	1.78	$ 23.98	
TOTALS	223.00	74.30	148.70	11.90	160.60	
AVERAGE	37.17	12.38	24.78	1.98	26.77	←
COUNT	6	6	6	6	6	
MAXIMUM	86.00	28.00	58.00	4.64	62.64	
MINIMUM	15.00	4.00	11.00	0.88	11.88	

KEYSTROKES

CHANGE ROW HEIGHT USING THE MENU

Sets row height to a specific size.

1. Select any cell in row(s) to size.
2. Click **Format** menu .... `Alt`+`O`
3. Click **Row** .... `R`
4. Click **Height**................................... `E`
5. Type number (0-409) in **Row Height** text box.
   ✓ *Number represents height in points.*
6. Click **OK**...................................... `Enter`

CHANGE ROW HEIGHT USING THE MOUSE

Change one row height:

1. Point to bottom border of row heading.
   Pointer becomes a ↕.
2. Drag ↕ up or down.
   Excel displays height on left side of formula bar.

Change several row heights:

1. Select rows to format.
   ✓ *Click **Select All** button to change all rows.*
2. Point to bottom border of any selected row heading.
   Pointer becomes a ↕.
3. Drag ↕ up or down.
   Excel displays height on left side of formula bar.

Set row height to fit tallest entry

Double-click row headings bottom border.

DRAW GRAPHIC OBJECTS

Draws objects such as rectangles, lines, arrows, and ellipses.

1. Click **Drawing** button.....................
   on Standard toolbar to show Drawing toolbar.
2. Click desired drawing tool on Drawing toolbar.
   Pointer becomes a + *and the status bar displays instructions.*
3. Point to an area where a corner or end of object will begin.
4. Drag object's outline until desired size and shape is obtained.
   ✓ *You can use the SHIFT, ALT and CTRL keys to constrain the objects you draw. For example, if you hold SHIFT while drawing an ellipse, you will draw a perfect circle.*

FORMAT GRAPHIC OBJECTS (SUMMARY)

Double-click object to access format options quickly.

To change colors or line styles:

1. Click **Colors and Lines** tab.... `Ctrl`+`Tab`
2. Click Fill **Color** box .... `Alt`+`C`
3. Select fill color.............................. `↕`
4. Select Line settings:
   - **Color** ....`Alt`+`O`, `↔`
   - **Dashed**................`Alt`+`D`, `↕`
   - **Style** ....`Alt`+`S`, `↕`
   - **Weight** ....`Alt`+`W`, `↕`

   Make desired setting using arrow keys or the mouse.

TO SET SIZE AND ROTATION FORMATS

1. Click **Size** tab.
2. Select size and rotation settings:
   - **Height** ....`Alt`+`E`
   - **Rotation**.........................`Alt`+`T`
   - **Width** ....`Alt`+`D`

   Make desired setting using arrow keys or the mouse.

3. Select scale settings:
   - **Height**............................`Alt`+`H`
   - **Width**..............................`Alt`+`W`

4. Click **OK**................................... `Enter`

INSERT CLIP ART OBJECT INTO WORKSHEET

1. Select cell where object will be inserted.
2. Click **Insert** menu .... `Alt`+`I`
3. Click **Object**.................................. `O`
4. Click **Create New** tab............. `Ctrl`+`Tab`
5. Select source application in Object Type list.
   Microsoft Clip Gallery
6. Click **OK**...................................... `Enter`
7. Select desired clip from gallery.
8. Click **Insert**............................ `Alt`+`I`
9. Size and place the object.

NEXT EXERCISE

Exercise

71

■ Add and Format a Text Box   ■ Add Callouts

NOTES

Add and Format a Text Box

- It is possible to add a **text box object**, in paragraph form, to both a worksheet and a chart. Clicking the **Text Box** button 🖾 on the Drawing toolbar allows you to drag and size the box to be created. Text within a text box object can be enhanced using the same font options used for cell data.

- As with objects, text boxes can be formatted. The border and background of a text box can be cleared so that the text box cannot be seen. A text box can also be enhanced by adding a drop shadow or an arrow. Adding an arrow to the text box creates a data label.

Add Callouts

- **Callouts**, one of the submenu options available on the AutoShapes menu, provides a series of boxes that can be used to explain or point out data on a chart, in a report, or for presentation use. Note the illustration of the callout shapes on the Callout menu.

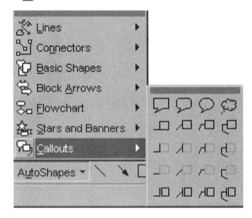

In this exercise, you will enhance the Umbrella Insurance Agency Quarterly Income Statement worksheet and charts. You will create a new chart and add explanatory paragraphs.

EXERCISE DIRECTIONS

1. Open 🖬 **INSQTRS** or 🖫 **71INSQTRS**.
   - Compare **INSQTRS**, as shown in Illustration A on the next page, with the enhanced version, as shown in Illustration B on page 278.

2. Move all charts except the column chart to Sheet2 of the workbook. Rename Sheet2, Charts.

3. Rename Sheet1, Income and Expense Analysis.

4. Create a stacked bar chart to analyze the sources of quarterly income. Use the selection shown in Illustration A.
   a. Use titles as illustrated.
   b. Place the chart in the range A24:F41.
   c. Adjust font sizes to 12 point for all text except for the main title (14 point).

5. Move the column chart directly below the stacked bar chart in the range A43:F60.

6. Make the changes to your worksheet indicated below:

a. Insert two rows above the title of the worksheet.

b. Move title and subtitle to column A.

c. Delete title.

d. Use WordArt to enter Umbrella Insurance Agency in the style illustrated, Row 1, Box 3, in Arial Black, 24 point.

e. Size and place the title as shown in Illustration B.

f. Subtitle: Set to 11 points bold. Center the subtitle over columns A to G.

g. Change fill color for the range A1:G5 to Light Blue, Row 3, Box 6.

h. Column titles: Use cell borders above and below the column titles as shown. Bold and right-align column headings. Change fill color to Yellow, Row 4, Box 3.

i. Bold the labels INCOME, EXPENSES and NET INCOME.

j. Include a single line above the Total Income and Total Expenses data, and a double line *below* NET INCOME data.

k. Change the fill color of the range A8:G62, to Gray-25%, Row 4, Box 8.

l. Worksheet text box: Create a text box containing the explanatory note for the stacked bar chart, as shown in the illustration. Size the text box so it fits in the range F27:G34. Set the text box text to 8 pt. Italics.

m. Callout: Use the Callouts submenu on the AutoShapes menu to include the text for the Expenses chart. Place the box and pointer as illustrated.

n. Select the callout and add a shadow.

o. Turn worksheet gridlines off, if necessary.

p. Select the column chart and move the chart legend to below the chart.

7. Use Print Setup to center worksheet horizontally and vertically.

8. Preview the worksheet.

9. Print a copy to fit on one page.

10. Save and close the file; name it **INSQTRS**.

Illustration A

	A	B	C	D	E	F	G
1			UMBRELLA INSURANCE AGENCY				
2			QUARTERLY INCOME STATEMENT				
3							
4			JAN-MAR	APR-JUNE	JULY-SEPT	OCT-NOV	COMBINED
5			TOTALS	TOTALS	TOTALS	TOTALS	TOTALS
6							
7	INCOME						
8	Agency Fees		38,052.39	41,566.18	42,402.51	42,314.40	164,335.48
9	Consultations		4,776.95	4,679.76	4,000.73	3,730.51	17,187.95
10	Total Income		42,829.34	46,245.94	46,403.24	46,044.91	181,523.43
11							
12	EXPENSES:						
13	Advertising		800.00	950.00	900.00	830.00	3,480.00
14	Rent		3,600.00	3,600.00	3,600.00	3,600.00	14,400.00
15	Salaries		18,750.00	18,750.00	18,750.00	18,750.00	75,000.00
16	Supplies		699.08	609.62	672.42	592.00	2,573.12
17	Utilities		655.72	703.61	790.62	700.98	2,850.93
18	Interest		75.00	75.00	75.00	75.00	300.00
19	Other		685.84	1,238.22	1,150.95	741.65	3,816.66
20	Total Expenses		25,265.64	25,926.45	25,938.99	25,289.63	102,420.71
21							
22	NET INCOME		17,563.70	20,319.49	20,464.25	20,755.28	79,102.72

Illustration B

Umbrella Insurance Agency
QUARTERLY INCOME STATEMENT

	JAN-MAR TOTALS	APR-JUNE TOTALS	JULY-SEPT TOTALS	OCT-NOV TOTALS	COMBINED TOTALS
INCOME					
Agency Fees	38,052.39	41,566.18	42,402.51	42,314.40	164,335.48
Consultations	4,776.95	4,679.76	4,000.73	3,730.51	17,187.95
Total Income	42,829.34	46,245.94	46,403.24	46,044.91	181,523.43
EXPENSES:					
Advertising	800.00	950.00	900.00	830.00	3,480.00
Rent	3,600.00	3,600.00	3,600.00	3,600.00	14,400.00
Salaries	18,750.00	18,750.00	18,750.00	18,750.00	75,000.00
Supplies	699.08	609.62	672.42	592.00	2,573.12
Utilities	655.72	703.61	790.62	700.98	2,850.93
Interest	75.00	75.00	75.00	75.00	300.00
Other	685.84	1,238.22	1,150.95	741.65	3,816.66
Total Expenses	25,265.64	25,926.45	25,938.99	25,289.63	102,420.71
NET INCOME	17,563.70	20,319.49	20,464.25	20,755.28	79,102.72

Income from Consultations has decreased this year. However, our total income and agency fees have continued to increase.

Salaries remain our largest expense. We are reviewing our employment policies.

KEYSTROKES

CREATE A TEXT BOX

1. Click **Text Box** button.....................

   on Drawing toolbar.

   Pointer becomes a +.

2. Position + where corner of box
   will be.

   To create a box without constraints:
   Drag box outline until desired size is
   obtained.

   To create a square box:
   Press **Shift** and drag box outline until
   desired size is obtained.

   **To create a box and align it to
   gridlines:**
   Press **Alt** and drag box outline until
   desired size is obtained.

3. Type text as desired.

4. Click outside text box to return to
   normal operations.

FORMAT TEXT BOX OBJECT

1. Select object to be formatted.

2. Select text and format for font, size,
   underline or style.

3. Click **OK** ....

Exercise 72

■ Summary

> *You have been asked to enhance the Furniture Showrooms, Inc. sales and salary report worksheet.*

EXERCISE DIRECTIONS

1. Open 🖮 **FURN** or 💾 **72FURN**.

2. Move the line and 3-D column chart to Sheet2.

3. Rename Sheet2, Charts.

4. Rename Sheet1, Sales and Salary Report.

5. Place **3-D stack** and **pie** charts side-by-side below the worksheet at row 21 at opposite ends of the worksheet. (Allow space for a note between the charts.)

6. The **3-D stack** chart should be to the left of the **pie** chart and both charts should be equal in size and fit within the width of the worksheet.

7. Include a text box object between the two charts. Set the text to Italics and create a shadow on the box. Size and place the box between the charts. Enter the following text:

   Tony Rivera was awarded "highest sales" awards for each quarter. Kelly Linsey won the "most-improved sales" award for the third quarter.

8. Enhance the worksheet and chart as desired or follow the suggestions listed below:
   a. Move the titles to column A.
   b. Set titles to Bookman Old Style font (or a serif font), 16 point, bold.
   c. Center titles over the width of the worksheet one at a time.
   d. Color the top three rows Color Scheme (Lavender), Row 5, Box 1.
   e. Bold column headings.
   f. Adjust column width as necessary.
   g. Format cells above and below column headings for borders.
   h. Color column headings Light Yellow, Row 5, Box 1.
   i. Color remaining worksheet, including chart area, a Gray-25%.

9. Print a copy of the file in landscape orientation to fit on one page.

10. Save and close the workbook file; name the file **FURN**.

Exercise 73

■ Summary

You work in the accounting department of the Network Extras Company, a computer firm. Each year, you create a balance sheet showing the total assets, liabilities, and capital of your company. Your supervisor, Mr. Harold Shirley, has asked you to create a balance sheet comparing 1995, 1996, and 1997 data, including charts. The worksheet and charts should be enhanced so that the report is ready to be presented to the bank officers.

EXERCISE DIRECTIONS

1. Create the worksheet on the next page as shown or open 📖 **73NET**. Format data and set column widths as necessary. Include the indicated cell borders.

2. Find:
   - Total Assets for each year.
   - Total Liabilities for each year.
   - CAPITAL (Total Assets-Total Liabilities).
   - TOTAL LIABILITIES AND CAPITAL.

3. Create an embedded **3-D column** chart below the worksheet comparing asset items (not totals) for 1995, 1996, and 1997. Place the chart in A24:F40. Include an appropriate heading, axis labels and titles, and a legend.

4. Create an embedded **3-D column** chart comparing liability items (not totals) for 1995, 1996, and 1997. Place the chart in A42:F58. Include an appropriate heading, axis labels and titles, and a legend.

5. Include the following text in a text box next to the Asset chart:

   There has been a significant increase in Accounts Receivable due to the economic downturn.

6. Add a drop shadow to the text box and insert an arrow pointing to the column showing the increase in Accounts Receivable.

7. Include the following text in a text box next to the Liability chart:

   The decrease in Loans Payable was due to the payment of a long-term note due in September.

8. Add a drop shadow to the text box and insert an arrow pointing to the decrease in Loans Payable.

9. Enhance the worksheet and charts, as desired, or follow the suggestions listed below:
   a. Use WordArt to create the title for the company name.
   b. Add rows if necessary.
   c. Set second and third title for Arial, 12 point, bold.
   d. Color title area Light Turquoise.
   e. Add a graphic at the right side of the title area.
   f. Bold ASSETS, LIABILITIES, and CAPITAL section titles.
   g. Color worksheet Pale Gray.

10. Print a copy of the worksheet to fit on one page.

11. Save and close the workbook file; name it **NET**.

	A	B	C	D	E	F	G
1	NETWORK EXTRAS COMPANY						
2	COMPARATIVE BALANCE SHEET						
3	December 31, 1997						
4							
5	ASSETS				1995	1996	1997
6		Cash			789,650	806,460	797,950
7		Investments			465,888	370,700	613,000
8		Accounts Receivable			1,321,700	1,342,690	1,545,500
9		Inventories			876,450	892,600	991,300
10		Other Assets			535,000	529,700	639,700
11	TOTAL ASSETS						
12							
13	LIABILITIES						
14		Accounts Payable			598,600	654,900	785,600
15		Loans Payable			623,800	793,500	384,500
16		Income Taxes Payable			276,000	287,050	345,200
17	Total Liabilities						
18							
19	CAPITAL						
20		Harold Shirley, Capital					
21	TOTAL LIABILITIES AND CAPITAL						

Excel

LESSON 10

ANALYZING DATA

Exercises 74-89

- Create a List/Database
- Add Records and Fields to a List
- Wrap Text
- Use a Data Form
- Name Lists
- Data Validation
- Sort Records in a List
- Undo a Sort
- Default Sort Order
- Create Valid Data List
- Update Database
- Add a Field to a List
- AutoFilter
- Maintain Original Record Order
- Advanced Filter
- Filter a List with Multiple Criteria
- Database (List) Functions

- Subtotals Feature
- Outline Feature
- Use Microsoft Query Wizard
- PivotTables
- Consolidate Data

Exercise 74

- ■ **Create a List/Database** ■ **Add Records and Fields to a List**
- ■ **Wrap Text** ■ **Use a Data Form**

NOTES

Create a List/Database

- While Excel is known mainly as spreadsheet software, it also has database capabilities that can help organize, manage, and locate information in a list. Data from external sources, such as database files or Web sites, may be brought into Excel, or lists may be exported from Excel to a database program for analysis. We will limit our discussion to creating and using the database functions provided in Excel.

- A **list** (or database) is a collection of related information.

- Excel automatically recognizes a labeled series of rows containing a set of data as a list. As shown in the illustration below, in a list:

  - Each row is a complete **record**, which usually consists of information about one person or one entity in the database.

  - Column labels are **field names**, or the name of a part of a record.

  - Columns of data are **fields**, which are parts of records.

- Fields are categories of information in a list. For example, the last name of the employee would be the data in the LAST field.

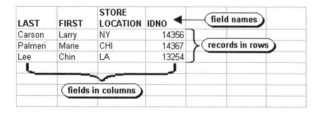

- When creating a list, keep the following guidelines in mind:

  - **Column Labels (Field Names)**

    - ◆ Type unique column labels in the first row of the list. The Excel Data feature utilizes this information to find and organize the data.

    - ◆ The column label format (font, alignment, cell borders, etc.) should be different from the record data.

    - ◆ If a column label is wider than the column, use the wrap text alignment format to insert a line break in the column label so that it fits in one cell. (See next page.)

    - ◆ Field data may be determined by a formula or function.

    - ◆ Do not insert a blank row between column labels and the records in the list.

  - **Row Data (Records)**

    - ◆ Do not include blank rows in a list.

  - **Location of List**

    - ◆ If you need to store more than one list in a workbook, it is best to store each on a separate worksheet.

    - ◆ Do not store other data in cells adjacent to the list data.

    - ◆ Avoid storing data to the left or right of a list because it may become hidden when you filter the records. *(See **AutoFilter**, Notes section, Exercise 79).*

Add Records and Fields to a List

■ A field (column of data) may be added in a list to the right of the last field, or you may insert a column and enter data.

■ A record may be added in a list below the last record, or you may insert a row and enter data.

Wrap Text

■ The **wrap text** alignment format will allow you to keep a longer column title or field name within one cell. This is necessary in a database list since the field name must be in the cell above the data for the field. To wrap text and allow a line break in a cell, click Format, Cells, the Alignment tab and then click the Wrap text option. Or, you can type the label and press Alt + Enter at the point you wish to wrap the text.

Use a Data Form

■ You can manage records in a list or database with a **data form**, which contains the data from one record. A data form displays one record at a time, whereas lists display all the records at once. You can create multiple lists in a workbook, and use a data form with any list.

■ From a data form you can:

• Browse or find records.

• Edit records.

• Add (append) new records.

• Delete records.

• Find records that match a criteria you specify.

■ Data forms are often used in business for customer service and other record oriented applications. The data is clearly organized, easy to read, and it is easy to enter and edit data. Note the illustration of a data form below.

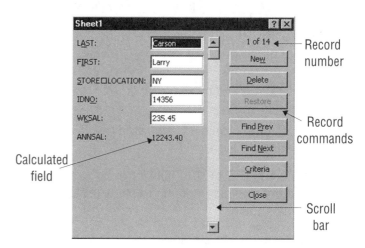

■ In a data form, calculated fields cannot be edited. However, Excel shows the contents of a calculated field and automatically calculates the field if you add a new record.

■ Use the following keys to work within a data form:

Tab	Positions insertion point in next field.
Shift + Tab	Positions insertion point in previous field.
Enter	Displays next record or inserts a new blank record.

■ To cancel changes made in a data form, press the Esc key or use the Close button ☒ in the top right corner.

In this exercise, you will create a database of Eiffel Records employees located in three cities. You will format field data, add records, add a field, and calculate values for the new field. You will create and use a data form to add records to the employee list.

EXERCISE DIRECTIONS

1. Create the list as shown in the worksheet at the bottom of the page, or open 🖫 **74EMPS.**

2. Format the WKSAL field data for two decimal places.

3. Align column labels as illustrated below and set them for bold type.

4. Set the STORE LOCATION label for wrap text alignment and size column to show label on two lines as shown.

5. Add the following employee records to the end of the list:

LAST	FIRST	STORE LOCATION	IDNO	WKSAL
Gregonis	Dimitri	LA	14395	275.00
Hopkins	George	NY	14396	310.00

6. To add an annual salary field, enter the field name ANNSAL in column F.

7. Enter a formula to calculate the annual salary.
   *Hint: WKSAL*52*

8. Format the ANNSAL column for two decimal places.

9. Use the Data, Form commands to display a data form for the list.

10. Use the Find Next and Find Prev buttons to view each record in the list.

11. Use the scroll box to move to the top and bottom of the list.

12. Display a New data form for the list and add the following records:

LAST	FIRST	STORE LOCATION	IDNO	WKSAL
Seltzer	Al K.	CHI	14931	255.00
Restivo	Mary	CHI	14932	295.00
Diamant	Sam	NY	14933	295.00

13. Delete the current record for Sam Diamant.

14. Close the data form.
    ✓ *Excel automatically added formulas for the new records to the calculated field ANNSAL.*

15. Print one copy of the list.

16. Close and save the workbook; name it **EMPS.**

	A	B	C	D	E	F
1	**LAST**	**FIRST**	**STORE LOCATION**	**IDNO**	**WKSAL**	**ANNSAL**
2	Carson	Larry	NY	14356	235.45	
3	Palmeri	Marie	CHI	14367	276.50	
4	Lee	Chin	LA	13254	345.00	
5	Baez	Franco	NY	14236	268.50	
6	Martino	John	LA	14289	342.90	
7	Carson	George	NY	14078	389.76	
8	Sawyer	Harriet	CHI	13290	358.60	
9	Samtanai	Perkash	LA	14354	215.45	
10	Tommei	Lori	NY	13852	376.00	
11	Watterson	Cathy	LA	14269	325.75	
12	Lee	Randy	CHI	13298	365.80	
13	Rogers	Jane	NY	14024	310.89	
14	Naidle	Adam	LA	14321	243.50	
15	Lee	Michael	CHI	14295	276.00	

KEYSTROKES

CREATE A LIST (DATABASE TABLE)

Excel automatically recognizes a labeled series of rows containing a set of data as a list. Many database operations, such as sorting and filtering records, can be done to a list.

1. Type field names (column labels) in adjacent cells of top row.
   - ✓ *If a label does not fit in a column, turn wrap text on in the cell or insert a line break.*

2. Enter data for first record below field names.

3. Enter data for each record in remaining rows.
   - ✓ *Do not leave empty rows between records.*

   The row containing the field names must be the first row of the range.

4. Format column labels as desired.

ADD A RECORD TO A LIST

Enter data for each field in row below last record in list.

OR

1. Insert a row where record will be entered in the list............................ Alt + I , R

2. Enter field data in row.

ADD A FIELD TO A LIST

1. Type field name (column label) in adjacent cell in top row of list.

2. Enter data for each record below field name.

OR

1. Insert a column where field will be entered in the list .... Alt + I , C

2. Type field name (column label) in first row of list in column.

3. Enter data for each record below field name.

WRAP TEXT IN CELLS

Wraps text to fit within cell. The row height changes to accommodate the text.

1. Select cell(s) containing text to wrap.

2. Click **Format** menu .... Alt + O

3. Click **Cells** .... E

4. Click **Alignment** tab .... Ctrl + Tab

5. Select **Wrap text** .... Alt + W

6. Click **OK** .... Enter

OPEN A DATA FORM FOR A LIST

Displays data in a list one record at a time.

1. Select any cell in list.

2. Click **Data** menu .... Alt + D

3. Click **Form** .... O

4. Select from available options. (See below.)

5. Click **Close** .... Alt + L

DISPLAY RECORDS USING A DATA FORM

1. Follow steps 1-3 of **OPEN A DATA FORM FOR A LIST**

2. To view next record:

   Click down scroll arrow ....

   OR

   Click **Find Next** .... Alt + N

3. To view previous record:

   Click up scroll arrow .... ▲

   OR

   Click **Find Prev** .... Alt + P

4. To scroll to record:

   Drag scroll box.

5. To move forward ten records:

   Click below scroll box.

6. Move back ten records:

   Click above scroll box.

ADD/DELETE RECORDS TO A LIST USING A DATA FORM

1. Follow steps 1-3 of **OPEN A DATA FORM FOR A LIST**.

2. Click **New** .... Alt + W

3. Type data in each record field.
   - ✓ *Press **Tab** to move to next field.*

   To add records:

   Repeat steps 2 and 3 for each new record.

   To delete current record:

   Click **Delete** .... Alt + D

EDIT RECORD IN A LIST USING A DATA FORM

1. Follow steps 1-3 of **OPEN A DATA FORM FOR A LIST**.

2. Display record to edit.

3. Select field to edit .... Tab

4. Edit data as desired.
   - ✓ *Do not press **Enter** after typing data in field.*

5. Repeat steps 2 and 3 for each field to change.

   To cancel changes made to current record:

   Click **Restore** .... Alt + R
   - ✓ *You must restore changes before moving to another record.*

   OR

   Press **Esc** .... Esc

Exercise

75

■ **Name Lists** ■ **Data Validation**

NOTES

Name Lists

■ If you name a range containing a list, and then add or delete records, the name will no longer accurately reference the list data. However, if you name a list DATABASE, the range will adjust when you add or delete records from a data form. The range for a database list should include the field names.

✓ *NOTE: You can name only one range*
DATABASE in a worksheet.

Data Validation

■ You can ensure that correct data is entered on a worksheet or in a database list by specifying what data is **valid** for individual cells or cell ranges. You can set the following types of validation tests:

• Restrict the data to a particular type such as whole numbers, percents, or text, and set limits on the valid entries.

• Specify a list of the valid entries.

• Limit the number of characters in entries.

• Use a formula to determine whether an entry is valid based on a calculation in another cell, such as checking that an entry for an account is not over the budgeted amount.

■ To include data validation tests, select the range for validation settings and click Data, Validation. The dialog box illustrated below will appear. You will note that when a data type is selected, decimals in this case, the minimum and maximum boxes display so you can limit the data.

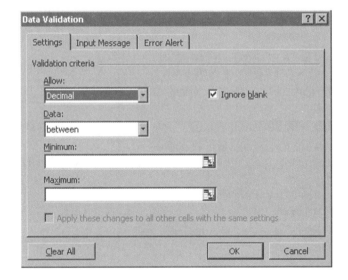

■ You can select the enforcement of the data validation settings as follows:

• Display a message that stops entry until data is within limits.

• Display warning and explanatory messages that allow entry of invalid data.

• Display input messages when the cell is selected.

- If you set limits and do not set warnings, select the **Circle Invalid Data** button 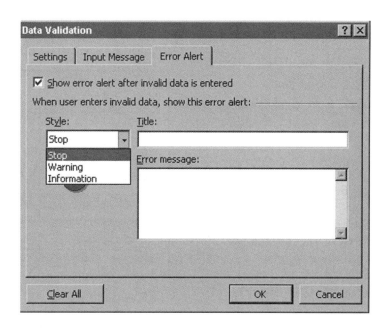 on the Auditing toolbar to find and correct invalid entries. Click Tools, Auditing, Show Auditing Toolbar to show the Auditing toolbar.

- Note the Error Alert tab on the Data Validation dialog box. You can set the alert to stop entry or to signal a warning or information message. On the Input Message tab, you can set a message to appear when the cell is selected.

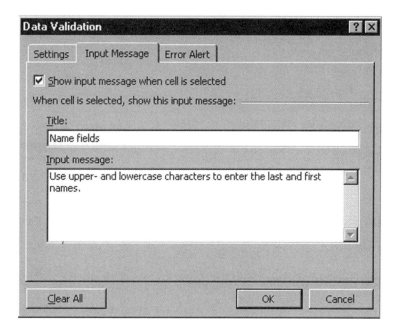

In this exercise, you will make data validation settings, including error alerts. You will add records to the Eiffel Records employee list.

EXERCISE DIRECTIONS

1. Open ⌨ **EMPS** or 💾 **75EMPS**.

2. Name the employee list (A1:F19) DATABASE.

3. Set data validation settings for the IDNO column as follows:
    a. Select range D2:D30.
    b. Click Data, Validation.
    c. On Settings tab, set validation criteria to allow Whole Numbers.
        Minimum value: 13000
        Maximum value: 17000
    d. On Error Alert tab, set a Stop Style warning titled: IDNO. Enter the Error Message: Enter IDNO from Employee Profile from Personnel.
    e. Click OK.

4. Set data validation settings for WEEKLY SALARY column as follows:
    a. Select range E2:E30.
    b. Click Data, Validation.
    c. On Settings tab, set validation criteria to allow Decimals.
        Minimum value: 200.00
        Maximum value: 500.00
    d. On Error Alert tab, set a Stop Style warning titled: SALARY. Enter the Error Message: Enter Salary from Employee Profile from Personnel.
    e. Click OK.

5. Set an input message for the Last column as follows:
    a. Select A2:A30.
    b. Click Data, Validation.
    c. On the Input message tab:
        Title: Name fields
        Message: Use upper- and lowercase characters to enter the last and first names.

6. Enter the following data in the table. Note that some entries are incorrect and will trigger alerts. Cancel the alert and enter the corrected entries listed below the incorrect data.

LAST	FIRST	STORE LOCATION	IDNO	WKSAL
Valdez	Lina	NY	**19385**	265.00
			14385	
Accosta	Anthony	LA	13929	375.55
Graham	Holly	NY	14402	**785.00**
				285.00
Esther	Polly	CHI	14235	286.50

7. Extend the ANNSAL formula for the new records.

8. In the name box, select the DATABASE range.

    ✓ *Note that the range includes the new records.*

9. Format the database of employees as follows:

10. Format columns E and F for two decimal places.
    • Center the column labels and data in columns C, D, and E.
    • Right-align the ANNSAL column label.

11. Print the worksheet containing the list.

12. Save the workbook file; name it **EMPS**.

13. Close the workbook file.

KEYSTROKES

DATA VALIDATION SETTINGS

1. Click **Data** menu .... `Alt`+`D`

2. Click **Validation** .... `L`

3. On Settings tab, click
   Allow and set criteria ..... `Alt`+`A`, `↓`

4. Click **Data** textbox and
   set control .... `Alt`+`D`, `↓`

5. Click **Minimum** and
   enter value .... `Alt`+`M`, *value*

6. Click **Maximum** and
   enter value .... `Alt`+`X`, *value*

7. To set error alert message:

8. Click Error Alert tab .... `Ctrl`+`Tab`

9. Click **Style** and set .... `Alt`+`Y`, `↓`

10. Click **Title** and
    type title .... `Alt`+`T`, *title*

11. Click **Error Message** and enter
    message .... `Alt`+`E`, *message*

12. Click **OK** .... `Enter`

SET INPUT MESSAGE

**To set an input message when cell is
selected:**

1. Click **Data** menu .... `Alt`+`D`

2. Click **Validation** .... `L`

3. Click **Input Message** tab .... `Ctrl`+`Tab`

4. Click **Title** and type title .. `Alt`+`T`, *title*

5. Click **Input message**
   and type message... `Alt`+`I`, *message*

6. Click **OK** .... `Enter`

Excel ■ Lesson 10 ■ Exercise 75   291

Exercise 76

■ Sort Records in a List ■ Undo a Sort

NOTES

Sort Records in a List

- Records in a list may be rearranged or sorted in a variety of ways, depending on what type of information is needed.

- For example, you can sort a list to find information arranged:

  - In alphabetical or numerical order.

  - Into groups (for example, all people in the list living in New York City or Chicago.)

  - In reverse alphabetical or numerical order.

- You can sort records in a list in two ways:

  - By selecting **Sort** from the **Data** menu.

  - By using the Sort Ascending 🔽 or Sort Descending buttons 🔽 on the Standard toolbar (quick sort).

- Using the Sort command from the Data menu. (Note the illustration of the Sort dialog box on the right):

  - You must first select any cell in the list. This tells Excel which list you want to sort. By default, when you sort a list, Excel will not sort the header row.

  - From the Sort dialog box, indicate the field(s) you wish to sort and the sort order. Excel will propose the Sort By field selected in the worksheet or the last field the list was sorted by.

- You must indicate whether you want the list sorted in **ascending** or **descending** order. Ascending order arranges labels alphabetically, values from the smallest to the largest, dates from the oldest to the most recent, and time from the earliest to the latest. Descending order accomplishes the reverse.

- You can sort records in a list by more than one field. For example, you could sort the employee list using LAST name (as the Sort By field) and FIRST name (as the Then By field). This would result in employees with the same last names arranged in alphabetical first name order.

  - To sort by more than three fields, first sort the list using the least important columns. Then, repeat the sort using the most important columns.

Sort Dialog Box

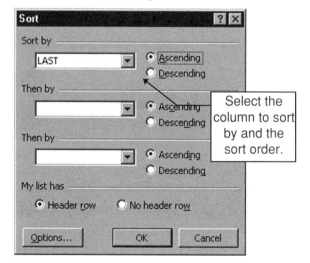

- The Options button in the Sort dialog box displays the dialog box below and contains the following:

  First Key Sort Order — Select a custom sort order, such as days of the week, or months in the year.

  Case Sensitive — Select to arrange duplicate items in case order.

  Orientation — Select to change the sort orientation from columns to rows.

- To use the sort buttons from the Standard toolbar:

  Sort Ascending

  Sort Descending

- You must first select any data cell in the column you wish to sort by.

- You can sort by only one column at a time. You can repeat the sort command on other columns (sorting least important columns first) to arrange records by more than one column.

- The sort buttons will apply any special options you have previously set from the Sort dialog box, such as Case Sensitive (see left).

Undo a Sort

- To undo a sort, Excel provides a one level Edit, **Undo Sort** option. This option must be used *immediately* after the sort.

- Conducting a sort will permanently change the record order unless the Edit, Undo Sort option is used. If you want to keep both the original order version and the sorted version, you can copy the original version to another sheet.

In this exercise, you will sort the EMPS file in a variety of ways. The three sorts are shown in the illustration below and on the next page.

EXERCISE DIRECTIONS

1. Open 📇 **EMPS** or 💾 **76EMPS**.

2. Use the Sort Ascending button, with the cursor in the IDNO column, to create SORT A shown below.

3. Use the Sort Descending button to sort the records by the ANNSAL column.

   ❓ Which employee earned the highest annual salary?

   ❓ Which earned the lowest annual salary?

4. Use the Sort command on the Data menu to create SORT B shown on the next page.
   - Sort the records by two fields: Use LAST name as the Sort By field in ascending order. Use FIRST name as the Then By field in ascending order.

5. Print one copy of the records showing the results of SORT B.

6. Use the Sort command on the Data menu to create SORT C shown on the next page.
   - Sort the data by three fields: Use STORE LOCATION as the Sort By field in descending order. Use LAST as the Then By field in ascending order. Use FIRST as the next Then By field in ascending order.

7. Undo the last sort so the records remain in Last/First name alphabetical order (SORT B).

8. Save and close the workbook file; name it **EMPS**.

Sort A

Ascending sort on IDNO column

LAST	FIRST	STORE LOCATION	IDNO	WKSAL	ANNSAL
Lee	Chin	LA	13254	345.00	17940.00
Sawyer	Harriet	CHI	13290	358.60	18647.20
Lee	Randy	CHI	13298	365.80	19021.60
Tommei	Lori	NY	13852	376.00	19552.00
Accosta	Anthony	LA	13929	375.55	19528.60
Rogers	Jane	NY	14024	310.89	16166.28
Carson	George	NY	14078	389.76	20267.52
Esther	Polly	CHI	14235	286.50	14898.00
Baez	Franco	NY	14236	268.50	13962.00
Watterson	Cathy	LA	14269	325.75	16939.00
Martino	John	LA	14289	342.90	17830.80
Lee	Michael	CHI	14295	276.00	14352.00
Naidle	Adam	LA	14321	243.50	12662.00
Samtanai	Perkash	LA	14354	215.45	11203.40
Carson	Larry	NY	14356	235.45	12243.40
Palmeri	Marie	CHI	14367	276.50	14378.00
Valdez	Lina	NY	14385	265.00	13780.00
Gregonis	Dimitri	LA	14395	275.00	14300.00
Hopkins	George	NY	14396	275.00	14300.00
Graham	Holly	NY	14402	285.00	14820.00
Seltzer	Al K.	CHI	14931	255.00	13260.00
Restivo	Mary	CHI	14932	295.00	15340.00

Ascending sort by LAST , then FIRST names.

Sort B

LAST	FIRST	STORE LOCATION	IDNO	WKSAL	ANNSAL
Accosta	Anthony	LA	13929	375.55	19528.60
Baez	Franco	NY	14236	268.50	13962.00
Carson	George	NY	14078	389.76	20267.52
Carson	Larry	NY	14356	235.45	12243.40
Esther	Polly	CHI	14235	286.50	14898.00
Graham	Holly	NY	14402	285.00	14820.00
Gregonis	Dimitri	LA	14395	275.00	14300.00
Hopkins	George	NY	14396	275.00	14300.00
Lee	Chin	LA	13254	345.00	17940.00
Lee	Michael	CHI	14295	276.00	14352.00
Lee	Randy	CHI	13298	365.80	19021.60
Martino	John	LA	14289	342.90	17830.80
Naidle	Adam	LA	14321	243.50	12662.00
Palmeri	Marie	CHI	14367	276.50	14378.00
Restivo	Mary	CHI	14932	295.00	15340.00
Rogers	Jane	NY	14024	310.89	16166.28
Samtanai	Perkash	LA	14354	215.45	11203.40
Sawyer	Harriet	CHI	13290	358.60	18647.20
Seltzer	Al K.	CHI	14931	255.00	13260.00
Tommei	Lori	NY	13852	376.00	19552.00
Valdez	Lina	NY	14385	265.00	13780.00
Watterson	Cathy	LA	14269	325.75	16939.00

Sort by STORE LOCATION in descending order, then by LAST name in ascending order, then by FIRST name in ascending order.

Sort C

LAST	FIRST	STORE LOCATION	IDNO	WKSAL	ANNSAL
Baez	Franco	NY	14236	268.50	13962.00
Carson	George	NY	14078	389.76	20267.52
Carson	Larry	NY	14356	235.45	12243.40
Graham	Holly	NY	14402	285.00	14820.00
Hopkins	George	NY	14396	275.00	14300.00
Rogers	Jane	NY	14024	310.89	16166.28
Tommei	Lori	NY	13852	376.00	19552.00
Valdez	Lina	NY	14385	265.00	13780.00
Accosta	Anthony	LA	13929	375.55	19528.60
Gregonis	Dimitri	LA	14395	275.00	14300.00
Lee	Chin	LA	13254	345.00	17940.00
Martino	John	LA	14289	342.90	17830.80
Naidle	Adam	LA	14321	243.50	12662.00
Samtanai	Perkash	LA	14354	215.45	11203.40
Watterson	Cathy	LA	14269	325.75	16939.00
Esther	Polly	CHI	14235	286.50	14898.00
Lee	Michael	CHI	14295	276.00	14352.00
Lee	Randy	CHI	13298	365.80	19021.60
Palmeri	Marie	CHI	14367	276.50	14378.00
Restivo	Mary	CHI	14932	295.00	15340.00
Sawyer	Harriet	CHI	13290	358.60	18647.20
Seltzer	Al K.	CHI	14931	255.00	13260.00

KEYSTROKES

SORT A LIST USING THE MENU

1. Select any cell in list to sort.
2. Click **Data** menu .... `Alt`+`D`
3. Click **Sort** .... `S`
4. Select the following sort options:

   To set the first key sort order:

   a. Click **Sort By** .... `Tab`+`↑↓`, `Enter`
      and select field.

   b. Select **Ascending** .... `Alt`+`A`

   c. Select **Descending** .... `Alt`+`D`

   To set second key sort order:

   a. Click **Then By** ..... `Tab`+`↑↓`, `Enter`

   b. Select **Ascending** .... `Alt`+`C`

   c. Select **Descending** .... `Alt`+`N`

   To set third key sort order:

   a. Click **Then By** ..... `Alt`+`↑↓`+`Enter`
      Click arrow and select field.

   b. Select **Ascending** .... `Alt`+`I`

   c. Select **Descending** .... `Alt`+`G`

To include or exclude header row from sort:

Select **Header Row** .... `Alt`+`R`
OR
Select **No Header Row** .... `Alt`+`W`

To select a custom sort order for first key:

a. Click **Options** .... `Alt`+`O`

b. Click
   first key sort order .... `Alt`+`F`

c. Select desired
   order .... `↑↓`+`Enter`

d. Click **OK** .... `Enter`

To change orientation of sort (columns to rows):

a. Click **Options** .... `Alt`+`O`

b. Select
   Sort left to right .... `Alt`+`L`

c. Click **OK** .... `Enter`

To set a case sensitive sort:

a. Click **Options** .... `Alt`+`O`

b. Select **Case Sensitive** .... `Alt`+`C`

c. Click **OK** .... `Enter`

5. Click **OK** .... `Enter`

SORT A LIST USING THE TOOLBAR

1. Select cell in column to sort by in the list.

   ✓ *Excel applies settings made in a previous sort, if one was made.*

   The active cell determines the column Excel will sort by.

2. Click **Sort Ascending** button .... `AↆZ`
   on Standard toolbar.
   OR

   Click **Sort Descending** button .... `ZↆA`
   on Standard toolbar.

UNDO A SORT

   ✓ *To successfully undo a sort, it is best to undo it immediately.*

1. Click **Edit** menu .... `Alt`+`E`

2. Click **Undo Sort** .... `U`

NEXT EXERCISE

Exercise

77

- ■ **Default Sort Order**
- ■ **Create Valid Data List**

NOTES

Default Sort Order

■ The default order for sorting data is as follows:

- Data is arranged according to the underlying value, not the data format.

- When a sort is in ascending order, Excel uses the following order:

  Numbers from the largest negative to largest positive number.

  Dates and times are sorted chronologically.

  Text and text that includes numbers, such as addresses, are sorted in ascending order as follows:

  0 1 2 3 4 5 6 7 8 9 (space) ! " # $ % & ' ( ) * + , - . / : ; < = > ? @ [\ ] ^ _ ` { | } ~ A B C D E F G H I J K L M N O P Q R S T U V W X Y Z

- Blank cells appear last whether the sort is in ascending or descending order.

Create Valid Data List

■ Data validation, as discussed in Exercise 75, attempts to improve the accuracy of data entered into an Excel database list. One of the data validation options is to create a list of the items that are valid for a field. This technique is used for fields that have a limited number of valid entries to save entry time and improve accuracy.

■ To create a data list:

- Enter a list of valid entries on an unused portion of the worksheet.

- Select **Data**, **Validation**, Settings tab, and then click List from the **Allow** pull-down menu.

- Select the data list range in the **Source** box.

In this exercise, you will use the procedures discussed in earlier exercises to create, modify, and add to a database—in list or data form format. A data list will be created for the type of homes for sale. The Micasa Real Estate Company will also require the sorting of the data list.

EXERCISE DIRECTIONS

1. Create the first four rows from Illustration A on the next page, or open 🖫**77HOME**.

2. Set column widths as follows:
   - Column A: 20
   - Column F: 12
   - ✓ *Adjust other column widths so that data can be fully viewed.*

3. Create a data list, as illustrated, in G1:G4 and set validation criteria for the TYPE field as follows:
   a. Select the field range D5:D30.
   b. Click Data, Validation.
   c. On the Settings tab, select List in the Allow box.
   d. Enter or select the data list range, G1:G4.
   e. Click OK.

4. Enter the remaining data from Illustration A. Use the data list arrow that appears in the TYPE field, to open the drop down list and select the appropriate value.

5. Format the money column data for currency with two decimal places.

6. Name the list range, including column headers, DATABASE.

7. Open a data form and add the data from Illustration B to the database list.

8. Use the Find Next and Find Prev buttons to view each record in the list.

9. Use the scroll box to move to the top and bottom of the list of forms. Return to the list.

10. Use the quick sort buttons to sort the list by PRICE in descending order.
    - ❷ Which house is the most expensive?
    - ❷ Which house is the least expensive?

11. Print one copy of this sort.

12. Use the Data, Sort method to sort the list by TOWN in ascending order, then by TYPE in ascending order, then by PRICE in descending order.
    - ❷ Which town has the most townhouse-type homes?
    - ❷ Which town has the most homes for sale?
    - ❷ Which townhouse is the least expensive in Springville?

13. Print one copy of this sort.

14. Sort the list so that the AVAIL dates are in ascending order.
    - ❷ Your client can't move in until February 15, 1998. How many homes are available after that date?

15. Print one copy of this sort.

16. Save and close the file; name it **HOME**.

Illustration A

	A	B	C	D	E	F	G
1		MICASA REAL ESTATE COMPANY					Colonial
2		CURRENT LISTINGS					Ranch
3							Split
4	ADDRESS	TOWN	AVAIL	TYPE	ROOMS	PRICE	Townhouse
5	45 Mintum Road	Arrochar	12/1/97	Colonial	10	$ 345,000.00	
6	125 Kelly Boulevard	Springville	1/1/98	Townhouse	7	$ 185,000.00	
7	670 Circle Loop	Sunset Hill	12/1/97	Split	10	$ 450,000.00	
8	89 Alberta Lane	New Dorp	2/2/98	Ranch	7	$ 195,000.00	
9	345 Jacques Avenue	Totten	1/1/98	Colonial	7	$ 190,000.00	
10	5 Flagg Terrace	New Dorp	2/1/98	Townhouse	6	$ 165,000.00	
11	29 Club Road	Sunset Hill	3/1/98	Colonial	8	$ 245,000.00	
12	914 Sand Lane	Totten	2/1/98	Ranch	7	$ 192,000.00	
13	823 Barrow Road	Springville	3/1/98	Split	7	$ 188,000.00	
14	92 Vellum Drive	New Dorp	2/1/98	Colonial	9	$ 287,500.00	
15	621 Blait Road	Arrochar	4/1/98	Ranch	8	$ 225,500.00	

List of valid entries for Type field

Illustration B

ADDRESS	TOWN	AVAIL	TYPE	ROOMS	PRICE
321 Englewood Drive	Totten	3/1/97	Townhouse	9	$279,000
89 Kingsley Street	Annadale	3/15/97	Colonial	11	$375,000
607 Miller Street	Springville	2/1/97	Townhouse	7	$210,000
90 Camden Road	Annadale	2/15/97	Split	8	$245,000
805 Nardino Road	New Dorp	3/15/97	Split	7	$180,000

KEYSTROKES

CREATE DATA LIST FOR A FIELD

1. Create list of valid entries for a field on an unused portion of the worksheet.

2. Click **Data** .... `Alt` + `D`

3. Click **Va̲lidation** .... `L`

4. On **Settings** tab, click **A̲llow** ... `Alt` + `A`

5. Select **List** setting .... `↓`

6. Click **S̲ource** .... `Alt` + `S`

7. Select or enter range of data list created in step 1.

8. Click **OK.** .... `Enter`

Exercise 78

- **Update Database (Find, Delete, and Modify Records Using a Data Form)**
- **Add a Field to a List**

NOTES

Update Database (Find, Delete, and Modify Records Using A Data Form)

- The accuracy of a database of records depends on maintaining and updating information. From a data form, you can search a list for records based on specified criteria. These records, once located, can be viewed, edited, or deleted.

- Search criteria are clues about field data used to search for a specific record or group of records. When you click the Criteria button in a data form, these options will appear:

Clear	Clears the current criteria.
Restore	Restores a cleared criteria.
Find Prev	Shows previous record meeting specified criteria. When the first record is reached, Excel sounds a beep.
Find Next	Shows next record meeting specified criteria. When the last record is reached, Excel sounds a beep.
Form	Returns form to show original options without using criteria. (When you select the Find Prev or Find Next button, the Form button becomes the Criteria button.)

- After selecting the Criteria button from the data form, you can select a field upon which to base the search, set the condition (operator) of the search (=, >, >=, <, <=, <>), and the data value(s) to search for. If no operator is typed, the search condition is set to find records that begin with the data value you typed. When you browse the records that match the search criteria, you can edit or delete them.

- A **wildcard** is a symbol used in a search value to substitute for unknown characters. Wildcards are particularly useful when working with large databases.

- There are two wildcard symbols available:

  - An **asterisk** (*) is used to indicate an unknown group of characters.

    - For example, if you were searching a list for a particular employee and you are certain only of the first two letters of the last name, you would indicate the search value for the LAST name field as *Pa**. This criteria will find all records in which the last name begins with *Pa*.

  - A **question mark** (?) is used to substitute for an unknown single character.

    - For example, if you were searching for a particular employee but were uncertain of one character in the name, the search value would be entered as *Na?dle*. This criteria will find all records with any letter in the question mark location.

- When you delete a record, Excel removes the entire row in the worksheet and the record cannot be restored. From a data form, you can click **Delete** to remove a record from a list.

- To remove or change the criteria, click the Criteria button again and select from available options.

Add a Field to a List

- Fields may be added to a list by inserting a column or field in the desired location. Column headings must be contained within one cell to qualify as a field name. After a field or column is added, it will appear in the form view of the record. When you add a column next to a column with data validation settings the settings will be copied to the new column. Unwanted data validation settings may be cleared by selecting the range, clicking Data, Validation, and clicking **Clear All**.

In this exercise, you will retrieve the EMP database, add two new fields to the list, and search and update it to reflect personnel changes within the company.

EXERCISE DIRECTIONS

1. Open ⌨ **EMPS** or 💾 **78EMPS**.

2. To include two new fields and data, as shown in the worksheet on the following page:
   a. Insert two columns between columns D and E.
   b. Enter the field names HIRED and DEPT.
   c. Highlight both new columns and click Data, Validation.
      ✓ Note that the IDNO settings have moved to the new columns.
   d. Clear all settings.
   e. Set a list validation field for DEPT. by entering the Admin, Sales, and Stock departments in I1:I3.
   f. Enter the data as shown.
      ✓ If you do not set the data list field, AutoComplete will also allow you to enter the DEPT. after typing the first few letters. See Exercise 21.
   g. Format columns E and F to center data.
   h. Using a data form, enter new employee records.
      IMPORTANT: Since the list was named DATABASE, Excel will include the new records in the list only if entered from a data form. If you want to add records directly to the worksheet, delete the name DATABASE before doing so.

3. Close the data form.

4. Select DATABASE from the name box to check that all records and the field names are selected. Then deselect the range.

5. From a data form:
   a. Find all the records of employees whose last name is Carson. Change the first name of Larry Carson to Laurence.
   b. Find all records that match Cars?n, and check that all are spelled Carson. Change any incorrect records.
   c. Find the records for employees whose last name begin with the letter P.
   d. How many employees fall into this category?
   e. Find the records of all employees hired before 01/03/95.
   f. How many employees fall into this category?
      HINT: Use < (less than) as the search operator. Do not type a space between operator and data value.
   g. Delete Franco Baez because he has left the company.

6. Close the data form.

7. Re-sort the records on LAST name (Sort By field) and FIRST name (Then By field) to place names in alphabetical order.

8. Print a copy of the list to fit on one page.

9. Save and close the workbook file; name it **EMPS**.

	A	B	C	D	E	F	G	H
1	**LAST**	**FIRST**	**STORE LOCATION**	**IDNO**	*HIRED*	*DEPT.*	**WKSAL**	**ANNSAL**
2	Accosta	Anthony	LA	13929	10/30/97	Sales	375.55	19528.60
3	Baez	Franco	NY	14236	11/1/94	Stock	268.50	13962.00
4	Carson	George	NY	14078	4/1/94	Admin.	389.76	20267.52
5	Carson	Larry	NY	14356	9/30/95	Stock	235.45	12243.40
6	Esther	Polly	CHI	14235	11/15/97	Admin.	286.50	14898.00
7	Graham	Holly	NY	14402	11/1/97	Sales	285.00	14820.00
8	Gregonis	Dimitri	LA	14395	5/25/97	Admin.	275.00	14300.00
9	Hopkins	George	NY	14396	6/10/97	Stock	275.00	14300.00
10	Lee	Chin	LA	13254	5/15/93	Sales	345.00	17940.00
11	Lee	Michael	CHI	14295	3/5/95	Stock	276.00	14352.00
12	Lee	Randy	CHI	13298	7/25/95	Stock	365.80	19021.60
13	Martino	John	LA	14289	11/1/95	Admin.	342.90	17830.80
14	Naidle	Adam	LA	14321	2/15/95	Sales	243.50	12662.00
15	Palmeri	Marie	CHI	14367	9/1/95	Stock	276.50	14378.00
16	Restivo	Mary	CHI	14932	10/1/97	Sales	295.00	15340.00
17	Rogers	Jane	NY	14024	5/18/96	Sales	310.89	16166.28
18	Samtanai	Perkash	LA	14354	11/25/96	Sales	215.45	11203.40
19	Sawyer	Harriet	CHI	13290	2/13/97	Admin.	358.60	18647.20
20	Seltzer	Al K.	CHI	14931	7/25/97	Stock	255.00	13260.00
21	Tommei	Lori	NY	13852	8/25/96	Admin.	376.00	19552.00
22	Valdez	Lina	NY	14385	10/15/97	Stock	265.00	13780.00
23	Watterson	Cathy	LA	14269	12/15/96	Sales	325.75	16939.00
24	Jackson	Martin	LA	14397	10/25/97	Stock	275.00	
25	Parsons	Lyle	NY	14398	10/31/97	Admin.	285.50	
26	Carsen	Penn	CHI	14399	11/5/97	Sales	225.75	

KEYSTROKES

FIND SPECIFIC RECORDS IN A LIST USING A DATA FORM

1. Select any cell in list.
2. Click **Data** menu .... `Alt`+`D`
3. Click **Form** ....`O`
4. Click **Criteria**.........................`Alt`+`C`
5. Select text box ....`Tab` of field to search.
6. Type a criterion.
   - ✓ *Wildcard characters (? or *) may be used to stand for one (?) or more (*) characters in the position of the wildcard character. To find an actual ? or *, precede ? or * character with a tilde (~).*

   EXAMPLES:

   Type pau or pau* in a text field to find records beginning with pau, such as Paul or Paula.

   Type >=1/1/89 in a date field to find records containing dates on or after 1/1/89.

Type (718) ???-???? in a character field to find phone numbers that have a 718 area code.

*Type * Shaw in a character field to find records that have **any** first name and Shaw as a last name.*

7. To add criteria to additional fields, repeat steps **5** and **6**.
8. Click **Find Next**......................`Alt`+`N`

   OR

   Click **Find Prev**.......................`Alt`+`P`
9. Repeat step **8** for each matching record to find.

   To obtain access to entire list:

   a. Click **Criteria** ....`Alt`+`C`
   b. Click **Clear**........................`Alt`+`C`
   c. Click **Form** ....`Alt`+`F`
   d. Click **Close** ....`Alt`+`L` to return to worksheet.

DELETE RECORDS IN A LIST USING A DATA FORM

CAUTION: Deleted records cannot be restored.

FROM DATA FORM:

1. Display record to delete.
2. Click **Delete** menu .... `Alt`+`D`
3. Click **OK** .... `Enter`

   Excel deletes records in list, and moves them up to close the space that has been left by the deletion.

To delete additional records:

Repeat steps **1–3** for each record to delete.

CLEAR VALIDATION SETTINGS

1. Click **Data Menu** .... `Alt`+`D`
2. Click **Validation** ....`L`
3. Click **Clear all**.......................`Alt`+`C`
4. Click **OK**. .... `Enter`

Exercise

79

■ **AutoFilter**

NOTES

AutoFilter

■ **AutoFilter**, which is selected from the <u>D</u>ata, <u>F</u>ilter menus, provides another way to find and work with records in a list. With AutoFilter you can show only the records from the list that meet a selected criteria. Therefore, unwanted records are filtered out. For example, you might want to show only records for employees in LA, as shown in the illustration below.

	A	B	C	D	E	F	G	H	
			STORE						
1	LAST	FIRST	LOCATIO	IDNO	HIRED	DEPT	WKSA	ANNS/	Ad
2	Accosta	Anthony	(All)	13929	10/30/97	Sales	375.55	19528.60	Sa
8	Gregonis	Dimitri	(Top 10...)	14395	525/97	Admin.	275.00	14300.00	
10	Lee	Chin	(Custom...) CHI	13254	5/15/93	Sales	345.00	17940.00	
13	Martino	John	LA	14289	11/1/95	Admin.	342.90	17830.80	
14	Naidle	Adam	NY LA	14321	2/15/95	Sales	243.50	12662.00	U
18	Samtanai	Perkash	LA	14354	11/25/96	Sales	215.45	11203.40	U
23	Watterson	Cathy	LA	14269	12/15/96	Sales	325.75	16939.00	
24	Jackson	Martin	LA	14397	10/25/97	Stock	275.00	14300.00	
27									

■ When you start AutoFilter, Excel adds a drop-down arrow to each field name. You can then set a **filter criteria** (specify which records to show) for any field by clicking a drop-down arrow and making a selection.

■ From any field name drop-down list you can select:

[All]   to end filtering for a field.

A specific data value, such as LA or NY.

[Custom...]   to specify a condition such as records within a range of dates or records containing two data values in a field.

[Blanks]   to show records with blanks (no data) in the field.

[NonBlanks] to show records with any data in the field.

■ When you select custom from the AutoFilter drop down list, the Custom AutoFilter dialog box displays. As illustrated below, you can set customized filters for the field by selecting the filter and value options.

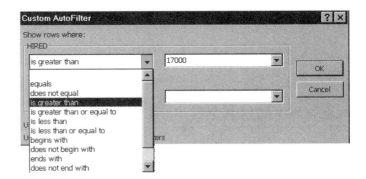

■ You can select or set a filter criterion in more than one column to find subsets of the records. For example, you can show only the records of Sales DEPT. employees in NY.

■ When you filter a list, Excel hides the data of the records that do not meet the criteria. This does not move or delete the records from the list. To restore the list to the original display, you must remove the filter criterion.

■ Removing criterion without ending AutoFilter:

• To remove a filter criterion for a single field, select **[All]** from the drop-down list for that field.

• To remove all filter criteria, select <u>F</u>ilter, <u>S</u>how All from the <u>D</u>ata menu.

EXERCISE DIRECTIONS

1. Open 🖳 **EMPS** or 🖫 **79EMPS**.

2. Use AutoFilter to show only employees who work in LA.

3. Print a copy of the list to fit on one page.

4. Filter the list to show employees who work in the sales department of the LA store.

5. Change the filter criterion for the DEPT. field to show only administrators (Admin.) in the LA store.

6. Print a copy of the list to fit on one page. (A)

7. Remove all filter criteria.

8. Filter the employee list, using a custom setting, to show only records for employees with an annual salary that is greater than or equal (>=) to 17000.

9. Print a copy of the filtered records. (B)

10. Remove all filter criteria.

11. Filter records to produce a list of employees hired after 1/1/96 who work in the Stock department.

12. Print a copy of all filtered records. (C)

13. Remove all filter criteria.

    Using filters, determine how many employees earn more than $300 per week and were hired after 1/1/96.

14. End AutoFilter.

15. Close the workbook file. You do not need to save the changes.

KEYSTROKES

FILTER A LIST AUTOMATICALLY

✓ *You can use **AutoFilter** with one list in a worksheet at a time but the list must have column labels. If you select criterion from more than one drop-down list, Excel will show only records meeting the criteria specified by both filters.*

1. Select any cell in list to filter all fields.

   OR

   Select cells containing field names in list to filter only selected fields.

2. Click **Data** menu .... [Alt]+[D]

3. Click **Filter** .... [F]

4. Click **AutoFilter** .... [F]

   ✓ *Excel adds drop-down list arrows next to column labels.*

5. Click drop-down arrow .... [▼] of field you want to filter.

6. Select item from list .... [↕], [Enter]

7. In addition to a specific item you can select:

   • **(All)**—to end filtering for the field.

   • **(Blanks)**—to show only records that have no data in the column.

   • **(NonBlanks)**—to show only records that have data in the column.

   • **(Custom...)**—to specify up to two comparison criteria for data in the column.

   If **Custom** was selected:

   a. Click criterion .... [Tab], [↓]

   b. Select a column item .... [↕], [Alt]+[↑]

   c. Click value .... [Tab], [↓]

   d. Select desired item operator .... [↕], [Alt]+[↑]

   To specify another criterion for column:

   a. Select **And** .... [Alt]+[A]

      OR

      Select **Or** .... [Alt]+[O]

   a. Click second criterion .... [Tab], [↓]

   b. Select a column item .... [↕], [Alt]+[↑]

   c. Click second value .... [Tab]

   d. Select desired item operator .... [↕], [Alt]+[↑]

SHOW ALL RECORDS IN A FILTERED LIST

1. Click **Data** menu .... [Alt]+[D]

2. Click **Filter** .... [F]

3. Click **Show All** .... [S]

END AUTOFILTER

1. Click **Data** menu .... [Alt]+[D]

2. Click **Filter** .... [F]

3. Click **AutoFilter** .... [F]
   to deselect it.

<table>
<tr><td>**Exercise**
80</td><td>■ **Maintain Original Record Order**
■ **Advanced Filter**</td></tr>
</table>

NOTES

Maintain Original Record Order

■ Once a set of records is sorted, the original order of the records is no longer intact. To retain the original order you may create a record number field with sequential numbers. By using the field that contains these numbers as the Sort By field, you may re-sort the records and return them to their original order.

■ If a sort result is not what you expected, check that the data in the Sort By column does not contain both values and text. Consider adding an apostrophe (') to numbers if this is the case.

Advanced Filter

■ Like AutoFilter, establishing guidelines for **advanced filter** criteria lets you filter records in a list. The criteria are typed in the worksheet, which allows for more complex filters, but the field names in the list will not contain drop-down arrows as in AutoFilter (see the illustration on page 311).

■ Records may be filtered in two ways:

  • The records that do not meet the criteria are hidden in the list (in-place filtering).

    OR

  • The records that meet the criteria are copied (extracted) to a worksheet range.

■ Guidelines for creating advanced filter criteria:

  • You must type the criteria in a range away from the data (above or below the list) in the worksheet. Note the illustration on page 311.

• Select Data, Filter, Advanced Filter.

• From the Advanced Filter dialog box you must specify:

  ♦ The action (to filter the list in-place or copy the result list to another location).

  ♦ The range containing the list.

  ♦ The worksheet cells containing the criteria range.

  ♦ The worksheet range to copy the results to, if the action requires it.

    ✔ NOTE: *The range can be the beginning cell or a range of cells for the result list. The ranges may be selected at each point in the dialog box, or they may be keyed into each location. See the illustration of the Advanced Filter dialog box below which relate to the illustrated worksheet on page 311.*

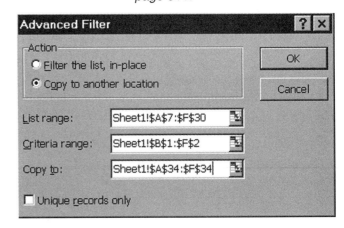

- Guidelines for setting up a simple criteria range:

  - You can copy the field names (column labels) to ensure that the labels in the criteria range are identical to the field names in the list.

  - Type the criteria below the criteria labels.

  - If the records must match the criteria, you can omit the = (equal sign) operator and just type the value.

  - The criteria range, specified in the Advanced Filter dialog box, cannot contain empty columns.

  - If more than one criteria is specified on one line, as in the illustration, the search will locate only records that match all criteria.

  - A criteria range can consist of one column with a field name and a criterion entry.

- The advantages of copying the results of a filter to another location are:

  - Records that meet the specified criteria are listed together.

  - Records in the result list can be sorted, filtered again, and formatted.

  - Records can be changed without affecting the records in the original list.

  - You can delete fields in the result list that you are not interested in.

  - The result list can be printed separately as a report.

- To end in-place filtering, select **Filter, Show All** from the **Data** menu.

- Result lists can be moved or copied to any worksheet. Column widths used by result lists are those that are current in the worksheet.

In this exercise, you will use and add to the list for the Micasa Real Estate Company. Use Advanced filter criteria to create alternate lists for clients who wish to purchase a particular type of house.

EXERCISE DIRECTIONS

1. Open 🖮 **HOME** or 💾 **80HOME**.

2. Additional homes have been listed by our agency. Add the following to the **HOME** database:

3. Sort the list by Price in descending order.

ADDRESS	TOWN	AVAIL	TYPE	ROOMS	PRICE
45 Point Road	Sunset Hill	4/1/98	Split	10	$448,500
16 Beverly Circle	Arrochar	4/15/98	Colonial	8	$325,000
71 Regis Avenue	Totten	3/15/98	Ranch	7	$175,000
87 Anthony Street	Springville	3/1/98	Townhouse	7	$155,000
236 Eighth Street	New Dorp	4/1/98	Colonial	8	$210,000
624 Clarke Road	Sunset Hill	4/30/98	Ranch	8	$255,000
90 Shore Road	Totten	5/1/98	Townhouse	6	$155,000

4. Create a criteria range and enter an advanced filter criterion:

   a. Insert three rows above the list and titles, and copy the field names (column headings) as shown in the illustration on the next page.

   b. Type a criterion to list houses located in New Dorp:

   B1:   TOWN

   B2:   New Dorp

   c. Select Data, Filter, Advanced Filter.

   d. Select option to filter list in-place.

   e. Specify the cells containing the criterion B1:B2.

   f. How many houses are available in New Dorp?

5. Show all records in the list (end in-place filtering).

6. Filter the list using the same criterion:

   a. Select Data, Filter, Advanced Filter.

   b. Select option to copy to another location.

   c. Specify the criteria range (B1:B2).

   d. Copy the result list to A34.

7. Print one copy of the range containing the result of the filter.

8. Delete the result list.

9. Filter the real estate list using an advanced filter criterion as follows:

   a. Type a criterion to list all ranch houses:

   D1:   TYPE

   D2:   Ranch

   b. Select Data, Filter, Advanced Filter.

   c. Select option to copy to another location.

   d. Specify the criteria range (D1:D2).

   e. Copy the result list to A34.

   ❷ How many Ranch-style homes are available?

10. Filter the result list by using an advanced filter criterion as follows:

   a. Type a criterion to list houses that cost less than $200,000.

   F1:   PRICE

   F2:   <200000

   b. Select Data, Filter, Advanced Filter.

   c. Select option to copy to another location.

   d. Specify range of the result list as the list range (A34:F39).

   e. Specify criteria range (F1:F2).

   f. Copy filtered list to A43.

   g. Type a heading on each result list that describe the contents, such as: RANCH-STYLE HOMES and RANCH-STYLE HOMES UNDER $200,000.

11. Print one copy of the range containing both result lists. (A)

12. Delete all result lists and all criteria entries.

13. Enter advanced filter criteria to filter the real estate list to find all Townhouse homes that cost less than $170,000. Copy the filtered list to A34.

   HINT: Enter both criteria on one line, as shown in the illustration, and use the entire area as the criteria range. Be sure to change the list range from the last filter back to the original list range.

12. Enter an appropriate heading above the result list and print one copy of the townhouses that cost less than $170,000. (B)

13. Delete result list and criteria entries.

14. Enter advanced filter criteria to filter the real estate list to find all New Dorp Ranches. Copy the filtered list to A34. (C)

   ❷ How many ranches are available in New Dorp?

15. Delete results and criteria entries.

16. Save the workbook file; name it **HOME.**

	A	B	C	D	E	F	G	H
1		**TOWN**	**AVAIL**	**TYPE**	**ROOMS**	**PRICE**		Advanced filter
2	Criteria labels	New Dorp		Ranch				criteria
3	entered away							
4	from data.	MICASA REAL ESTATE COMPANY					Colonial	
5		CURRENT LISTINGS					Ranch	
6							Split	
7	**ADDRESS**	**TOWN**	**AVAIL**	**TYPE**	**ROOMS**	**PRICE**	Townhouse	
8	45 Mintum Road	Arrochar	12/1/97	Colonial	10	$ 345,000.00		
9	670 Circle Loop	Sunset Hill	12/1/97	Split	10	$ 450,000.00		
10	125 Kelly Boulevard	Springville	1/1/98	Townhouse	7	$ 185,000.00		
11	345 Jacques Avenue	Totten	1/1/98	Colonial	7	$ 190,000.00		
12	92 Vellum Drive	New Dorp	2/1/98	Colonial	9	$ 287,500.00		
13	5 Flagg Terrace	New Dorp	2/1/98	Townhouse	6	$ 165,000.00		
14	607 Miller Street	Springville	2/1/98	Townhouse	7	$ 210,000.00		
15	914 Sand Lane	Totten	2/1/98	Ranch	7	$ 192,000.00		
16	89 Alberta Lane	New Dorp	2/2/98	Ranch	7	$ 195,000.00		
17	90 Camden Road	Annadale	2/25/98	Split	8	$ 245,000.00		
18	823 Barrow Road	Springville	3/1/98	Split	7	$ 188,000.00		
19	29 Club Road	Sunset Hill	3/1/98	Colonial	8	$ 245,000.00		
20	321 Englewood Drive	Totten	3/1/98	Townhouse	9	$ 279,000.00		List range
21	89 Kingsley Street	Annadale	3/15/98	Colonial	11	$ 375,000.00		
22	805 Nardino Road	New Dorp	3/15/98	Split	7	$ 180,000.00		
23	621 Blait Road	Arrochar	4/1/98	Ranch	8	$ 225,500.00		
24	45 Point Road	Sunset Hill	4/1/98	Split	10	$ 448,500.00		
25	16 Beverly Circle	Arrochar	4/15/98	Colonial	8	$ 325,000.00		
26	71 Regis Avenue	Totten	3/15/98	Ranch	7	$ 175,000.00		
27	87 Anthony Street	Springville	3/1/98	Townhouse	7	$ 155,000.00		
28	236 Eighth Street	New Dorp	4/1/98	Colonial	8	$ 210,000.00		
29	624 Clarke Road	Sunset Hill	4/30/08	Ranch	8	$ 255,000.00		
30	90 Shore Road	Totten	5/1/98	Townhouse	6	$ 155,000.00		
31								
32								
33								
34	**ADDRESS**	**TOWN**	**AVAIL**	**TYPE**	**ROOMS**	**PRICE**		Results copied to
35	89 Alberta Lane	New Dorp	2/2/98	Ranch	7	$ 195,000.00		another location.
36								

KEYSTROKES

SET UP A CRITERIA RANGE

Tells Excel how to filter a list, prior to using Advanced Filtering.

1. If necessary, insert blank rows above the list you want to filter.
2. Type or copy desired field names to a blank row above list.

   These labels are called **criteria labels** *and must be identical to the column labels in the list you want to filter.*

3. Enter criteria in row(s) directly below criteria labels.

To show only records (rows) matching a value, date, or text:

Enter text, number, date, or logical value to find in column.

EXAMPLE:

Below **Town***, type* **New Dorp***.*

✓ *When you enter text, Excel will find all items beginning with the text criteria. For example, if you enter* **Sam***, Excel will include records such as* **Samuel** *and* **Sammy***.*

EXAMPLES:

To find:

An exact text match	="exact text"
Any character in a specific position	Topic?
Consecutive characters in a specific position	Sa*y
An actual question mark, asterisk, or tilde (~)	What is that~?
A value greater than a specified number	>1000

To show items that compare to a specified value:

Use one of the following comparison operators before a value, date, or text criterion.

- = (equal to or matches)
- <> (not equal to)
- > (greater than)
- < (less than)
- >=(greater than or equal to)
- <=(less than or equal to)

EXAMPLE: Enter <170000 *below the Price criteria label to show only records containing values less than 170000 for that column.*

Filter list with Advanced Filtering *(see left)* to show results of criteria.

FILTER A LIST WITH ADVANCED FILTERING

✓ *List must have column labels.*

1. Set up criteria range *(see above)*.
2. Select any cell in list to filter.
3. Click **Data** menu .... Alt + D
4. Click **Filter** .... F
5. Click **Advanced Filter** .... A
6. To change proposed list range:

   Select range to filter in worksheet.

   OR

   Type reference of list to filter in **List range** text box.

7. Click **Criteria Range:** .... Alt + C
8. Select criteria range in worksheet.

   OR

   Type criteria range.

   ✓ *Include the criteria label(s) with the criteria.*

9. Select **Filter the list,**

   in-place .... Alt + F

   OR

   a. Select **Copy to another**

      location .... Alt + O

   b. Click **Copy to:** .... Alt + T

   c. Select destination range for result list in worksheet.

      OR

      Type destination reference for result list.

      CAUTION: If you indicate a single cell, Excel copies the filtered results to cells below and to the right of the cell, overwriting existing data without warning.

To hide duplicate records:

1. Select **Unique records only** .... Alt + R
2. Click **OK** .... Enter

SHOW ALL RECORDS IN A FILTERED LIST

1. Click **Data** menu .... Alt + D
2. Click **Filter** .... F
3. Click **Show All** .... S

NEXT EXERCISE

Exercise 81

■ Extract Records Using Advanced Filter ■ Edit Result List

NOTES

Extract Records Using Advanced Filter

■ When you use advanced filter criteria to extract records from one location within a worksheet and place them in another, the extracted records are not linked to the original list. Therefore, if you need to edit the records, do so prior to conducting an advanced filter.

Edit Result List

■ To meet requirements for a report, irrelevant fields may be deleted from a result list. As noted earlier, you can edit any list from a data form or from the list itself. Data forms may be used to edit the original list or the result list.

> In this exercise, you will create a supplies inventory list for Chandler Community College.
> Your supervisor wants reports extracted from this inventory to show specific sets of records.

EXERCISE DIRECTIONS

1. Create the list shown on the right, or open 🖫 **81STORE**.

   a. Set column widths A to 11 and B and C to 20.

   b. Format the money column for two decimal places.

   c. Left-align the date column entries.

   d. Right-align the PRICE and TOTAL column labels.

   e. Find the total cost of each item in the list. Format the results for two decimal places.

2. Sort VENDOR (Sort By field) in ascending order and DESCRIPTION (Then By field) in ascending order.

3. Print a copy. (A).

4. Enter advanced filter criterion to extract to A30 items that are purchased in Package format. (We hope to purchase in larger units in the future.) Use cells in rows 1-2 for the criteria range (A1:G2).

5. In the result list, delete the UNIT data and label.

   ✓ *Delete the cells, do not clear them. When prompted, select Shift Cells Left, to move remaining columns in the result list.*

6. Enter a two-line heading above the result list:

   CHANDLER COMMUNITY COLLEGE

   SUPPLIES PURCHASED IN PACKAGE UNITS

7. Use the menu to sort the result list data by DESCRIPTION in ascending order.

8. Print a copy of the report. (B)

9. Delete the result list and criteria, but not the result list title.

10. Edit the September 2 record to correct the vendor from Forest Stationery to Treehouse Paper.

11. Enter advanced filter criteria to extract to A30 all Paper City purchases that were received in a Box format.

12. In the result list, delete the columns containing VENDOR and UNIT data and label.
    Use Shift cells left to delete the columns and move the remaining columns over into the blank areas.

13. Adjust column widths as necessary.

14. Move the report titles left one column.

15. Edit the report's subheading to:

    BOX UNIT PURCHASES FROM PAPER CITY

16. Print a copy of the report. (C)

17. Delete the result list and criteria but not the result list title.

18. Adjust column width in the database list.

19. Select a cell in the database list and use a data form and the Find procedures to change the (8.5X11) entries in the Description column to (Letter) and the (8.5X14) entries to (Legal).

20. Enter advanced filter criteria to extract to A30 all box unit purchases from School Central, Inc.

21. Edit the report's subheading to:

    BOX UNIT PURCHASES FROM SCHOOL CENTRAL, INC.

22. In the result list, delete the columns containing VENDOR and UNIT data and label. Adjust column widths as necessary.

23. Print one copy of the report. (D)

24. Delete the result list, the related headings, and criteria.

25. Adjust column widths as necessary.

26. Save and close the workbook; name it **STORE**.

Criteria labels

Type advanced filter criteria below labels as needed.

	A	B	C	D	E	F	G
1	DATE	DESCRIPTION	VENDOR	UNIT	QUANTITY	PRICE	TOTAL
2							
3							
4							
5			CHANDLER COMMUNITY COLLEGE				
6			SCHOOL STORE - SUPPLIES INVENTORY				
7							
8	DATE	DESCRIPTION	VENDOR	UNIT	QUANTITY	PRICE	TOTAL
9	15-May-97	Folders (8.5X11)	Paper City	Box	4	12.50	
10	15-May-97	Folders (8.5X14)	Paper City	Box	2	18.65	
11	15-May-97	Paper (8.5X11)	Paper City	Case	10	45.00	
12	15-May-97	Paper (8.5X14)	Paper City	Case	4	49.60	
13	12-Jul-97	Index cards (3x5)	Treehouse Paper	Box	3	32.86	
14	14-Jul-97	Binders - Large	School Central, Inc.	Box	8	53.79	
15	19-Jul-97	Binders - Small	School Central, Inc.	Box	5	47.89	
16	22-Jul-97	Adhesive notes	Stickum Bros.	Package	15	5.49	
17	22-Jul-97	Adhesive tape	Stickum Bros.	Box	5	23.50	
18	10-Aug-97	Pens - Speedroll	J & J Discount	Box	20	15.75	
19	15-Aug-97	Pencils - #2	J & J Discount	Box	16	12.95	
20	25-Aug-97	Pads (5x8)	Treehouse Paper	Package	6	8.49	
21	2-Sep-97	Envelopes #10	Forest Stationery	Box	5	3.49	
22	6-Sep-97	Looseleaf - large	School Central, Inc.	Package	200	2.49	
23	6-Sep-97	Looseleaf - small	School Central, Inc.	Package	125	2.10	
24	10-Sep-97	Paper (Bond)	Paper City	Box	85	6.89	

Exercise 82

■ Filter a List with Multiple Criteria

NOTES

Filter a List with Multiple Criteria

■ In the previous exercises you filtered a list to find records that met criteria for two or more conditions. This meant that only records that met *all* the criteria were filtered. It is often necessary to filter records that meet *any* of a series of criteria for one field. The difference between these filters is as follows:

All This is often referred to as an AND condition. That is, the records must meet the first criteria (condition) *and* the second condition. The AND condition was used in previous exercises when two items were entered on the same line in the criteria range.

Any This is often referred to as an OR condition. That is, the records can meet the first *or* the second criteria.

■ In a criteria range you tell Excel the records must meet **all** the criteria by typing the criteria in the *same row*, as we have done in previous exercises.

EXAMPLE: This results in all New Dorp ranches.

TOWN	TYPE
New Dorp	Ranch

■ If the records can meet either (**any**) condition, type the criteria in *separate rows*.

EXAMPLE: This results in any homes in New Dorp and any Ranches from the entire list.

TOWN	TYPE
New Dorp	
	Ranch

■ If the records can meet different criteria for the same column, set up duplicate criteria labels.

EXAMPLE: This results in any Ranches or Townhouses from the list.

TYPE	TYPE
Ranch	
	Townhouse

■ If the records can meet different criteria within the same field, you must repeat the field that is required.

EXAMPLE: This results in any Townhouses or Ranches in Springville.

TOWN	TYPE
Springville	Townhouse
Springville	Ranch

■ **Comparison operators** can be used to set individual criterion:

SYMBOL (CONDITION)		EXAMPLE	WILL PRODUCE A LISTING OF
=	(equal to)	=Ranch	Ranch style houses.
<>	(not equal)	<>Townhouse	House types except Townhouses.
>	(greater than)	>200000	Houses priced greater than $200,000.
<	(less than)	<200000	Houses priced less than $200,000.
>=	(greater than or equal to)	>=200000	Houses that are $200,000 and higher.
<=	(less than or equal to)	<=200000	Houses that are $200,000 and lower.

> *In this exercise, you will search the Micasa Real Estate Company's listings to answer clients' requests.*

EXERCISE DIRECTIONS

1. Open ⌨ **HOME** or 💾 **82HOME**.

2. Center the field names in the list.

3. Add an additional row to the criteria range for "ANY/OR" conditions, as illustrated.

   ✓ *Set advanced filter criteria to do all of the filtering operations that follow. Determine if the filter requires an AND condition (criteria in one row) or an ANY/OR condition (criteria in separate rows.) Be sure the added row is in the criteria range.*

4. Filter the list in-place to show homes that are Split type.

   ❷ How many such listings exist?

5. End in-place filtering (show all records in the list).

6. Filter the list in-place to show Townhouses in Springville or New Dorp.

   ❷ How many such listings exist?

   HINT: *The TOWN and TYPE criteria labels will each have two entries below them.*

7. End in-place filtering for the list.

8. Filter the list in-place to show all houses in New Dorp *except* Townhouses.

   ❷ How many such listings exist?

9. End in-place filtering for the list.

10. Filter the list in-place to show Ranch style houses less than $200,000 that will become available on or after February 1, 1997.

    ❷ How many such listings exist?

11. End in-place filtering for the list.

12. Filter the list and extract (copy) to A35 all the Townhouse or Ranch style houses.

    ❷ How many such listings exist?

13. Filter the list and extract to A50 all the Townhouse or Ranch style houses that are located in New Dorp. Compare the result list created in step 12 with the result list in the illustration below.

    ❷ How many such listings exist?

    HINT: *The TOWN and TYPE criteria labels will each have two entries below them.*

14. Filter the list and extract to A56 all Ranch or Colonial style houses under $250,000.

    ❷ How many such listings exist?

15. Sort the records in *each* result list in ascending PRICE order.

16. Add appropriate titles for each of the result lists.

17. Print all the result lists on one page.

18. Save and close the workbook file; name it **HOME**.

Advanced filter criteria for Ranch
or Townhouses in New Dorp.

	A	B	C	D	E	F	G	H
1		**TOWN**	**AVAIL**	**TYPE**	**ROOMS**	**PRICE**		
2		New Dorp		Ranch				
3		New Dorp		Townhouse				
4								
5		MICASA REAL ESTATE COMPANY					Colonial	
6		CURRENT LISTINGS					Ranch	
7							Split	
8	ADDRESS	TOWN	AVAIL	TYPE	ROOMS	PRICE	Townhouse	
9	45 Mintum Road	Arrochar	12/1/97	Colonial	10	$ 345,000.00		
10	670 Circle Loop	Sunset Hill	12/1/97	Split	10	$ 450,000.00		
11	125 Kelly Boulevard	Springville	1/1/98	Townhouse	7	$ 185,000.00		
12	345 Jacques Avenue	Totten	1/1/98	Colonial	7	$ 190,000.00		
13	92 Vellum Drive	New Dorp	2/1/98	Colonial	9	$ 287,500.00		
14	5 Flagg Terrace	New Dorp	2/1/98	Townhouse	6	$ 165,000.00		
15	607 Miller Street	Springville	2/1/98	Townhouse	7	$ 210,000.00		
16	914 Sand Lane	Totten	2/1/98	Ranch	7	$ 192,000.00		
17	89 Alberta Lane	New Dorp	2/2/98	Ranch	7	$ 195,000.00		
18	90 Camden Road	Annadale	2/25/98	Split	8	$ 245,000.00		
19	823 Barrow Road	Springville	3/1/98	Split	7	$ 188,000.00		
20	29 Club Road	Sunset Hill	3/1/98	Colonial	8	$ 245,000.00		
21	321 Englewood Drive	Totten	3/1/98	Townhouse	9	$ 279,000.00		
22	89 Kingsley Street	Annadale	3/15/98	Colonial	11	$ 375,000.00		
23	805 Nardino Road	New Dorp	3/15/98	Split	7	$ 180,000.00		
24	621 Blait Road	Arrochar	4/1/98	Ranch	8	$ 225,500.00		
25	45 Point Road	Sunset Hill	4/1/98	Split	10	$ 448,500.00		
26	16 Beverly Circle	Arrochar	4/15/98	Colonial	8	$ 325,000.00		
27	71 Regis Avenue	Totten	3/15/98	Ranch	7	$ 175,000.00		
28	87 Anthony Street	Springville	3/1/98	Townhouse	7	$ 155,000.00		
29	236 Eighth Street	New Dorp	4/1/98	Colonial	8	$ 210,000.00		
30	624 Clarke Road	Sunset Hill	4/30/08	Ranch	8	$ 255,000.00		
31	90 Shore Road	Totten	5/1/98	Townhouse	6	$ 155,000.00		
32								
33								
34								
35	ADDRESS	TOWN	AVAIL	TYPE	ROOMS	PRICE		
36	5 Flagg Terrace	New Dorp	2/1/98	Townhouse	6	$ 165,000.00		
37	89 Alberta Lane	New Dorp	2/2/98	Ranch	7	$ 195,000.00		

Result list

Exercise

83

■ Use Database (List) Functions

NOTES

Use Database (List) Functions

■ Entries in a list are the same as any entries in a worksheet. Therefore, regular functions and formulas may be used on list data. By using Excel's **database functions**, you can select records that meet a certain criteria and perform calculations on those records in one step.

■ Excel contains twelve database functions, each of which have the following format:

=Dfunction name(*list range,field,criteria***)**

- The **list range** argument is the range that identifies the entire list. It can be a named list or a reference to the range containing the list.

- The **field** argument is the field whose entries are involved in the function calculation. You may click on the field label (which will enter the cell address of the field label) or substitute the field number, which is the position of the field in the list. The first field number is 1, the second field number is 2, etc.

- The **criteria** argument is the range that contains the typed criteria. Database functions are set up in the same way as advanced filter criteria.

    ✓ NOTE: *As with all formulas, Excel adjusts all relative cell references when a function is copied to a new location. If you plan to copy these functions, make the references in the functions absolute, or name the references that will be retained in the copied function.*

- For example, the list function =DSUM (INPUT, H8, C1:C2) would find the total of the H8 column in the INPUT database for the VENDOR criteria in C1:C2.

■ When you use a database function, the result is linked to the list and criteria range data.

Therefore, if you edit a criteria, it changes the results in functions that reference it. To prevent this, create duplicate criteria labels when setting up additional criteria for the same field name. Note the illustration on page 322.

■ Excel provides the following functions that can be applied to any list:

DAVERAGE	Finds average value in field for records meeting criteria.
DCOUNT	Counts cells in field for records meeting criteria.
DCOUNTA	Counts only nonblank cells in field for records meeting criteria.
DGET	Returns value for a single record in field for records meeting criteria. Returns #NUM! if more than one record meets criteria.
DMAX	Finds maximum value in field for records meeting criteria.
DMIN	Finds minimum value in field for records meeting criteria.
DPRODUCT	Multiplies the values in a field for records meeting criteria.
DSTDEV	Estimates the standard deviation of a population based on a sample for values in a field for records meeting criteria.
DSTDEVP	Calculates the standard deviation based on the entire population for values in a field for records meeting criteria.
DSUM	Finds sum of values in a field for records meeting criteria.
DVAR	Estimates variance based on a sample for values in a field for records meeting criteria.
DVARP	Calculates variance based on the entire population for values in a field for records meeting criteria.

In this exercise, you will use database functions to obtain information about the supplies inventory for Chandler Community College.

EXERCISE DIRECTIONS

1. Open ⌨ **STORE** or 💾 **83STORE**.

2. Add the additional columns illustrated for ITEMS PER and ITEM PRICE as shown in Illustration A on the next page.

3. Enter the number of items in each box, package or case as shown in Illustration A.

4. Enter a formula to find the ITEM PRICE.
   HINT: TOTAL/(ITEM PER*QUANTITY)

5. Format the results for two decimal places.

6. Add the data in Illustration B on the next page for additional supplies purchased.

7. Find the TOTAL and ITEM PRICE for each new item on the list.

8. Name the database range INPUT, as outlined in Illustration A.

9. Set up all criteria labels in row one.

10. Find the Average Price per item.
    ✓ *Since this average is of all the data, and does not require a criteria filter, a regular formula may be used.*

11. Find the Total Items Purchased. (Use the total of column F.)

12. To find Total Value of Purchases from School Central, Inc:
    a. Type a criteria to show School Central, Inc., in the VENDOR field.
    b. Using the DSUM function in the appropriate cell, enter the INPUT list range, the "TOTAL" field label address, and the criteria range.
    c. Format the result for two decimal places.

13. Using the DAVERAGE function in the appropriate cell, find the average value of purchases from School Central, Inc. Format the results for two decimal places.

14. To find Total Value of Purchases from Paper City, repeat step 12 for Paper City in the appropriate cell.
    HINT: Create a second criteria label for VENDOR to the right of the criteria labels and change the criteria range. If you change the first criteria label, the School Central, Inc., result will also change.

15. Find the average purchase for Paper City by repeating step 13 in the appropriate cell.

16. Print a copy of the information determined by steps 10-15. (A)

17. Delete rows 31–38.

18. Find CASE SUMMARY DATA:
    a. Create a formula in the appropriate cell to find the number of cases in inventory. Format the result for no decimal places.
       HINT: Set up a criteria range for the UNIT field, then use the DSUM function to total values in the QUANTITY column meeting the criteria set up for the UNIT field.
    b. Create a formula to find the number of products shipped in cases.
       HINT: Use the DCOUNT function to find total values in the QUANTITY column meeting a criteria set up for the UNIT field.
    c. Create a formula to find the highest value of a case item.
       HINT: Use DMAX function to find highest value in the PRICE column meeting a criteria set up for the UNIT field.
    d. Create a formula to find the lowest value of a case item.
       HINT: Use DMIN function to find lowest value in the PRICE column meeting a criteria set up for the UNIT field.

19. Find the same information as found in step 18 for purchased boxed items:
    a. Copy the labels used for the CASE SUMMARY DATA, leaving a blank row between the sections.
    b. Edit the heading to read BOX SUMMARY DATA; edit labels to include boxes rather than cases.
    Set up and use a duplicate field for the criteria range, then apply the function to find answers for boxes.

20. Print a copy of the CASE SUMMARY DATA and the BOX SUMMARY DATA on one page. (B)

21. Save and close the workbook file; name it **STORE**.

Illustration A

DATE	DESCRIPTION	VENDOR	ITEMS PER	UNIT	QUANTITY	PRICE
15-Oct-97	Adhesive notes	Stickum Bros	6	Box	1	28.95
15-Oct-97	Pads (5 x 8)	Treehouse Paper	60	Box	1	75.95
20-Oct-97	Folders (Letter)	Paper City	2500	Case	1	60.95
20-Oct-97	Folders (Legal)	Paper City	2500	Case	1	75.95
20-Oct-97	Looseleaf - large	School Central, Inc.	10	Box	3	22.50

Illustration B

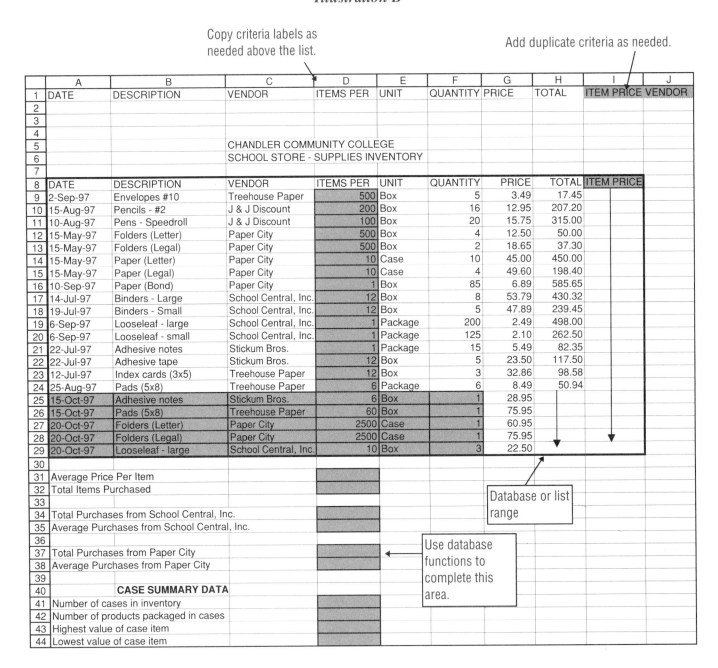

Copy criteria labels as needed above the list.

Add duplicate criteria as needed.

	A	B	C	D	E	F	G	H	I	J
1	DATE	DESCRIPTION	VENDOR	ITEMS PER	UNIT	QUANTITY	PRICE	TOTAL	ITEM PRICE	VENDOR
2										
3										
4										
5			CHANDLER COMMUNITY COLLEGE							
6			SCHOOL STORE - SUPPLIES INVENTORY							
7										
8	DATE	DESCRIPTION	VENDOR	ITEMS PER	UNIT	QUANTITY	PRICE	TOTAL	ITEM PRICE	
9	2-Sep-97	Envelopes #10	Treehouse Paper	500	Box	5	3.49	17.45		
10	15-Aug-97	Pencils - #2	J & J Discount	200	Box	16	12.95	207.20		
11	10-Aug-97	Pens - Speedroll	J & J Discount	100	Box	20	15.75	315.00		
12	15-May-97	Folders (Letter)	Paper City	500	Box	4	12.50	50.00		
13	15-May-97	Folders (Legal)	Paper City	500	Box	2	18.65	37.30		
14	15-May-97	Paper (Letter)	Paper City	10	Case	10	45.00	450.00		
15	15-May-97	Paper (Legal)	Paper City	10	Case	4	49.60	198.40		
16	10-Sep-97	Paper (Bond)	Paper City	1	Box	85	6.89	585.65		
17	14-Jul-97	Binders - Large	School Central, Inc.	12	Box	8	53.79	430.32		
18	19-Jul-97	Binders - Small	School Central, Inc.	12	Box	5	47.89	239.45		
19	6-Sep-97	Looseleaf - large	School Central, Inc.	1	Package	200	2.49	498.00		
20	6-Sep-97	Looseleaf - small	School Central, Inc.	1	Package	125	2.10	262.50		
21	22-Jul-97	Adhesive notes	Stickum Bros.	1	Package	15	5.49	82.35		
22	22-Jul-97	Adhesive tape	Stickum Bros.	12	Box	5	23.50	117.50		
23	12-Jul-97	Index cards (3x5)	Treehouse Paper	12	Box	3	32.86	98.58		
24	25-Aug-97	Pads (5x8)	Treehouse Paper	6	Package	6	8.49	50.94		
25	15-Oct-97	Adhesive notes	Stickum Bros.	6	Box	1	28.95			
26	15-Oct-97	Pads (5x8)	Treehouse Paper	60	Box	1	75.95			
27	20-Oct-97	Folders (Letter)	Paper City	2500	Case	1	60.95			
28	20-Oct-97	Folders (Legal)	Paper City	2500	Case	1	75.95			
29	20-Oct-97	Looseleaf - large	School Central, Inc.	10	Box	3	22.50			
30										
31	Average Price Per Item									
32	Total Items Purchased									
33										
34	Total Purchases from School Central, Inc.									
35	Average Purchases from School Central, Inc.									
36										
37	Total Purchases from Paper City									
38	Average Purchases from Paper City									
39										
40		**CASE SUMMARY DATA**								
41	Number of cases in inventory									
42	Number of products packaged in cases									
43	Highest value of case item									
44	Lowest value of case item									

Database or list range

Use database functions to complete this area.

KEYSTROKES

INSERT A DATABASE FUNCTION USING PASTE FUNCTION

✓ *You can also type a function to insert.*

1. Set up criteria range in worksheet.

   ✓ *The criteria range is a location in the worksheet containing one or more criteria labels. Below these you must type data values that indicate a condition that must be met. Guidelines for setting up a criteria range were discussed in* **Exercises 80** *and* **82**.

2. Select cell to receive function.

3. Click **Paste Function** button ....
   on Standard toolbar.

4. Select **Database** ....
   in **Function category** list.

5. Select desired database function
   in **Function name** list ...

6. Click **OK** .... Enter

7. Type reference or name of list range in **database** box.

   OR

   Select cells in worksheet containing field labels and list data.

8. Click **field** box .... Tab

9. Type field name containing data the function will calculate.

   OR

   Select cell in worksheet containing desired field label.

10. Click **criteria** box........................... Tab

11. Type reference or name of criteria range.

12. Click **OK** .... Enter

Exercise 84

- **Subtotals Within a List** ■ **Nested Subtotals**
- **Remove Subtotals**
- **Copy Subtotals** ■ **Outline Feature**

NOTES

Subtotals Within a List

- Excel enables you to create **subtotals** to quickly summarize sorted data within a list. Subtotals may be used instead of database functions to summarize specific groups of data. (See Illustration A on the right.)

- Creating a subtotal within a list will automatically:

  - Calculate and insert subtotals below grouped fields.

  - Calculate and insert grand totals.

  - Label the calculated values.

  - Outline the data families in the list.

- Follow these guidelines when subtotaling a list:

  - First, sort the list so that the fields for which you want subtotals are grouped together.

  - Select **Subtotals** from the **Data** menu, then select the following from the Subtotals dialog box, as illustrated below:

    At each change in: Select a field name.
    Use function: Select a function.
    Add subtotal to: Select one or more fields to calculate.

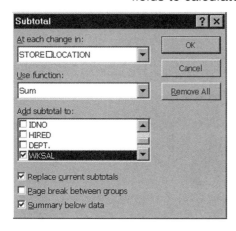

- You can also use the subtotals command on a filtered list. When you do so, Excel only calculates the values that are visible in the filtered list.

- If you change the details in a list, the subtotals and grand totals will also change.

Illustration A

123		A	B	C	D	E	F	G	H
	1	LAST	FIRST	STORE LOCATION	IDNO	HIRED	DEPT.	WKSAL	ANNSAL
	2	Carson	Penn	CHI	14399	11/5/97	Sales	225.75	11739.00
	3	Esther	Polly	CHI	14235	11/15/97	Admin.	286.50	14898.00
	4	Lee	Michael	CHI	14295	3/5/95	Stock	276.00	14352.00
	5	Lee	Randy	CHI	13298	7/25/95	Stock	365.80	19021.60
	6	Palmeri	Marie	CHI	14367	9/1/95	Stock	276.50	14378.00
	7	Restivo	Mary	CHI	14932	10/1/97	Sales	295.00	15340.00
	8	Sawyer	Harriet	CHI	13290	2/13/97	Admin.	358.60	18647.20
	9	Seltzer	Al K.	CHI	14931	7/25/97	Stock	255.00	13260.00
	10			CHI Total				2339.15	
	11	Accosta	Anthony	LA	13929	10/30/97	Sales	375.55	19528.60
	12	Gregonis	Dimitri	LA	14395	5/25/97	Admin.	275.00	14300.00
	13	Jackson	Martin	LA	14397	10/25/97	Stock	275.00	14300.00
	14	Lee	Chin	LA	13254	5/15/93	Stock	345.00	17940.00
	15	Martino	John	LA	14289	11/1/95	Admin.	342.90	17830.80
	16	Naidle	Adam	LA	14321	2/15/95	Sales	243.50	12662.00
	17	Samtansi	Perkash	LA	14354	11/25/96	Sales	215.45	11203.40
	18	Watterse	Cathy	LA	14269	12/15/96	Sales	325.75	16939.00
	19			LA Total				2398.15	
	20	Carson	George	NY	14078	4/1/94	Admin.	389.76	20267.52
	21	Carson	Laurence	NY	14356	9/30/95	Stock	235.45	12243.40
	22	Graham	Holly	NY	14402	11/1/97	Sales	285.00	14820.00
	23	Hopkins	George	NY	14396	6/10/97	Stock	275.00	14300.00
	24	Parsons	Lyle	NY	14398	10/31/97	Admin.	285.50	14846.00
	25	Rogers	Jane	NY	14024	5/18/96	Sales	310.89	16166.28
	26	Tommei	Lori	NY	13852	8/25/96	Admin.	376.00	19552.00
	27	Valdes	Lina	NY	14385	10/15/97	Stock	265.00	13780.00
	28			NY Total				2422.60	
	29			Grand Total				7159.90	
	30								

Nested Subtotals

- You can find subtotals within subtotals (nested subtotals) if you do the following:

  - Sort the list by both fields for which you want subtotals.

    EXAMPLE: *Sort By DEPT., then by STORE LOCATION.*

  - Find subtotal for first field you sorted by.

- From the Subtotal dialog box, deselect the Replace Current Subtotals option, then find subtotals for second field you sorted by.

Remove Subtotals

■ You can remove subtotals in three ways:

- Select **Remove All** button from the Subtotal dialog box.

- Replace existing subtotals by selecting new subtotal options, then select Replace current subtotals from the Subtotal dialog box.

- Select **Undo Subtotals** from the **Edit** menu.

Copy Subtotals

■ If you want to copy a subtotal result, use the Copy and Paste Special commands. Be sure to paste the result as a value.

Outline Feature

■ You can use the **outline controls** to hide or show the **details** (families of records) in the subtotaled list. To show the detail data within a group, click the show detail button **+**. To show a specific level in an outline, click the row or column level symbol **1 2 3**. If you click level 3, the lowest level, all details will display. To hide levels in an outline, click the hide detail button **−**.

■ Note Illustration B below which shows the summary of a subtotaled worksheet, or level 2 data. If you click the level 1 hide button, only the Grand Total will display. You could then print or chart only the visible cells — just the subtotals, for example.

Illustration B

		A	B	C	D	E	F	G	H
	1	LAST	FIRST	STORE LOCATION	IDNO	HIRED	DEPT.	WKSAL	ANNSAL
+	10			CHI Total				2339.15	
+	19			LA Total				2398.15	
+	29			NY Total				2691.10	
−	30			Grand Total				7428.40	
	31								

Outline controls

Column level buttons

Show Detail button

Hide Detail button

> *In this exercise, you will use subtotals to summarize the data in the EMPS database.*

EXERCISE DIRECTIONS

1. Open ⌨ **EMPS** or 💾 **84EMPS**.

2. Add summary label data below the list as shown on page 327, in Illustration C.

3. Bold the SUMMARY DATA heading labels.

4. Make sure the list is sorted by LAST (Sort By field) and FIRST (Then By field) in ascending order as shown.

5. Find the answers for the SUMMARY DATA-ADMINISTRATION DEPARTMENT:

   a. Since you want subtotals for the ADMINISTRATION DEPARTMENT, sort the DEPT. field in ascending order.

   b. Use the Subtotals command to find the total weekly salary paid to members of each department.

   > HINT: From Subtotal dialog box, set:
   >   At Each Change in: DEPT.
   >   Use Function: Sum
   >   Add Subtotal to: WKSAL

   c. Click the row level 2 outline symbol to hide all rows except the subtotal rows and the Grand Total row.

   d. Use Copy and Paste Special to copy the Admin. subtotal to the appropriate cells in the summary area as a value.

   e. Remove all subtotals from the list.

   f. Repeat step b using the Average function.

   g. Format the copied values to show two decimal places.

6. Find the answers for the SUMMARY DATA-LOS ANGELES STORE area:

   a. Since you want subtotals for the Los Angeles locations, sort the STORE LOCATION field in ascending order.

   b. Use Sum, Average, Min, and Count functions as needed to answer each question.

   c. Use the row level 2 outline symbol to hide details.

   d. Use Copy and Paste Special command to copy LA subtotal to the appropriate cell as a value.

   e. Remove all subtotals after each calculation.

   > ✓   *You can also select Replace Current Subtotals when performing the next subtotal command to reduce the number of steps.*

   f. Format each copied result in the summary area for the appropriate number of decimal places.

7. Find the answers for SUMMARY DATA-LOS ANGELES ADMINISTRATION DEPARTMENT:

   a. Since you want subtotals for a subgroup (Administration for Los Angeles stores), sort the records by DEPT., then by STORE LOCATION.

   b. Use two Subtotal commands to find each summary answer for the Los Angeles Administration subgroup.

   > HINT: To find total weekly salaries:
   >   Find sum for WKSAL on each change in DEPT.
   >   Select Subtotals again, deselect Replace Current Subtotals, and find sum for WKSAL on each change in STORE LOCATION.

   c. Use the row level 2 outline symbol to hide details.

   d. Use Copy and Paste Special commands to copy the appropriate subtotal result to the summary area as a value.

   e. Remove all subtotals before repeating Step b.

   f. Format copied results in the summary area as needed.

8. Remove subtotals in the list.

9. Print a copy of entire worksheet to fit on one page.

10. Save and close the workbook file; name it **EMPS**.

Illustration C

	A	B	C	D	E	F	G	H
1	**LAST**	**FIRST**	**STORE LOCATION**	**IDNO**	**HIRED**	**DEPT.**	**WKSAL**	**ANNSAL**
2	Accosta	Anthony	LA	13929	10/30/97	Sales	375.55	19528.60
3	Carson	George	NY	14078	4/1/94	Admin.	389.76	20267.52
4	Carson	Laurence	NY	14356	9/30/95	Stock	235.45	12243.40
5	Carson	Penn	CHI	14399	11/5/97	Sales	225.75	11739.00
6	Esther	Polly	CHI	14235	11/15/97	Admin.	286.50	14898.00
7	Graham	Holly	NY	14402	11/1/97	Sales	285.00	14820.00
8	Gregonis	Dimitri	LA	14395	5/25/97	Admin.	275.00	14300.00
9	Hopkins	George	NY	14396	6/10/97	Stock	275.00	14300.00
10	Jackson	Martin	LA	14397	10/25/97	Stock	275.00	14300.00
11	Lee	Chin	LA	13254	5/15/93	Sales	345.00	17940.00
12	Lee	Michael	CHI	14295	3/5/95	Stock	276.00	14352.00
13	Lee	Randy	CHI	13298	7/25/95	Stock	365.80	19021.60
14	Martino	John	LA	14289	11/1/95	Admin.	342.90	17830.80
15	Naidle	Adam	LA	14321	2/15/95	Sales	243.50	12662.00
16	Palmeri	Marie	CHI	14367	9/1/95	Stock	276.50	14378.00
17	Parsons	Lyle	NY	14398	10/31/97	Admin.	285.50	14846.00
18	Restivo	Mary	CHI	14932	10/1/97	Sales	295.00	15340.00
19	Rogers	Jane	NY	14024	5/18/96	Sales	310.89	16166.28
20	Samtanai	Perkash	LA	14354	11/25/96	Sales	215.45	11203.40
21	Sawyer	Harriet	CHI	13290	2/13/97	Admin.	358.60	18647.20
22	Seltzer	Al K.	CHI	14931	7/25/97	Stock	255.00	13260.00
23	Tommei	Lori	NY	13852	8/25/96	Admin.	376.00	19552.00
24	Valdez	Lina	NY	14385	10/15/97	Stock	265.00	13780.00
25	Watterson	Cathy	LA	14269	12/15/96	Sales	325.75	16939.00
26								
27	**SUMMARY DATA - ADMINISTRATION DEPARTMENT**							
28	Total weekly salaries							
29	Average weekly salaries							
30								
31	**SUMMARY DATA - LOS ANGELES STORE**							
32	Total weekly salaries							
33	Average weekly salaries							
34	Highest weekly salary							
35	Lowest weekly salary							
36	Number of employees							
37								
38	**SUMMARY DATA - LOS ANGELES ADMINISTRATION DEPARTMENT**							
39	Total weekly salaries							
40	Average weekly salaries							
41	Highest weekly salary							
42	Lowest weekly salary							
43	Number of employees							

Enter summary labels and values here.

KEYSTROKES

SUBTOTAL A LIST AUTOMATICALLY

Creates subtotals for groups of data in specified columns, and a grand total at the bottom of the list. Excel automatically applies outlining to the resulting list.

✓ *You can also subtotal a filtered list.*

1. Sort column(s) in list to subtotal.
   ✓ *List must contain labeled columns in its first row. Items to subtotal should be grouped together.*

2. Select any cell in list.

3. Click **Data** menu .... `Alt`+`D`

4. Click **Su̱btotals** .... `B`

5. Click **At each change in**: .... `Alt`+`A`

6. Select field .... `⇅`, `Alt`+`↑` containing groups to subtotal.

7. Click **Use Function**: .... `Alt`+`U`

8. Select desired function .... `⇅`, `Alt`+`↑`

9. Select **Add Subtotal to**: .... `Alt`+`D`

10. Click fields .... `⇅`, `Space` containing values to calculate.

11. Repeat steps 9 and 10 for each field to calculate.

   To replace current subtotals:

   Select **Replace c̱urrent subtotals** .... `Alt`+`C`

   To force page breaks between subtotaled groups:

   Select **P̱age break between groups** .... `Alt`+`P`

   To place subtotals and grand totals above data:

   Deselect **S̱ummary below data** .... `Alt`+`S`

12. Click **OK** .... `Enter`

REMOVE ALL AUTOMATIC SUBTOTALS IN A LIST

1. Select any cell in subtotaled list.

2. Click **Data** menu .... `Alt`+`D`

3. Click **Su̱btotals** .... `B`

4. Click **Ṟemove All** .... `Alt`+`R`

5. Click **OK** .... `Enter`

CREATE A SUBTOTAL WITHIN A SUBTOTALED GROUP IN A LIST

1. Sort all columns in list to subtotal.

2. Subtotal first group in list.

3. Follow steps to subtotal second group in list.

4. Deselect **Replace c̱urrent Subtotals** .... `Alt`+`C`

5. Click **OK** .... `Enter`

USE OUTLINE SYMBOLS TO SHOW OR HIDE OUTLINE GROUPS AND LEVELS

Show group details:

Click show detail symbol .... `+` of group to expand.

Hide group details:

Click hide detail symbol .... `−` of group to hide.

Show all outline groups for a level:

Click row level symbol .... for lowest level to show.

NEXT EXERCISE

Exercise

85

■ Use Microsoft Query Wizard

NOTES

Use Microsoft Query Wizard

■ The Microsoft Query feature, which contains the Query Wizard, is an optional feature that must be installed using the Custom installation option. If you installed Excel using the Typical installation option, Microsoft Query was not included in the install. Use the Help menu and the Installing Microsoft Query topic for assistance on installing this option.

■ The query feature allows you to ask a question of databases that exist in Excel, on Web sites, or in external databases, such as Microsoft Access. The Query Wizard makes it easy to select data from various data sources and then bring the results into Excel for analysis.

■ Microsoft Query allows you to get data from the following data sources: Microsoft Access, dBASE, Microsoft FoxPro, Microsoft Excel, Paradox, SQL Server, or a text database. You can also get data from a Web site if you are connected to the Internet. To run a Web query, select **Data**, **Get External Data**, and then click **Run Web Query**. You can select sample queries that are in the Queries folder of your Microsoft Excel directory.

■ One of the data sources you can use is a Microsoft Access database. In the Microsoft Office suite, Access is the database software and Excel is the spreadsheet software. You can query database tables from Access even if you don't have the software installed, question it for data, and then show the results within an Excel workbook.

■ To bring data from an external source into a Query you must create the data source file, which attaches the appropriate driver to convert the file for Excel. Query Wizard will assist you in this process. Once the data source file is created you can sort, filter, and select the data you want from the table(s) you select as your data source. There are multiple steps and screens in the creation of the data source file and the query. For this exercise, the screens will be illustrated in the Exercise directions.

In this exercise, you will query the Chandler Community College database, which was created in Microsoft Access 97, and which has a Teacher's table. Each teacher's budget has been increased due to a grant. The Access database file is provided in the DDC Data Folder on the DDC CD-ROM that accompanies this book. The steps to create the data source, query the data, report and enhance the results in Excel will be provided in the directions that follow.

EXERCISE DIRECTIONS

1. Open a new spreadsheet.

2. Use the <u>D</u>ata, Get External <u>D</u>ata, Create <u>N</u>ew Query commands.

   ✓ *Microsoft Query must be installed to complete this exercise. If you get an error message here, you must install the feature using your software disks or CD-ROM. Check the Help menu (Installing Microsoft Query) for this procedure.*

3. On the Choose Data Source dialog box, click <New Data Source> and click OK to use Query Wizard to help you create the data source.

4. Complete the Create New Data Source dialog box as illustrated below:

   Step 1. College

   Step 2. Microsoft Access Driver (*.mdb) Note the other drivers that are provided in this dialog box.

   Step 3. Click Connect and on the ODBC Microsoft Access 97 Setup dialog box, click Database: Select. Then select 🖫 **85COLLEGE.MDB**, from the data disk. Click OK to accept the selection. Click OK to accept the completed Setup box. The database filename will be entered in box 3.

   Step 4. Click the drop down arrow and select the TEACHERS table as the default table in box 4. Click OK.

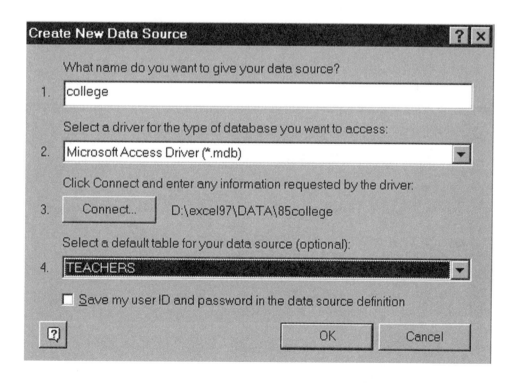

5. The college data source was created and will appear on your Choose Data Source dialog box.

6. Select college and click OK.

7. On the Query Wizard-Choose Columns dialog box, illustrated below, select the fields for the query and click the right arrow button. Include the following fields in the query: TITLE, LAST, FIRST, DEPT, BUDGET, and BLDG. Click Next.

8. On the Query Wizard-Filter Data dialog box, select the BLDG field and use the drop down arrows to set the filter for equals M, as illustrated below. Click Next.
    This filters only main building teachers.

9. On the Query Wizard-Sort Order dialog box, select DEPT in ascending order, and then LAST and FIRST names. Click Next.

10. On the Query Wizard-Finish dialog box, accept the default setting to Return data to Microsoft Excel and click Finish.

11. Place the data in cell A4 of the blank worksheet, as illustrated below.

12. Add titles in cells A1 and A2 as follows:
    CHANDLER COMMUNITY COLLEGE
    GRANT EXTENSIONS FOR MAIN BUILDING BUDGETS

13. Delete the BLDG. column.

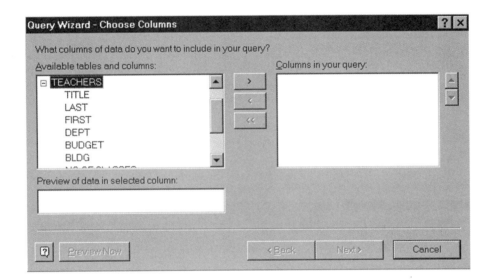

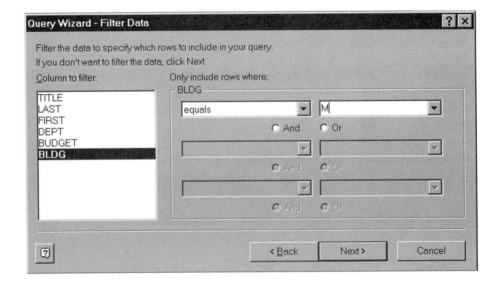

14. Add two new column headings in columns F and G:
GRANT   TOTAL

15. In the GRANT column, enter a formula to find 75% of the present budget.
HINT: Budget*.75.

16. In the TOTAL column, enter a formula to find the total of the Budget and the Grant values.

17. Use the subtotal feature to find the totals of the BUDGET, GRANT, and TOTAL columns by DEPT.

18. Use the outline feature to select outline level 2 to summarize all the departmental data.

19. Close and save the file; name it **BUDGET**.

	A	B	C	D	E	F	G
1	CHANDLER COMMUNITY COLLEGE						
2	GRANT EXTENSIONS FOR MAIN BUILDING BUDGETS						
3							
4	TITLE	LAST	FIRST	DEPT	BUDGET	GRANT	TOTAL
5	Dr.	Fernandez	Ricardo	Bus	180.00		
6	Mr.	Keltz	Mel	Bus	200.00		
7	Dr.	Browning	Paula	Eng	150.00		
8	Dr.	Fernandez	Jose	Eng	200.00		
9	Ms.	Hargrave	Sally	Eng	250.00		
10	Ms.	Marcus	Diana	Eng	250.00		
11	Mr.	Brown	Donald	For. Lang.	140.00		
12	Ms.	Greene	Ralph	Math	140.00		
13	Ms.	Blane	Jaime	PE	120.00		
14	Dr.	Anderson	Harvey	S.S.	200.00		
15	Dr.	Blanc	Pamela	Sci	200.00		
16	Ms.	Chen	Julie	Sci	160.00		

Exercise 86

■ Use a PivotTable to Summarize List Data

NOTES

Use a PivotTable to Summarize List Data

- Excel provides a powerful tool for summarizing data in a list called a **PivotTable**.

- This exercise will provide an introduction to PivotTables.

- With a PivotTable you can:

  - Use functions to summarize data fields.

  - Show only the fields you specify.

  - Hide or show details in the PivotTable.

  - Change (pivot) label orientation to rows or columns.

  - Filter the results to summarize only the records you specify.

- Guidelines for creating a PivotTable:

  - Select any cell in a list. The list must have labeled columns (field names).

  - Determine how you want to summarize the list.

  - Select the PivotTable Report command from the Data menu.

  - Follow the prompts provided by the PivotTable Wizard:

    Step 1 of 4: Indicate source of data. In this exercise it is a Microsoft Excel list, however, you will note that you can also use external data sources for this feature.

    Step 2 of 4: Change or accept proposed range that contains the data. If you named the range, the range name will appear.

    Step 3 of 4: Drag field buttons onto appropriate part of layout area and assign a function to summarize fields placed in the <u>D</u>ATA area. Note the illustration of the Step 3 screen below.

    Step 4 of 4: Specify where to place the PivotTable (the starting cell).

    ✓ NOTE: *Excel places the PivotTable on a new worksheet if you do not specify the starting cell for the PivotTable.*

- The Step 3 of 4 PivotTable Wizard screen (illustrated on the next page) is used to drag each field button to a layout area as follows:

  <u>P</u>AGE area Provides a drop-down list of fields from which you can select data to display in the PivotTable (filter the PivotTable).

  <u>R</u>OW area Creates row labels for each unique item in field.

  <u>C</u>OLUMN area Creates column labels for each unique item in field.

  <u>D</u>ATA area Specifies field to summarize.

  ✓ NOTE: *You must include at least one field in the DATA area. You can drag more than one field button into a layout area, but it's best to limit the number of fields when starting out.*

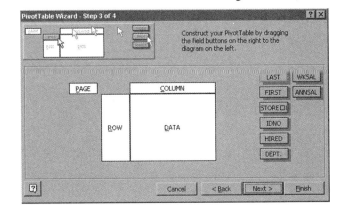

- When you create a PivotTable, you may wish to display the **PivotTable toolbar**. This toolbar provides buttons and a menu you can use to customize the PivotTable.

Query and PivotTable Toolbar

IMPORTANT: *Be sure to understand what a command does before trying it. For example, if you click the **Show Pages** button, Excel will create a new PivotTable for each Page Field item on a separate worksheet.*

- In a PivotTable, you can drag the field buttons to change their position and, therefore, the view of your data. For example, you can drag a row field button to the column or page position. When you drag the button, the pointer changes as listed below, to show the result of dropping the button in various areas of the PivotTable.

  - Move field to column
  - Move field to row
  - Move field to page
  - Remove field from PivotTable

- When you change a PivotTable or refresh the data in it, the resulting cells will *not* retain the formatting you may have applied to it.

- You can undo the last PivotTable change by selecting **Undo PivotTable** from the **Edit** menu.

- Note the PivotTable in Illustration B on the next page created by the settings made in Illustration A below.

Illustration A

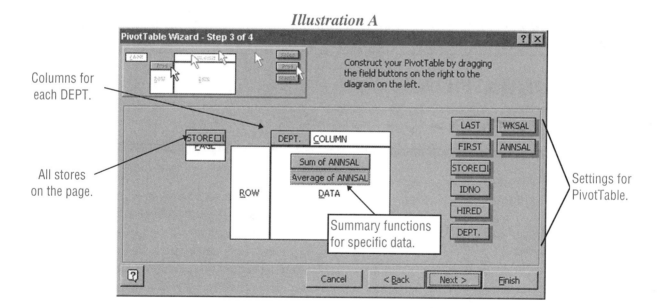

Columns for each DEPT.

All stores on the page.

Summary functions for specific data.

Settings for PivotTable.

Illustration B

	A	B	C	D	E	F	G	H	I
1	LAST	FIRST	STORE LOCATION	IDNO	HIRED	DEPT.	WKSAL	ANNSAL	Admin.
2	Accosta	Anthony	LA	13929	10/30/97	Sales	375.55	19528.60	Sales
3	Carson	George	NY	14078	4/1/94	Admin.	389.76	20267.52	
4	Carson	Laurence	NY	14356	9/30/95	Stock	235.45	12243.40	
5	Carson	Penn	CHI	14399	11/5/97	Sales	225.75	11739.00	
6	Esther	Polly	CHI	14235	11/15/97	Admin.	286.50	14898.00	
7	Graham	Holly	NY	14402	11/1/97	Sales	285.00	14820.00	
8	Gregonis	Dimitri	LA	14395	525/97	Admin.	275.00	14300.00	
9	Hopkins	George	NY	14396	6/10/97	Stock	275.00	14300.00	
10	Jackson	Martin	LA	14397	10/25/97	Stock	275.00	14300.00	
11	Lee	Chin	LA	13254	5/15/93	Sales	345.00	17940.00	
12	Lee	Michael	CHI	14295	3/5/95	Stock	276.00	14352.00	
13	Lee	Randy	CHI	13298	7/25/95	Stock	365.80	19021.60	
14	Martino	John	LA	14289	11/1/95	Admin.	342.90	17830.80	
15	Naidle	Adam	LA	14321	2/15/95	Sales	243.50	12662.00	
16	Palmeri	Marie	CHI	14367	9/1/95	Stock	276.50	14378.00	
17	Parsons	Lyle	NY	14398	10/31/97	Admin.	285.50	14846.00	
18	Restivo	Mary	CHI	14932	10/1/97	Sales	295.00	15340.00	
19	Rogers	Jane	NY	14024	5/18/96	Sales	310.89	16166.28	
20	Samtanai	Perkash	LA	14354	11/25/96	Sales	215.45	11203.40	
21	Sawyer	Harriet	CHI	13290	2/13/97	Admin.	358.60	18647.20	
22	Seltzer	Al K.	CHI	14931	7/25/97	Stock	255.00	13260.00	
23	Tommei	Lori	NY	13852	8/25/96	Admin.	376.00	19552.00	
24	Valdez	Lina	NY	14385	10/15/97	Stock	265.00	13780.00	
25	Watterson	Cathy	LA	14269	12/15/96	Sales	325.75	16939.00	
26									
27	STORE LOCATION	(All)							
28									
29		DEPT.						PivotTable	
30	Data	Admin.	Sales	Stock	Grand Total				
31	Sum of ANNSAL	100789.52	119399.28	101855.00	322043.80				
32	Average of ANNSAL2	16798.25	14924.91	14550.71	15335.42				

Data for all stores.

Arranged by DEPT.

Summary data

In this exercise, you will create PivotTables that summarize salary data for New York, Chicago, and Los Angeles employees. You will place each PivotTable on a separate sheet tab.

EXERCISE DIRECTIONS

1. Open ⌨ **EMPS** or 💾 **86EMPS**.

2. Delete summary data below the employee list and remove subtotals if any exist.

3. Sort list by LAST and then FIRST name.

4. Create a PivotTable to summarize weekly salaries for each department for all employees:

   a. Design the layout, dragging the field buttons as follows:

   PAGE area: STORE LOCATION
   ROW area: blank
   COLUMN area: DEPT.
   DATA area: Sum of WKSAL

   ✓ *Sum is the default function for a field containing values. When you drag WKSAL to the data area it automatically creates the Sum function.*

   b. PivotTable starting cell: Sheet2!$A$1

   c. Format the totals to show two decimal places and size columns as needed.

5. Click the drop down arrow in the Store Location Page value section to view the different values for the weekly salaries for each store. Leave the PivotTable set to All values.

6. Modify the PivotTable in Sheet2 so that it also displays average weekly salaries for all employees:

   a. Select any cell in the PivotTable.

   b. Display the PivotTable Toolbar, if not visible by clicking View, Toolbars, PivotTable.

   c. Click the PivotTable Wizard button.

   d. Add a second WKSAL to the DATA area.

   ✓ *Excel names it Sum of WKSAL2.*

   e. Change the function used by WKSAL2 to AVERAGE (double-click the Sum of WKSAL2 button and select the AVERAGE function.) Click OK.

   f. Click Next.

   g. Place the table on the existing worksheet in A1 and click Finish.

h. Format the totals as currency and size columns as needed.

i. Print one copy of the PivotTable.

7. Create a PivotTable to summarize the salary data for each Store Location or Page value by clicking the Show Pages button on the PivotTable toolbar.

8. Select any cell in the PivotTable.

a. Click the Show Pages button on the PivotTable toolbar.

b. When Store Location is suggested as the pages, click OK.

Each store's data will be on a separate PivotTable on separate labeled sheets.

9. Rename Sheet2; name it All Locations.

10. Create a new PivotTable to summarize employees for all store locations by department.

a. Select any cell in the data list and select PivotTable Wizard.

b. Design the layout as follows:

DATA area: Average of ANNSAL
                    Max of ANNSAL
                    Min of ANNSAL
                    Count of ANNSAL

ROW area: DEPT.

c. Place the PivotTable in cell A1 on Sheet3.

d. Edit the data labels in the PivotTable as follows:

Average Annual salary

Highest Annual salary

Lowest Annual salary

Number of employees

✓   *To edit an item in a PivotTable, press **F2** or click in the formula bar. You cannot double-click a cell to edit in a PivotTable. When you edit the first four labels, all repeated labels will be edited.*

a. Adjust column width as necessary.

b. Format dollar values as currency.

c. Format totals as currency and size columns as needed.

d. Name the sheet Dept. Salary Data.

e. Print one copy of this PivotTable.

11. Rename Sheet1; name it Employee List.

12. Save and close the workbook file; name it **EMPS**.

	A	B	C	D	E	F	G	H
1	LAST	FIRST	STORE LOCATION	IDNO	HIRED	DEPT.	WKSAL	ANNSAL
2	Esther	Polly	CHI	14235	11/15/97	Admin.	286.50	14898.00
3	Sawyer	Harriet	CHI	13290	02/13/97	Admin.	358.60	18647.20
4	Gregonis	Dimitri	LA	14395	05/25/97	Admin.	275.00	14300.00
5	Martino	John	LA	14289	11/01/95	Admin.	342.90	17830.80
6	Carson	George	NY	14078	04/01/94	Admin.	389.76	20267.52
7	Parsons	Lyle	NY	14398	10/31/97	Admin.	285.50	14846.00
8	Tommei	Lori	NY	13852	08/25/96	Admin.	376.00	19552.00
9	Carson	Penn	CHI	14399	11/05/97	Sales	225.75	11739.00
10	Restivo	Mary	CHI	14932	10/01/97	Sales	295.00	15340.00
11	Accosta	Anthony	LA	13929	10/30/97	Sales	375.55	19528.60
12	Lee	Chin	LA	13254	05/15/93	Sales	345.00	17940.00
13	Naidle	Adam	LA	14321	02/15/95	Sales	243.50	12662.00
14	Samtanai	Perkash	LA	14354	11/25/96	Sales	215.45	11203.40
15	Watterson	Cathy	LA	14269	12/15/96	Sales	325.75	16939.00
16	Graham	Holly	NY	14402	11/01/97	Sales	285.00	14820.00
17	Rogers	Jane	NY	14024	05/18/96	Sales	310.89	16166.28
18	Lee	Michael	CHI	14295	03/05/95	Stock	276.00	14352.00
19	Lee	Randy	CHI	13298	07/25/95	Stock	365.80	19021.60
20	Palmeri	Marie	CHI	14367	09/01/95	Stock	276.50	14378.00
21	Seltzer	Al K.	CHI	14931	07/25/97	Stock	255.00	13260.00
22	Jackson	Martin	LA	14397	10/25/97	Stock	275.00	14300.00
23	Carson	Laurence	NY	14356	09/30/95	Stock	235.45	12243.40
24	Hopkins	George	NY	14396	06/10/97	Stock	275.00	14300.00
25	Valdez	Lina	NY	14385	10/15/97	Stock	265.00	13780.00
26								
27	SUMMARY DATA - ADMINISTRATION DEPARTMENT							
28	Total weekly salaries			2314.26				
29	Average weekly salaries			330.61				
30								
31	SUMMARY DATA - LOS ANGELES STORE							
32	Total weekly salaries			2398.15				
33	Average weekly salaries			299.77				
34	Highest weekly salary			375.55				
35	Lowest weekly salary			215.45				
36	Number of employees			8				
37								
38	SUMMARY DATA - LOS ANGELES ADMINISTRATION DEPARTMENT							
39	Total weekly salaries			617.90				
40	Average weekly salaries			308.95				
41	Highest weekly salary			342.90				
42	Lowest weekly salary			275.00				
43	Number of employees			2				
44								
45								

Delete summary data.

KEYSTROKES

CREATE A PIVOTTABLE

1. Select any cell in list to summarize.
2. Click **Data** menu .... `Alt`+`D`
3. Click **PivotTable Report** .... `P`
4. **PIVOTTABLE WIZARD – STEP 1 OF 4:**
   a. Select source of data:
      - **Microsoft Excel list or database** .... `M`
      - **External data source** .... `E`
      - **Multiple consolidation ranges** .... `C`
      - **Another PivotTable** .... `A`
   b. Click **Next** .... `Enter`
4. **PIVOTTABLE WIZARD – STEP 2 OF 4:**
   a. Select cells in worksheet containing data source.

      OR

      Type cell reference of data source in **Range** text box.
      - ✓ Select the **Browse** button if the data source is external. Then select the file containing the data.
   b. Click **Next** .... `Enter`
6. **PIVOTTABLE WIZARD – STEP 3 OF 4:**
   a. Create PivotTable layout:

      To add a field to PivotTable:

      Drag field button onto desired layout area.

      To remove a field from PivotTable:

      Drag field button off the layout area.

      To move a field to another layout area:

      Drag field button onto desired layout area.
7. To change function to apply to field:
   a. Double-click field button in **D**ATA area.
   b. Select **Summarize by list** .... `Alt`+`S`
   c. Select desired function .... `↕↓`
   d. Click **OK** .... `Enter`

---

   e. Click **Next** .... `Enter`
8. **PIVOTTABLE WIZARD – STEP 4 OF 4:**
   a. Select upper-left destination cell of table in worksheet.

      OR

      Type reference to upper-left destination cell of table in **PivotTable Starting Cell** text box.
      - ✓ If you leave this blank, Excel creates the PivotTable on a new worksheet. Do not place the PivotTable where it can overwrite existing data.
   b. Select or deselect **PivotTable Options**:
      - **Grand totals for columns** .... `Alt`+`G`
      - **Grand totals for rows** .... `Alt`+`T`
      - **Save data with table layout** .... `Alt`+`W`
      - **AutoFormat Table** .... `Alt`+`A`
9. Click **Finish** .... `Enter`
10. PivotTable appears.

DISPLAY SPECIFIC PAGE ITEMS IN A PIVOTTABLE

1. Click page field drop-down button .... `▼`
2. Select desired field item .... `↕↓`, `Enter`

DISPLAY ALL PAGE ITEMS IN A PIVOTTABLE

1. Click page field drop-down button .... `▼`
2. Select **(All)** .... `↕↓`, `Enter`

UPDATE A PIVOTTABLE

Updates a PivotTable to show changes made to source data.
   - ✓ If rows or columns were removed or added to the source data range, you may have to follow the steps to modify a PivotTable and change the reference to the source data.

1. Select any cell in the PivotTable.
2. Click **Refresh Data** button .... `!` on PivotTable toolbar.

   OR

   a. Click **Data** menu .... `Alt`+`D`
   b. Click **Refresh Data** .... `R`

MODIFY A PIVOTTABLE

1. Select any cell in the PivotTable.
2. Click **PivotTable Wizard** button .... `⊞` on PivotTable toolbar.

   OR

   a. Click **Data** menu .... `Alt`+`D`
   b. Click **PivotTable** .... `P`
3. If desired, make changes to field layout:

   AND/OR

   Click **Next** .... `Enter`

   OR

   Click **Back** .... `Alt`+`B`
4. Make additional changes as desired.
5. Click **Finish** .... `Alt`+`F`

MOVE OR REMOVE FIELDS ON A PIVOTTABLE

1. In PivotTable, drag field button onto desired area in or off PivotTable.
   - ✓ Pointer indicates the result of the move as follows:
2. Move field to column ....
3. Move field to row ....
4. Move field to page ....
5. Remove field from PivotTable ....

| **Exercise** | ■ **Consolidate Data** ■ **Create a Consolidation Table** |
| **87** | |

NOTES

Consolidate Data

■ Another way to handle data is to consolidate it. Database lists and/or multiple worksheets can be consolidated to condense and summarize the data from one or more source ranges into a consolidation table. The source ranges can be on one worksheet, several worksheets in the same workbook, or in different workbooks.

■ You can use the consolidation feature to summarize data from several database lists. For example, you may have a separate database for each branch that can be summarized with a consolidation table. As long as the data items have the same labels, you can select the source ranges and summarize the data. This is called a **consolidation by category**.

■ You can also use the consolidation feature to summarize data from several non-database worksheets that are identical in layout and have data from different departments. For example, a template may be completed by each department for an expense analysis that can then be summarized on a consolidation table. This is called a **consolidation by position**.

Consolidate Dialog Box

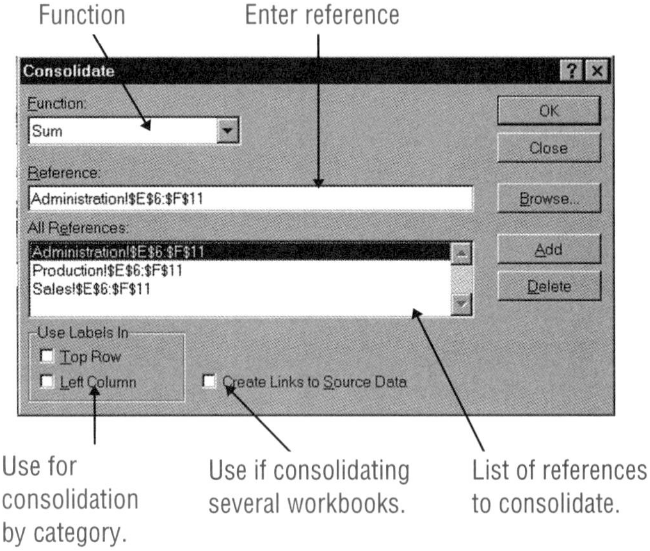

Create a Consolidation Table

■ To create a consolidation table, place the cursor in the top left cell of the consolidation table range. Select **Data, Consolidate** and the Consolidate dialog box will display. As shown in the illustration above, you can select the **Function** and the **Reference** to be used. The illustration above shows the same range on three departmental worksheets being combined. After each source range is selected, the Add button is clicked and the range moves into the All References box. Note that links to the source data may be selected that will update the consolidation table if the source data changes. This feature cannot be used if the data is all in one workbook. The label selections are used for consolidation by category consolidations.

In this exercise, Pringle Publishers, Inc. would like to consolidate expense analysis data from the production, sales, and administration departments into a consolidated expense report.

EXERCISE DIRECTIONS

1. Insert one sheet and then group Sheets 1-4. Create the template as shown on the next page or open 💾 **87EXPENSES**.

2. Ungroup sheets and select Sheet1. Rename Sheet1; name it Production.

3. Modify the subtitle to read:

   Expense Analysis-Production

4. Enter the data below:

1997 Actual	1998 Estimate
72,956.00	83,500.00
8,950.00	10,150.00
3,865.00	4,400.00
1,751.00	2,000.00
950.00	1,020.00

5. Rename the next two sheets Sales and Administration.

6. Modify the subtitles to reflect each department.

7. Enter the data below on the Sales sheet and on the Administration sheet:

Sales 1997 Actual	1998 Estimate	Administration 1997 Actual	1988 Estimate
86,457.00	99,500.00	121,670.00	125,500.00
10,569.00	12,100.00	14,483.00	15,300.00
4,586.00	5,200.00	6,448.00	6,600.00
2,145.00	2,400.00	2,920.00	3,000.00
1,549.00	1,700.00	1,532.00	1,750.00

8. Group the Production, Sales, and Administration sheets and total the two columns.

9. On Sheet4, change the subtitle to:

   Consolidated Expense Analysis

10. Rename the sheet Consolidated Analysis.

11. Consolidate the data from the department sheets onto the consolidation table.
    a. Place cursor at E6 on the Consolidated Analysis sheet.
    b. Click Data, Consolidate.
    c. Sum is the default, do not change the function.
    d. Click the Reference: box. Select the Production sheet and the range with numeric data (E6:F10).
    e. Click Add.
    f. Repeat the last two steps for the Sales and Administration sheets.
    g. Click OK.

12. Print a copy of the workbook.

13. Save and close the workbook; name it **EXPENSES**.

	A	B	C	D	E	F
1	PRINGLE PUBLISHERS, INC.					
2	Expense Analysis-Production					
3						
4	Expenses				1997 Actual	1998 Estimate
5	Number	Account				
6	510	Salaries				
7	520	Employer Taxes				
8	530	Benefits Plan				
9	580	Office Supplies				
10	590	Telecommunications				
11	Total					

KEYSTROKES

CONSOLIDATE DATA—BY POSITION

Consolidate by position when source data is in the same order and uses identical category labels.

1. If data is in separate workbooks, open and arrange workbooks.

2. Make sure data to consolidate is arranged in the same order.

3. Select destination worksheet.

4. Select range to receive consolidated data.

5. Click **Data** menu .... `Alt`+`D`

6. Click **Consolidate** .... `N`

7. Click **Function** and select summary function .... `F`

8. Click **Reference:** and select (from worksheet) or type source area reference .... `R`

9. Click **Add** .... `Alt`+`A`
   ✓ *Reference is added to All References list.*

10. Repeat steps 7 and 8 for each source reference to add.

   To create a link to source data:

   Select **Create links to source data** .... `S`
   ✓ *You cannot link the data if the destination range is on the same worksheet as the source data.*

11. Click **OK** .... `Enter`

NEXT EXERCISE

■ **Summary**

Exercise 88

Anthony Jordan, a friend of yours, has asked you to assist him in organizing a section of his checkbook. You will create a database list that will make it easier for Anthony to prepare his taxes and keep track of his expenditures.

EXERCISE DIRECTIONS

1. Create the worksheet on the following page, or open 📁 **88CKBK**.

2. Do the following:
   a. Set column B to 20, column E to 15, and column F to 11.
   b. Use Fill, Series on the Edit menu to enter the check numbers, then center these values.
   c. Center all column titles and data in columns A, C, and F.

3. Sort the database so the FOR entries are in alphabetical order and the date of the checks are in order within each category.

4. Create a database range name.

5. Insert five rows above the worksheet to use for criteria rows.

6. Below the database enter the following title:

   SUMMARY OF EXPENSES

7. Enter the following pairs of row labels, in column B, with a blank line between each pair:

   Total expenses
   Number of checks written
   Total non-deductible expenses

Number of non-deductible checks
Total deductible expenses
Number of deductible checks

8. Calculate the value referred to by each label and place the result in column D of that row. Use the blank rows at the top for criteria rows.

9. Use advanced filter criteria to create a result list of the deductible expense checks.
   • Place the table three rows below the summary labels.
   • Enter the following heading: DEDUCTIBLE EXPENSES

10. Using advanced filter criteria and a new set of criteria rows at the top of the worksheet, create a result list that will list the payments made for telephone as well as heat and light.
    • Place this table five rows below the previous table.
    • Enter the following heading: UTILITY EXPENSES

11. Print a copy of the entire worksheet to fit on one page.

12. Re-sort the database data so the checks are in check number order.

13. Save and close the file; name it **CKBK**.

344

	A	B	C	D	E	F
1			Anthony Jordan			
2			Check Register			
3						
4	NUMBER	PAYEE	DATE	AMOUNT	FOR	DEDUCTIBLE
5	235	Merry Mortgage Co.	10/01/97	553.65	mortgage	N
6	236	FoodShop Grocery	10/05/97	186.65	groceries	N
7		LA Fitness Center	10/07/97	45.50	entertainment	N
8		Sally Gregory	10/10/97	25.00	gift	N
9		Dr. Jane Friend	10/15/97	75.00	medical	Y
10		Cancer Care	10/17/97	55.00	donation	Y
11		Glow Utility Co.	10/20/97	103.86	heat and light	N
12		Mr. and Mrs. J. Soto	10/20/97	100.00	gift	N
13		West Telephone Co.	10/29/97	95.43	telephone	N
14		Merry Mortgage Co.	11/01/97	553.65	mortgage	N
15		LA Fitness Center	11/07/97	45.50	entertainment	N
16		Dr. William Keene	11/08/97	140.00	medical	Y
17		FoodShop Grocery	11/12/97	192.45	groceries	N
18		Bitex Computer Inst.	11/15/97	850.00	tuition	Y
19		Jason Park Township	11/18/97	475.98	taxes	Y
20		Glow Utility Co.	11/21/97	121.98	heat and light	N
21		Homeless Shelter	11/28/97	100.00	donation	Y
22		Merry Mortgage Co.	12/01/97	553.65	mortgage	N
23		West Telephone Co.	12/05/97	129.87	telephone	N
24	▼	LA Fitness Center	12/07/97	45.50	entertainment	N

Exercise

89

■ Summary

The Royale Auto Sales dealership needs to organize their transaction data to plan for bonuses, reorders, and potential profits. You have been asked to prepare a database list so that Mr. Kingsley, the manager of the dealership, can easily get this and other information.

EXERCISE DIRECTIONS

1. Create the database shown on the following page, or open 💾 **89ROYALE**.
   - ✓ *The transactions are coded: S for Sold, L for Leased.*
   a. Set columns C and E to 14.
   b. Left-align column A data.
   c. Center column E entries.
   d. Format the price data with commas and no decimal places.

2. Sort the data so the salespeople and the items they sold are listed in alphabetical order.

3. Name the database range and insert 5 rows above the worksheet for criteria rows.

4. Use Advanced Filter to create a result list of only the cars that were sold.
   a. Place the table four rows below the existing data.
   b. Enter an appropriate heading for this table.
   c. Clear the TRANSACTIONS field from the table.
   d. Enter the row label TOTAL below this listing.
   e. Calculate the total value of cars sold below the PRICE column.

5. Use Advanced Filter to create a result list of the cars that were leased.
   a. Place the table four rows below the existing data listing.
   b. Enter an appropriate heading for this table.
   c. Clear the TRANSACTION field from the table.
   d. Enter the row label NUMBER OF LEASES below this listing.
   e. Calculate the count of cars leased and place this value to the right of the NUMBER OF LEASES label.

6. Use filters to answer the following questions:
   - ❷ How many cars were sold by Jim?
   - ❷ How many Tigers were leased?
   - ❷ How many Tigers were sold?
   - ❷ How many Road Runners were sold in December?
   - ❷ How many Panthers were sold in December?

7. Use Advanced Filter to create a result list of all the transactions involving the two models of the TIGER.
   a. Place the table four rows below the existing data listing.
   b. Enter an appropriate heading for this table.

8. Enter the following summary labels in an available area of the worksheet, and calculate the results using database (list) functions or by using summary totals:

   SALES SUMMARY–RON
   Total $ Sales
   Average Sale Price
   Number of Sales
   Highest Sale Price
   Lowest Sale Price

9. Format money values for commas and no decimal places.

10. Re-sort the file so that all items are in chronological order.

11. Print a copy of the worksheet to fit on one page.

12. On a new sheet, create a PivotTable to summarize the data as follows:

    Page: AGENT
    Row: ITEM
    Data: Sum of PRICE

13. Format the data for commas.

14. Use the PivotTable toolbar to Show Pages and create a page for each agent.

15. Rename Sheet2; name it Summary.

16. Print a copy of the PivotTable.

17. Save and close the file; name it **ROYALE**.
    OPTIONAL: Add enhancements as desired.

	A	B	C	D	E
1			ROYALE AUTO SALES		
2			TRANSACTIONS DATABASE		
3					
4	DATE	AGENT	ITEM	PRICE	TRANSACTIONS
5	11/04/97	JAIME	BARACUDA	17,689	S
6	12/22/97	JAIME	PANTHER	15,345	S
7	11/13/97	JAIME	TIGER	22,698	L
8	11/28/97	JAIME	TIGER	22,435	L
9	11/08/97	JIM	BARACUDA	17,565	L
10	12/04/97	JIM	PANTHER	15,999	S
11	11/04/97	JIM	TIGER	21,760	L
12	12/12/97	JIM	TIGER ZX	26,540	L
13	11/24/97	KAREN	BARACUDA	17,986	S
14	12/05/97	KAREN	BARACUDA	17,476	L
15	12/15/97	KAREN	ROAD RUNNER	13,765	S
16	12/29/97	KAREN	TIGER ZX	25,476	L
17	11/07/97	PAT	PANTHER	15,430	L
18	11/18/97	PAT	ROAD RUNNER	13,675	L
19	12/08/97	PAT	ROAD RUNNER	13,999	S
20	11/04/97	PAT	TIGER	22,550	S
21	12/18/97	RON	BARACUDA	17,999	L
22	11/10/97	RON	PANTHER	15,765	S
23	11/04/97	RON	ROAD RUNNER	13,545	S
24	11/22/97	RON	TIGER ZX	25,489	S

NEXT LESSON

Excel

LESSON 11

MACRO BASICS AND HYPERLINKS

Exercises 90-93

- Create, Name, Record, and Run Simple Macros
- Stop Recording Toolbar
- Delete Macros
- Open Files Containing Macros
- Visual Basic
- Edit a Macro
- Assign Macro to a Graphic Control
- Select a Macro Button without Running the Macro
- Hyperlinks
- Hyperlinks to the Internet

Exercise

90

- **Create, Name, Record, and Run Simple Macros**
- **Stop Recording Toolbar** ■ **Delete Macros**

NOTES

Create, Name, Record, and Run Simple Macros

- A **macro** is a series of actions used to accomplish a task quickly and efficiently. The actions are recorded and then stored for reuse at a later time. Macros provide a way to automate a set of instructions that you need to perform often, such as the entry of commands, formats, formulas and/or labels. An entire list of commands can then be performed with one mouse click or several keystrokes. For example, you can write a macro to create your business heading.

- Recording a macro involves the following steps:

  - Plan the keystrokes or commands needed to complete the task.

  - Select the cell where the recording will begin.

  - Decide if the macro should use relative references.   Select this option if you want the macro to be carried out anywhere on the worksheet in relation to the previously selected cell. Deselect it if the macro should always act on the specific cells in which the macro was recorded.

  - Click **Tools**, **Macro**, **Record New Macro**. When the record macro dialog box appears do the following:

    - Assign a **Macro name**.
    - Assign a **Shortcut key** for playing back the macro.
    - Specify a location to **Store macro in** (either in the current workbook or the Personal Macro Workbook).
    - Provide a **Description** (optional) of the task the macro will perform.
    - Click OK.

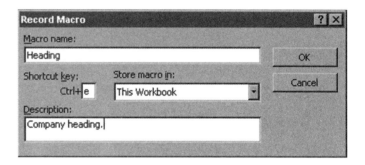

  - Perform the steps to complete the task and/or type data to record when the **Ready Recording** message is on the status bar.

  - Stop the macro when you are done, by clicking **Tools**, **Macro**, **Stop Recording** or by clicking the Stop Recording button on the Stop Recording toolbar.

- When you record a macro, it is stored in a Visual Basic module attached to the location you specify. Visual Basic is the programming language Excel uses for macros. Excel can run any macro contained in any open workbook.

- As you will note in the Record New Macro dialog box above, you can select the Store macro in: box, which displays the following selections for macro storage:

  - **Personal Macro Workbook**—stores macros in a *hidden* workbook that is always open. Use this option to store macros you want available when working in Excel with all workbooks. You can use the **Unhide** command on the Window menu to view the hidden Personal Macro workbook.

- **This Workbook**—stores macros in the current workbook. Use this option if the macro applies to tasks you will do only on the current workbook.

- **New Workbook**—stores macros on a new or specified workbook. Use this option if you will sometimes apply the macro to tasks in other jobs. You will have to open the workbook containing the macro before running it.

■ When creating a macro, you should describe the macro in the space provided so that you (or another user) can easily identify its purpose at a later time.

■ When you play back your macro recording or run a macro, Excel carries out the instructions in the macro program. Once a macro has been created and named, you can run (invoke) the macro by completing one of the following procedures:

- Press the shortcut key, if you assigned one.

- Select Tools, Macro, Macros, or press Alt + F8, and then select the macro from the list.

Stop Recording Toolbar

■ As previously discussed, you can stop recording a macro by using the menu, or by using the Stop Recording toolbar which has a Stop Recording button. This toolbar automatically displays when you are recording a macro or can be displayed at anytime by selecting **Stop Recording** from on

the View, Toolbars menu, in the Customize section.

■ The toolbar, illustrated below, contains the Stop Recording button and the Relative Reference button.

■ The Relative Reference button may be clicked to enable recording with relative cell references. This is useful so that your macro will work in any location. If the Relative Reference button is indented or sunken, as illustrated above, relative recording is activated. It will remain in this position until it is disabled.

Delete Macros

■ If you no longer need a macro, or wish to record it again, you can delete it. To delete a macro, click Tools, Macro, Macros, then select the macro and click Delete. When you delete a macro, Excel deletes the lines in the module.

■ If you use the Personal notebook to store macros, you will need to unhide it to view or delete a macro.

In this exercise, you will create a vendor list for Gourmet Depot. Since this list will be updated with new names frequently, certain tasks can be automated using macro commands.

EXERCISE DIRECTIONS

1. Create the partial worksheet as shown on the right, or open 🖫 **90LIST**.

2. Adjust column widths as necessary.

3. To create a macro for the company heading, place the cursor in A1 and use the information provided below:

   a. Click <u>T</u>ools, <u>M</u>acro, <u>R</u>ecord New Macro and set:

Macro name:	Heading
Description:	Company heading
Shortcut Key:	Ctrl + E (suggested)
Store in:	This Workbook

   b. Click OK button.

   c. Enable Relative Reference recording by clicking the button on the Stop Recording toolbar.
   The button should appear three-dimensional and indented.

   d. Record the following steps:
   - Type heading "Gourmet Depot" (use upper and lower case) in current cell.
   - Format for Bold, 14 point, Century Gothic font.
   - Center across columns A1:F1.
   - Highlight A2:F2 and format the cells for a heavy line across the bottom of the cells.

   e. Stop recording by clicking the Stop Recording button on the Stop Recording toolbar.

4. To test and run the macro, switch to Sheet2, place the cursor in cell A1 and press Ctrl+E.

   ✓ *The heading should appear on Sheet2. The width of the heading may vary since there are no columns of data. If there is an error, you can delete the macro using the Tools, Macro dialog box and then record it again. You will learn how to edit a macro in the next exercise.*

5. To run the macro from the Tools menu, switch to Sheet3, cell A1, and select Heading from the bottom of the Tools menu.

6. To create a macro for credit limit format, place the cursor on the first CREDIT LIMIT number and use the information provided below:

   a. Relative Reference should be enabled on the Stop Recording toolbar.

   b. Record a new macro as follows:

Macro name:	Limit
Description:	Format credit limit for commas, currency, and no decimals.

Shortcut Key:	Ctrl + L (suggested)
Store in:	This Workbook

   c. Record formatting for currency, commas, and no decimals. (Toolbar buttons can be used.)

   d. Stop recording.

7. To test the macro, highlight the remainder of the credit limit numbers, and press Ctrl+L.

8. Add the following data to the list using AutoComplete to enter the product:

COMPANY	LAST	FIRST	TELEPHONE	PRODUCT	CREDIT LIMIT
China Tea	Wong	Samuel	212-555-2376	Coffee/Tea	5000
Organics, Inc.	Aloe	Sally	908-555-9812	Produce	6000

9. Use the Limit macro (Ctrl+L) to format the credit limit data.

10. To create a macro to print the list in compressed format with gridlines, use the information provided below:

    a. Relative Reference should be enabled on the Stop Recording toolbar.

    b. Record a new macro as follows:

Macro name:	Printsmall
Description:	Prints list with gridlines to fit in daily calendar.
Store in:	This Workbook

    c. Record page setup commands for 75% scaling and gridlines. Record print command.

    d. Stop recording.

    ✓ *To test the macro, you must be connected to a printer.*

11. To check options set for macros:

    a. Select Tools, Macro, Macros.
    b. Select the Limit macro.
    c. Click Options.
    d. Click OK.
    e. Close the Macro dialog box

12. Rename Sheet1; name it Vendor List.

13. Save and close the workbook file; name it **LIST**.

	A	B	C	D	E	F
3	VENDORS					
4						
5	COMPANY	LAST	FIRST	TELEPHONE	PRODUCT	CREDIT LIMIT
6	Merlin Products	Florham	Marie	201-555-6598	Specialty	5000
7	TRG Provisions	Bowman	Bill	212-555-6589	Meat/Poultry	9000
8	Coffee Depot	Roast	Sam	212-555-5487	Coffee/Tea	5000
9	Produce Central	Weimer	Carol	617-555-7687	Produce	7000
10	Penzina Candy	Trent	David	908-555-2376	Confections	5000
11	Golly Farms	King	Peter	201-555-1242	Meat/Poultry	10000

KEYSTROKES

DISPLAY STOP RECORDING TOOLBAR

1. Click **View** menu .... `Alt`+`V`
2. Click **Toolbars**.............................. `T`
3. Click **Customize** .... `C`
4. Select **Stop Recording** toolbar...... `↖↘`
5. Click **Close**................................. `Enter`

RECORD A MACRO

1. If necessary, mark position for recording macro (*see below*).
2. Click **Tools** menu .... `Alt`+`T`
3. Click **Macro**................................... `M`
4. Click **Record new macro** .... `R`
5. Click **Macro Name** text box.... `Alt`+`M`
6. Type macro name.
   ✓ *A macro name cannot contain spaces.*
7. Click **Description**: .... `Alt`+`D`
8. Type macro description.
9. To assign a shortcut key:
   a. Select **Shortcut key** .... `Alt`+`K`
   b. Click in **Ctrl** + box..................... `Tab`
   c. Type shortcut letter.
   ✓ *If letter is already in use, Excel will notify you.*

10. To specify where macro will be stored:
    a. Select
       Store macro in box........... `Alt`+`I`
    b. Select a location:
       Personal Macro Workbook....... `↖↘`
       OR
       New Workbook...................... `↖↘`
       OR
       This Workbook...................... `↖↘`
11. Click **OK**.................................... `Enter`
12. To set recording references to relative or absolute:
    Select or deselect **Relative Reference** button on the Stop Recording toolbar .... `▦`
13. Execute commands to record.
14. Click **Stop Macro** button................ `▪` to end recording.

RUN A MACRO

1. Press assigned
   shortcut key .... `Ctrl`+*letter*
   OR
   a. Click **Tools** menu .... `Alt`+`T`
   b. Click **Macro** .... `M`
   c. Click **Macros** .... `M`
   d. Select macro
      in **Macro**
      Name List ...... `Alt`+`M`+`Tab`, `↖↘`
   e. Click **Run**.

DELETE A MACRO

   ✓ *If macro is stored in the Personal Macro Workbook.*

1. Click **Window** menu .... `Alt`+`W`
2. Click **Unhide** .... `U`
3. Click **Tools** menu .... `Alt`+`T`
4. Click **Macro**................................... `M`
5. Click **Macros**................................. `M`
6. Select Macro in **Macro Name** list.
7. Click **Delete** .... `Alt`+`D`

CHANGE OPTIONS FOR EXISTING MACRO

1. Click **Tools** menu .... `Alt`+`T`
2. Click **Macro**................................... `M`
3. Click **Macros**................................. `M`
4. Select Macro in **Macro Name** list.
5. Click **Options**........................ `Alt`+`O`
6. Click **Shortcut key** .... `Alt`+`K`
7. Change Key.
8. Click **Description** .... `Alt`+`D`
9. Type Description.
10. Click **OK**.................................... `Enter`

Exercise 91

- Open File Containing Macros ■ Visual Basic ■ Edit a Macro
- Assign Macro to a Graphic Control

NOTES

Open File Containing Macros

- If Macro virus protection has been enabled for your system, you will get a warning message when you open a workbook that contains a macro. This check does not determine whether the macro is a virus, just that a macro is present. If the workbook is from an uncertain source, click the **Disable Macros** button, otherwise click **Enable Macros** to allow macros to work. Note the illustration of the warning screen below:

Visual Basic

- Excel records your actions in a language called **Visual Basic** in modules that are attached to the worksheet you specified. If you specified the Personal Macro Workbook as the storage location, the macros are available when you work in all Excel workbooks. Excel provides online help about the Visual Basic macro language by selecting **Help**, **Contents and Index,** and Visual Basic Help.

Edit Macros

- You can edit the macro commands Excel records if you know how to write the Visual Basic Language. For example, when Excel records your command to turn gridlines off, it writes the following line:

ActiveWindow.DisplayGridlines = False

You can edit this line to make the macro turn gridlines on or off depending upon the current state of the active window. To do this you would change the line to read:

ActiveWindow.DisplayGridlines = Not ActiveWindow.DisplayGridlines

- The **Not** operator tells Excel to change the Display Gridlines property to its opposite state, which acts as a toggle when the macro is invoked.

- To edit a macro, click Tools, Macro, Macros (or click Alt+F8), select the desired macro and click Edit. This brings you into Visual Basic Editor mode where you can read and edit the visual basic code in the macro. Return to Excel by clicking the File, Close and Return to Microsoft Excel commands.

Assign Macro to a Graphic Control

- In the previous exercise, macros were assigned to shortcut keys or accessed from the bottom of the Tools menu.

- In addition, you can assign a macro to a graphic button or a control that you place in the worksheet. (Note the illustration of the labeled button in the worksheet on the right.) The mouse cursor changes to a pointing hand when you click a graphic control and the macro assigned to the button is activated.

- To create the button, you will need to use the Forms toolbar. Display the Forms toolbar (click View, Toolbars, Forms) and then select the **Button** button ▢. Click and drag within the worksheet to create the button. After the button is placed on the worksheet, the Assign Macro dialog box displays, as illustrated on the right. You can then select macro to assign to that button. The "Button" text can be edited to include the macro name.

- The macro button can be moved, sized and edited as you would any object. You can right-click the object and use the shortcut menu to edit or assign macros to the button.

- You can use the Select Object tool ▷ available on the Drawing toolbar to select a macro button without executing the macro.

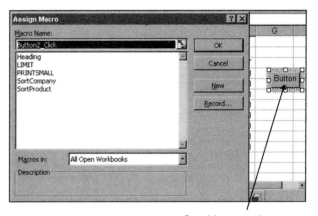

Graphic control

In this exercise, you will update the LIST worksheet for Gourmet Depot. You will create macros to automate several tasks and assign the new macros to graphic buttons.

EXERCISE DIRECTIONS

1. Open 🗄 **LIST** or 🖫 **91LIST**.
   - ✓ *If you have enabled virus protection, click Enable Macros to open the file with macros enabled.*

2. Name the database list: DATABASE.

3. Set Options name and then record two macros to perform the tasks indicated below:
   a. Options for each macro:
      - Disable Relative Reference on the Stop Recording toolbar.
      - Do not assign macros to a shortcut key—you will assign macros to graphic buttons later on.
      - Set option to store macros in the current workbook.
      - Type a brief description that describes the task each macro will perform.

b. Macro names and tasks:

• Macro name	Task Description
SortCompany	Sorts list by company, turns on print preview, and zooms in to view output.
SortProduct	Sorts list by product, turns on print preview, and zooms in to view output.

4. Display the Form toolbar.

5. Use the Button icon to create two graphic buttons and assign one to the SortCompany Macro and the other to the SortProduct Macro.

6. Label the graphic buttons as indicated in Illustration A on the following page and adjust button size as necessary.

7. Add the two new vendors from Illustration B to the list.

8. Format the credit limit figures using the Limit macro shortcut keys, Ctrl+L.

9. Place the cursor on the list and test the new macro button for SortProduct.

10. Do not print the worksheet. Close the Preview window.

11. Test the SortCompany button, but do not print the worksheet. Close the Preview window.

12. Record and name a macro to perform the task indicated below:
    a. Options:
       - Set no options since a button will be created.
       - Store the macro in this workbook.
    b. Macro Name and task:

Macro name	Description
Gridlines	Turns worksheet gridlines off.

    HINT: Use the Tools, Options menu to remove worksheet gridlines.

13. Create and label a graphic button for the Gridlines macro. Right-click the graphic button and view the shortcut menu.

14. Edit the Gridlines macro as follows:
    a. Click Tools, Macro, Macros.
    b. Select the Gridlines macro.
    c. Click Edit. *This brings you into Visual Basic Editor.*
    d. In the main window to the right, edit the Gridlines macro so that it reads:
       `ActiveWindow.DisplayGridlines = Not ActiveWindow.DisplayGridlines`
       ✓ *The line should appear on one line. Do not include line breaks in the module. There is a space after the word "Not" and before and after the equals sign.*
    e. Click File.
    f. Click Close and Return to Microsoft Excel.

15. Test the Gridlines macro button. It should turn gridlines on or off each time you click it.

16. Create and label a graphic button for the PrintSmall macro. Name it Print Small.

17. Use the Print Small button to print the worksheet in compressed format with gridlines.

18. Save and close the file; name it **LIST**.

Illustration A

	A	B	C	D	E	F	G	H
1			Gourmet Depot					
2								
3	VENDORS							
4								
5	COMPANY	LAST	FIRST	TELEPHONE	PRODUCT	CREDIT LIMIT	Sort Company	
6	China Tea	Wong	Samuel	212-555-2376	Coffee/Tea	$ 5,000		
7	Coffee Depot	Roast	Sam	212-555-5487	Coffee/Tea	$ 5,000		
8	Golly Farms	King	Peter	201-555-1242	Meat/Poultry	$ 10,000	Sort Product	
9	Merlin Products	Florham	Marie	201-555-6598	Specialty	$ 5,000		
10	Organics, Inc.	Aloe	Sally	908-555-9812	Produce	$ 6,000		
11	Penzina Candy	Trent	David	908-555-2376	Confections	$ 5,000	Gridlines	
12	Produce Central	Weimer	Carol	617-555-7687	Produce	$ 7,000		
13	TRG Provisions	Bowman	Bill	212-555-6589	Meat/Poultry	$ 9,000		
14							Print Small	
15								
16								

Illustration B

COMPANY	LAST	FIRST	TELEPHONE	PRODUCT	CREDIT LIMIT
Kate's Cookies	Krumble	Kate	201-555-5923	Confections	1000
Globe Trading	Mariner	Tug	212-555-1200	Specialty	5000

KEYSTROKES

DISPLAY FORM TOOLBAR

1. Click **View** menu .... `Alt`+`V`
2. Click **Toolbars** .... `T`
3. Click **Forms** .... `↓`

ASSIGN MACRO TO A GRAPHIC BUTTON

1. Click **Button** button .... `□`
   on Form toolbar.
   Pointer becomes a +.
2. Position pointer at any corner of button.
   Pointer becomes a ↖.
3. Drag button outline to desired size.
4. Select macro .... `Tab`, `↑↓`
   in **Macro Name** list.
5. Click **OK** .... `Enter`
6. Click text in button.
7. Edit text as desired.
8. Click anywhere in worksheet.
   ✓ *If you need to change the button text, size, or position, you need to select the button without running the macro (see below).*

SELECT A MACRO BUTTON WITHOUT RUNNING THE MACRO

1. Click **Drawing** button .... `↺`
   on Standard toolbar to display Drawing toolbar.
2. Click **Select Objects** button .... `↳`
   to activate it.
3. Click any part of button.
   Excel marks button with a selection outline and handles.
4. Click in button to edit the button text.
   ✓ *When you have finished editing the button, be sure to click the **Select Objects** button again to deactivate it. This will let you work with data in cells and allow you to run a macro assigned to the button.*

EDIT A MACRO

1. Click **Tools** menu .... `Alt`+`T`
2. Click **Macro** .... `M`
3. Click **Macros** .... `M`
   Select macro .... `Tab`, `↑↓`
   in **Macro Name** list.
4. Click **Edit** .... `Alt`+`E`
   This brings you into the Visual Basic Editor.
5. Edit macro commands as desired.
   ✓ *Appendix C contains additional information about the Visual Basic Macro language.*
6. Click **File** .... `Alt`+`F`
7. Click **Close and Return to Microsoft Excel** .... `C`

Exercise

92

■ Hyperlinks ■ Create Hyperlinks in Excel
■ Hyperlink to the Internet

NOTES

Hyperlinks

- A **hyperlink** is a "hot spot," or shortcut, that allows you to jump to another location. For example, by clicking on a hyperlink, you can jump to another worksheet or range within the current workbook, another file on your hard drive or network, or to an Internet address.

  ✓ NOTE: You do not have to be on the Internet to use hyperlinks.

- You can create a hyperlink from cell text or from graphic objects such as pictures. A hyperlink is a field that includes the path to the file and/or range, and may include switch codes for options during the linking process. When hyperlinks are text based, they are represented by display text which is usually blue and underlined.   When you rest the pointer over a hyperlink, the pointer changes to a hand 🖑. When you return to the workbook after visiting the hyperlink location, the hyperlink text color changes to purple to indicate that you have already visited the link.

Create Hyperlinks in Excel

- To create a hyperlink to another location in Excel, first create the text or graphic that will be used to represent the hyperlink. You can create a hyperlink by selecting the cell that contains the text or the graphic object and clicking the Insert

  Hyperlink button 📖 on the Standard toolbar or clicking **Insert, Hyperlink**. The Insert Hyperlink dialog box, illustrated on the right, appears. Enter the file or URL path (Internet address) in the **Link to file or URL** text box. Instead of typing the path, you can use the Browse button to search for the file. The file that you select must be closed and saved.

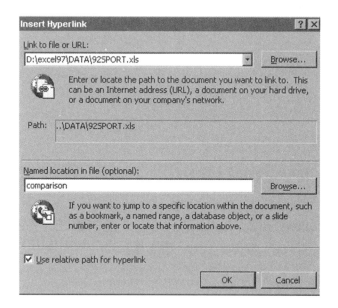

- You can also enter a named range or specific location in the file in the **Named location in file** box. If you wish to link a chart or specific data from a worksheet with several sheets, you should name the ranges you wish to use for hyperlink data. When you click the Browse button, the Browse Excel Workbook dialog box appears. Clicking the Sheet name or Defined name selections will display the sheet names or named ranges in the file selected.

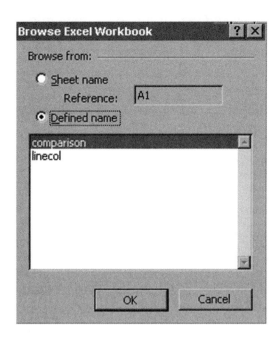

• A hyperlink can also be created by copying the destination data and using the Edit, Paste As Hyperlink commands or by dragging and dropping the destination data.

■ Editing a hyperlink can present a problem since clicking on it automatically jumps you to the location specified. To edit a hyperlink, *right-click* on the hyperlink text or object, display the shortcut menu, and select Hyperlink, Select Hyperlink. Copy, edit, and other features can be initiated from the Hyperlink menu as illustrated on the right. The default blue color and format of the hyperlink can be changed by clicking on Select Hyperlink and using the Format, Cells dialog box.

Hyperlink to the Internet

■ If you are connected to the Internet, you can click on hyperlinks that connect you to Internet addresses and automatically take you to the linked location. If you are not currently signed onto the Internet, clicking on an Internet link should take you to your Internet service provider's sign-on screen, and then to the specified location once you are on the Internet. When you enter an Internet address in an Excel worksheet, it automatically formats it as a hyperlink. By default, text that contains a hyperlink is blue and underlined. The mouse pointer becomes a hand ☝ and the Internet address displays in a box when you point to the hyperlink.

✓ Note: Connecting to the Internet through Excel 97 will be discussed further in Lesson 12.

> *In this exercise, Sport Togs, Inc. is preparing its annual Income Statement. They would like to include hyperlinks to another workbook that includes the breakdown of the Sales data and projected sales for 1999.*

EXERCISE DIRECTIONS

1. Create the worksheet as illustrated on the right, or open ⌨**92TOGS**.
   a. Place an asterisk in F6, next to the Sales Income value.
   b. Use the indent alignment feature to enter the note under the Income Statement, as illustrated.
   c. Enter single lines under the following values: Direct Variable Costs, Less: Ending Inventory, Cost of Goods Sold, Selling, and Total Expenses.
   d. Enter double lines under Net Profit.

2. Enter formulas to find the following information and to complete the worksheet:
   - Find: Total Costs
     Hint: Beginning Inventory+Direct Materials+Direct Labor+Direct Variable Costs
   - Cost of Goods Sold
     Hint: Total Costs-Ending Inventory
   - Gross Profit
     Hint: Sales Income-Cost of Goods Sold
   - Total Expenses
   - Net Profit
     Hint: Gross Profit-Expenses

3. Enter the hyperlink text display data as illustrated:

   Production Analysis   Production Chart
   ✓ *The text will not be underlined until the hyperlink is inserted.*

4. Save the file; name it **TOGS**.

5. Open ⌨**SPORTS** or ⌨**92SPORTS**.

6. On the Data sheet, select the worksheet data and name the range; name it COMPARISON.

7. On the Embedded Charts sheet, select the combination line-column chart and copy it to Sheet3.

8. Select Sheet3 and name the range; name it LINCOL.

9. Save and close the file; name it **SPORTS**.

10. In the **TOGS** document, go to the first hyperlink location, Production Analysis.

11. Insert a hyperlink to the **SPORTS** worksheet as follows:
    a. Click Insert.
    b. Click Hyperlink.
    c. Enter 92SPORTS in the Link to File box or Browse to locate the file on the appropriate drive.
    d. Click Browse in the Named location in file box.
    e. Click Defined name on the Browse Excel Workbook dialog box.
    f. Select the Comparison range.
    g. Click OK. *A blue underlined hyperlink will be created with the display text.*

12. Practice an edit to the hyperlink display text as follows:
    a. Right-click the hyperlink text.
    b. Select Hyperlink, Select Hyperlink to highlight the hyperlink text.
    c. Type: Production Data.
    d. Click on another location to stop displaying text entry.

13. Move to the second hyperlink location and insert a hyperlink for the Line-Column worksheet in the SPORTS workbook, as follows:
    a. Click the Insert Hyperlink button on the toolbar.
    b. Link to 92SPORTS.
    c. Select the Lincol defined name location.
    d. Click OK.

14. Check the hyperlinks:
    a. Click the Production Data hyperlink.
    b. The SPORTS worksheet data will display. Close the worksheet.
    c. Click the Production Chart hyperlink.
    d. The SPORTS Line-Column chart will display.
    e. Close the worksheet.

15. Close and save the file; name it **TOGS**.

	A	B	C	D	E	F	G	H
1	SPORTS TOGS, INC.							
2	INCOME STATEMENT							
3	For the Fiscal Year Ended July 1, 1998							
4								
5	Income:							
6		Sales Income			2,834,587	*		
7								
8	Cost of Goods Sold:							
9		Beginning Inventory		1,353,676				
10		Direct Materials		1,043,224				
11		Direct Labor		1,123,454				
12		Direct Variable Costs		65,876				
13		Total Costs						
14		Less: Ending Inventory		1,644,575				
15		Cost of Goods Sold						
16	Gross Profit							
17								
18	Expenses:							
19		Administrative		98,654				
20		Manufacturing		123,423				
21		Selling		342,678				
22		Total Expenses						
23								
24	Net Profit							
25								
26	* The breakdown of sales by product shows an increase for most products.							
27	The projected sales figures were calculated based on customer patterns and standing orders.							
28	Click on Production Analysis to view comparison data for 1997, 1998 and projected 1999 data,							
29	and on Production Chart to view charted data.							
30								
31	Production Analysis			Production Chart				
32								
33								
34								
35								

> Type text, then insert hyperlinks to connect to named ranges in another workbook.

KEYSTROKES

INSERT A HYPERLINK

1. Place your cursor on a graphic object, text box or, cell containing text.
2. Click **Insert** .... `Alt`+`I`
3. Click **Hyperlink** .... `I`
4. In the **Link to File or URL:** box, enter filename or URL

   OR

   Click **Browse** to locate file ...... `Alt`+`B`

5. If desired, in **Named location in the file**, ... `Alt`+`N`
   type range name, or bookmark.

   OR

   Click **Browse** .... `Alt`+`W`
   to locate location within file.

6. Click **OK** .... `Enter`

EDIT AND SELECT HYPERLINK TEXT

1. Right–click hyperlink text.
2. Click **Hyperlink** .... `Alt`+`H`
3. Click **Select Hyperlink** .... `S`
4. Type display text.

Exercise

93

■ Summary

You will create a macro in a new workbook and then apply it to other worksheets. You will create several macros on Rochelle Martling's investment analysis and attach them to buttons.

EXERCISE DIRECTIONS

1. Open a new workbook.

2. Since the purpose of this workbook is to record and store macros, delete all sheet tabs except Sheet1.

3. Save and name the workbook **MYMACS**.

4. In Sheet1, record a macro that will type your name and enter the current date and time.

   a. Set these macro options:
   - Macro name: Author
   - Description: Type name and insert date and time.
   - Store in: This Workbook
   - Shortcut key: Ctrl+A

   b. Record these commands and entries:
   - Disable the Relative References feature.
   - Use Go To command to activate cell A1.
   - Enter your full name.
   - Select cell A2.
   - Insert current date (Press Ctrl + ;).
   - Set width of column A to fit the longest entry.
   - Stop recording the macro.

5. Select the Author macro and edit the macro line that types in the date to:

   ActiveCell.FormulaR1C1 = Now()
   Close the Visual Basic Editor.

6. Clear the text in A1 and A2.

7. Place your cursor in any other cell.

8. Test the macro on Sheet1. Edit the macro, if necessary.

9. Resave the **MYMACS** file; do not close the file.

10. Open ⌨ **REDUCE** or 💾 **93REDUCE** and run the Author macro to insert your name and current date and time.

11. Open and save the file; name it **REDUCE**.

12. Open ⌨ **INVEST** or 💾 **93INVEST**.

13. Record a macro that will format data for currency with commas.

   a. Set these macro options:
   - Enable the Relative References feature.
   - Macro name: FormatVal
   - Description: Formats money values for currency.
   - Store in: This Workbook
   - Record commands.
   - Stop recording.

14. Create a macro button and assign the FormatVal macro to the button. Name the button, Format Values.

15. Use the button to format the remaining money values.

16. Record a macro to print the data sheet with 105% scaling in landscape mode without gridlines.
   - Macro name: PrintLarge
   - Description: Prints worksheet in landscape mode with 105% scaling without gridlines.
   - Store in: This Workbook
   - Record commands.
   - Stop recording.

17. Create a macro button and assign the PrintLarge macro to the button. Name the button Print Data.

18. Since **MYMACS** is still open, run the Author macro (Ctrl+A) to insert your name and current date and time.

19. Save and close the file; name it **INVEST**.

20. Close all files.

Excel

LESSON 12

SUMMARY EXERCISES

Exercises 94-100

- Internet Basics
- Use Internet Features
- Finance/Portfolio Analysis
- Accounting/Balance Sheet
- Economics/Decision Making
- Sales Marketing
- Accounting/Depreciation
- Accounting/Financial Reports

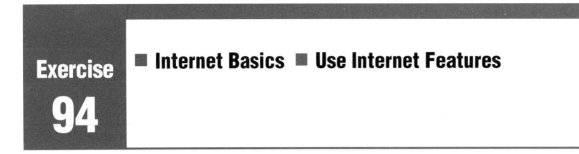

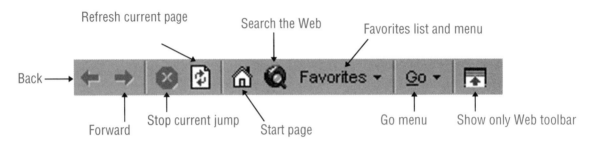

The Web Toolbar

Refresh current page

Search the Web

Favorites list and menu

Back

Forward

Stop current jump

Start page

Go menu

Show only Web toolbar

NOTES

Internet Basics

- The **Internet** is a world-wide network of computers. These computers may be located in businesses, schools, research foundations, individual's homes, etc. Those who are connected to this network can share information with each other, communicate via e-mail, and search for information.

- Unless you have direct access to the Internet through a school, businesses, organization, etc. you will need to access the Internet through the use of a **modem** and an **Internet Service Provider (ISP)**. A modem enables your computer to go through standard telephone lines to log onto a server that is maintained by your Internet Service Provider. Your ISP then connects you directly to the Internet. ISPs usually charge a standard monthly fee for limited or unlimited Internet usage. In addition, they typically provide the necessary software for logging onto their system as well as a Web browser for viewing the World Wide Web.

- The **World Wide Web (WWW)** is a service of the Internet in which pages, created by companies, individuals, schools, and government agencies around the world, are linked to each other.

- A **browser** is a graphic interface program that displays the information you retrieve from the World Wide Web in a readable format. Two of the most popular Web browsers today are Microsoft Internet Explorer and Netscape Navigator.

- **Hyperlinks** commonly found on Web pages— are text or graphic objects that link you from one location to another. When you move your cursor across a hyperlink, the cursor transforms into a hand 🖑. Clicking on an Internet hyperlink can take you to another page within the current site or to another site altogether. Text-based hyperlinks usually appear in a different color, underlined, or **both**.

- A **Uniform Resource Locator**, or URL, is a World Wide Web address. The URL system is like an enormous card catalog that lets computers that are connected to the World Wide Web find a designated site.

364

- When you enter an address on the URL line, you will frequently start the address of the site with **http** or **ftp**. Http stands for **HyperText Transfer Protocol**, which refers to the communication protocol that allows web pages to connect to one another, regardless of what type of operating system is used to display or access the files. **File Transfer Protocol (ftp)** lets you transfer files from one computer to another over a network (or across the Internet).

- When you want to locate information on the Internet, you will access a **search site**. Search sites (Yahoo!, AltaVista, Excite, etc.) are Web sites that contain catalogs of Web resources that can be searched by headings, URLs and key words. Such sites use search engines to continuously search and catalogue information available on the Web.

Use Internet Features

- The Internet provides access to countless Web sites, many of which contain information and documentation that can be used for researching a particular subject.

- Excel 97 provides easy access to the Internet through the menus and toolbar buttons. When you click the Web toolbar button 🐫 or click View, Toolbars, Web, the Web toolbar displays. Note the illustration of the toolbar on the previous page.

- On the right is an explanation of the buttons on the Web toolbar.

← →	The **Back** and **Forward** buttons move you among the pages that are stored in the recent history of your hyperlinks.
⊗	The **Stop** button interrupts a page from loading or refreshing button reloads current Web page. Use this button when a page is taking too long to load or when you decide to take a different action.
⟳	The **Refresh Current Page** button reloads the current Web page. This is convenient when a page doesn't seem to load completely or correctly.
⌂	The **Start Page** button returns you to your default start (or home) page. The current start page can be changed at anytime.
🔍	The **Search the Web** button, connects you to the main search page on the Microsoft World Wide Web site.
Favorites ▾	The **Favorites** button displays the current contents of your Microsoft Internet Explorer Favorites folder. Use the Favorites folder to store WWW addresses that you visit frequently. You can add folders and addresses using this option, even if you are off line.
Go ▾	The **Go** button opens a menu that provides additional ways to interact with Internet Explorer.
📰	The **Show Web Toolbar Only** button conceals all other toolbars. Clicking the button again redisplays the hidden toolbars.

■ The Go menu on the Web toolbar, illustrated in the table on the previous page, is used to expedite movement to specific locations on the Web. You can open Internet sites using the Open command on the Go menu. When you click Open, the Open Internet Address dialog box displays and is used to enter the http or ftp server address.

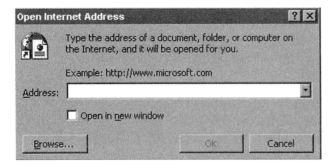

■ If you do not have a specific address and wish to search the Web for information, click Search the Web on the Go menu or click the Search the Web button on the toolbar. If you are not already connected to the Internet, you will be prompted to sign onto your Internet Service and to launch your Web browser. Once you are connected to the Internet, you will jump directly to the main search page of the Microsoft Web site. You can type the information you are seeking and begin your search.

  • You will gather information from the Internet for the rest of the exercises in this lesson. If you are connected to the Internet, use the suggested sites or select other appropriate Web sites.

  • If you are not connected to the Internet, use the CD-ROM that accompanies this book. All the Internet actions described in the exercises have been simulated on the CD. You can use the information on the CD-ROM to complete the exercises in this book.

■ If you want to use the Excel Internet Simulation for these exercises, follow the CD-ROM installation directions on page vi in the Introduction section at the beginning of this book.

To launch the simulation from your system once it has been installed:

  • On the Web toolbar, Click **Go**, then select **Open**.

  • Type **C:\DDCPUB\EX97INT.IMR** on the address line. If you installed the files to a drive other than C:, use the letter of that drive. For example, if you installed the program on the D: drive, enter D: instead of C:.

  • Click **OK** to open the simulation.

The Poseidon Import/Export Company is involved in foreign trade of food items. Since many foreign companies use the metric system for measurements, and we show both measures on our labels, your supervisor has asked you to create a record of the conversion of metric measurements to U.S. Customary Weights and Measures and vice versa.

Your supervisor would also like a price list developed for each lot of merchandise. The markup depends on the number of items in a lot. There is a 35% markup on all items except for those that we have ordered in lots of 1000 units or more, where the markup is only 30%.

Finally, on the third sheet you will use the prices and conversion rates from the Internet to determine the product prices in the currencies of our foreign trading partners. An Internet Web site will be used to find the name of the foreign currency and the current conversion rate.

EXERCISE DIRECTIONS

1. Create the worksheet as shown in Illustration A on page 368, or open 🖫 **94TRADE**.

   a. Set column widths, as necessary.

   b. Use a series for the Lot numbers.

   c. Name the lookup table range, TABLE.

   d. Enhance title rows as desired.

2. Find:

   - FACTOR

     HINT: Use a vertical lookup function to search the TABLE for the desired conversion and the associated factor. The format for a lookup formula is =VLOOKUP(search item, range to search, column position in range, FALSE).

   - PKG. WT.

     HINT: ORIGINAL PKG. WT * FACTOR

   - UNIT

     HINT: Use a vertical lookup formula to search the TABLE for the desired "CONVERT TO" associated unit.

3. Copy the heading and the first two columns of this report to Sheet2 and create the second worksheet as shown in Illustration B on page 369. Or, move to Sheet2 on 🖫**94TRADE**.

4. Enter the NUMBER of items in the lot and the PRICE per item as per the illustration.

5. Find:

   - TOTAL: The total price for the lot of merchandise.

   - MARKUP: Enter an IF statement that produces a 30% markup on lots of 1000 units or more or a 35% markup on all other lots.

   - RESALE PRICE: TOTAL+MARKUP.

6. Find the Totals for this report.

7. Use cell borders of single and double lines to enhance the reports.

8. Copy the heading and the first two columns of this report to Sheet3.

9. Create the third worksheet as shown in Illustration C on page 369. Or, move to Sheet3 in 🖫**94TRADE**.

10. Copy the PRICE data from Sheet2.

11. Use the Internet or the **Excel Internet Simulation CD-ROM** to complete the Currency Conversion chart on Sheet3. Find the names of foreign currencies and the current value of the U.S. dollar in that currency by following one of the sets of steps below:

    USING THE INTERNET

    a. Sign on to your Internet service provider.

    b. Select your Web browser.

    c. Use the Yahoo! search engine to search on the words "currency convert."
    The URL for Yahoo! Is: http://www.yahoo.com.
    You may use other search methods, if desired.

    d. View the sites that might provide currencies and conversion rates.

    e. Select a site, go to that site and then search for the currencies and conversion rates for the countries listed in the conversion table.

    OR

    USING THE EXCEL INTERNET SIMULATION

    a. Click **Go**, **Open** on the Web toolbar.

    b. Type **C:\DDCPUB\EX97INT.IMR**

    *If the Excel Internet Simulation has been installed on another drive, replace **C:** with the accurate letter representing the drive.*

c. Click **OK** to launch the simulation.

d. Select Exercise 94: Currency Conversion.

e. Click the Search button ☐ at the top of the screen.

f. At the simulated Yahoo! search site, click in the Search text box, type *Universal Currency Converter,* and click Search.

g. Follow the onscreen directions.

12. Note, copy or print the desired information.

13. Exit from your browser and disconnect from your Internet service provider, or exit the Excel Internet Simulation.

14. Enter the COUNTRY CURRENCY and FOREIGN EXCHANGE data into the worksheet that you obtained as a result of your Internet search.

15. Name the currency conversion table EXCHANGE.

16. Enter a vertical lookup formula to search EXCHANGE for the desired "CURRENCY" data.

17. Enter a vertical lookup formula to search EXCHANGE for the desired "RATE" data.

18. Find the foreign price using the US price and the foreign conversion rate.
*HINT: US price * Exchange rate.*

17. Edit the subtitle to read: PRICE CONVERSION AS OF (enter today's date).

18. Rename the worksheets as follows:
- Sheet1: LABELING RECORD
- Sheet2: PRICE LIST
- Sheet3: PRICE CONVERSION

19. Save and close the workbook file; name it **TRADE**.

20. Hide the lookup tables on the Labeling Record and the Price Conversion sheets and print a copy of the workbook.

Illustration A

POSEIDON IMPORT/EXPORT COMPANY
LABELING RECORD

LOT NO.	PRODUCT	PKG. WT.	UNIT	FACTOR	PKG. WT.	UNIT
23452	Sardines	100	grams			
23453	Fish sauce	715	grams			
23454	Olive oil	3.785	Liters			
23455	Flour	2.27	Kilograms			
23456	Rice	11.35	Kilograms			
23457	Vinegar	950	Milliliters			
23458	Coffee	16	Ounces			
23459	Tuna	6	Ounces			
23460	Fruit Juice	1	Gallons			
23461	Maple Syrup	2.5	Pints			
23462	Choc. Sauce	1.5	Quarts			

CONVERSION TABLE		
CONVERT FROM:	MULT. BY FACTOR	CONVERT TO:
Gallons	3.785	Liters
Grams	0.035	Ounces
Kilograms	2.2	Pounds
Liters	33.8	Ounces
Milliliters	0.0338	Ounces
Ounces	28.3495	Grams
Pints	0.473	Liters
Pounds	0.454	Kilograms
Quarts	0.946	Liters

Illustration B

POSEIDON IMPORT/EXPORT COMPANY
PRICE LIST

LOT NO.	PRODUCT	NUMBER	PRICE	TOTAL	MARKUP	RESALE PRICE
23452	Sardines	1440	0.35			
23453	Fish sauce	2400	1.10			
23454	Olive oil	288	5.40			
23455	Flour	500	0.95			
23456	Rice	200	3.65			
23457	Vinegar	720	1.95			
23458	Coffee	1800	0.95			
23459	Tuna	1440	0.38			
23460	Fruit Juice	288	0.96			
23461	Maple Syrup	500	2.20			
23462	Choc. Sauce	288	1.85			
TOTALS						

Illustration C

	A	B	C	D	E	F	G
1	POSEIDON IMPORT/EXPORT COMPANY						
2		PRICE CONVERSION AS OF (DATE)					
3			U.S.			CONVERSION	FOREIGN
4	LOT NO.	PRODUCT	PRICE	COUNTRY	CURRENCY	RATE	PRICE
5	23452	Sardines	0.35	Portugal			
6	23453	Fish sauce	1.10	Japan			
7	23454	Olive oil	5.40	Italy			
8	23455	Flour	0.95	Spain			
9	23456	Rice	3.65	Japan			
10	23457	Vinegar	1.95	Italy			
11	23458	Coffee	0.95	Brazil			
12	23459	Tuna	0.38	Portugal			
13	23460	Fruit Juice	0.96	Brazil			
14	23461	Maple Syrup	2.20	Korea			
15	23462	Choc. Sauce	1.85	Brazil			
16							
17							
18							
19							
20							
21			CONVERSION TABLE				
22					EXCHANGE		
23			COUNTRY	CURRENCY	RATE		
24			Brazil			Use the Internet to	
25			Italy			research foreign	
26			Japan			currency name and	
27			Korea			current exchange rate.	
28			Spain				
29			Portugal				
30			Spain				

Exercise
95

- ■ **Finance/Portfolio Analysis (Formulas, Charting, Enhancements)**
- ■ **Use Internet Financial Services**

NOTES

Finance/Portfolio Analysis, (Formulas, Charts, Enhancements)

- ■ A **portfolio** is a varied group of investments in stocks and/or bonds.

- ■ **Commission** is a fee charged for buying stock. It is added to your cost.

- ■ **Market value** is the current price of a traded security. If you compare market value to the cost of your security, you can determine your "paper" profit or loss. This is known as a paper profit or loss since you must sell the stock to actually earn the profits.

Use Internet Financial Services

- ■ The Internet provides a vast array of current financial information. All the major financial publications have Web sites that provide market data, data on specific companies, and business news. The equity market prices are updated several times each hour and reflect the actual prices for that day.

- ■ In most market quote Web sites you must search for the stock using the ticker symbol. There is usually a search procedure for the ticker symbol as well. Your service provider may have a Web site that saves the entry of your stock symbols so that all you need do is sign on to get the latest prices of your portfolio stocks. The DDC Simulation will provide stock prices, but actual current prices must be obtained from the Internet.

As an active investor in the stock market, you would like to evaluate your portfolio each month. In this exercise, you will create a portfolio analysis for October and chart your paper profits and losses. You will use the Internet to update the current unit price value for current market prices.

EXERCISE DIRECTIONS

1. Create the worksheet shown on the right, using wrapped column headings, or open 🖫 **95FOLIO**.

2. Use your name as the owner of the portfolio.

3. Set column widths as necessary.

4. Find:
   - TOTAL COST.
   - CURRENT VALUE.
   - $ PROFIT OR LOSS.
   - % PROFIT OR LOSS (based on TOTAL COST).

   - Totals of TOTAL COST, CURRENT VALUE, $ PROFIT OR LOSS columns.
   - % OF PORTFOLIO (based on total CURRENT MARKET VALUE).
   - Total of % OF PORTFOLIO column.

5. Use the Internet or the **Excel Internet Simulation CD-ROM** to determine the ticker symbols for new investments and the current market price of each investment. Follow one of the sets of steps below:

   USING THE INTERNET
   a. Sign on to your Internet service provider.

370

b. Select your Web browser.

c. Use the Excite search engine to search on the words "stock prices."
   The URL address is http://www.excite.com.
   You may use other search methods, if desired.

d. View the sites that might provide stock quotes.

e. Select Money Quick Quotes, if available.

f. Find the ticker symbols for Pfizer and Microsoft.

g. Find the current quotes for all stocks listed on the worksheet.

OR

USING THE EXCEL INTERNET SIMULATION

a. Click **Go**, **Open** on the Web toolbar.

b. Type **C:\DDCPUB\EX97INT.IMR**

   *If the Excel Internet Simulation has been installed on another drive, replace **C:** with the accurate letter representing the drive.*

c. Click **OK** to launch the simulation.

d. Select **Exercise 95: Stock Prices**.

e. Click the Search button at the top of the screen.

f. At the simulated Excite search site, click in the Search text box, type *Quick Quotes,* and click Search.

g. Follow the onscreen directions.

6. Note, copy or print the last price for each stock.

7. Exit from your browser and disconnect from your Internet service provider, or exit the Excel Internet Simulation.

8. Enter the current prices, using fraction format, into the CURRENT UNIT PRICE column of the worksheet, overwriting outdated values. *Note that the calculated values will change to reflect the current valuation.*

9. Enhance the worksheet using Autoformat and make any additional format and alignment changes.

10. Create an embedded pie chart illustrating the % OF PORTFOLIO column. Add appropriate titles and labels. Explode the pie section of the largest investment.

11. Place the chart below the worksheet and add the following text note to the left of the graph: (Enter the appropriate data to replace parenthetical explanations.) *The (Stock name representing largest portion of portfolio) investment is showing over (rounded percent of return) profit (loss, if applicable).*

12. Create an embedded 3-D column chart using stock symbols and comparing the Unit Cost and Unit Price columns. Add appropriate legends, titles and data labels.

13. Save the workbook file; name it **FOLIO**.

14. Print a copy in landscape mode.

15. Close the workbook file.

16. From the printed copy of **FOLIO**, determine the following:

   ❓ Which stock is most profitable? Least profitable?

   ❓ Which stock represents the largest percentage of the portfolio? Smallest percentage?

   ❓ What is your recommendation for future sales/purchases of your currently held stocks? (You can use the Internet to research the companies whose stock you own.)

	A	B	C	D	E	F	G	H	I	J	K	L
1					(YOUR NAME)							
2					MONTHLY PORTFOLIO ANALYSIS - OCTOBER							
3												
4	DATE BOUGHT	STOCK NAME	SYMBOL	QUANTITY	UNIT COST	COMMIS-SION	TOTAL COST	CURRENT UNIT PRICE	CURRENT VALUE	$ PROFIT OR LOSS	% PROFIT OR LOSS	% OF PORTFOLIO
5	11/7/91	Norwest Corp	NOB	500	11 1/4	0.00		46 3/4				
6	1/25/93	Phillips Petroleum	P	200	25 1/2	98.40		39 5/8				
7	12/15/93	NYNEX Corp.	NYN	300	40 3/4	0.00		44 3/8				
8	4/15/94	Colgate-Palmolive	CL	100	57 1/2	35.00		106 1/2				
9	11/23/94	Xerox Corp	XRX	150	105 3/4	127.50		59 5/8				
10	3/7/95	Texas Utilities	TXU	250	37 1/4	135.76		31 2/3				
11	10/12/95	Wrigley	WWY	125	49 3/4	48.25		57 1/2				
12	5/30/96	International Paper	IP	50	38 1/4	52.55		42				
13	10/2/96	Microsoft		200	76 3/4	56.00		113 3/8				
14	2/1/97	Pfizer		100	92 1/2	35.00		92 7/8				
15												
16		TOTALS										

Exercise 96

- **Accounting: Balance Sheet**
  (Copy Template sheet, 3-D references, Consolidate Data)
- **Internet Research Using Current Periodicals**

NOTES

Accounting Balance Sheet (Copy Template Sheet, 3-D References, Consolidate Data)

- A **balance sheet** is an accounting form that shows what a company owns (ASSETS), what the company owes (LIABILITIES), and how much the owners are worth (EQUITY) if the company were to pay its debts and go out of business.

Internet Research Using Current Periodicals

- Most periodical publications have instituted Web sites where you can research current articles on topics of interest. A selection of past issues may be available and there may be topic indices to help in your search for data. You may also access regular feature sections of a magazine that you know will provide the information you need.

> Web Electronics is a large company that has several separate divisions. Each division requires its own balance sheet each month. As an assistant in the Accounting Department, you have been asked to prepare a balance sheet for each division, a consolidated balance sheet, and a comparative balance sheet which compares divisions. You will access the Internet to provide a listing of the recently awarded government contracts in the electronics industry for the sales department.

EXERCISE DIRECTIONS

1. Create the worksheet template for a balance sheet shown in Illustration A on page 372.
   a. Set column widths as necessary.
   b. Create lines exactly as shown.
   c. Enhance the title lines as desired.
   d. Enter a formula to find TOTAL ASSETS, TOTAL LIABILITIES, and, TOTAL LIAB and EQUITY.
   ✓ *Zeros will appear until data is entered.*

2. Rename Sheet1; **BAL**.

3. Copy the BAL sheet five times.

4. Rename sheets as follows:

BAL (1)	**SUMMARY**
BAL (2)	**MODEM**
BAL (3)	**SOFTWARE**
BAL (4)	**REPAIR**
BAL (5)	**COMPARISON**

6. Select the MODEMS sheet and add data for the MODEM DIVISION using the data shown in Illustration B on page 374.
   - Change second line of the title to read: MODEM DIVISION.

7. Select the SOFTWARE sheet and add data for the SOFTWARE DIVISION using the data shown in Illustration B on page 374.
   - Change second line of the title to read: SOFTWARE DIVISION.

8. Select the REPAIR sheet and add data for the REPAIR DIVISION using the data shown in Illustration B on page 374.

   • Change second line of the title to read: REPAIR DIVISION.

9. On the COMPARISON sheet:
   a. Move the Liabilities and Capital sections below the assets so that all the labels are in column A.
   b. Change the second line of the title to read: COMPARATIVE BALANCE SHEET.
   c. Create four column headings, using word wrap, beginning in Column D, under the date, that read:

   MODEM   SOFTWARE   REPAIR   TOTAL
   DIVISION   DIVISION   DIVISION

10. Copy the Balance Sheet data from each division sheet into the appropriate column on the Comparison sheet. (Since data is arranged in two columns on the division sheets, each copy will be a two-step process.)

11. Find the horizontal TOTAL for each item.

12. Find the TOTAL ASSETS, TOTAL LIABILITIES, and TOTAL LIABILITIES and CAPITAL for all columns.

13. Create a stacked column chart comparing the Assets for the three divisions. Add appropriate labels, headings, and legends.

14. Add a text note with a shadow below the chart as follows:

   ✓ *We are beginning an effort to capture subcontractor business from firms that have recently been awarded government contracts. Sales personnel please note the Contracts Reference page for the contracts awarded this month.*

15. Select the Summary sheet.

16. Use the consolidation feature or 3-D references to consolidate all the Asset ranges into the summary sheet.

17. Use the consolidation feature or 3-D references to consolidate all the LIABILITY and CAPITAL ranges into the summary sheet.

18. Format all money values for two decimal places.

19. Add a new sheet to the workbook and rename it Contracts Reference.

20. Use the Internet or the **Excel Internet Simulation CD-ROM** to research electronic industry news to obtain a list of recently awarded government contracts. Follow one of the sets of steps below:

   USING THE INTERNET
   a. Sign on to your Internet service provider.
   b. Select your Web browser.
   c. Use the Excite search engine to search on the words "electronics industry news".
      The URL address is http://www.excite.com.
      You may use other search methods, if desired.
   d. Select E-Source, Electronics OEM's, Distributors and News, if available, or a comparable site.
   e. Find the Government Contracts feature in Electronics News, if available.
   f. Copy the latest government contract list.

   OR

   USING THE EXCEL INTERNET SIMULATION
   a. Click **Go**, **Open** on the Web toolbar.
   b. Type **C:\DDCPUB\EX97INT.IMR**
      If the Excel Internet Simulation has been installed on another drive, replace C: with the accurate letter representing the drive.
   c. Click **OK** to launch the simulation.
   d. Select **Exercise 96: Electronics**.
   e. Click the Search button [Search] at the top of the screen.
   f. At the simulated Excite search site, click in the Search text box, type *electronics industry news,* and click Search.
   g. Follow the onscreen directions.

21. Exit from your browser and disconnect from your Internet service provider, or exit the Excel Internet Simulation.

22. Paste the copied information onto the Contracts Reference sheet of your workbook.

23. On the Contracts Reference sheet, delete extra blank rows and references to pictures.

24. Save and close the workbook file; name it **WEB**.

Illustration A

	A	B	C	D	E	F	G
1			**WEB ELECTRONICS**				
2			**CONSOLIDATED STATEMENTS**				
3			**BALANCE SHEET**				
4			**JUNE 30, 19--**				
5							
6		**ASSETS**				**LIABILITIES**	
7							
8	CASH				ACCOUNTS PAYABLE		
9	ACCOUNTS RECEIVABLE				NOTES PAYABLE		
10	INVENTORY				TOTAL LIABILITIES		
11	FURNITURE						
12	EQUIPMENT				**CAPITAL**		
13	BUILDINGS						
14	LAND				NED WEBER, CAPITAL		
15							
16	**TOTAL ASSETS**				**TOTAL LIAB AND CAPITAL**		
17							

Illustration B

	A	B	C	D	E	F	G	H	I	J	K
1				MODEM DIVISION			SOFTWARE DIVISION			REPAIR DIVISION	
2	ASSETS										
3	CASH			9000			5600			12000	
4	ACCOUNTS RECEIVABLE			15680			22450			39600	
5	INVENTORY			12500			9600			5990	
6	FURNITURE			4300			5500			14000	
7	EQUIPMENT			16900			11400			61000	
8	BUILDING			84500						72000	
9	LAND			65000						50000	
10											
11	LIABILITIES										
12	ACCOUNTS PAYABLE			12900			10400			15678	
13	NOTES PAYABLE			115000			8000			134780	
14											
15	NED WEBER, CAPITAL			79980			36150			104132	

NEXT EXERCISE

Exercise 97

■ Economics/Decision Making (Formulas, Copying, Editing, Multiple Worksheets, AutoFormat, Charting, Enhancements)

Marvin Gold, the owner of the Yellow Star Cab Company, leases three cabs and employs three drivers. Until now, the cabs have been operating for one eight hour shift with a one hour meal break. The company has been losing money and the owner would like to test the break even point and profit points for multiple shifts, drivers, and even for adding another cab.

The important data you need to complete this analysis is as follows:

Cabs generate revenue of approximately $40 per operating hour.
Cab leases are $80 per day per cab, and office rent is $60 per day for fixed costs.
Each driver is paid $100 per day plus 30% of revenue.
Gasoline costs amount to $3.00 per hour.

EXERCISE DIRECTIONS

1. Create the worksheet as shown, or open 🖫 **97CAB**.

2. Find:
   - No. of Drivers (use fill series to create numbers 1 to 12).
   - Hours of Operation
     *HINT: 7*No. of Drivers.*
   - Revenue
     *HINT: 40*Hours of Operation.*
   - Driver Earnings
     *HINT: (100*No. of Drivers)+(Revenue*30%).*
   - Gasoline
     *HINT: Hours of Operation*3.*
   - Total Variable Costs
     HINT: Driver Earnings+Gasoline.
   - Fixed Costs
     *HINT: No. of Cabs*80+60.*
   - Total Costs
     HINT: Total Variable Costs+Fixed Costs.
   - Profit
     HINT: Revenue-Total Costs.

3. Extend the formulas to each driver row.

4. Rename the sheet containing the data; **Analysis**.

5. Bold the worksheet and column titles.

6. Create a column chart showing the No. of Drivers, Revenue, and Total Costs. Use appropriate titles and place the chart on Sheet2.

7. Use the Chart, Data Source commands to enter the series names in the Legend box.

8. Add a subtitle: Break Even Analysis.

9. Format the font size of the Number of Driver axis data to 9 points.

10. Size the column chart so that data is clearly visible.

11. Copy the column chart to a blank space below the first chart.

12. Change the chart type to a line chart.

13. Adjust chart sizes as necessary.

14. Rename Sheet2; name it CHARTS.

15. Using AutoFormat, format the Analysis sheet for Classic 3 format.

16. Change the font size of the main title to 14 points.

17. Center the subtitle across the range A2:H2.

18. Enter a star graphic in I1:J3.

19. Using the chart or worksheet data, answer the following questions:

❓ How many drivers would result in the maximum profit with three cabs?

❓ How many shifts should there be each day?

❓ What number of hours constitutes the "break even" point?

❓ How would leasing a fourth cab affect profits?

20. Save the workbook file; name it **CAB**.

21. Print one copy of the workbook.

	A	B	C	D	E	F	G	H	I	J
1			YELLOW STAR CAB COMPANY							
2			Break Even Analysis							
3										
4							Total			
5	No. of	No. of	Hours of		Driver		Variable	Fixed	Total	
6	Drivers	Cabs	Operation	Revenue	Earnings	Gasoline	Costs	Costs	Costs	Profit
7	1	3								
8		3								
9		3								
10		3								
11		3								
12		3								
13		3								
14		3								
15		3								
16		4								
17		4								
18		4								

Exercise

98

■ Sales Marketing (Lists, Subtotals, Database Functions, Filters, PivotTables)

You are the owner of a local sneaker store, Jogger's Circle, with a small department selling sportswear apparel. Since this is a new line to the shop, the garments have not yet been inventoried. You are to create a list to record all purchases in this department as of March 31, 1998. You will then create reports to summarize the list information.

In addition, you will need to determine the items that should be reduced in price to promote quick sale. According to store policy, prices must be marked down 20% on items in stock over 40 days, and garments must be reordered when inventory falls below 50%.

EXERCISE DIRECTIONS

1. Create the list shown on the right, or open 💾 **98JOG.**
   - Set column widths appropriately.
   - Format the COST column for two decimal places.
   - Enter the labels SELL PR., NO. SOLD, % SOLD, GROSS PROFIT in columns G through J.

2. Find SELL PR. for each item.

   HINT: Markup is 40% of cost. Selling price is COST x 40% + COST or COST x 1.4.

3. Format appropriately.

4. Find remaining items:
   - NO. SOLD
     HINT: NO. PURC. - ON HAND.
   - % SOLD
     HINT NO. SOLD/NO. PURCHASED.
   - GROSS PROFIT
     HINT: (SELLING PRICE - COST) x NO. SOLD.

5. Format appropriately.

6. Name the list ITEMS. Include column titles.

7. Sort the list so all vendors (Sort By field) are in alphabetical order and items (Then By field) are in alphabetical order within vendor names.

8. Use Advanced Filter to extract from the list items to be reordered (items that sold more than 50% of inventory).

   a. Insert four rows above the list and set up a criteria range there to indicate % SOLD>.50 condition.
   b. Copy the extracted records to the range beginning at A40.
   c. Label the extracted list appropriately.
   d. Print a copy of this report.

9. Set up advanced filter criteria to extract from the original list items that have been in stock for more than 40 days as of March 31, 1998. We would like to reduce the selling price of these items by 20%.

   a. Set up criteria range as follows:
      DATE REC.
      ="<"&DATE(98,3,31)-40

      ✓ *In the criteria, the & (ampersand) combines the less than sign (<) with the result of the date expression (DATE(98,3,31)-40. The serial value resulting from the date expression appears.*

      ✓ *If you see #VALUE! and not <35845, check that the Transition Formula Evaluation setting is deselected. To do this, click Options on the Tools menu. Select the Transition tab, then click the option to deselect it.*

   b. Copy the records to the range beginning at A58.
   c. Label the extracted list appropriately.
   d. Delete the last three fields in the extracted list.
   e. Add a new field to the extracted list in column H; name it NEW SELL PR.
   f. Find new selling price (SELL PR. x .8).
   g. Format appropriately.

10. Print a copy of the new list.

11. To analyze purchases and sales of merchandise from OLYMPICS, one of our vendors, enter the summary labels below in an available area of the worksheet:
    - RUNNER'S WORLD
    - SPORTSWEAR SUMMARY DATA
    - ANALYSIS OF OLYMPICS PURCHASES AND SALES
    - Total Items Purchased
    - Total Items Sold
    - Total Gross Profit
    - Average % Sold
    - Average Gross Profit per item

12. Format appropriately.

13. Print a copy of the summary data.

14. Use the data list range and create a PivotTable on a new sheet with the following settings:
    - PAGE: Vendor
    - DATA: Sum of Cost
    - Sum of Selling Price
    - Sum of Number Sold
    - Sum of Number Purchased
    - Average of % Sold

15. Format Cost and Selling Price data for currency.

16. Format Average of % Sold data for percents.

17. Rename Sheet1 and Sheet2; name them Data List and PivotTable.

18. Print a copy of the PivotTable sheet.

19. Save and close the workbook file; name it **JOG**.
    OPTIONAL: Add enhancements to the lists and summary data.

	A	B	C	D	E	F	G	H	I	J	K
1			JOGGER'S CIRCLE								
2			SPORTSWEAR DIVISION								
3											
4	ITEM	VENDOR	NO. PURC	ON HAND	DATE REC.	COST	SELL PR.	NO. SOLD	% SOLD	GROSS PROFIT	
5	JOG SUIT-WOMEN/XL	ADIOS	4	2	02/15/98	30.00					
6	T-SHIRT/L	CHAMP	40	10	02/28/98	6.00					
7	T-SHIRT/M	CHAMP	30	2	02/28/98	6.00					
8	T-SHIRT/S	CHAMP	15	5	02/28/98	6.00					
9	T-SHIRT/XL	CHAMP	15	4	02/28/98	6.00					
10	JOG SUIT-WOMEN/L	DCNY	10	3	02/15/98	30.00					
11	JOG SUIT-WOMEN/M	DCNY	15	7	02/15/98	30.00					
12	JOG SUIT-WOMEN/S	DCNY	15	12	02/15/98	30.00					
13	BODY LEOTARD/L	JUMPSKIN	10	1	01/19/98	20.00					
14	BODY LEOTARD/M	JUMPSKIN	25	12	01/19/98	20.00					
15	BODY LEOTARD/S	JUMPSKIN	10	2	01/19/98	20.00					
16	SWEATPANTS/L	OLYMPIC	20	17	03/14/98	7.00					
17	SWEATPANTS/M	OLYMPIC	25	19	03/14/98	7.00					
18	SWEATPANTS/S	OLYMPIC	12	7	03/14/98	7.00					
19	SWEATPANTS/XL	OLYMPIC	12	10	03/14/98	7.00					
20	SWEATSHIRT/L	OLYMPIC	60	20	01/29/98	10.00					
21	SWEATSHIRT/M	OLYMPIC	50	20	02/28/98	10.00					
22	SWEATSHIRT/S	OLYMPIC	30	20	01/29/98	10.00					
23	SWEATSHIRT/XL	OLYMPIC	25	15	01/29/98	10.00					
24	JOG SUIT-MEN/L	SPIKEE	20	4	01/10/98	25.00					
25	JOG SUIT-MEN/M	SPIKEE	15	12	01/10/98	25.00					
26	JOG SUIT-MEN/XL	SPIKEE	10	8	01/10/98	26.00					
27	NYLON SHORTS/L	SPIKEE	10	6	02/09/98	8.00					
28	NYLON SHORTS/M	SPIKEE	15	11	02/09/98	8.00					
29	NYLON SHORTS/S	SPIKEE	10	9	02/09/98	8.00					
30	NYLON SHORTS/XL	SPIKEE	8	8	02/09/98	8.00	▼	▼	▼	▼	

Exercise 99

■ Accounting/Depreciation (Formulas, IF Statements)

NOTES

- An **asset** is something of value that is owned.

- **Depreciation** is a decrease in value of an asset because of use and passage of time.

- **Salvage value** is the estimated amount that can be recovered at the end of the life of an asset.

- **Book value** is the current value of an asset. It is calculated by subtracting the total depreciation (from all years owned) from the asset cost.

- **Straight-line depreciation** is a method of calculating annual depreciation that results in charging an equal amount of annual depreciation expense for every year.

  For example, an asset costs $1,000, has a salvage value of $200 and has an estimated life of eight years. Using the straight-line method, the annual depreciation would be $100 per year (1000-200)/8=100.

- Depreciation is calculated for this problem based on the **Half Month method**. This states that if the equipment is purchased between the first and fifteenth of a month, depreciation is calculated for the entire month. If equipment is purchased between the sixteenth and end of the month, depreciation is not calculated until the next month.

- The IRS allows businesses to use accelerated depreciation methods that result in higher depreciation amounts in the early years of an asset's life. One of these accelerated methods is the **Double Declining Balance** method. If an asset has a five year life, it would normally depreciate 20% per year. However, when you use the Double Declining Balance method, you would deduct 40% of the declining balance each year.

- Depreciation is an expense for a business, and it can be deducted as an expense on the business tax return. If you use accelerated depreciation methods, your tax deduction is limited by Internal Revenue rules.

EXERCISE DIRECTIONS

1. Create the worksheet on Sheet1, as shown in Illustration A on page 383, and the worksheet on Sheet3 as shown in Illustration B on page 383. Or, open 🖫 **99DEPR**.

2. Do the following on Sheet1:
   a. Set column widths as necessary.
      ✓ *Note that each part of the date (month, day, year) is in its own column.*
   b. Underline the row six column titles.
   c. Use fonts, styles, and color to enhance the heading area.
   d. Format the money columns for two decimal places.

3. Do the following on Sheet2:
   a. Set column widths as necessary.
   b. Underline the row ten column titles.
   c. Use fonts, styles, and color to enhance the heading area.
   d. Format the money columns for two decimal places.

4. Find for all assets on sheet 1:
   • ANNUAL DEPR.
      Depreciation is calculated using straight-line method.
      HINT: *(COST - SALVAGE VALUE)/ LIFE OF ASSET IN YEARS.*
   • FIRST YR. NO. OF MONTHS
      Depreciation is calculated for the time that the equipment is owned using the half month method (see notes above).
      HINT: *=IF(DAYS>15,12-MONTH, 12-(MONTH-1))*
   • FIRST YR. PARTIAL DEPR.
      The depreciation for the first year of ownership based on the number of ownership months and the established annual depreciation.
      HINT: *(ANNUAL DEPR./12) x FIRST YR. NO. OF MONTHS.*

   • DEPR. 1995, DEPR. 1996, and DEPR. 1997
      The appropriate depreciation value for each asset is determined by when that asset was purchased. If the asset was purchased in the current year, the depreciation value is the same as the FIRST YR. PARTIAL DEPR. If the asset was purchased in a prior year, the depreciation value is the ANNUAL DEPR. An IF statement can be used, copied, and edited for each of the different depreciation years.
      HINT: *=IF(YR=DEPR. year, FIRST YR. PARTIAL DEPR., ANNUAL DEPR.)*
      ✓ *You should enter DEPR. year as a constant (i.e, 95, 96 or 97).*
   • BOOK VALUE
      The cost of the asset less the total depreciation from all ownership years represents the current book value.

5. Find:
   • COST TOTALS for 1995, 1996, 1997 and ASSETS.
   • TOTALS for DEPR.1995, DEPR.1996, DEPR.1997, in the appropriate columns.
   • BOOK VALUE at the end of 1997.

6. Format all money columns for two decimal places and delete extraneous zeros that may have appeared after formulas were entered.

7. Rename sheets:
   Sheet1: Office Equipment
   Sheet2: Automobile

8. On the Automobile sheet, enter a formula to calculate depreciation in C12.
   *Hint: Book Value Jan-94*40%.*

9. Find 1994 Book Value.
   Hint: Jan 94-Depreciation.

10. Copy formulas for the remaining years.

11. Find 1994 IRS Valuation.
    Hint: Book Value Jan-94-IRS Allowance.

12. Copy the formula for the remaining years.

13. Use the Internet or the **Excel Internet Simulation CD-ROM** to research the current market value of the business automobile.
    USING THE INTERNET
    a. Sign on to your Internet service provider.
    b. Select your Web browser.
    c. Use the Excite search site to search on the words "Kelley Blue Book."
       The URL address is http://www.excite.com.
       You may use other search methods, if desired..
    d. View the sites that might provide values for used cars.
    e. Select the Kelley Blue Book home page to research the current value of the 1994 Chrysler Concorde.

    OR

    USING THE EXCEL INTERNET SIMULATION
    a. Click **Go**, **Open** on the Web toolbar.
    b. Type **C:\DDCPUB\EX97INT.IMR**
       *If the Excel Internet Simulation has been installed on another drive, replace **C:** with the accurate letter representing the drive.*
    c. Click **OK** to launch the simulation.
    d. Select **Exercise 99: Market Values**.
    e. Click the Search button at the top of the screen.
    f. At the simulated Excite search site, Click in the Search text box, type *Kelly Blue Book,* and click Search.
    g. Follow the onscreen directions.

14. Copy or note the available information.

15. Exit from your browser and disconnect from your Internet service provider, or exit the Excel Internet Simulation.

16. Enter the Current Market Value on this year's line. Add the current year if it is not on the sheet.

17. Print a copy of the Automobile sheet.

18. Print a copy of the Office Equipment sheet so it fits on one page.

19. Save and close the workbook file; name it **DEPR**.

   ❷ What was the total value of all Office Equipment assets at the time of purchase?

   ❷ What is the total depreciation or loss in value for the years 1995? 1996? 1997?

   ❷ What is the book value of all Office Equipment assets?

   ❷ Which value is the highest for our automobile for the current year (Book Value, IRS Valuation, or Current Market Value)?

Illustration A (sheet 1)

	A	B	C	D	E	F	G	H	I	J	K	L	M	N
1						MARK AND JANE THOMASVILLE, ATTORNEYS AT LAW								
2						DEPRECIATION SCHEDULE								
3														
4		D				ESTIMATED	LIFE OF		FIRST YR.	FIRST YR.				
5	M	A	Y	ASSET		SALVAGE	ASSET IN	ANNUAL	NO. OF	PARTIAL	DEPR.	DEPR.	DEPR.	BOOK
6	O	Y	R	DESCRIPTION	COST	VALUE	YEARS	DEPR.	MONTHS	DEPR.	1995	1996	1997	VALUE
7														
8	4	3	95	DESK AND CHAIR	1020.00	200.00	8							
9	5	16	95	FILE CABINET #25	375.00	75.00	8							
10	6	14	95	FILE CABINET #48	750.00	150.00	8							
11	10	15	95	TYPEWRITER	600.00	100.00	8							
12	12	10	95	CALCULATOR	150.00	45.00	5							
13				TOTAL 1995										
14														
15	5	2	96	DESK AND CHAIR	650.00	125.00	8							
16	6	20	96	COMPUTER	2700.00	700.00	5							
17	7	10	96	LASER PRINTER	1300.00	300.00	5							
18	9	19	96	FILE CABINET #34	540.00	100.00	8							
19	11	5	96	CONSOLE	1200.00	225.00	8							
20				TOTAL 1996										
21														
22	1	28	97	COMPUTER TABLE	485.00	95.00	5	78.00	11	71.50				
23	5	5	97	FILE CABINET #42	550.00	100.00	8	56.25	8	37.50				
24				TOTAL 1997										
25														
26				TOTAL ASSETS	-									

Illustration B (sheet 2)

	A	B	C	D	E	F	G	H
1	MARK AND JANE THOMASVILLE, ATTORNEYS AT LAW							
2	DEPRECIATION SCHEDULE							
3								
4	Automobile:		1994 Chrysler Concorde Sedan					
5	Date:		1/4/94					
6	Depreciation:		5 year, 200% DDB					
7	Cost:		18000					
8						Current		
9		Book		IRS	IRS	Market		
10	Year	Value	Depreciation	Allowance	Valuation	Value*		
11	Jan-94	18000.00						
12	1994			2960.00				
13	1995			4700.00				
14	1996			2850.00				
15	1997			1675.00				
16	1998			1675.00				
17								
18								
19	* Kelley Blue Book Wholesale Value - Average Condition							

Exercise

100

■ Accounting/Financial Reports
(3-D Reference, Worksheets, Enhancements)

Home Beautiful, an interior design firm, summarizes their records each month using a Trial Balance. All the account balances are entered on the Trial Balance and then used in the financial reports. Mr. Draper would like you to set up a Trial Balance sheet that would automatically send the values to the appropriate locations on the Financial reports as the Trial Balance is created.

EXERCISE DIRECTIONS

1. Open 💾 **100DECOR** or create the worksheets from the illustrations provided on pages 385 and 386 as listed below:

    a. Create the Trial Balance on Sheet1, as shown in Illustration A (page 385).

    b. Create the Income Statement on Sheet2, as shown in Illustration B (page 386).

    c. Create the Balance Sheet on Sheet3, as shown in Illustration C (page 386).

    ✓ *The shading shows the location for data. Do not shade your worksheets.*

2. Group all three sheets:
    *   Enhance the three heading lines to 14 point Bold.
    *   Ungroup the sheets.

3. On the Trial Balance:

    a. Enter a formula to find the balance totals.

    b. Format borders as illustrated.

    c. Format numbers for commas with no decimal places.

    d. Name the sheet: Trial Balance–May.

4. In the Income Statement:

    a. Bold each section heading (Income, Expenses, Net Income).

    b. Enter a 3-D reference to enter the Fees Income from the Trial Balance to the location indicated.

    c. Copy the formula down for Rental Income.

    d. Enter a sum formula to find Total Income in Column F.

    e. Enter a 3-D reference to enter the Salary Expense from the Trial Balance sheet to the location indicated.

    f. Copy the formula down for all expenses.

    g. Enter a formula to find Total Expenses in Column F.

    h. Enter a formula to find Net Income in Column F.

    i. Format borders as indicated.

    j. Format numbers for commas with no decimal places.

    k. Rename the sheet: Income Statement–May.

5. On the Balance Sheet:

    a. Bold each section heading (Assets, Liabilities, Capital).

    b. Enter a 3-D reference to enter Cash from the Trial Balance to the location indicated.

    c. Copy the formula down for Accounts Receivable and Supplies.

    d. Continue entering 3-D references for remaining Assets and Liabilities. The Building and Accumulated Depreciation of Building values should be in column E.

    e. Find the book value of the building by subtracting the Accumulated Depreciation from the Building value and enter the answer in Column F.

    f. Enter a formula to find Total Assets.

    g. Enter a formula to find Total Liabilities.

    h. Enter a 3-D reference for Pierre Draper, Capital and Pierre Draper, Withdrawals to enter the values from the Trial Balance.

    i. On the Net Income/Net Loss line enter a 3-D reference to enter the number from the bottom line of the Income Statement.

    j. Enter a formula to find Total Capital using the Capital, Withdrawals and Net Income data.
    Hint: Capital - Withdrawals and Net Income.

k. Enter a formula to find Total Liabilities and Capital.

l. Format the borders as indicated.

m. Format numbers for commas with no decimal places.

n. Rename the sheet: Balance Sheet–May.

6. Copy the three sheets so that they follow these sheets.

7. Rename the sheets:

Trial Balance–June

Income Statement–June

Balance Sheet–June

8. Enter the June Balances on the Trial Balance sheet, as shown in Illustration D (page 387).

9. Change Dates to June 30 on all June reports.

10. Check June statements for accuracy.

11. Print a copy of May and June Statements with footers that include filename and sheet name.

12. Save and close the file; name it **DECOR**.

Illustration A

	A	B	C	D	E	F
1			**Home Beautiful**			
2			**Trial Balance**			
3			**May 31, 199-**			
4						
5	**Account**				**Debit**	**Credit**
6	**Number**	**Account**			**Balances**	**Balances**
7	101	Cash			18,000	
8	110	Accounts Receivable			8,000	
9	120	Supplies			1,500	
10	150	Building			57,000	
11	155	Accumulated Depreciation				12,000
12	201	Accounts Payable				6,300
13	202	Mortgage Payable				15,000
14	301	Pierre Draper, Capital				34,000
15	305	Pierre Draper, Capital			10,000	
16	401	Fees Income				42,400
17	402	Rental Income				2,000
18	501	Salary Expense			12,000	
19	502	Utilities Expense			2,500	
20	503	Interest Expense			1,200	
21	504	Advertising Expense			1,000	
22	505	Miscellaneous Expense			500	
23						

Illustration B

	A	B	C	D	E	F	G
1			**Home Beautiful**				
2			**Income Statement**				
3			**For the month ended May 31, 199-**				
4							
5	Income:						
6		Fees Income					
7		Rental Income					
8		Total Income					
9							
10	Expenses:						
11		Salary Expense					
12		Utilities Expense					
13		Interest Expense					
14		Advertising Expense					
15		Miscellaneous Expense					
16		Total Expenses					
17	Net Income						
18							

Illustration C

	A	B	C	D	E	F
1			**Home Beautiful**			
2			**Balance Sheet**			
3			**May 31, 199-**			
4						
5		**Assets**				
6	Cash					
7	Accounts Receivable					
8	Supplies					
9	Building					
10	Accumulated Depreciation of Building					
11	Total Assets					
12		**Liabilities**				
13	Accounts Payable					
14	Mortgage Payable					
15	Total Liabilities					
16		**Capital**				
17	Pierre Draper, Capital					
18	Less: Pierre Draper, Withdrawals					
19	Add: Net Income/Net Loss					
20	Total Capital					
21	Total Liabilities and Capital					

Illustration D

101	Cash	12000	
110	Accounts Receivable	21000	
120	Supplies	3280	
150	Building	57000	
155	Accumulated Depreciation		13000
201	Accounts Payable		4480
202	Mortgage Payable		14500
301	Pierre Draper. Capital		51200
305	Pierre Draper, Withdrawals	18000	
401	Fees Income		55000
402	Rental Income		4000
501	Salary Expense	22000	
502	Utilities Expense	5000	
503	Interest Expense	2000	
504	Advertising Expense	1200	
505	Miscellaneous Expense	700	

Excel

APPENDIX

Appendices A-E

- Glossary
- Functions
- Toolbars
- Error Messages
- Worksheet Planning Grid

GLOSSARY

3-d reference A reference to cells in other sheets in a workbook.

absolute reference A type of cell reference that will not change when copied or moved.

active cell The cell that is ready to receive data or a command.

advanced filter An Excel feature that displays or extracts records from a list based on a specified criteria such as employees that live in New York.

Autofilter An Excel feature that makes it easy to show specific records in a list.

buttons Symbols on a toolbar which represent tasks or actions and are used in conjunction with a mouse to access the tasks or actions.

cell A single location on a worksheet.

cell reference A column letter and row number, e.g., A1 or F12.

charting Preparing a visual interpretation of data in the form of columns, lines, pie charts, etc.

Chartwizard An Excel feature that provides a series of steps with prompts that guide you through the process of creating a chart.

column(s) The vertical portions of the worksheet, e.g., A, B, C, etc. There are 256 columns in a worksheet.

column heading(s) The area at the top of a worksheet that indicates the column letters. Column headings also act as controls for sizing or hiding columns.

column width Refers to the size of a cell. A cell may be made wider or more narrow than its default size of nine characters.

copying Reproducing data from one location to another.

data form A special dialog box that lets you edit or add data to fields in a list one record at a time.

data table A data table used to evaluate different solutions to a problem based on specific input values or variables.

database functions A set of built-in formulas that perform calculations or special operations on records in a list.

default Settings which are preset by Excel but may be modified by the user. For example, column width settings.

dialog box   A box which appears on the screen after a menu item is selected and contains settings to be changed.

drag-and-drop editing   An action that lets you perform tasks, such as copying a cell, by using the mouse to move an object or data to another object or location.

editing   Changing the contents of a cell.

external reference   A reference to cells in another workbook.

extract data   The process of copying a subset of a data range to another worksheet or workbook.

field names   Column labels that appear in the first row of a list and identify the content of each column.

file   A saved workbook.

filename   The name given to a saved workbook.

fill series   An Excel feature that allows for fast entry of sequential numbers in a column or row.

font   A set of characters that share a design and name. Fonts come in varying sizes and styles.

format   Using special commands to display worksheet data in the style, numeric format or alignment that makes the best presentation.

formula   A mathematical expression that makes new values by combining numerical values with operators (plus, minus, etc.) Formulas may contain cell references, operators and functions.

freeze panes   An Excel feature that keeps row or column titles in view while you scroll to other parts of a worksheet.

function   A built-in formula that performs calculations or special operations.

global   A command affecting the entire worksheet.

Goal Seek   An Excel feature that changes a value in a problem so a formula using the value results in a specified answer.

graphic objects   Items, such as pictures and shapes, that you can add to a worksheet or chart.

graphing   Preparing a visual interpretation of data in the form of columns, lines, or pie charts, etc.

label   A cell entry that begins with a letter or label prefix. Labels cannot be used in ordinary calculations.

label prefix	The apostrophe (') character that precedes a cell entry to format a number as text.
link	A feature enabling the user to connect two or more files so the linked file automatically updates when changes are made to the source file.
list (database)	A table containing similar sets of data. Excel treats each row in a list as a record and each column as a field. Labels in the first row indicate the field names.
lock cells	An Excel feature that lets you restrict use of specific cells in a worksheet when worksheet protection is on.
logical function	A function that answers a true/false question and calculates data according to the answer.
logical operator	Symbols, such as > <, used in formulas or criteria ranges to evaluate a condition.
lookup function	A type of function that you can use to retrieve data from a list.
macro	A series of recorded actions that automates a task.
named range	A defined area of a worksheet that has been given a name.
non-adjacent range	A selection of cells that do not exist next to each other in a worksheet.
numerical data	Data that can be calculated.
office assistant	Animated help screen provided in Excel 97 that provides search and index features and context-sensitive questions. Click F1 or click the Help button on the toolbar to open the Office Assistant.
open	The process of accessing a saved file.
page break	A division in a worksheet that marks the end of one printed page and the beginning of another.
Paste function palette	An Excel feature that helps you enter a function into a formula by displaying each of its arguments, a description of the function and each argument as well as the result of the function and of the entire formula.
PivotTable	An interactive tool used to analyze information in a list.
protect	A feature that restricts access to worksheet data or a workbook file.
range	A group of adjacent cells in a worksheet that may be identified with a cell reference such as AB:D5.
record	A row in a list that makes up a related set of data, such as an employee's name, address and phone number.

relative reference	A type of cell reference that will change when copied or moved.
row(s)	The horizontal portions of the worksheet, e.g., 1, 2, 3, etc. There are 65,536 rows in a worksheet.
row headings	The area to the left of a worksheet that indicates row numbers. Row headings also act as controls for sizing or hiding rows.
save	Stores a copy of the workbook on disk.
scroll	A vertical or horizontal screen movement which displays portions of the spreadsheet that exist beyond the limits of the screen.
series	A set of values that are grouped together.
sheet tabs	Controls that let you select sheets in a workbook.
sheets	Units of a workbook, such as worksheets, charts and modules.
sort	The process of arranging records in a list in a particular order according to the contents of one or more columns.
template	A skeleton worksheet containing labels and possibly formulas which may be reused with different data.
toolbar	A set of buttons that carry out commands when clicked.
transpose	The layout of data will be changed from row to column orientation or vice versa.
typestyle	A selected font attribute such as bold, italic or underlined, for example.
value	A numerical or formula entry on the worksheet used in calculations.
Web (or World Wide Web)	A service of the Internet in which pages of information are linked together by the use of Hyperlink text and objects. Use the Web toolbar to connect to your Internet service provider and locate the desired Web site.
Web browser	A graphic environment that displays the information you retrieve from the Web in a readable format.
windows	The graphic environment that allows you to use Excel and other Windows-based programs simultaneously.
workbook	An Excel document which may contain worksheets, charts and module sheets.
worksheet	A columnar spreadsheet, containing 256 columns and 65,536 rows, used to calculate or analyze data. By default there are sixteen worksheets in a workbook.
wrap text	A method of formatting text so that it fits on more than one line in a cell or other text area.

FUNCTIONS

- A **function** is a built-in formula that performs a special calculation automatically. Like formulas, functions require an *equal sign* (=) as the first character in the cell entry. Excel identifies functions by the *function name* followed by a *left and right parentheses* which may include a *set of arguments*. No spaces separate a function name from the first parenthesis.

- The **arguments** are the variable names that the function needs (references to values or the values themselves) to return an answer. *Commas* are used to separate the arguments (shown in bold below) in a function.

    *EXAMPLE: =AVERAGE(**B2,B3,70**) + SUM(**A1:A20**)*

- In this example, the first character is an equal sign (=) and the results of two functions (AVERAGE and SUM) are totaled. The arguments in the AVERAGE function are B2, B3, and 70. The argument in the SUM function is the range A1:A20.

- Functions may be typed directly or may be entered by using the Paste Function. The **Paste Function** will take you through the necessary steps for entering the function and its arguments.

To Use Paste Function to Create a Function:

1. Select cell to contain formula.

    OR

    a. Double-click cell containing formula.
    b. Click formula where function will be inserted.

2. Click **Paste Function** button f_x on Standard toolbar.

    OR

    a. Select **Insert** menu.
    b. Select **Function**.

3. Select a category in **Function category** list.

4. Select a function in **Function name** list.

5. Click **OK**.

6. Select desired argument box.

7. Type data.

    Depending on the function, enter or use the Collapse box to select the following kinds of data:

    Numbers (constants)   type numbers (integers, fractions, mixed numbers, negative numbers) as you would in a cell.

    References   type or insert cell references.

    Named references or formulas   type or insert named references or formulas.

Functions

type a function or click **Paste Function** button [fx] to insert another function into an argument (nest functions). The resulting screens describe the current argument, indicate if the argument is required, and show you the result of the values you have supplied.

8. Repeat steps 6-7, as needed.

9. Click **OK**.

10. Type or insert remaining parts of formula, or press **Enter**.

Paste Function Dialog Box

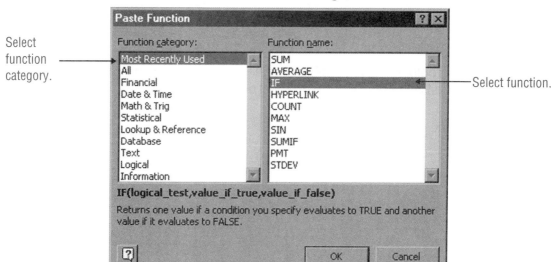

Select function category. ⟶

Select function.

Paste Function Example for If Function

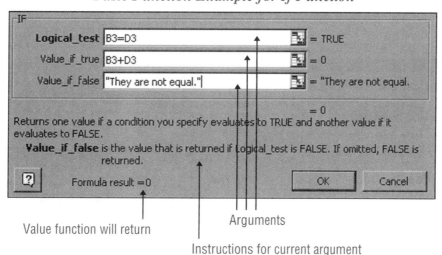

Value function will return

Arguments

Instructions for current argument

TOOLBARS

- A **toolbar** is a group of related buttons that allow mouse users to select frequently used commands without accessing the menu system.

- By default, Excel automatically displays the Standard and Formatting toolbars just below the menu bar.

Standard toolbar

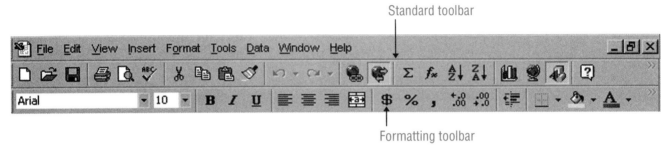

Formatting toolbar

- Excel comes with thirteen toolbars. Each toolbar contains buttons that can help you do specific tasks quickly. Note the illustration below of the **View**, **Toolbars** menu.

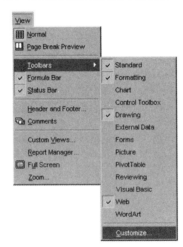

- The Toolbars command on the View menu contains a Customize option that lets you create custom toolbars that modify existing ones. Note the illustration below.

Select category.

Select toolbar to show.

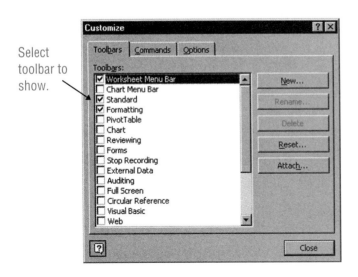

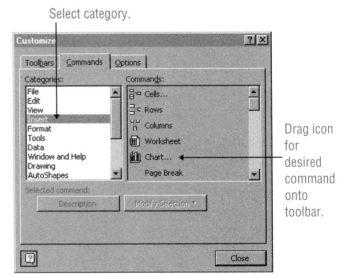

Drag icon for desired command onto toolbar.

■ The following are features that let you use your Excel toolbars to maximize and customize your work area.

- Show the purpose of a toolbar button.
- Use a toolbar button.
- Access the toolbar shortcut menu.
- Show or hide a toolbar.
- Move a toolbar.
- Switch between a floating or docking toolbar.
- Size a floating toolbar.
- Set general toolbar options, such as color and size.
- Create a customized toolbar.
- Delete a customized toolbar.
- Reopen a built-in toolbar.
- Move a toolbar button.
- Copy a toolbar button.

To show purpose of a toolbar button:
Rest pointer on desired toolbar button.
The button name or function appears below the button.

To use a toolbar button:
Click the button or drop-down arrow to the right of the button.

To access the toolbar shortcut menu:
1. Right–click a anywhere on any toolbar.
2. Click desired menu option:
   - Built-in toolbars: Standard, Formatting, Chart, Control Toolbox, Drawing, External Data, Forms, Picture, PivotTable, Reviewing, Visual Basic, Web, WordArt
   - Customize

To show or hide a toolbar:
1. Click **View** menu.
2. Click **Toolbars**.
3. Select or deselect desired toolbar(s) in **Toolbars** list.

   OR

   Drag toolbar down the screen until it is floating then click the close ☒ button.

4. Click **OK**.

To move a toolbar:
✓ *You can dock a toolbar (between the menu bar and the formula bar or on the edges of the Excel window), or have it float as a separate window. However, toolbars containing a drop-down list (i.e., the Formatting toolbar) cannot be docked on the left or right edge of the Excel window.*

1. Point to a blank area on a toolbar.

   OR

   Point to the title bar of a floating toolbar.

2. Drag the toolbar outline onto a desired workspace or docking position.
   ✓ *Excel shifts nearby toolbars when you move a new one into a docking position.*

To switch between a floating or docking toolbar:
Double-click a blank area on the toolbar.

To size a floating toolbar:
1. Point to border or corner of floating toolbar.
   Pointer becomes a double-sided arrow.
2. Drag toolbar outline to desired size.

To set general toolbar options:

1. Click **View** menu.
2. Click **Toolbars**.
3. Click **Customize**.
4. Click **Options** tab.
5. Select or deselect toolbar options:
   - **Large Icons**
   - **Show ScreenTips on toolbars**
   - **Menu animations**
6. Click **Close**.

To create a customized toolbar:

1. Click **View** menu.
2. Click **Toolbars**.
3. Click **Customize**.
4. Click **New**
5. Name new toolbar
6. Click **OK**
7. Click **Commands** tab.

   To add a button to the new toolbar:
   a. Click a category in **Categories** list.

   To see a button's description:
   1. Click desired button in **Commands** list.
   2. Click **Description**.
   3. Read description in pop-up window.

   b. Drag desired icon on to destination toolbar.
   c. Repeat steps a–b, as needed.

   To remove a button:
   Drag button off toolbar.

   Click **Close**.

To delete a customized toolbar:

1. Click **View** menu.
2. Click **Toolbars**.
3. Click **Customize**.
4. Click **Toolbars** tab.
5. Select name of toolbar to delete in **Toolbars** list.
6. Click **Delete**.

7. Click **OK** to confirm deletion.
8. Click **Close**.

To restore a built-in toolbar to its original configuration:

1. Click **View** menu.
2. Click **Toolbars**.
3. Click **Customize**.
4. Click **Toolbars** tab.
5. Select name of toolbar to restore in **Toolbars** list.
6. Click **Reset...**
   - ✓ If reset button is grayed-out, you have selected a customized toolbar, which cannot be reset.
7. Click **OK** to confirm reset.
8. Click **Close**.

To move a toolbar button:

✓ Groups a button with other buttons, adds space between buttons, moves a button to a new position on a toolbar, and move a button to another toolbar. If you are moving a button to another toolbar, both toolbars must be in view.

1. Right-click toolbar.
2. Click **Customize**.
3. While the **Customize** dialog box is open, drag button on toolbar to desired location on current or other toolbar.
4. Click **Close**.

To copy a toolbar button:

✓ If you are copying a button to another toolbar, both toolbars must be in view.

1. Right-click toolbar.
2. Click **Customize**.
3. While the **Customize** dialog box is open, press **Ctrl** and drag button on toolbar to desired location on current or other toolbar.
4. Click **Close**.

ERROR MESSAGES

■ Below is a list of error values that may appear in a cell when Excel cannot calculate the formula value.

#DIV/0! Indicates that the formula is trying to divide by zero.
In formula: • Divisor is a zero. • Divisor is referencing a blank cell or a cell that contains a zero value.

#N/A Indicates that no value is available.
In formula: • An invalid argument may have been used with a LOOKUP function. • A reference in an array formula does not match range in which results are displayed • A required argument has been omitted from a function.

#NAME? Indicates that Excel does not recognize the name used in a formula.
In formula: • A named reference has been deleted or has not been defined. • A function or named reference has been misspelled. • Text has been entered without required quotation marks. • A colon has been omitted in a range reference.

#NULL! Indicates that the intersection of two range references does not exist.
In formula: • Two range references (separated with a space operator) have been used to represent a non-existent intersection of the two ranges.

#NUM! Indicates a number error.
In formula: • An incorrect value has been used in a function. • Arguments result in a number too small or large to represent.

#REF! Indicates reference to an invalid cell.
In formula: • Arguments refer to cells that have been deleted or overwritten with non-numeric data. The argument is replaced with #REF!.

#VALUE! Indicates the invalid use of an operator or argument.
In formula: • An invalid value, or a referenced value, has been used with a formula or function (i.e., SUM("John")).

Circular A message that indicates formula is referencing itself.
In formula: • A cell reference refers to the cell containing the formula result.

The number value calculated or entered is too large for the cell width.

✓ NOTE: *If a circular reference is intended, you can select Options from the Tools menu, then select Iteration from the Calculation tab. Iteration is an instruction to repeat a calculation until a specific result is met.*

WORKSHEET PLANNING GRID

	A	B	C	D	E	F	G	H
1								
2								
3								
4								
5								
6								
7								
8								
9								
10								
11								
12								
13								
14								
15								
16								
17								
18								
19								
20								
21								
22								
23								
24								
25								
26								
27								
28								
29								
30								
31								
32								
33								
34								
35								
36								
37								
38								
39								
40								
41								
42								
43								
44								
45								
46								
47								
48								
49								
50								
51								
52								
53								
54								
55								
56								
57								
58								
59								
60								

3

3-D
charts 234
formulas 144
references 144

A

ACCESS SCREEN TIPS 20
accounting...372
ADD A FIELD TO A LIST....................................287
ADD A RECORD TO A LIST 287
ADD CUSTOM BORDERS TO CELLS 259
ADD DATA SERIES TO A CHART.......................221
ADD/DELETE RECORDS TO A LIST
    USING A DATA FORM..................................287
ADJUST WORKSHEET PANES 116
ALIGN (JUSTIFY) LABELS USING THE MENU 53
ALIGN LABELS USING THE TOOLBAR.................39
ALIGN LABELS USING THE MENU 39
alignment
    buttons..38
    label 36, 38
    titles over selected range 261
APPLY AUTOFORMAT 181
APPLY COLOR TO Cell Font 181
APPLY COLOR TO Fill CELL 181
APPLY STYLES..255
arguments 70
ARRANGE WORKBOOK WINDOWS 143
ARRANGE WORKBOOKS 116, 133
arrow 10
asset 380
ASSIGN MACRO TO A GRAPHIC BUTTON 357
ATTACH COMMENT TO A FORMULA..................171
audit formulas 170
AUDIT WORKSHEET..171
auditing feature 170
AutoCalculate..74
    box 3
AUTOCALCULATE VALUES IN A WORKSHEET ...76
AutoComplete 79
AutoCorrect...109
AutoFilter...306
AutoFit...78
AutoFormat 178
AutoShapes feature 257
AutoSum 83

B

balance sheet...372
BOLD TEXT 94
BOLD TEXT USING THE MENU............................94
BOLD, ITALICIZE OR UNDERLINE DATA
    USING THE TOOLBAR 254
book value...380
browser 364

C

callouts...276
category labels 202
cell...4
    active...4, 24
    addresses 28
    block of..51
    change borders 256
    colors and patterns 250
    comment 82
    label 32
    reference..4, 24, 44
    status 32
CENTER TITLES OVER SELECTED RANGE.......264
CHANGE ACTIVE CELL USING GO TO 29
CHANGE ACTIVE CELL USING
    THE KEYBOARD..27
CHANGE ACTIVE CELL USING THE MOUSE........27
CHANGE ACTIVE CELL USING THE NAME BOX..29
CHANGE AREA FORMAT OF A DATA SERIES OR
    DATA POINT 232
CHANGE CATEGORY SHADING........................241
CHANGE CELL BORDERS
    USING THE TOOLBAR 259
CHANGE CHART OPTIONS................................225
CHANGE CHART SUBTYPE 213
CHANGE CHART TYPE FOR ENTIRE CHART 208
CHANGE COLOR AND/OR PATTERN OF CELLS
    USING THE MENU..255
CHANGE COLOR OF CELLS
    USING THE TOOLBAR 254
CHANGE COLUMN WIDTHS USING THE MENU ..81
CHANGE COLUMN WIDTHS
    USING THE MOUSE 81
CHANGE FONT COLOR USING
    THE TOOLBAR 254
CHANGE FONT SIZE USING
    THE FONT SIZE BOX 249
CHANGE FONT USING THE FONT BOX.............249
CHANGE FONT, FONT SIZE, AND FONT STYLE
    USING THE MENU..249
CHANGE OFFICE ASSISTANT OPTIONS 20
CHANGE OPTIONS FOR EXISTING MACRO 353
CHANGE ORIENTATION OF CHART TEXT 225
CHANGE ORIENTATION OF DATA SERIES 225
CHANGE PAGE ORIENTATION...........................264
CHANGE PRINT MARGINS 264
CHANGE PRINT MARGINS
    BY DRAGGING MARGIN HANDLES.................264
CHANGE ROW HEIGHT USING THE MENU........274
CHANGE ROW HEIGHT USING THE MOUSE 274
CHANGE SCALE OF PRINTED DATA 89, 169, 269
chart
    change location...222
    colors and patterns 214
    create 203
    edit chart in its own window 212
    editing 205, 211

elements 203
embedded 202
   move 214
options 223
set scale of value axis.................................227
sheet 202
size plot area or legend...............................230
text 222
toolbar 205, 211
types
   3-D 234
   area..230
   column 204
   combination...211
   custom 210
   line 204
   pie 204
   pie, exploded......................................230
   stock..226
   subtypes..210
  update 219
  with two value axes...............................227
check box..11
check mark..10
Circle Invalid Data button............................170
Clear Validation Circles button....................170
CLEAR VALIDATION SETTINGS 305
click...5
Clip Art...266
  download from the Internet 267
CLOSE A DUPLICATE WORKBOOK WINDOW....147
CLOSE A MENU...9
CLOSE A WORKBOOK...................................35
close button
  application window............................3, 16
  workbook window....................................4
close full screen box 13
codes 90
Collapse button...87
collapse dialog box 70
Color buttons (Fill/Font Color)......................178
column
  headings 4
  width..78
column and row
  insert and delete 104
  titles...96
column-position...183
Comma button 79
command buttons 11
commands 6
commission 370
Conditional Sum Wizard 166, 169
consolidate data..340
CONSOLIDATE DATA- BY POSITION 342
copy 112
  button 54
  data 54

formulas 58
  part of a cell 74
  worksheets 144
COPY (DRAG AND DROP)............................107
COPY AND PASTE SPECIAL
  (COMBINE DATA) 129, 131
COPY AND PASTE SPECIAL (EXTRACT DATA) .116
COPY FORMATS USING FORMAT PAINTER......254
COPY MULTIPLE SHEETS BY DRAGGING 147
COPY ONE SHEET BY DRAGGING 147
COPY OR MOVE PART OF A
  CELL'S CONTENTS 76
COPY SHEETS USING THE MENU 147
COPY SHEETS WITHIN A WORKBOOK 147
COPY USING THE MENU 57
correct errors (strikeover) 32
CREATE A CHART FROM WORKSHEET DATA..207
CREATE A LINE-COLUMN CHART....................213
CREATE A LIST (Database Table) 287
CREATE A PIVOTTABLE.................................339
CREATE A SCENARIO 181
create a series 78
CREATE A SERIES OF NUMBERS, DATES, OR
  TIMES USING THE MENU.................81
CREATE A SUBTOTAL WITHIN A SUBTOTALED
  GROUP IN A LIST 328
CREATE A TEMPLATE WORKBOOK 143
CREATE A TEXT BOX 280
CREATE A TWO-INPUT DATA TABLE 157
CREATE BACKUP 49
CREATE CHART WITH CHART WIZARD.............207
CREATE CUSTOM VIEWS 194
CREATE DATA LIST FOR A FIELD......................301
CREATE NEW WORKBOOK 116
CREATE TEXT CELL COMMENTS 85
cut and paste 104

D

data
  form..285
  labels..234
  markers 226
  series 202
    change orientation 222
  tables 154, 158
  validation..126, 288
    list..298
DATA VALIDATION......................................129
DATA VALIDATION SETTINGS............................291
database
  create 284
  functions...320
  update 302
decrease decimal button..................................50
DELETE A MACRO......................................353
DELETE COLUMNS/ROWS................................107
DELETE RECORDS IN A LIST
  USING A DATA FORM......................305

DELETE SHEETS...121
dependent workbook..140
dependents 170
depreciation 380
    straight-line 380
DESELECT GROUPED SHEETS 121
dialog box...10, 11
    options 11
directional arrow keys 6
DISABLE CHART EDITING.................................208
DISPLAY ALL PAGE ITEMS IN A PIVOTTABLE ...339
DISPLAY DRAWING TOOLBAR 259
DISPLAY FORM TOOLBAR 357
DISPLAY RECORDS USING A DATA FORM........287
DISPLAY SPECIFIC PAGE ITEMS
    IN A PIVOTTABLE...................................339
DISPLAY STOP RECORDING TOOLBAR.............353
Double Declining Balance method.........................380
double–click 5
drag 5
drag and drop..104
    between workbooks 132
DRAG AND DROP BETWEEN WORKBOOKS......133
DRAW GRAPHIC OBJECTS.................................274
Drawing toolbar.......................................270
drop-down
    list...11
    menu 6, 10

E

edit 74
    cell colors and patterns 250
    cell formats...261
    chart titles and axis labels................................214
    linked chart text..214
    maps 238
    result list..314
EDIT A MACRO 357
EDIT AND SELECT HYPERLINK TEXT 361
EDIT CELL COMMENTS.................................85
EDIT CELL CONTENTS..76
EDIT CELL CONTENTS AFTER DATA IS ENTERED
    (ENABLE CELL EDITING)..................................76
EDIT CHART TEXT 217
EDIT CHART TEXT IN CHART 208
Edit Formula button.......................................70
EDIT FUNCTIONS USING FORMULA PALETTE....73
EDIT LINKED CHART TEXT IN WORKSHEET 217
EDIT RECORD IN A LIST
    USING A DATA FORM....................................287
ellipsis 10
ENABLE CHART EDITING.................................208
ENABLE MAP EDITING 241
ENABLE OR DISABLE CHECK FOR VIRUSES......37
END AUTOFILTER...307
ENTER A DATE AS NUMERICAL DATA 175
ENTER A FORMULA USING
    CELL REFERENCES 45

ENTER A FORMULA USING
    NATURAL LANGUAGE 45
ENTER A FUNCTION USING THE KEYBOARD 73
ENTER A LABEL 35
ENTER A NUMERIC LABEL 37
ENTER A VALUE..37
ENTER DATA LABELS 237
enter dates as numerical data.................................174
ENTER FORMULAS FOR ABSOLUTE
    CONDITIONS 60
Enter keys 6
ENTER LINE BREAKS IN A CELL ENTRY...........237
ENTER MIXED NUMBERS 65
ENTER NUMBERS AS FRACTIONS 65
ERASE CONTENTS OF CELL.............................76
Error Alert..289
Escape key 6
Excel
    exit 7
    start 2
Excel 97 window 2
EXIT EXCEL 35
EXIT EXCEL USING THE MENU 15
EXIT HELP OR HELP SCREENS 20
EXIT WITHOUT SAVING 9

F

field names...284
fields..284
file 32
    create backup 47
    open 46
    save 47
    save as...47
    send 47
File Transfer Protocol (ftp) 365
filename 32
    extension...32
fill handle..78
FILTER A LIST AUTOMATICALLY 307
FILTER A LIST WITH ADVANCED FILTERING 312
filter criteria 306
    advanced 308, 314
finance/portfolio analysis.............................370
FIND A SPECIFIC SOLUTION TO A FORMULA
    (GOAL SEEK)...................................157
FIND SPECIFIC RECORDS IN A LIST
    USING A DATA FORM.....................................305
format
    cells..247
    characters 58
    comma 79
    currency 50
    data 50, 58
    font...246
    graphic objects.................................271
    negative numbers 127
    number...50

INDEX

numerical dates...174, 175
   sheet background 251
   styles 251
FORMAT AUTO SHAPE 259
Format Cells dialog box 50
FORMAT DATA MARKERS IN A LINE CHART.....229
FORMAT DATA SERIES 217
FORMAT FOR BOLD, ITALICS AND
   UNDERLINE 61
FORMAT GRAPHIC OBJECTS (Summary)...........274
FORMAT NEGATIVE VALUES 129
FORMAT NUMBERS FOR FRACTIONS 65
FORMAT NUMBERS USING THE MENU 53
FORMAT NUMBERS USING THE TOOLBAR...53, 61
Format Painter 251
FORMAT SHEET BACKGROUND.........................255
FORMAT TEXT BOX OBJECT................................280
Formatting toolbar.................................38, 50, 58, 250
formula 44
   bar..3, 44
Formula bar 70
Formula Palette 70
fractions 62
FREEZE PANES ON A SPLIT WORKSHEET 117
freeze titles..112, 117
function keys 5
functions...70

G

Go To 28
   Special button 28
Goal Seek 154
graphic objects...270
gridlines..234
group sheets 119

H

Half Month method..380
Headers and footers 90
headings 4
help features 16
   contents and index 18
   exit 18
   menu 16
   Microsoft on the Web 16
hide
   cell contents 192
   columns..192
   gridlines...251
HIDE COLUMNS BY DRAGGING..........................194
HIDE COLUMNS USING THE MENU 194
HIDE CONTENTS OF CELL 194
HIDE WORKSHEET GRIDLINES.........................254
HLOOKUP 182, 188
hyperlinks..358, 364
HyperText Transfer Protocol (http) 365

I

IF
   function 166
      insert 162
   statement 162
IMPORT CLIP ART FROM OFFICE
   SOFTWARE 269
increase decimal button 50
increment box 11
indent button 38
indent text 38
insert
   objects...270
   pictures..266
INSERT 3-D REFERENCE IN FORMULA 147
INSERT A DATABASE FUNCTION
   USING FUNCTION WIZARD................................323
INSERT A FUNCTION IN A FORMULA 73
INSERT A FUNCTION USING
   FUNCTION WIZARD 73
INSERT A HYPERLINK..361
INSERT A VLOOKUP OR HLOOKUP FUNCTION
   USING FUNCTION WIZARD................................185
INSERT AN IF FUNCTION USING PASTE
   FUNCTION 164
INSERT AND USE A DATA MAP...........................241
INSERT CLIP ART OBJECT INTO
   WORKSHEET..269, 274
INSERT COLUMNS/ROWS 107
INSERT COLUMNS/ROWS USING
   THE MOUSE 107
INSERT IF FUNCTION USING KEYBOARD AND
   MOUSE..164
INSERT LIST OF NAMED RANGES......................124
INSERT MANUAL PAGE BREAKS 94
INSERT OR REMOVE GRIDLINES 237
INSERT SHEETS 121
insertion point..5
Internet...364
Internet financial services 370
Internet research...372
Internet Service Provider (ISP) 364
item 182

K

keyboard 5
Keyboard Template..7

L

label prefix...36
labels...32
   align 38
line breaks in a cell entry 234
LINK WORKBOOKS USING PASTE LINK.............143
list (see Database)
   filter with multiple criteria....................................316

list box 11
lock/unlock cells 188
LOCK/UNLOCK CELLS IN A WORKSHEET 191
Look Up Reference 62
lookup functions 182

M

macros 350, 354
Map
   feature 238
   toolbar 239
market value 370
mathematical operators 44
MAXIMIZE A WINDOW 20
maximize button
   application window..3, 16
   workbook window..4
menu bar 3
menus 6
Microsoft Query Wizard 330
MINIMIZE A WINDOW...21
minimize button
   application window..3, 16
   workbook window..4
mixed numbers 62
modem 364
modifier keys 5
MODIFY A PIVOTTABLE 339
mouse 5
   pointer 3, 5
MOVE (CUT/PASTE) USING THE MENU 107
MOVE (DRAG AND DROP) 107
MOVE AN EMBEDDED CHART 217
MOVE BETWEEN WORKSHEET PANES.............117
MOVE CHART ELEMENT—EXPLODE A PIE
   SECTION...232
move data (cut and paste) 104
MOVE MULTIPLE SHEETS 121
MOVE OR REMOVE FIELDS
   ON A PIVOTTABLE..339
MOVE SHEETS WITHIN A WORKBOOK 121

N

NAME A RANGE USING THE NAME BOX............124
name box 3, 24, 28
name lists 288
NAME/MODIFY A RANGE USING THE MENU 124
named ranges 122
named tab 11
natural language formulas 44
New Comment button 170
New Workbook button..113
non-consecutive references in a function 192
number signs (######) 36
numeric
   keys..6
   labels...36

values..36

O

Office Assistant 3, 17
OPEN A DATA FORM FOR A LIST 287
OPEN A NEW DUPLICATE WORKBOOK
   WINDOW 147
OPEN A WORKBOOK FILE 49
OPEN EMBEDDED CHART IN A WINDOW..........213
OPEN ORIGINAL TEMPLATE FILE......................139
option buttons 11
options, black/dimmed 10
outline feature 325

P

PAGE BREAK PREVIEW 94
page breaks 90
   manual 90
page setup 86
   header/footer 87
   margins 87
   orientation 86
   page order...87
   paper size 86
   print quality..87
   scaling...86
Page Setup options...260
paste
   button 54
   function feature 162
   options 112
   special...108, 112, 127, 130
Paste Function 71
percentage button 58
Personal Macro Workbook..................................350
PivotTable 334
PMT function 158
point to 5
pop-up menu 6
portfolio 370
POSITION LEGEND IN CHART 213
precedents 170
preview button..54
print
   a worksheet..54
   button 54
   charts 218
   compressed worksheet......................................166
   dialog box..54
   embedded charts 219
   options 54, 82
   preview...82
   preview charts..218
   titles...96
   workbook..119
PRINT A NAMED RANGE 124
PRINT A WORKSHEET 57

INDEX

PRINT CHARTS 221
PRINT EMBEDDED CHART SEPARATELY.........221
PRINT RANGE OF CELLS 85
PRINT WORKBOOK 121
printers 219
printout, enlarge 266
program control menu icon 3
PROTECT A SHEET 191
protect worksheet..188

R

ranges 51
record..284
RECORD A MACRO 353
REDISPLAY HIDDEN CELL 194
redo..105
reference
    3-D 144
    absolute 58
    cell...4, 24, 44
    external 140
    relative 58
Relative Reference button 351
REMOVE ALL AUTOMATIC SUBTOTALS
    IN A LIST 328
REMOVE ALL BORDERS FROM CELLS 259
REMOVE ALL TRACER ARROWS 171
REMOVE DEPENDENT TRACER ARROWS........171
REMOVE MANUAL PAGE BREAKS......................94
REMOVE PRECEDENT TRACER ARROWS........171
REMOVE SPLIT BARS...116
RENAME A SHEET 121
replace 132, 133
RESAVE/OVERWRITE A WORKBOOK FILE..........49
RESET COLUMNS TO STANDARD
    COLUMN WIDTH 81
RESTORE A MAXIMIZED WINDOW 21
restore button
    application window...3
    workbook window...4
right–click 5
right–drag 5
rotate text 247, 249
row
    headings 4
    height 271
row-position..188
RUN A MACRO 353

S

salvage value 380
SAVE A FILE AS A TEMPLATE 139
SAVE A NEW WORKBOOK..................................35
SAVE AS..49
save button 33
SAVE FILE AS A TEMPLATE WITH READ-ONLY
    RECOMMENDATION..143

SAVE WORKSPACE..116
scaling option 166
scenario feature 178
Scenario Manager dialog box 178
scroll bar 5, 11
SCROLL TIPS..117
SCROLL USING THE KEYBOARD........................27
SCROLL USING THE MOUSE...............................27
ScrollTip 25, 108
search
    criteria 302
    item 188
    site 365
select
    chart items 211
    command from the drop-down menu 6
    command from the pop-up (shortcut) menu...........6
    command from toolbar 6
    menu 6
    shortcut menu commands....................................6
SELECT (HIGHLIGHT) A RANGE OF CELLS
    USING THE KEYBOARD 39, 53
SELECT (HIGHLIGHT) A RANGE OF CELLS
    USING THE MOUSE 39, 53
SELECT A MACRO BUTTON WITHOUT RUNNING
    THE MACRO 357
SELECT A MENU BAR ITEM................................9
SELECT A NAMED RANGE..................................124
SELECT A SHORTCUT MENU ITEM 9
Select All button 5
SELECT CHART Elements 213
SELECT NON-ADJACENT CELLS
    USING THE KEYBOARD 207
SELECT NON-ADJACENT CELLS
    USING THE MOUSE 207
SELECT SHEETS...121
SELECT WORKBOOK 116
serial value 174
series labels 202
    for pie charts 214
SET AN AUTOCORRECT REPLACEMENT.........111
SET CHART PRINT OPTIONS 221
SET COLUMN WIDTH TO FIT LONGEST
    ENTRY..81
SET FONT AND FONT ATTRIBUTES
    USING THE MENU..254
SET HEADER AND FOOTER OPTIONS.................94
SET INPUT MESSAGE 291
SET PAGE ORIENTATION OF PRINTED PAGE ..221
SET PRINT AREA FOR A NAMED RANGE 124
SET PRINT OPTIONS FOR WORKSHEET............89
SET REPEATING PRINT TITLES
    FOR WORKSHEET 98
SET SCALE OF VALUE AXIS 229
SET STANDARD COLUMN WIDTH........................81
SET STYLES BY EXAMPLE 255
SET UP A CRITERIA RANGE...............................312

SET VIEW OPTIONS FOR A 3-D CHART
(Change Rotation and Elevation)......................237
SET VIEW PREFERENCES....................................15
SET WINDOW OPTIONS.....................................117
SET WORKSHEET TO PRINT ON SPECIFIED
NUMBER OF PAGES..121
SET/CLEAR PRINT AREA......................................85
sheet tabs..5
SHOW ALL RECORDS IN A FILTERED
LIST..307, 312
SHOW AUDITING TOOLBAR...............................171
SHOW HIDDEN COLUMNS BY DRAGGING........194
SHOW HIDDEN COLUMNS USING THE MENU...194
Show/hide Microsoft Map Control button..................238
SIZE AND MOVE CLIP ART OBJECTS................269
SIZE EMBEDDED CHARTS.................................208
SIZE PLOT AREA OR LEGEND IN A CHART.......232
sort
in ascending/descending order..........................292
maintain original record order..........................308
order..298
records in a list..292
SORT A LIST USING THE MENU........................296
SORT A LIST USING THE TOOLBAR...................296
source workbooks..140
SPECIFY NUMBER OF COPIES TO PRINT.........264
SPELL CHECK...65
spelling feature..62
split panes..112
SPLIT WORKSHEET INTO PANES
USING SPLIT BOXES......................................116
SPLIT WORKSHEET INTO PANES
USING THE MENU...116
START EXCEL..9
START OFFICE ASSISTANT..................................20
status bar..3
submenu..10
substitution values...154
SUBTOTAL A LIST AUTOMATICALLY.................328
subtotals..324

T

tab
scrolling buttons...5, 118
split box...5, 118
table-range..183, 188
templates...140
spreadsheets..136
text
bold...90
text box..11
text box, add and format....................................276
title bar
application window...3
dialog box...11
workbook window...4
TO CREATE A SCENARIO SUMMARY.................181

TO SET SIZE AND ROTATION FORMATS..........274
TO VIEW A SCENARIO.......................................181
toolbars...3, 6
TRACE DEPENDENT FORMULAS......................171
Trace Error button...170
TRACE PRECEDENT DATA AND FORMULAS....171
transpose data...108, 111
two-input data tables...154
TWO-INPUT DATA TABLES (What-If Tables).....157
TYPE A 3-D REFERENCE IN FORMULA.............147

U

undo
a command...105
a sort...293
UNDO A COMMAND...107
UNDO A SORT..296
UNDO LAST CHANGE...232
UNFREEZE PANES...117
UNFREEZE TITLES..117
unhide column...192
Uniform Resource Locator (URL).........................364
UNPROTECT A SHEET.......................................191
UPDATE A PIVOTTABLE....................................339
USE AN EXCEL TEMPLATE................................139
USE AUTO SHAPES..259
USE AUTOSUM..85
USE CONTENTS AND INDEX...............................20
USE LOOK UP REFERENCE.................................65
USE OFFICE ASSISTANT......................................20
USE OUTLINE SYMBOLS TO SHOW OR HIDE
OUTLINE GROUPS AND LEVELS....................328
USE THE PMT FUNCTION..................................160
USE WORD ART FEATURE..................................264

V

view
custom views option..192
default settings..12
full screen...13
menu..12
set preferences..12
tab..12
VIEW CUSTOM VIEWS......................................194
VIEW TOOLBAR BUTTON DESCRIPTIONS.............9
VIEW TOOLBARS..15
viruses..36
Visual Basic...354
VLOOKUP..182, 186

W

Web toolbar button..365
What-if worksheet..154
wildcard symbols...302
WordArt feature...261

INDEX

workbook..4
   arrange workbooks window 113
   close...33
   create 113
   duplicate workbooks window 144
   link..140
   save 32
   sheets 118
   window 4
workbook control menu icon 4
worksheets...4, 118
   protect 188
workspace file
   create 113
   save 113
World Wide Web (WWW) 364

wrap text 285
WRAP TEXT IN CELLS..287

X

x-axis..203

Y

y-axis..203

Z

z-axis..234
zoom 13, 15

Notes

Notes

Notes

Notes

Notes

Notes

Notes

Notes

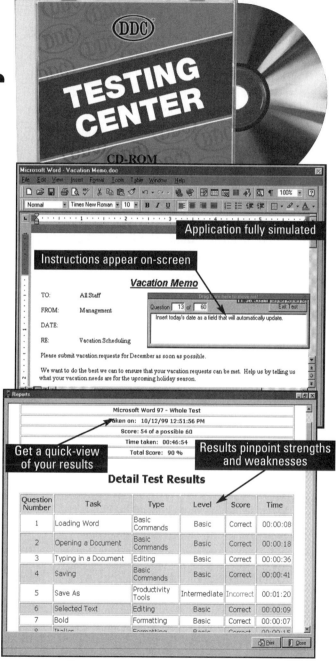

INSTALLATION DIRECTIONS:

To install the Excel Internet Simulation, the Multimedia Internet Browser Tutorial, or the Demo of DDC's Office 97 Multimedia tutorial:

A separate installation is required for each program. At the designated prompt, indicate which program you wish to install: Excel Internet Simulation, Office 97 CBT or Internet Browser Tutorial. When installation of one program is complete, you may begin again from step one to install another.

System Requirements

Software	Windows 95 or Windows NT 3.51 (or higher)
Hardware	80486DX or higher, 16 MB RAM, 256 Color Monitor, and CD-ROM Drive-
Disk Space	30 MB available hard disk space for a Typical installation.

To install a program, place the DDC CD-ROM in your CD-ROM drive and follow the listed steps below:

1. **To install from Windows 95:**
   Click Start on the desktop and click Run.
   OR
   To install from Windows NT:
   Go to Program Manager in Main, click File.

2. In the Run window, begin a program installation by typing one of the following:

   - *CD-ROM drive letter:*\EX97INT\SETUP to install the **Excel Internet Simulation**.
   - CD-ROM drive letter:\OFFICE97\SETUP to install the **Office 97 CBT**.
   - CD-ROM drive letter: \NETSIM\SETUP to install the **Browser tutorial**.

3. Click NEXT at the Setup Wizard screen.

4. At the following screen, click NEXT to create a DDCPUB directory for storing program files. Then click YES to confirm the directory choice.

5. At the following screen, allow the default folder to be named DDC Publishing, and click NEXT. At the next screen, choose one of the following options based on your individual system needs:
   - ✓ NOTE: *A **Typical** installation is standard for most individual installation.*

   - **TYPICAL**: installs a minimum number of files to the hard drive with the majority of files remaining on the CD-ROM.

   - **COMPACT**: installs the fewest required files to the hard drive. This is the best option for portable computers and computers with little available hard disk space.

   - **CUSTOM**: installs only those files that you choose to the hard drive. This is generally only recommended for advanced users of Innovus Multimedia software.

   - **SERVER**: installs the programs on a network server and enables you to then do workstation installations to any computer connected to your network. **(A separate Network Site License purchase is required for this option.)**
      - ✓ NOTE: *With a typical or compact installation, the CD must remain in the CD-ROM drive when running the program.*

7. Click NEXT to begin copying the necessary files to your system.

8. Click OK at the Set Up status Window and then click YES to restart Windows.

To launch a program, click the Start button on the Windows 95 desktop, select Programs, DDC Publishing, and then select one of the following:

- **Ex97INT** (to start the Internet Simulation)
- **DEMO97** (to start the Office97 CBT)
- **NETCBT** (to start the Browser tutorial)

To Copy the Data Files:

1. Open Windows 95 Explorer (Right-click on **Start** button and click **Explore**).

2. Be sure that the CD is in your CD-ROM drive. Select the CD-ROM drive letter in the **All Folders** pane of Windows 95 Explorer.

3. Click to Select the **Ex97data** folder in the **Contents of (CD-ROM Drive letter)** pane of Windows 95 Explorer.

Drag the folder to the letter representing your hard drive (usually **C:**) in the **All Folders** pane of Windows 95 Explorer.

Network Site Licence

If you wish to install the programs and data files that accompany this book on a network server, a Network Site License may be purchased separately from DDC Publishing. This would enable any computer workstation that is connected to the main server to access the programs and data files.

FREE CATALOG
AND
UPDATED LISTING

We don't just have books that find your answers faster; we also have books that teach you how to use your computer without the fairy tales and the gobbledygook.

We also have books to improve your typing, spelling and punctuation.

Return this card for a free catalog and mailing list update.

275 Madison Avenue,
New York, NY 10016

☐ Please send me your catalog and put me on your mailing list.

Name

Firm (if any)

Address

City, State, Zip

Phone (800) 528-3897   Fax (800) 528-3862

SEE OUR COMPLETE CATALOG ON THE INTERNET @: http://www.ddcpub.com

---

FREE CATALOG
AND
UPDATED LISTING

We don't just have books that find your answers faster; we also have books that teach you how to use your computer without the fairy tales and the gobbledygook.

We also have books to improve your typing, spelling and punctuation.

Return this card for a free catalog and mailing list update.

DDC Publishing

275 Madison Avenue,
New York, NY 10016

☐ Please send me your catalog and put me on your mailing list.

Name

Firm (if any)

Address

City, State, Zip

Phone (800) 528-3897   Fax (800) 528-3862

SEE OUR COMPLETE CATALOG ON THE INTERNET @: http://www.ddcpub.com

---

FREE CATALOG
AND
UPDATED LISTING

We don't just have books that find your answers faster; we also have books that teach you how to use your computer without the fairy tales and the gobbledygook.

We also have books to improve your typing, spelling and punctuation.

Return this card for a free catalog and mailing list update.

DDC Publishing

275 Madison Avenue,
New York, NY 10016

☐ Please send me your catalog and put me on your mailing list.

Name

Firm (if any)

Address

City, State, Zip

Phone (800) 528-3897   Fax (800) 528-3862

SEE OUR COMPLETE CATALOG ON THE INTERNET @: http://www.ddcpub.com

BUSINESS REPLY MAIL
FIRST-CLASS MAIL   PERMIT NO. 7321   NEW YORK, N.Y.

POSTAGE WILL BE PAID BY ADDRESSEE

275 Madison Avenue
New York, NY 10157-0410

BUSINESS REPLY MAIL
FIRST-CLASS MAIL   PERMIT NO. 7321   NEW YORK, N.Y.

POSTAGE WILL BE PAID BY ADDRESSEE

275 Madison Avenue
New York, NY 10157-0410

BUSINESS REPLY MAIL
FIRST-CLASS MAIL   PERMIT NO. 7321   NEW YORK, N.Y.

POSTAGE WILL BE PAID BY ADDRESSEE

275 Madison Avenue
New York, NY 10157-0410